List of Abbreviations

ALMP	active labour market policies
Cedefop	European Centre for the Development of Vocational Training
CME	coordinated market economy
EC	European Commission
EMU	European Monetary Union
EPL	employment protection legislation
EQUALSOC	Economic Life, Quality of Work and Social Cohesion Network
ESRI	Economic and Social Research Institute
ESS	European Social Survey
EU	European Union
EULFS	European Union Labour Force Survey
FGLS	feasible generalized least square
GDP	gross domestic product
GRR	gross replacement rate
ICTWSS	Institutional Characteristics of Trade Unions, Wage Setting, State Intervention and Social Pacts (database)
ILO	International Labour Organization
IMF	International Monetary Fund
ISCED	International Standard Classification of Education
ISCO	International Standard Classification of Occupations
LME	liberal market economy
MP	member of parliament
NRR	net replacement rate
OECD	Organisation for Economic Co-operation and Development
OLS	ordinary least squares
QNHS	Quarterly National Household Survey
SA	social assistance
SWB	subjective well-being

List of Contributors

Martina Dieckhoff is a Senior Research Fellow at the Social Science Research Centre Berlin (WZB).

Duncan Gallie is an Official Fellow of Nuffield College, Oxford, and Professor of Sociology at the University of Oxford.

Vanessa Gash is Senior Lecturer in Sociology at City University London.

Hande Inanc is a Junior Analyst, Directorate of Statistics, OECD.

Frances McGinnity is Senior Research Officer at the Economic and Social Research Institute (ESRI) and Adjunct Associate Professor, Trinity College Dublin.

Javier Polavieja is Professor of Sociology, Universidad Carlos III, Madrid.

Helen Russell is Associate Research Professor at the Economic and Social Research Institute (ESRI) and Adjunct Professor, Trinity College Dublin.

Nadia Steiber is researcher and lecturer at the Department Socioeconomics of the Vienna University of Economics and Business.

Michael Tåhlin is Professor of Sociology at the Swedish Institute for Social Research (SOFI), Stockholm University.

Dorothy Watson is Associate Research Professor at Economic and Social Research Institute and Adjunct Professor at Trinity College Dublin.

Ying Zhou is Lecturer of Human Resource Management, University of Surrey.

1

Economic Crisis, the Quality of Work, and Social Integration: Issues and Context

Duncan Gallie

Introduction

Theory and research on employment and the quality of work over the last fifty years has been premised in the main on a long-term trend of economic growth, driven by increasingly sophisticated technologies and expanding markets. It was widely assumed that this would lead to higher employment rates, favouring the increased integration into the labour market of both women and older workers. At the same time, although this was more controversial, it was argued that it was a trend that was likely to be associated with improvements in the quality of work. An economy that was more knowledge intensive and involved increasingly complex technologies required more skilled employees (and the evidence did indeed point to rising skill levels in the workforce). This in turn was seen as likely to lead to a long-term enhancement of the quality of work. A more skilled workforce would need better ongoing training provision to enable it to take full advantage of new innovations. It would need to be given greater control over the way work was carried out to ensure full use of its knowledge. It would have greater job security, as employers would wish to retain employees with firm-specific skills that they had invested in and were difficult to replace. Improvements in the quality of work, with the introduction of new forms of work organization, were thought then to be no longer a cost to employers, but an essential condition of their objectives of higher levels of work performance. Given this convergence of interests, there could be a reasonable expectation of rising work quality.

It is true that there were some caveats to the generalizability of this scenario. In the increasingly competitive conditions of the closing decades of the twentieth century, there was a growing awareness that not all sectors of

1

the workforce might benefit from these developments to the same degree. Those in low-skilled work were likely to be increasingly vulnerable as skill requirements rose. Older workers might find their status downgraded in conditions of rapid technical change and a continuing need for skill development. There were also concerns that there might be increasing labour market dualism, with the general improvements in the conditions of the core workforce offset by deteriorating conditions among an insecure peripheral sector of employees on non-standard contracts (temporary or part-time). But even in these more pessimistic scenarios, it was generally accepted that the periphery would constitute a minority of the workforce and that, at least for some, there would be pathways for transition from peripheral to core employment.

It also became evident from comparative research that the scenario of rising skills driving improved work organization and work quality was more pronounced in some countries, or sets of countries, than others. In particular, the Nordic countries stood out for their improvements in job design and their much higher level of involvement of employees in decision-making within their organizations. In contrast, work conditions in the Southern European countries were notably less good. This pointed to an important role for macro-institutional factors in moderating the implications of underlying economic trends. But even though the pace of developments might vary considerably between countries, it was commonly believed that, in the longer term, the pressures of economic change were likely to favour a shift towards more progressive employment policies.

The prolonged economic crisis that was unleashed in 2008 placed a major question mark over the core assumptions that had underpinned such predictions about changes in both employment rates and the quality of work. The sharp fall in employment could not be contained solely by shedding the peripheral workforce. It led to unemployment and higher job insecurity in some of the hitherto most protected parts of the workforce (not least in the public sector). The rapid and radical restructuring to deal with the sharp falls in demand for products and services was also likely to have chased the issue of quality of work off employers' agendas. Implementing new types of job design and work organization are likely to require long-term planning and are tricky to implement in times of market turbulence and workforce instability.

The crisis also affected the salience of the quality of work on the political agenda. The most urgent pressures on policy-makers were to devote resources to handling the employment consequences of the crisis, through measures to stimulate employment creation and to equip the unemployed to find new jobs, rather than on schemes to encourage better work quality. This was clearly evident in discussions at the higher levels of EU policy-making. Since the inauguration of the Lisbon Strategy in 2000, improving the quality of work had become a central pillar of the EU's Employment Strategy, with the introduction in 2001 of a range of indicators for measuring the progress of member states. There were plans just before the crisis for a major updating of these policy indicators, but these had to be put on hold. As was noted in a report to the EU's Employment Committee (EMCO): 'Due to the downturn, the attention from quality of jobs has shifted to sustaining employment levels. Thus, as a prerequisite to the quality of work, inclusion and access to the labour market are obviously essential in this respect' (Employment Committee (EMCO) 2010; see also European Commission 2011b).

But, while predictions based on the old assumptions about economic growth clearly had become very problematic, it was far from clear what developments were to be expected under the new conditions. The major post-war theoretical visions of the future of work had simply not anticipated the possibility of an economic collapse on such a scale. Yet an understanding of the effects of the crisis is arguably of central importance not only for employees' experiences of their jobs and of the labour market, but for their broader social inclusion. It has long been accepted that work is a central component of male identity and that unemployment and job insecurity can have devastating consequences for people's psychological well-being and their ability to relate to others. But one of the most important developments in recent decades has been the progressive integration of women into the labour market. While there has been debate about the extent to which women's commitment to employment has converged with that of men, it seems plausible that the new economic crisis may have undermined the personal well-being of both men and women.

The objective of this book is to explore both the way that the quality of work was affected by the crisis and its implications for social integration. It focuses on nineteen European countries for which we have good comparative data both before the great recession of 2008/9 and in its aftermath, at a time (2010) in which most of the countries were emerging from the recession but were still suffering from the economic crisis that it had generated. These include the two North Western countries—Ireland and the UK; four Nordic countries—Denmark, Finland, Norway, and Sweden; four Continental countries—Belgium, France, Germany, and the Netherlands; three Southern countries—Greece, Portugal, and Spain; and six Eastern countries—the Czech Republic, Estonia, Hungary, Poland, Slovenia, and Slovakia.

With respect to the quality of work the book focuses on changes in the skill structure of the workforce, in opportunities for skill development, in the control that employees can exercise over their work, in the intensity of work, in job security, and in work–family conflict. With regard to social integration, it examines the implications of changed economic conditions for employees' commitment to employment, their subjective well-being, and finally their attitudes to the political system. The next sections of this chapter first consider the severity of the crisis in different European countries, then outline some possible scenarios of the effects of the crisis for the quality of work and their potential implications for social integration, third describe the institutional contexts that may have mediated the crisis in different countries, and finally present the data used and structure of the following chapters.

The Severity of the Economic Crisis

It is important to distinguish the recession in a technical sense and the broader period of economic crisis. A recession is conventionally defined as a period with two consecutive quarters or more of GDP decline. But the difficulties faced by employers and employees can persist well beyond the end of the recession. It may be a long time before production returns to the level of the previous peak. Employers will still be confronting reduced product markets, and employees will continue to suffer from greater job insecurity than in the past. Indeed, unemployment rates tend to be lagged and can continue to rise sharply after the economy has started growing again. We use the notion of 'economic crisis' to refer to the period between the start of the recession and the recovery of the level of GDP to the previous peak.

It is clear from Figure 1.1 that there were considerable differences in the experience of the nineteen countries both in the depth and duration of the

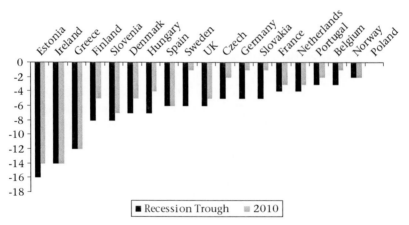

Figure 1.1. Percentage decline of GDP per capita from 2008 to (a) year of recession trough and (b) 2010

Note: Figures taken from Groningen Total Economic Database_Jan 20121(1).xls. <http://www.rug.nl/research/ggdc/data/total-economy-database>: GDP-capital EKS.

initial recession and in the extent of recovery from the economic crisis by 2010. In three (Estonia, Ireland, and Greece), recession led to a drop of more than 10 per cent in per capita GDP and the decline was still far from over in Ireland and Greece by 2010. In contrast, Poland escaped recession altogether, while GDP decline was 4 per cent or less in France, the Netherlands, Portugal, and Belgium. It is notable that, with the exception of the Continental countries (Germany, Belgium, and the Netherlands), the extent of the initial shock of the recession did not show strong differences by European region. The countries that had particularly sharp falls in GDP (declines of 5 per cent or more) included countries from the Eastern, Southern, Nordic, and North Western regions.

By 2010, all of the countries, apart from Ireland and Greece, had moved out of recession, but at the same time all but Poland were still in economic crisis in the sense that GDP had not recovered to its pre-crisis level. Some countries, however, had recovered much more rapidly than others—notably Sweden and Finland among the Nordic countries, Germany and Belgium among the Continental, and Hungary, the Czech Republic, and Slovakia among the East European.

Perhaps the most salient indicator of economic crisis for the general population is the change in the unemployment rate. As can be seen from Figure 1.2,

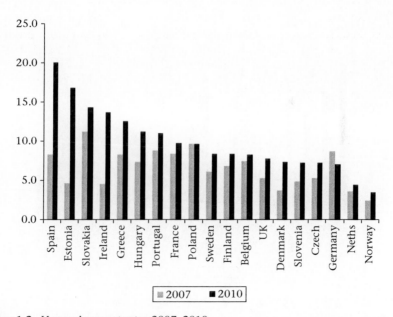

Figure 1.2. Unemployment rates 2007–2010

Source: OECD *Employment Outlook* 2012: Statistical Annex. Table A. Harmonized unemployment rates.

it rose between 2007 and 2010 in all countries other than Poland, where it was stable, and in Germany where it fell. By far the sharpest percentage point rises were in Spain (+11.8), Estonia (+12.2), and Ireland (+9.1). But it also increased in Greece, Hungary, Denmark, and Slovakia by more than three percentage points. The experiences of unemployment change across the economic crisis varied strongly across the different regions of Europe. In the Nordic and Continental countries, an initial rise levelled off quite quickly and remained at a relatively low level. In the East European countries, an initially very sharp rise in Estonia, Slovakia, and Hungary began to reverse before 2010, while in the Southern countries (and to a lesser extent in Ireland) there was a sharp and continuing rise in unemployment across the whole period.

By 2010, then, there were very marked differences in the state of the labour market in different parts of Europe, with the countries with the highest levels of unemployment predominantly in Southern Europe (Spain, Greece, and Portugal) and in Eastern Europe (Estonia, Slovakia, Hungary, and Poland).

A final point important to bear in mind is that some countries had seen substantial improvements in the level of unemployment in the years immediately prior to the recession. While unemployment generally rose with the recession, the level it had reached by 2010 was lower in certain countries than it had been in 2004. As can be seen in Figure 1.3, this was the case with Slovakia, the Czech Republic, and Germany, where unemployment rates were

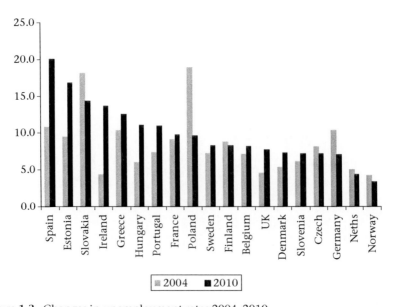

Figure 1.3. Changes in unemployment rates 2004–2010

Source: OECD *Employment Outlook* 2012: Statistical Annex. Table A. Harmonized unemployment rates.

three to four percentage points lower than they had been in 2004. Poland, which did not experience recession, had an even greater decline in unemployment over the period (by nine percentage points).

Whereas there were countries in most regions of Europe that had suffered heavily from the initial decline in GDP with the recession, the longer-term picture with respect to unemployment was one of sharp regional differences both in the level and experience of increase in unemployment. In the early 2000s, unemployment rates in France and Germany were as high as in the Southern countries and the majority of the East European countries. But by 2010 there was a much sharper differentiation between the richer 'core' countries and a Southern and Eastern 'periphery', joined by the isolated case of Ireland in Northern Europe.

From the point of view of those still in employment, rising rates of unemployment are likely to be reflected in the experience of high levels of workforce reductions. We can take a measure of this from the 2010 European Social Survey. People were asked 'During the last three years, would you say that the number of people employed at the organization for which you work has decreased a lot, decreased a little, not changed, increased a little or increased a lot?' We show in Figure 1.4 the difference between the proportion reporting workforce increases and the proportion reporting decreases.

This reveals a broadly similar pattern of the severity of the crisis to that of the rise in unemployment rates. The countries with the highest level of reductions in workplace numbers are again primarily those of Southern and Eastern Europe, together with Ireland. The four countries that had the highest level

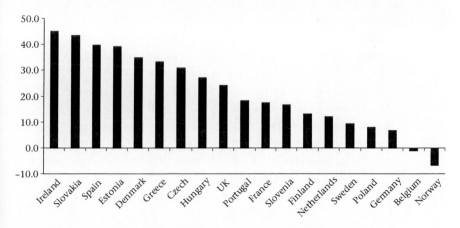

Figure 1.4. Net reductions in workforce reported by employees

Source: European Social Survey 2010. Net reductions = % employees reporting reductions—% reporting increases in size of workforce.

of unemployment in 2010—Estonia, Ireland, Slovakia, and Spain—were also those where employees were the most likely to report workforce reductions.

Economic Crisis, Institutional Regulation, and the Quality of Work: The Issues

Although there has been little consideration in the literature of the potential effects of economic crisis on the quality of work, a number of scenarios can be drawn from influential accounts of the determinants of work processes. These point in sharply divergent directions: economic crisis may have led to a significant decline in work quality; it may have led to changes in work organization that resulted in improvements to jobs; it may have contributed to polarization between the experiences of different sectors of the workforce; and, finally, it may have had very limited effects because of the inertia of existing institutional structures.

Economic crisis and deteriorating work conditions?

Arguments that economic crisis is likely to have led to a decline of job quality can draw on a long tradition of neo-Marxian sociological thought about the conflictual nature of employer and employee interests and the propensity of employers to seek to enhance their control over the workforce and to intensify the work process (Braverman 1974; Edwards 1979; Smith 1994). Within this perspective, the key determinants of work relations are the relative power resources available to employers and workers. The level of employment is a vital factor that affects the balance of power. Where the demand for employment is high and labour markets are tight, employees have greater leverage to secure improvements in work conditions. But in times of economic crisis and rising unemployment, their capacity to resist unilateral management initiatives is heavily diminished as a result of the fear of job loss. This premise underlay the early Marxian conception of the growth of 'a reserve army of labour' in conditions of recession. The increase of those out of work would undermine the work conditions of those in jobs by providing employers with a ready pool of cheap labour for replacing existing employees who were unwilling to make concessions. The expectation then is that employers will use times of crisis to impose tighter controls over the way employees do their jobs. Higher levels of employer control over work performance will lead to work intensification—increased pressure on employees in terms of both the amount and speed of work.

A pessimistic expectation is reinforced by the argument in some versions of flexibility theory that, when faced by more competitive and uncertain product markets, employers would seek greater numerical flexibility, increasing their ability to dismiss workers at short notice to offset declines in demand. Priority to being able to rapidly hire and fire in turn is likely to be conducive to strategies of work simplification, reinforcing tendencies to deskilling and the reduction in employee discretion.

Economic crisis and improved work conditions?

The argument that economic crisis might improve rather than undermine work quality can draw on the Schumpeterian conception of capitalism as a 'process of creative destruction' (Schumpeter 1970). As the argument was developed in *Capitalism, Socialism and Democracy*, first published in 1943, capitalism is an evolutionary system whose 'essential fact' is the process of creative destruction (Schumpeter 1970: 83). It is revolutionized from within by the 'perennial gale' of destruction of old structures by new methods of production, markets, and forms of organization. Major crises, for instance war or large-scale economic crises, act as 'accelerators' of this process (Schumpeter 1970: 420–4). Schumpeter's view was that the long-term outcomes of creative destruction involved the elimination of archaic forms of capitalism and their replacement by more socialized forms of organization.

A first implication of this argument is that in times of economic crisis the major beneficiaries will be those who have the capacity to innovate. The research literature on innovation and organizational structures suggests that this should have significant consequences for patterns of work organization and hence for the quality of work. Conditions of uncertain product markets and rapidly changing technologies, it is suggested, give major advantage to organizations that are designed to provide a high level of horizontal communication, team work, and internal flexibility (Burns and Stalker 1961; Kern and Schumann 1987; Womack et al. 1990). One of the classic studies on innovation—Burns and Stalker's *Management of Innovation* (1961) argued that bureaucratic forms of organization are dysfunctional where predictability is low, while such conditions are conducive to *organic* forms of organization where hierarchical control is reduced and decision-making is decentralized to employees. A rather similar argument has been made more recently by social psychologists of work, who have suggested that team work and employee discretion are most effective under conditions of uncertainty (Wall et al. 2002). Economic crisis involves a sharp increase in such uncertainty and heightens the need for adaptability faced by a rapidly changing environment. A substantial research literature has confirmed the benefits of greater employee participation for facilitating organizational change (Blumberg 1968; Brannen 1983; Heller et al. 1998). Arguably, then, in responding to the accelerated uncertainty of crisis, employers may move towards more

9

decentralized and participative forms of work organization. Moreover, an emphasis on innovative capacity should also mean a greater willingness to increase employee training, to achieve the full benefits of technological change and gain competitive advantage during economic recovery.

There is also a literature on technology and work organization that points in the same direction. Economic crises in the perspective of 'creative destruction' entail an accelerated replacement of old technologies by new, which in the current context is likely to involve increased computerization and automation. A number of researchers have argued that work conditions tend to be better in more advanced technical settings (Blauner 1964; Woodward 1970; Piore and Sabel 1984). Labour costs represent a lower proportion of overall costs, so workforce reductions provide fewer economic benefits and labour tends to be treated more as a fixed cost. Increasing computerization and automation, it is suggested, reduce physical work hazards, make it easier to enrich job tasks, provide greater returns to training, and encourage the introduction of forms of semi-autonomous team working.

The other side of the coin of 'creative destruction' is the selective nature of the jobs that are eliminated. In past recessions, less-skilled employees and those in technologically less sophisticated sectors have tended to be disproportionately vulnerable to unemployment (Gershuny and Marsh 1993; Gallie et al. 1998). Employers are likely to give priority to retaining their skilled employees, because they have invested more in their skill development and they are more difficult to replace. The disproportionate reduction then of less-skilled employees and those in less technologically advanced sectors removes from the workforce those with the lowest quality of working conditions. The result is that the average job quality of the 'survivors' is likely to rise.

Overall, then, the combination of improving work conditions among the survivors and disproportionate elimination of those in the least skilled and most backward sectors of industry should mean that a period of economic crisis raises the average quality of work among those still in employment.

Economic crisis and workforce polarization?

A third possibility is that economic crisis may accelerate a long-term process of labour market polarization in advanced societies. This has been a central preoccupation of research from at least the 1990s (Kalleberg 2011). It can be seen as a development from earlier theories of labour market segmentation, which depicted a sharp divide between employees in a primary labour market who benefited from multiple advantages in terms of employment conditions and those in a secondary labour market who suffered from cumulative disadvantage. The new element in theories that developed from the 1990s was that the divisions between labour market sectors were not static, but rather were growing greater over time. Arguments within this general perspective, however, could take two rather different forms.

The first was that there was a progressive 'hollowing out' of the employment structure, in which the most highly skilled employees at the one extreme and the least skilled at the other were increasing their shares of the workforce, while employees with intermediary skills had a declining share. This argument has been particularly influential in analyses of labour market change in the United States (Wright and Dwyer 2003; Kalleberg 2011), but has become increasingly important in discussions of developments in Europe (Goos and Manning 2007; Goos et al. 2009; Oesch and Rodriguez Menes 2011; Fernandez-Macias et al. 2012). There have been diverse views about the factors that underlie this process, but it is most commonly attributed to the effects of increasing computerization and automation. Such advanced technologies, it has been suggested, are particularly effective at displacing jobs that involve clearly defined and fixed work routines (Autor et al. 2003). The procedures involved in such 'routinized' jobs can be programmed into the technological equipment itself, thereby eliminating the job tasks previously carried out by employees. In contrast, computerization adds to the value of highly skilled jobs rather than supplanting them, since they involve complex decision-making in conditions of uncertainty. At the other end of the scale, many unskilled jobs are also considered difficult to 'program' out of existence since work routines tend to be relatively unsystematic.

The second variant of the polarization argument has been concerned not with the overall shape of the employment structure, that is to say the relative proportions of employees in different skill categories, but with the increasing divergence in the quality of work between those in highly skilled and those in low-skilled work (Kalleberg 2011). The spread of computer technologies again has been central to some of these accounts. While developments in computerization add to the value of the work of those in highly skilled occupations, they decrease the value of low-skilled workers who have difficulty assimilating new technical developments. Such 'skill-biased' technological development has been seen as one of the sources of the sharp rise in pay inequalities in the United States.

Another source of growing inequality in work conditions, it has been suggested, is the divide between employees on standard and those on non-standard contracts—in particular temporary and part-time contracts (Atkinson 1986; Barker and Christensen 1998; Capelli et al. 1997; Kalleberg 2011). A number of researchers have pointed to the increasing use by employers of workers on 'precarious' or fixed-term contracts, where low job security is compounded with poorer opportunities for skill development, worse physical working conditions, and low levels of task discretion. The expansion of the precarious workforce is thought to reflect the need to be able to reduce labour costs rapidly under conditions of product market volatility. As economies became more interdependent and competitiveness more severe, it seemed likely that the employment conditions of such workers would grow worse over time.

These theories of polarization were developed in a period of economic prosperity. At that time there had been considerable controversy about whether they were confirmed by the empirical trends in workforce development (Auer and Cazes 2003; McGovern et al. 2007). But the economic crisis could be seen as giving them a strongly heightened new relevance. If the growth of precarious work was a response to product market volatility, then, in conditions of economic crisis, it could be expected that employers would push for a considerable expansion of the temporary workforce. Whereas in times of prosperity a significant proportion of temporary workers could be expected eventually to find permanent jobs, in conditions of economic crisis they were likely to be the first choice option for dismissals, thereby becoming increasingly entrapped in cycles of temporary work and unemployment.

Institutional mediation of the effects of the crisis?

A fourth possibility is that the effects of economic crisis may be relatively limited because institutional structures will be resistant to change. Instead there will be enduring differences in the quality of work between countries or sets of countries. However, such arguments may also imply that economic crisis will lead to differential costs to particular types of employee depending on the prevailing type of institutional regime. There are two main theories that could potentially provide accounts of stability and difference in employer responses—production regime theory on the one hand and employment regime theory on the other.

Production regime (or varieties of capitalism) theory has suggested that a crucial difference between societies is the level of employer coordination (Soskice 1999; Hall and Soskice 2001). Where employers are well coordinated (that is to say in Coordinated Market Economies), they will have longer-term planning horizons, produce more complex and high-quality products (diversified quality production), and place an emphasis on the development of a highly skilled workforce that has both occupational- and firm-specific skills. Where employers are highly fragmented in their bargaining practices (liberal market economies), they will work to relatively short-term horizons, produce relatively standardized mass products, and rely for the greater part on a relatively low-skilled workforce with little specialized vocational training.

These very different skill formation strategies are thought to have important implications for the quality of working conditions. Where employers opt for high and specialized skills, employees will be given greater discretion over their work and will adopt policies aimed at the retention of the workforce. Where employers rely on general skills, employee discretion will be low and the priority will be given to ease of hiring and firing to save costs in times of economic difficulty.

An alternative account of institutional difference is the employment regime perspective, which is rooted in welfare regime theory with its emphasis on the relative power resources of employers and employees (Korpi 1983, 2006; Esping-Andersen 1990; Gallie 2007b). This points to a broad distinction between inclusive systems of employment regulation, where policies are designed to protect vulnerable sectors of the workforce, dualist systems where there is a relatively sharp distinction between core and peripheral workers (those on standard and non-standard contracts), and liberal systems where work conditions will depend primarily on market power.

In production regime theory the Scandinavian countries and Germany are held to be examples of coordinated market economies, Britain and Ireland of liberal market economies. In the employment regime perspective the Scandinavian countries are held to be the principal examples of inclusive regimes, the Continental countries of dualist regimes, and Britain and Ireland of Liberal regimes. The principal differences in expectation between the theories relates to the degree of similarity or difference between the Scandinavian and Continental countries, with production regime theory postulating a broad similarity of pattern between them and employment regime theory a significant difference. It is notable that neither perspective has provided a clear view of how France and the Southern and East European countries are to be integrated within such frameworks. There has been a suggestion that France constitutes a distinctive form of coordinated market economy (a state coordinated economy) where government influence is central to the coordination process (Soskice 1999). The argument has also been made that the Southern countries and France constitute a distinct 'Mediterranean' type of capitalism (Hall and Soskice 2001; Amable 2003).

If the main prediction of these theories is stability of pattern, they nonetheless imply that some types of employees may be more vulnerable than others, potentially leading to increased internal polarization in periods of economic difficulty. Estevez-Abe (2005) has argued that within the production regime perspective, given its emphasis upon skill specificity as the factor underlying good work and employment conditions, women may be expected to be disadvantaged in relation to men in coordinated market economies, since they are likely to find it more difficult to acquire specific skills. Employment regime theory would imply that the costs of the crisis would be relatively evenly shared in inclusive societies, but would be linked to polarization primarily by contract status in dualist societies and by market power or class in liberal societies.

Economic Crisis, Welfare Regimes, and Social Integration

The implications of economic crises may extend beyond the sphere of work to undermine social integration more widely. In contrast to the case for work quality, most scenarios point primarily to the potentially negative effects of economic crisis on social integration. Even the theory of creative destruction underlined the dilemma that, while economic crisis could have positive effects in terms of the development of production, these were at the cost of the severe disruption of people's lives and a possible threat to the broader social fabric.

We know a good deal more about the impact of earlier recessions on the lives of the unemployed than on the quality of work. It has been shown to cause severe economic and psychological deprivation, raising the risks of social marginalization. But the extent to which this is the case has been found to vary between countries. Earlier research has suggested that one factor that underlies this is the relative generosity of the welfare system, in particular how far it provides protection of people's incomes faced by job loss.

Potentially the effects of economic crisis on social integration may reach further than those most directly affected by the loss of their jobs. For those in work, it is likely to bring heightened insecurity and some studies have suggested that the psychological effects of job insecurity may be as damaging as those of unemployment itself. Arguably its effects may be wider still, affecting people's understanding of their society and their commitment to its underlying principles. The limited research on the political effects of recession in post-war recessions found little evidence of such radicalization. But concern about such wider effects can clearly draw on the experience of the Great Depression in the 1930s, where the most severe economic crisis prior to the recession of 2008/9 appears to have led in many countries to a widespread delegitimation of prevailing institutions, the emergence of radical movements on both the left and the right of the political spectrum, and in several countries the collapse of democratic regimes.

In examining the wider implications of the crisis for social integration, we focus on three main issues. These are its implications for commitment to employment, for psychological well-being and finally for political legitimacy.

Employment commitment

Commitment to employment has been regarded as a key aspect of social integration for people of working age because of the importance of work for personal well-being. But it has also been seen as an important determinant of social integration more widely, given the benefits of work for protection from poverty and opportunities for social relationships.

There has been long-standing research interest in the potential effects of unemployment on people's commitment to work. Starting from the assumption that work is a disutility and that people would naturally prefer to give priority to leisure if they can afford to, economists have examined the effects of unemployment benefit rates on the time it takes for unemployed people to find another job and return to work. In general the evidence indicates relatively minor effects in delaying job acquisition, mainly concentrated among young workers in the early parts of their unemployment spells (Nickell et al. 1989; Narendranathan and Stewart 1993; Arulampalam and Stewart 1995; Spiezia 2000). Studies focusing directly on employment commitment have generally shown that employment commitment among the unemployed is actually higher than among the employed (Gallie and Vogler 1993; Gallie and Alm 2000). This has been accounted for by the new awareness the experience of unemployment brings of the value of taken-for-granted or 'latent' benefits of employment for people's everyday life patterns—for instance its value in providing a structure of time and connectedness to others (Jahoda 1982).

Such conclusions were based on research carried out in periods of much less severe crisis than that triggered by the recession of 2008/9. A difference in a situation of major economic crisis lies in the sheer scale of unemployment, which arguably may produce a distinctive effect on attitudes to work. High levels of unemployment may increase a sense of fatalism as a result of the sheer dearth of job vacancies and the experience of repeated rejection when making job applications. It also increases the numbers of unemployed in the local community and this may reduce the stigmatic nature of unemployment.

There is an almost complete lack of research on the effects of economic crisis on the employment commitment of those who remain in work. It could be that it reinforces commitment to employment, as those in work become more sharply aware of the good fortune of having a job in conditions where others are experiencing redundancy. Alternatively, the increased pressures at work for the 'survivors'—whether in terms of higher levels of work intensity, the disruption of long-standing working patterns, a deterioration in the social environment at work, or a curtailment of career opportunities—may undercut the intrinsic rewards of work and reduce longer-term employment commitment (Dordevic 2004). It is notable that a US study concluded that people who had experienced recessions in their formative years were more likely to believe that luck rather than effort was the most important factor behind individual success (Giuliano and Spilimbergo 2009). Arguably scepticism about the rewards for effort is likely to be subversive of work motivation.

15

Subjective well-being

Subjective well-being can be seen as a summary indicator of people's sense of social integration with respect to their everyday personal lives. Given previous research, the assumption would be that economic crisis would have high costs in terms of personal well-being. The literature on unemployment has shown consistently that it creates psychological distress for both men and women. This has been shown using both relatively simple indicators of life satisfaction and well-validated multi-item scales of anxiety and depression (Warr 1987; Clark and Oswald 1994; Gallie and Russell 1998). Longitudinal research has shown that the effect is causal and cannot be accounted for by prior differences in the psychological well-being of employed and unemployed people (Linn et al. 1985; Warr 1987). With respect to those in work, research on job insecurity has provided a very similar picture (De Witte 1999; Burchell et al. 2002; Ferrie et al. 2002; Sverke et al. 2002, 2006; Burchell 2011). Indeed there is some evidence that the duration of strong negative effects on well-being is greater with respect to job insecurity than is the case even with unemployment.

There is still much disagreement, however, on the relative importance in accounting for the distress associated with job loss of economic deprivation on the one hand and the dissolution of social networks on the other. The latter was particularly emphasized in the literature on social exclusion and could draw on the classic interwar study of the social consequences of unemployment *Marienthal*, which showed the increasing isolation of the unemployed from community life (Jahoda et al. 1972). Using data from eleven countries in the EU-15, Gallie et al. (2003) argued that economic deprivation is the major factor underlying psychological distress and that there was little evidence of change in the strength of social support with entry to unemployment. But a German panel study concluded that non-pecuniary effects were stronger than income effects (Winklemann and Winklemann 1998). It has also been shown that unemployment does enhance social isolation by increasing the risk of the dissolution of partnerships (Lampard 1993; Inanc 2012). It remains possible that the relative importance of financial and non-financial sources of distress varies between different countries and different parts of Europe. As yet, there has been no study with a relatively comprehensive coverage.

Moreover, an area that still remains largely uncharted by research is the relationship between the general level of unemployment and its consequences for psychological distress. Do the higher rates of unemployment that accompany economic crisis make the experience of being without work easier or more difficult to bear? Arguably, the very bleak labour prospects in a period of economic crisis could accentuate the risks of anxiety and depression, and longer spells of unemployment will reinforce this by eroding

people's financial reserves and increasing the severity of financial deprivation. But there is also an argument that, with longer-term unemployment, a
process of adaptation sets in, as people grow accustomed to being without a
job and adjust to the constraints of their new economic situation. A higher
level of local unemployment may also reduce the sense of personal failure
and encourage greater solidarity towards the unemployed within the local
community.

Political trust and legitimacy

The wider concern about the potential implication of economic crisis for social
integration is that people's experiences of employment insecurity and financial deprivation may lead to the erosion of normative support for the political
institutions of their society. These are conditions that are thought to favour
extremist movements, political violence, and loss of confidence in democratic
institutions. The spectre of the interwar period where economic crisis facilitated
the rise of both extreme right and extreme left anti-democratic movements
inevitably casts its shadow over thinking about the potential consequences of
the current crisis.

Research in the post-war period, covering a period of relative prosperity,
has provided some support for the view that unemployment has significant
negative effects for political attitudes. A study in the US found that people
who had experienced a recession in their formative years (18–25) were less
likely to have confidence in public institutions and that recessions had long-
lasting effects on people's beliefs (Giuliano and Spilimbergo 2009). Similarly,
a cross-national study concluded that personal experience of unemployment
led to negative opinions about the effectiveness of democracy (Altindag and
Mocan 2010). Results for Europe showed that these effects were particularly
strong among the long-term unemployed: those who were unemployed for
more than a year were significantly more likely to indicate that democracy is
bad for the economy, to think that democracies were indecisive and involved
too much quibbling, and to approve of 'having a strong leader who does not
have to bother with parliament and elections'.

Such research on the political effects of job loss was carried out in a context of relative prosperity. There is clearly a need to chart rigorously the
impact of the much more severe economic difficulty that began with the
recession of 2008/9. One issue in particular that has not been examined is
how widely across the population such negative political effects are found.
Research has focused primarily on those who have personally experienced
job loss. But arguably, with an economic crisis of far greater scale, doubts
about the adequacy of current institutions may spread much further, given

the highly visible and prolonged failure of the political elites. The negative effects resulting from people's personal experiences of deprivation may be reinforced, then, by more general changes in attitudes due to perceptions of the inefficacy of economic policy-making

Welfare regimes and social integration

The institutional sphere that is likely to be most important for mediating the effects of the economic crisis with respect to social integration is that of the welfare state. There are grounds for expecting that the extent to which economic crisis affects social integration will be in part dependent on the strength of the safety net for the unemployed provided by the welfare system. The most influential formulation of a typology of welfare regimes is that of Esping-Andersen (1990), which distinguished three types of welfare regime differentiated by the extent to which welfare provision derived from the state, the market, or households. His schema contrasted the 'social-democratic' regime characteristic of the Nordic countries with an emphasis on universalism and de-commodification, with the dualist 'corporatist' regimes of the Continental and Southern countries, where the generosity of welfare provision was tied to employment status, and the 'Liberal' regimes prevailing in the Anglo-Saxon countries, which emphasized minimal state provision and a reliance on the market. The appropriateness of considering the Continental and Southern countries as constituting a single type of regime has been the subject of much critical discussion (Leibfried 1992; Castles 1993; Saraceno 1994; Ferrera 1996; Rhodes 1997).

There also has been doubt about the similarity of principles underlying different aspects of welfare provision within countries. In considering different types of unemployment-related welfare provision, Gallie and Paugam (2000) restricted the notion of welfare regime more specifically to the nature of public provision. Their schema separated out the Southern countries as a distinct category, giving a typology of four types of regime, which differed in terms of benefit coverage, level and duration of cover, and investment in active employment policy. The universalistic, employment-centred and Liberal categories mapped onto the original distinctions highlighted in Esping-Andersen's typology. But it was argued that the Southern countries were better conceived as part of a sub-protective welfare system where the coverage of benefits was very incomplete, the level and duration of cover was weak, and active employment policy virtually non-existent.

The last decade has seen major reforms to the welfare system in many countries, so it is problematic how far such differences between country groups persist. Moreover, the East European societies were not included in these analyses and their categorization within such schemas is unclear.

Country Variations in Institutional Patterns

Arguments about the potential role of institutions in mediating processes of economic change have developed broad typologies for classifying countries within a limited number of regime types. But a notable feature of such schemas is that the examples they cite include a relatively limited number of countries and the location of others has been a matter of considerable controversy. In particular, as has been seen, there has been little agreement about the proper allocation of the Southern European countries and virtually no consideration of how the East European countries can be fitted into the different typologies. This has reflected in part the limited availability in the past of comparative institutional data. The evidence, however, has been substantially improved with the development of a comparative database (the ICTWSS) providing indicators of industrial relations characteristics for the full range of European countries (Visser 2011). It is now possible to consider how the wider range of countries relates to the key classifying criteria of the different institutional schemas.

Production regimes and bargaining coordination

Taking first production regime theory, the central institutional characteristic is taken to be the degree of bargaining coordination between employers. The prime examples of Coordinated Market Economies are the Nordic countries on the one hand and Germany, Austria, and the Benelux countries on the other. The examples in Europe of Liberal market economies are Britain and Ireland.

A first issue, then, is whether these initial distinctions are well grounded empirically and how other countries can be situated in relation to these exemplar cases. The original argument (Soskice 1999) drew on detailed but qualitative knowledge of a small number of countries with relatively clear-cut patterns of bargaining procedure. But obtaining good and comparable measures of effective bargaining coordination across a wide range of countries was a much trickier process, as it had to take account of tacit understandings as well as formal agreements. Although Soskice did produce an intuitive scoring for a number of countries, a more systematic attempt to produce a measure that included informal bargaining coordination was provided by Kenworthy (2001). Kenworthy was sceptical about the possibility of measuring wage coordination practices as such, but opted for a measure based on institutional features that could be predicted to generate greater or lesser coordination. These combined information on the level of bargaining with the extent of regularized pattern bargaining or bargaining synchronization as a result either of employer coordination or of union concentration. The schema allowed then for coordination to be generated by qualitatively different institutional arrangements.

This schema was adopted in a modified form in the ICTWSS database. It should be noted that the typology allows for coordination to be strongly influenced by state intervention, so in principle it covers the notions both of corporatist and state coordination. Like Kenworthy's, it distinguishes five levels of coordination:

5 = economy-wide bargaining, based on (a) enforceable agreements between the central organizations of unions and employers affecting the entire economy or entire private sector, or on (b) government imposition of a wage schedule, freeze, or ceiling.

4 = mixed industry and economy-wide bargaining : (a) central organizations negotiate non-enforceable central agreements (guidelines) and/or (b) key union and employers' associations set the pattern for the entire economy.

3 = industry bargaining with no or irregular pattern setting, limited involvement of central organizations, and limited freedoms for company bargaining.

2 = mixed industry- and firm-level bargaining, with weak enforceability of industry agreements.

1 = none of the above, fragmented bargaining, mostly at company level.

Figure 1.5 presents the pattern of bargaining coordination by country, with scores averaged over the years 2000 to 2009. As can be seen, the picture of high levels of employer coordination in the Continental European countries

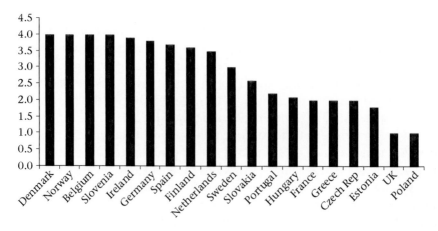

Figure 1.5. Bargaining coordination 2000–2009
Source: Derived from ICTWSS Database, Version 4.0 (Visser 2012: updated tables from author).

certainly fits well the cases of Germany, the Netherlands, and Belgium. The Nordic countries have medium high levels of coordination, with the exception of Norway which is close to the level of the Continental countries. Turning to the countries that were allocated to the category of 'Liberal market economies', the characterization of the UK as having low levels of bargaining coordination is confirmed. But Ireland stands out as quite distinct from the UK and is among the countries with relatively high levels of coordination. In these terms, it would appear that the 'Liberal' category should be restricted to the UK.

What is the level of bargaining coordination of the countries whose position was less clearly defined in the original schema? It has been suggested that France and the Southern countries could also be regarded as coordinated market economies, albeit more heavily dependent on state intervention to bring the social partners together. As can be seen, this is not supported by the evidence. France clearly is quite distinct from the Continental European group, with only relatively weak coordination. Among the Southern countries, Spain is comparable in bargaining coordination to the Continental countries, but Portugal and Greece have rather low levels. Thus there seems no simple way of classifying either France or the Southern European countries within a broader conception of 'coordinated market economy'. There had been no attempt to allocate the East European (or Transition) countries in the schema. But their position seems relatively clear-cut. They predominantly fall towards the lower end of the scale of coordination. The major exception is Slovenia, which has a level of bargaining coordination comparable with the Continental countries.

Overall, while there is support for the description of the Continental and Nordic countries as Coordinated Market Economies and for the description of the UK as a Liberal market economy, the allocation of other countries within the production regime schema proves rather problematic. Ireland fits poorly the 'Liberal' category and the provisional allocation of France and the Southern European countries to a form of 'coordinated market economy' seems unviable.

Employment regimes and inclusiveness

The employment regime perspective places the emphasis not on the level of coordination but on the degree of inclusiveness of the regulative system (Gallie 2007b; European Commission 2009). Inclusiveness can be taken to involve two principal dimensions—the scope of collective bargaining and its depth. Plausible proxies of these are bargaining coverage (the proportion of dependent employees covered by wage bargaining agreements) and the level of union density. Bargaining coverage is an indicator of the scope of joint regulation—and implies the prevalence of a norm about its appropriateness.

Union density can be considered a proxy of the depth of joint regulation—the extent to which it is likely to involve effective negotiation and to be implemented at workplace level.

The ICTWSS dataset provides an adjusted measure of bargaining coverage, which removes any groups from the employment count who are formally excluded from the right of bargaining.[1] It represents a measure of how complete coverage is relative to potential coverage. It is taken as reflecting the actual influence of industrial relations regulation (European Commission 2009: 77) or the extent to which the terms of employment are negotiated by trade unions (European Commission 2011a: 35). The same dataset also includes a measure of union density which is net union membership as a proportion of wage and salary earners in employment. This excludes any union members who are outside the active, dependent, and employed labour force—for instance retired workers, independent workers, students, and the unemployed. In both cases, we again take the average over the period 2000 to 2009.

The relative position of countries with respect to the two dimensions can be seen in Figure 1.6. Countries cluster in three quite distinct quadrants of

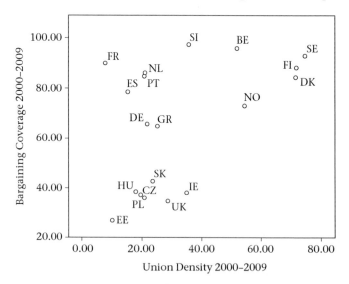

Figure 1.6. Bargaining coverage and union density

Source: Derived from ICTWSS Database, Version 4.0 (Visser 2012: updated tables from author). Figures for bargaining coverage and union density are averages for the period between 2000 and 2009.

[1] Adjusted and unadjusted rates are generally very close, but they differ for some countries where public employees without bargaining rights are excluded—for instance Austria, Germany, Hungary, Luxembourg, and Spain. More generally coverage rates exclude those not in the formal sector (for instance family workers), a category which estimates suggest is substantially higher in Southern European countries (European Commission 2011a).

the chart. Taking first the EU-15 countries, there are those that are inclusive in terms of both coverage and union density (primarily the Nordic countries), those that are inclusive with respect to coverage but not unionism (the Continental coordinated and Southern European countries), and finally those that have low inclusiveness with respect to both dimensions (Great Britain and Ireland). These groupings broadly coincide with the three types of employment regime that have been identified—inclusive, dualistic, and liberal regimes. With the exception of Slovenia, the East European countries are predominantly located in the low inclusive, Liberal, quadrant.

Country variations in welfare regimes

Gallie and Paugam's (2000) analysis of welfare generosity for the unemployed suggested that the Nordic countries came closest to a universalistic regime, the UK and Ireland to a Liberal-minimal regime; France, Netherlands, Germany, and Belgium to an employment-centred regime; and the Southern countries to a sub-protective regime. There was no attempt to classify the East European countries. The data underlying these allocations, however, were drawn from the 1980s and 1990s. In the course of the 2000s, reform of welfare funding has been one of the major objectives of policy in many countries. How far, then, do the earlier patterns of country difference in the EU-15 persist and what type of unemployment support is available in the East European countries?

In examining the similarities or differences between countries with respect to welfare generosity, we take three main criteria: the proportion of the unemployed in receipt of benefits (the coverage rate), the extent to which benefits replace income when in work (the net replacement rate), and finally expenditure on active employment policies (ALMP) as a percentage of per capita gross domestic product. Estimates of country positions in terms of these indicators are given in Table 1.1.

Taking first coverage rates, the Continental, the Nordic countries, and the Liberal countries all have relatively high levels of coverage. In contrast, the Southern and especially the East European countries have very low levels of coverage. The differences in coverage in the different regions of Europe is very substantial—ranging from two-thirds of the unemployed in the Continental countries to less than a third in the Southern and East European countries.

The second aspect of welfare generosity is how far benefits for the unemployed replace lost income from work. Replacement rates are notoriously tricky to calculate, given the problem of assessing what the income from work of the unemployed person is likely to be if they were able to get a job (for a detailed discussion, see Atkinson and Mickelwright 1985). The generosity of

Table 1.1. Welfare protection for the unemployed

		OECD net replacement rate short-term u/e 2009	Overall net replacement rates with social assistance	Coverage: % unemp. in receipt of unemp. payments 2009	Income poverty Unemployed 2007	ALMP expenditure % of GDP
Nordic	Denmark	76.9	68	73.3%	31	1.9
	Finland	70.6	62	88.4%	41	1.0
	Norway	75.4	61	30.6%	44	0.6
	Sweden	65	60	45.4%	26	1.1
	Mean	*72*	*63*	*59.4%*	*35.5*	*1.2*
Continental	Belgium	72.6	65	93.9%	56	1.5
	Germany	73	54	87.7%	51	0.9
	Netherlands	69	68	27.2%	27	1.2
	France	79.5	57	62.8%	33	1.1
	Mean	*73.5*	*61*	*67.9%*	*41.8*	*1.2*
Liberal	UK	61.1	49	49.7%	58	0.4
	Ireland	58.6	71	67.9%	43	1.0
	Mean	*59.9*	*60*	*58.8%*	*50.5*	*0.7*
Southern	Greece	65.1	31	12.4%	35	0.9
	Spain	71.5	50	47.3%	36	0.9
	Portugal	77.4	58	33.1%	32	0.7
	Mean	*71.3*	*46*	*30.9%*	*34.3*	*0.8*
Transition	Czech Rep.	73.5	51	20.9%	48	0.3
	Estonia	56.9	42	22.7%	62	0.2
	Slovenia	79	53	12.4%	36	0.5
	Slovakia	64.6	39	14.7%	45	0.3
	Hungary	70.1	37	54.7%	46	0.6
	Poland	61.4	43	17.8%	43	0.7
	Mean	*67.6*	*44*	*23.9%*	*46.7*	*0.4*

Note: Coverage data are drawn from EU-SILC 2010, with the exception of Ireland which is 2009. Figures relate to people who have been unemployed for at least six months in the previous 12 months, who have received unemployment-related benefits in the previous 12 months. Unemployment is self-defined. Note: The NRR summary measure is defined as the average of the net unemployment benefit (including SA and cash housing assistance), replacement rates for two earnings levels, three family situations, and 60 months of unemployment (see Stovicek and Turrini 2012).

Source: <http://www.oecd.org/social/socialpoliciesanddata/49971171.xlsx>. ALMP figures from OECD <http://dx.doi.org/10.1787/lmpxp-table-2012-1-en>. Figures are for 2010 with the exception of the UK (2009) and Norway (2007). Poverty figures from Eurostat 2010, table 3.1.

benefits can also vary substantially depending on the duration of unemployment and the composition of the household. The OECD has estimated measures of average net unemployment benefit replacement rates, both for the short-term unemployed and for the unemployed as a whole taking account of social assistance and housing benefits.

Countries have broadly similar levels of net replacement for the short-term unemployed. The exceptions are the Anglo-Saxon countries, both of which have rather lower levels of support. There is considerably more variation in terms of the replacement rates of the unemployed as a whole, taking account of the various forms of social assistance available when initial insurance benefits have run out. This shows that the Nordic countries (Denmark, Finland, Norway, and Sweden) are all at the higher end of the spectrum. The Continental countries have widely differing replacement rates, with Netherlands and Belgium among the countries with high replacement rates, but France and Germany intermediate. The three Southern countries have relatively low income support, in particular Greece, as is the case for all the East European countries. The Liberal countries emerge as quite different from each other, with Ireland having the highest and the UK a relatively low replacement rate.

It should be noted that these differences in the financial generosity of welfare systems do not translate in a simple way into differences in income poverty among the unemployed. While the more generous Nordic and Continental systems were associated with substantially lower income poverty than either the Liberal or the East European countries, this was not the case with respect to the Southern countries. This probably relates to the distinctive role of the family in the protection of the unemployed in the Southern countries (Gallie and Paugam 2000).

Turning to the third aspect of welfare protection for the unemployed, it is clear that the broad differences in financial generosity are paralleled by differences in spending on active labour market policies. The Nordic and Continental countries have much higher levels of expenditure than any of the other groups of countries. The Liberal (although again with substantial differences between the UK and Ireland) and the Southern countries have intermediate levels and the East European countries very low levels of expenditure.

In comparison to the picture in the 1990s, the pattern in 2010 suggests a significant convergence of the level of protection offered in the Nordic and Continental countries. In part, this reflects the programme of welfare reform in the Nordic countries which was aimed at reducing costs and placing greater emphasis on incentives to work (for developments in Sweden, see Anxo and Ericson 2011). With respect to unemployment provision, the Nordic countries now appear closer to an employment-centred model of welfare than a universalistic one. There is a marked divergence between the two Anglo-Saxon countries, which is likely to have been accentuated by the cuts to welfare provision for the unemployed in the UK. They remain similar only in the low support they give to those who are relatively short-term unemployed. Finally, the East European countries, which were previously unclassified, can now be seen to be a relatively extreme version of the sub-protective regime, with low coverage rates and low overall replacement rates.

Assessing the Patterns of Change

The analyses in the book draw on two principal data sources to assess the implications of the economic crisis for work quality and social integration. The first of these is the European Union Labour Force Survey series (EULFS), which provides the most robust evidence about changes in employment structure. It provides the main source of data for the analyses of employment reduction, changes in the distribution of employment, as well the assessment of changes in the composition of the workforce with respect to contract status. It also provides the contextual data for measures of the severity of the economic crisis in terms of employment reduction (along with measures of GDP decline from Eurostat and OECD data sources).

The second source of evidence is the European Social Survey (ESS). This has been used for assessing changes in the quality of work and in social integration from the standpoint of those directly affected—people in employment and the unemployed. In 2004, the ESS included a module on family, work, and well-being. In 2010 a substantial part of the module was replicated to provide a picture of change from the pre-recessionary to the post-recessionary period. Further details on the sample sizes, interview dates, and weighting can be found in the appendix to this chapter.

In addressing the impact of the crisis, the ESS 2010 provides two ways of assessing change: comparison of patterns with respect to 2004 and a number of retrospective questions asking people about their personal experiences of change in the previous three years. The analyses have focused on the nineteen countries for which there were data available for both the 2004 and 2010 waves of the ESS. In many of the chapters, the authors use indicators of the severity of the crisis in terms either of the change in GDP or of the rate of unemployment to assess whether these account for the extent of change or the differences between country patterns. But it is important to remember that the data available only allow us to take the story up to a certain point. The initial recession triggered by the banking crisis of 2008 was over in most of the countries by 2010. But the economic crisis in the sense of a level of per capita GDP still below the previous peak was still ongoing. Indeed, many countries were to experience a return to recession in the following year. Our analyses, then, should be regarded as provisional assessments of the consequences of the economic crisis generated by the recession of 2008/9.

In exploring country variations and the potential effects of institutional differences, the chapters give analyses both of the patterns for individual countries and for six country groups. The groups were constituted to take account of the theoretical discussions of institutional types, but they have been kept relatively disaggregated so that it is possible to examine the relationship between France, the Southern, and Transition or East European countries, whose classification in institutional terms has been problematic, and the more conventional Nordic, Continental, and Liberal groupings. Rather than accepting a priori the relevance of such groupings, our approach has been to explore empirically their utility for understanding variations in experiences of the quality of work and social integration. The country groupings are shown in Table 1.2.

The next two chapters of the book set the context in terms of the patterns of employment reduction in the European countries between 2008 and 2010. In Chapter 2 Michael Tåhlin focuses on the overall extent of employment reduction and assesses how far this can be related to changes in GDP levels and the types of institutional system prevalent in different countries. In Chapter 3 he turns to look at how reductions in employment affected different categories of employee, in particular whether reductions led to a more pronounced polarization of the employment structure.

The following four chapters examine the implications of the economic crisis for the quality of work. In Chapter 4 Martina Dieckhoff looks at what has happened to training opportunities for employees; in Chapter 5 Duncan Gallie and Ying Zhou take up the interconnected issues of job control, work intensity, and work stress; in Chapter 6 Vanessa Gash and Hande Inanc consider whether the economic crisis has led to increased structural polarization of the workforce in terms of job security; and in Chapter 7 Frances McGinnity and Helen Russell examine the impact of changes at work on work–family conflict.

The last three substantive chapters are concerned with the implications of the economic crisis for social integration. In Chapter 8 Nadia Steiber examines whether higher levels of unemployment and job insecurity are corrosive of commitment to employment; in Chapter 9 Helen Russell, Dorothy Watson, and Frances McGinnity assess the impact of the rise of unemployment on subjective well-being; and finally in Chapter 10 Javier Polavieja turns to the issue of whether the economic crisis has affected support for democratic and welfare institutions. The final chapter provides an overview of the main findings from the volume.

Table 1.2. Countries and country groups

Liberal	Nordic	Continental	France	Southern	Transition
Ireland	Denmark	Belgium		Greece	Czech Republic
UK	Finland	Germany		Portugal	Estonia
	Norway	Netherlands		Spain	Hungary
	Sweden				Poland
					Slovakia
					Slovenia

Appendix

The 2010 module

The 2010 module was constructed by a questionnaire design team coordinated by Duncan Gallie. It included Martina Dieckhoff, Helen Russell, Nadia Steiber, and Michael Tåhlin. Duncan Gallie, Helen Russell, and Michael Tåhlin had also been involved in the design of the work questions for the 2004 module, for which the overall team coordinator was Robert Erickson. The sample numbers for the two years (overall and for the subsample of employees) are given in Table A1.1.

Weighting the ESS data

The ESS data, particularly when the analysis is focused on employees, need additional weighting to the basic weights provided. This was carried out for the team by Dorothy Watson of the ESRI, using the EULFS. The purpose of

Table A1.1. Sample numbers

	2004		2010	
	All	Employees	All	Employees
Belgium	1778	738	1704	748
Czech	3026	1255	2386	1018
Germany	2870	1184	3031	1393
Denmark	1487	775	1576	774
Estonia	1989	931	1793	780
Spain	1663	708	1885	724
Finland	2022	912	1878	748
France	1806	777	1728	790
UK	1897	789	2422	1005
Greece	2406	613	2715	693
Hungary	1498	567	1561	656
Ireland	2286	941	2576	766
Netherlands	1881	912	1829	871
Norway	1760	1006	1548	899
Poland	1716	619	1751	726
Portugal	2052	716	2150	668
Sweden	1948	997	1500	728
Slovakia	1512	634	1856	695
Slovenia	1442	589	1403	565
Total	37039	15663	37292	15247

survey weighting is to compensate for any imbalances in the distribution of characteristics in the completed survey sample compared to the population of interest, whether such imbalances occur because of sampling error, from the nature of the sampling frame used, or due to differential response rates within population subgroups. The weights were constructed for the population age 20–64.

Weighting was a two-stage process:

1. Construction of a design weight to compensate for the over-representation or under-representation of individuals as a consequence of the sampling frame or sample design used in each country. The design weight was already provided with the ESS data.

2. Beginning with the design weight, and calibrating the design-weighted sample distribution to population totals within country and year (2004 and 2010) along a number of dimensions that were of key importance for the analyses in this book:[2]

   – age by sex (nine 5-year age groups)

   – age by sex for the population at work (two age groups, 20–39 and 40–64)

   – ISCO 1 digit by sex for employees. Due to small cell sizes in several countries, ISCO codes were combined for 0 (armed forces), 6 (farming employees), and 9 (not stated).

The control totals for the calibration were obtained from the EULFS Survey tables published on the Eurostat website, for 2004 and 2010.

For analysis involving country groups, an important weighting decision is whether to include countries in proportion to their size or to treat each country as an equal unit. For testing regime type accounts, equal unit weighting is to be preferred. The ESS sample numbers are neither proportional to size nor equal between countries. The data were then reweighted to given an overall sample size of 1,000 for each country for each wave.

---

[2] This involved using GROSS, a program using a minimum distance algorithm and iterative process to calibrate to external controls from the European Labour Force Survey data for 2004 and 2010 from the Eurostat website.

2

Economic Crisis and Employment Change: The Great Regression

Michael Tåhlin

Introduction

The introductory chapter of the book gave an overview of how the economic crisis evolved from its early phase in 2007 to more recent years. In this and the following chapter we will focus on the first part of the contraction, from 2007 through 2010, and we will compare developments across the eighteen countries that were included in the European Social Survey (ESS) waves of 2004 and 2010. The data from ESS then form the empirical basis for all other chapters of the book.

There are two main questions to be answered in the present chapter. First, what countries were hit hardest, in GDP and un/employment, by the economic crisis? Second, why were some countries hit harder than others? With regard to the second question, we attempt to distinguish between economic and institutional factors that might have been of importance for the magnitude of employment decline.

We use the word 'explain' in a cautious way, as a synonym of 'account for' in the sense of assessing the degree of empirical association between outcomes and potential explanatory factors. Hence, we provide evidence of correlation, not causation. Our topic is much too broad, and our data much too coarse, to allow any rigorous test of which causal mechanisms are at work. Nonetheless, some of the patterns that emerge from our empirical analysis are sufficiently clear to indicate promising lines of explanation that might be pursued further in future research.

The present chapter deals with cross-national variation in general developments of the labour market during the crisis, while the next chapter looks at differences in adverse employment change across population groups and examines how these differences vary by country. We begin by briefly outlining a conceptual frame to be used in the empirical analysis, drawing a distinction between economic and institutional factors of interest when accounting for international variance in contraction magnitude and impact. Descriptive and more explanatory empirical patterns are then reported in tandem as the story unfolds. The chapter concludes with a summary and some remarks on how the general picture painted by the data and our analysis of them can be interpreted.

The magnitude and labour market impact of the crisis—a conceptual frame

Economic life in general and the labour market in particular has two fundamental properties: growth and distribution. These two stand in a complex relationship to each other. To economists of an orthodox variety, there is an inevitable trade-off between efficiency and equality, implying that very narrow distributions of rewards reduce rates of economic growth by destroying micro-level incentives. While economic incentives are obviously important to some degree, the more exact nature of the trade-off is not easily determined. In the other causal direction, rising rates of growth might lead to increasing inequality (at least in the short run) to the extent that expansion is driven by actions of uneven intensity across the economic structure.

In this conceptual context, what is an economic recession? The standard definition is negative growth (falling output) over some extended period of time (like two consecutive quarters). In itself, this definition is thus related to growth only, without any reference to distribution. But even if there is no logical (conceptual or definitional) link between recession and distribution, is there nonetheless a strong empirical connection?

In thinking about this issue it is useful to consider the concept of institutions, defined as rules of the game, both formal and informal (cf. North 1990). Institutions are formed, reformed, and moulded on the basis of purposeful action (including the unintended consequences of such action). Growth and distribution therefore relate differently to institutions: while growth is essentially uncontested (with few exceptions, high growth is always preferred over low growth, *ceteris paribus*), the wideness of distribution is highly contested, with large differences in preferences across population groups and between organized interests (partly on the basis of beliefs about how distribution affects growth). Labour market institutions are formed mainly to affect distribution, not growth. To achieve or maintain a high growth rate (a general desire) is a restriction on the design and redesign of labour market institutions, but the main purpose of institutions is to modify distribution (a contested desire).

Still, some aspects of growth are socially contested. First, some argue that growth—at least in most of its current forms—is detrimental for the natural environment, and should therefore be kept low. Second, some argue that while high growth is desirable, it is less important to achieve than is a more equal distribution, so even if equality reduces growth it is a price worth paying (see e.g. Layard 2005). This view is based on the belief that individual well-being is more affected by relative than absolute rewards. Third, growth rate volatility—the frequency and width of cyclical swings—is typically less tolerated by those who prefer relatively equal distributions, because worker categories with low labour market rewards to begin with tend to be more harshly treated than others by economic downturns.

Of these three aspects we will disregard the first two since they concern the value and costs of long-run growth which in turn is a structural characteristic of the economy. As such it is not directly linked to recessions, by definition expected to be cyclical (temporary or short-term) events rather than structural (more permanent). Recessions are negative deviations from long-run growth, and our interest here lies in the deviation—its causes, magnitude, and consequences—not the trend.

The institutional connection between distribution and recessions leads us to expect the following empirical regularity: in countries with an institutional structure favouring low inequality in labour market rewards, the magnitude of the recent contraction has been relatively small. Minimizing cyclical swings around a given long-run growth rate is desirable for the same reasons as minimizing inequality in job rewards more generally, since low monetary rewards tend to go together with high unemployment risks (a pattern closely tied to inequalities in skill).

There are several mechanisms that link equalizing institutions and low employment volatility, including trade union strength and employment protection. Low wage inequality may reduce the variance in worker productivity (Acemoglu and Pischke 1999; Tåhlin 2004) and thereby the relative number of marginal workers. High rates of social insurance provide automatic stabilizers that help maintain general demand in economic downturns. However, there are also mechanisms that may lead to negative employment effects of equality-promoting institutions. For example, high replacement rates and long entitlement periods in unemployment insurance, without active measures to encourage job search, are empirically associated with relatively long durations of individual unemployment, perhaps due to reduced incentives to look for work (see e.g. Nickell 1997). High wage floors raise the productivity hurdles that workers must pass to get a job. In general, equalizing institutions might produce barriers between insiders with good employment conditions and outsiders who are not allowed to compete by offering to work at lower reward levels (Lindbeck and Snower 1988). But note that mechanisms of the insider–outsider kind can be expected to adversely affect employment levels rather than employment fluctuations. Indeed, although the overall impact of raising reward floors on the rate of labour market inequality may be theoretically mixed and empirically uncertain, its specific impact on employment volatility should go in the same direction as the mechanisms mentioned earlier, i.e. reducing fluctuations.

The reduction of volatility produced by equality works similarly in downturns and upturns. Just as lay-off rates during recessions can be expected to be relatively low if equality-promoting institutions are in place, hiring rates in periods of recovery can likewise be expected to be relatively low, to a large extent for the same reasons. While the expected overall impact on long-run employment is therefore not positive (but may be negative according to some views), the net outcome of low rates of both lay-offs and hiring is nonetheless desirable because the negative effect of losing a job is seen as larger than the positive effect of finding one. In part, this may be an instance of what Kahneman and Tversky (1984) call loss aversion, but also reflects a real (rather than merely subjective) difference in value: the average job lost has a longer realized duration than the expected duration of an average job found, and is correspondingly difficult to replace.

Aside from the hypothesis that distribution affects volatility (via institutions) we expect that growth affects volatility. This may be called the regression hypothesis: in countries where recent growth has been relatively high, the magnitude of the downturn as well as its employment consequences will be relatively large. As in the distributional (or institutional) case, there are several mechanisms involved. The first is statistical and is called regression to the mean (see e.g. Tversky and Kahneman 1974; Stigler 1997). Any two variables that are imperfectly correlated will display the tendency that the more extreme (higher or lower) the value of one variable, the larger will be the difference in value between the variables. In our case, this means that the higher the rate of growth was in a given country just before the recession, the larger (on average) the fall in growth will be in the recession, and vice versa. The tendency comes about due to the role of chance variation. Think of a test of some kind, with individual performance measured at two occasions. For each individual and occasion, the test result is the joint outcome of two factors, ability and luck (such as guessing the right answer). Luck is by definition randomly distributed across individuals, but will be concentrated among individuals with relatively good results on the test, since luck increases the proportion of correct responses. While luck may randomly hold for any individual across occasions, by definition it will not hold on average and therefore benefit other individuals at the second occasion. Hence, while ability produces a positive correlation of test results across occasions, luck produces a negative correlation between the test result at the first occasion and the

33

change in results between occasions. The latter tendency is called regression to the mean, and will be stronger the larger the role played by random factors in producing the outcome of interest. Since random factors play at least some role for almost all outcomes, and often play a large role, regression to the mean is a practically universal phenomenon and is in many cases (or even typically) of considerable numerical size.

A second kind of mechanism producing a negative correlation between growth rates before and during recessions is related to systematic rather than random variation. There are two main instances of such mechanisms which may metaphorically be labelled bursting bubbles and infant mortality. Bubbles are price increases that exceed sustainable levels. While easy to observe after bursting they are notoriously difficult to identify beforehand. Indeed, the identification problem is present almost by definition, since the price increase occurs due to a continued rise in demand. Even observers who believe that the price increase is unsustainable in the long run are tempted to invest in the short run in order not to forgo profits that other investors are conspicuously making and, by giving in to temptation, contribute to blowing up the bubble. At the micro level this behaviour may certainly be rational, which would appear to be the main reason for why it occurs, but may in the aggregate lead to strongly undesirable consequences. The evolution of housing and real estate markets in some (but far from all) countries is the chief example of the recent recession. When bubbles burst, dramatic repercussions throughout the economy and the labour market may occur, especially if the bubble is located in a central economic position such as housing and construction. Sudden brakes on construction activity are an important direct cause of rapidly increasing unemployment. Indirect effects may be even bigger. Since housing is the major component of personal wealth, large falls in its value—perhaps below the mortgage level—may heavily curtail the spending capacity of households and hence general domestic demand.

By infant mortality is meant the strong tendency of new jobs and firms to last a shorter period of time than older ones (see e.g. Dunne et al. 1989; Brüderl et al. 1992; Rosenfeld 1992; Cressy 2006). For many reasons, new jobs and firms are relatively vulnerable. For firms, the market's weeding out of non-competitive units is especially harsh among newcomers, since a relatively large fraction of these are trying their luck for the first time with correspondingly immature products and methods. For jobs, many of the newly formed matches between employers and employees are try-outs or otherwise time-limited in their contract form, and even if not formally temporary are typically vulnerable in the face of weakened labour demand due to their short tenure. In economic recessions, negative employment change will therefore tend to be especially large in labour markets with a large fraction of recent hires, i.e. in markets with strong employment expansion in the years preceding the downturn.

To sum up, we have two main expectations regarding cross-national varia-tion in the magnitude of the recent recession and its labour market outcomes. First, countries with an institutional structure favouring equality in labour market rewards have experienced comparatively mild deteriorations in their employment levels. Second, countries with a relatively strong economic expansion in the period preceding the recession have experienced compara-tively large subsequent falls in output and employment.

These two expectations are linked in the sense that the first predicts a nega-tive association between equality and volatility and the second predicts a pattern of continuing volatility over time with positively correlated sizes of upturns and downturns. Hence, an additional expectation is that countries with a strong economic expansion before the recession (and a correspond-ingly strong contraction in the recession) are relatively unequal societies.

There is, however, a possible counter-argument concerning the effects of equality on employment reduction. It appears reasonable to expect that the size of the employment fall during the crisis *given* pre-recession growth rates has been relatively large in countries with equality-promoting institutions. The presumed mechanisms are related to labour market rigidities of which at least three aspects are relevant here, concerning wages, working hours, and employment contract form, respectively. As an alternative to laying workers off (or ceasing to hire) in the face of weakened demand for the firm's output, employers might consider reducing employment costs by cutting wages or working hours. These options would seem to be more available in contexts where organized labour is relatively weak, since trade unions are typically not prepared to accept significant reductions in benefit levels. Therefore reduced labour demand translates to a relatively large extent into reductions of employment (rather than wages or hours) in countries with strong labour organizations. This line of reasoning is commonly referred to as Krugman's unified theory, intended to account for rising wage inequality but fairly low unemployment in the United States in the 1980s and the converse pattern—rising unemployment but low wage inequality—in Europe (Krugman 1994). The third aspect of flexibility, contract form, is directly related to dealing with the rigidity problems created by sharp insider–outsider boundaries. Expanding the scope for time-limited employment contracts as a middle form between insiders and outsiders has been a common way to deal with unemployment in some countries, notably Spain but also, for example, in Scandinavia. Workers on temporary contracts, by definition as well as in prac-tice, run much higher risks than others of losing their job.

All these mechanisms—downwardly inflexible wages, downwardly inflex-ible working hours, and a sizeable proportion of workers on temporary contracts—would appear to lead to comparatively large employment reductions in economic downturns in countries with equality-promoting institutions. This tendency, then, runs counter to the one spelled out above, that equality reduces employment volatility. The combined expectation is that the employment fall during the crisis has been relatively small in equal countries due to a fairly low degree of employment volatility, but given volatility, employment reduction has been relatively large in equal countries.

A General Picture of Employment Fall in the Crisis

When examining how employment has changed during the economic crisis, it is relevant to consider both the employment rate, expressed as the proportion employed of the population, and the unemployment rate, expressed as the proportion unemployed of the labour force (where the labour force consists of all employed and unemployed but excludes the remaining population). The employment rate alone is not sufficient because many individuals have chosen not to work, due to involvement in other activities, such as education or child care, while others may be unable to work for health reasons. The unemployment rate is not sufficient either, since many individuals who would prefer to work are not in the labour force because they have given up (at least temporarily) on trying to find a job.

Reporting both employment and unemployment rates, however, leads to a rather inaccessible presentation, with large amounts of information to digest. In addition, much of the presentation would be redundant due to overlap, since the pattern of variation across countries or population groups tends to be fairly (though not completely) similar for employment and unemployment rates.

We therefore use a summary indicator of employment and unemployment rates by subtracting the unemployed share of the labour force from the employed share of the population. This measure can take values from 100 (per cent), when everyone in the population is employed and no one is out of work, to minus 100 when no one is employed and everyone is looking for work. In practice, most countries in most years have values between 40 and 75 on this summary indicator. In the years prior to the recession, the top performers on the employment index were Denmark, Sweden, the Netherlands, and the UK, all with a value of around 70, while Poland and Slovakia (around 45) and Greece and Spain (around 55) were at the bottom end.

The starting year of the contraction is set at 2007 if unemployment rose from 2007 to 2008, which was the case for six countries (Estonia, Hungary, Ireland, Spain, Sweden, and the UK), while the starting year is set at 2008 if unemployment fell from 2007 to 2008, which was the case for the other twelve countries. In all eighteen countries unemployment rose from 2008 to 2009 and in all countries except Germany unemployment continued to rise from 2009 to 2010.

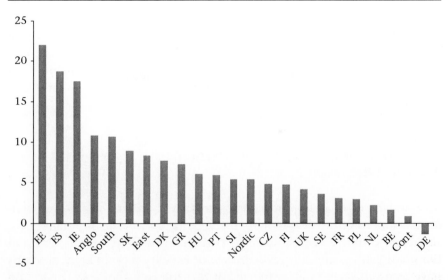

Figure 2.1. Employment fall 2007/8–2010 in 18 European countries. Percentage points, summary indicator of employment and unemployment

In addition to distinguishing individual countries, we group them into traditional clusters or 'regimes'. In the following figures, 'Anglo' includes Ireland and the UK, 'Cont' (for Continental) includes Belgium, Germany, and the Netherlands, 'East' includes the Czech Republic, Estonia, Hungary, Poland, Slovakia, and Slovenia, 'Nordic' includes Denmark, Finland, and Sweden,[1] and 'South' includes Greece, Portugal, and Spain. France is not included in any country group due to its special pattern of institutional characteristics, essentially a mix of Continental and Southern elements.

Figure 2.1 shows the change from 2007/8 to 2010 in the overall employment indicator (the employment rate minus the unemployment rate) by individual country as well as averages for country groups. (Unless otherwise indicated, all numbers in the following are based on aggregate data from the European Union Labour Force Surveys, EULFS.) It is striking that three countries—Estonia, Spain, and Ireland—have been hit much harder than all others. (In the diagram, these countries' large employment losses affect the country group averages more or less strongly, depending on the number of countries in each group. The Anglo group, with Ireland and just one other country, the UK, is affected the most.)

---

[1] Norway is excluded in this chapter and the next due to its highly special economic situation, with large long-run surpluses in government budgets arising from abundant natural resources (oil), greatly reducing vulnerability to external economic shocks.

Aside from Ireland and Denmark, all the countries of Europe's rich north-west have seen total employment losses of less than 5 per cent, a stark contrast to the fate of the three hardest hit. The positively extreme country group is the Continental category, with all its members—Germany, Belgium, and the Netherlands—being better performers on this score than all other fifteen countries.

Accounting for Cross-National Variation, Part 1: The Great Regression

We now turn to an attempt to explain (or at least account for) the large variation across countries in the labour market outcomes of the economic crisis. As discussed above, we have two main expectations regarding the pattern of cross-national variation: (a) countries with equality-promoting institutions have seen relatively small employment reductions in the crisis period and (b) countries with relatively strong rates of economic expansion before the recession have suffered from relatively large subsequent employment reductions. We start by empirically evaluating the second of these expectations.

Figure 2.2 shows rates of economic growth from 1990 to 2010. The three countries with extremely large falls in employment are singled out in the

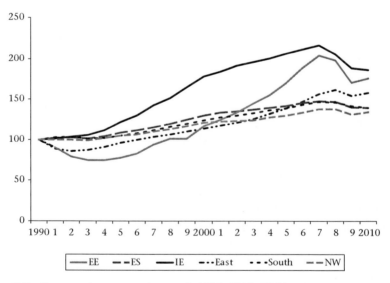

Figure 2.2. Comparative economic growth 1990–2010. GDP/capita in constant prices, 1990 = 100

Source: The Conference Board Total Economy Database™, January 2012, <http://www.conference-board.org/data/economydatabase/>.

figure, with the remaining countries grouped as above, except that the Continental and Nordic countries together with France and the UK form a large North Western category with fairly small internal variation in this regard. In this way, each of the three cases of largest interest—Estonia, Spain, and Ireland—are compared to their respective geographical or institutional cluster.

It is immediately evident that Estonia and Ireland are truly exceptional in their outstandingly high pre-recession growth rates relative to all others. These two countries had—by far—the highest rates of economic growth of all eighteen countries considered, as measured by the change in GDP per capita from the 1990s to the 2000s until 2007. Spain apparently fits less well into this pattern. While its growth rate in the period considered was higher than in most other countries, the difference is not large.

Among the three country groups, it can be noted that the richest category, the North West, had the slowest growth, while the poorest category, the East, had the fastest growth. But the variation across these categories pales in comparison to the extreme growth rates of Estonia and Ireland.

The very steep downturns in GDP in Estonia and Ireland as the recession hits are also evident from the figure. If all individual countries are considered (not shown in the figure), the overall correlation between the GDP rise from the 1990s to 2007/8 and the GDP fall from 2007/8 to 2010 is 0.60. Poland is an outlier in this respect, being the only country of all eighteen with a positive growth rate through 2010, despite a relatively high growth rate from the 1990s into the 2000s. With Poland excepted, the correlation between pre-recession economic growth and subsequent economic contraction rises from 0.60 to 0.86. This high correlation is not only due to the difference between Estonia/Ireland and all others. All countries except Poland line up in a rather orderly fashion to produce the strong association. Hence, a general pattern of regression is clear.

A second factor that was singled out above as potentially important when accounting for the magnitude of employment reduction in the wake of the recession is the housing sector. As an indicator of boom and bust—or bubble bursting—we look at how employment size in the construction industry evolved in the years leading into and through the recession. Figure 2.3 clearly shows how all the three cases of main interest had construction booms before the recession that were much stronger than among their neighbours. Here Spain fits the picture better than in the GDP comparison. It is striking that all of the strong construction expansion in Ireland and Spain was lost during the economic crisis, and a very large fraction in Estonia as well. As evident from the figure, none of the comparison country groups comes close to the dramatic development of the extreme trio. This remains true if all countries are examined individually (not shown in the figure).

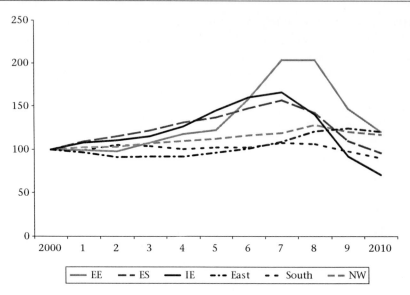

Figure 2.3. Comparative growth of construction industry employment, 2000–2010, 2000 = 100

The third factor of interest in predicting employment reduction in the crisis is the evolution of general employment levels prior to the recession. Due to limited space the pattern of cross-national variation is not shown in figure form. While the differences between countries in pre-recession employment growth are smaller than the differences in GDP growth and construction expansion shown above, Estonia and Spain stand out as having added many more jobs than other countries in the pre-recession years and then losing all of them in net terms by 2010. In contrast, Ireland did not expand its employment numbers much more than others did, but still suffered comparatively large losses in the following crisis.

In summary, Estonia, Ireland, and Spain all showed strong signs of booming economies before the recession. This sets them clearly apart from all comparison countries and is likely to have contributed greatly to the very large reductions of their employment numbers during the course of the crisis. Although at much lower levels, the pattern of expansion magnitude before the recession mirroring contraction magnitude in the crisis appears to hold even in the larger set of countries in the comparison. To examine how strong this overall pattern is, we run a regression with employment change from 2007/8 to 2010 as outcome and three predictors: (a) GDP fall in the crisis (in turn strongly correlated with GDP rise pre-recession), (b) the size of the construction sector at the eve of the recession (2007), and (c) employment rise preceding the recession, 2004–7 (the lagged dependent variable). Table 2.1 shows the results.

Table 2.1. Employment fall 2007/8–2010 predicted by three factors (R = 0.96, R^2 = 0.91; n = 18)

	B	SE	beta	t	sign.
GDP fall 2007–10	0.68	0.12	0.50	5.6	0.000
Construction ind. size 2007	1.58	0.22	0.62	7.3	0.000
Employment rise 2004–7	0.33	0.09	0.27	3.5	0.004

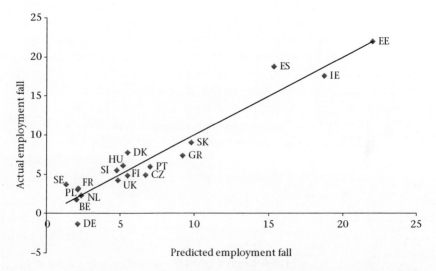

Figure 2.4. Predicted (from Table 2.1) and actual employment change 2007/8–2010

The predictive power of this regression is very large: more than 90 per cent of the variance in employment change is accounted for by the three predictors.[2] Figure 2.4 provides the country pattern.

The expectation that the magnitude of employment reduction in the crisis can be accounted for by the strength of economic expansion before the recession is hence clearly borne out by the data. We refer to this development of boom and bust across the downturn border as The Great Regression. Next, we examine our second main expectation regarding how to explain employment fall by looking at the impact of institutional structure.

[2] An alternative specification limited to predictors referring to pre-recession years only would be to replace GDP change 2007/8–10 with GDP change 1990–2007 (i.e. the time perspective applied in Figure 2.2). In this alternative specification as well, the multiple correlation with the outcome (employment decline 2007/8–10) is very high (R = 0.92, adj. R^2 = 0.82), with large impacts of GDP change (partial correlation 0.39, t = 2.9) and construction industry size (partial correlation 0.66, t = 5.2), although the coefficient of employment rise 2004–7 is not significant.

Accounting for Cross-National Variation, Part 2: Labour Market Institutions

Constructing a scale of equality-promoting institutions

A common point of departure in examining the role of institutional factors in cross-nationally comparative research is regime models of various kinds (see Gallie 2011 for a recent and comprehensive overview). The regimes typically resemble the country groups we distinguished above, with institutionally based clusters of nations that also tend to be geographically proximate. Despite their merits, such models suffer from well-known weaknesses of which one is regime internal heterogeneity.

Here, we use a different approach. The idea is to build, via factor analysis, a continuous scale of institutional traits on which each country has a value rather than produce a set of country categories. There are several advantages of the scale approach. First, regime internal heterogeneity is not a problem, since each country has its own value. Second, a continuous scale is easier and more efficient to use statistically than is a set of categories, especially when estimating associations with other variables. Third, a scale based on a number of items is more reliable than single items, since it is based on the common variance of the items and thus excludes item-specific error variance. Fourth, by using only common variance across indicators, measurement validity is enhanced because theoretical interest in a set of related items is typically tied to an underlying concept which cannot be measured perfectly but is reflected approximately by each item; the partial validities of individual indicators are thus combined into a theoretically superior common factor. Fifth, related to validity, extracting a common factor from a set of individual items accords well with the notion of institutional structure, i.e. with interrelated parts forming a larger entity rather than an aggregate of independent pieces.

The defining feature of labour market regimes is the institutional structure of inequality, i.e. the structural modification of market distribution. There are two main aspects of inequality in the labour market: prices (wages) and quantities (employment). Labour market regimes are located in a space defined by these two dimensions of inequality. As it happens, the wage (price) dimension is more readily measured by a single scale than the employment (quantity) dimension turns out to be. We return to the quantity dimension in a later section of the present chapter, in the context of looking at flows between labour market states. But we concentrate on the wage dimension by following the route laid out below.

On the basis of previous research on labour market and welfare state regimes, a set of indicators were selected each of which is related to the modification of inequality in labour market rewards. From an initial set of around a dozen items, seven were selected to form a single scale (based on factor analysis in its principal component form). There were two guiding principles of item selection: (a) each selected item should be strongly associated (correlated) with wage dispersion (since the scale should reflect equality-promoting institutions), and (b) the selected items should form a single factor. In addition, given that the particular purpose of the present analysis is to examine the importance of labour market institutions for the change in employment and unemployment rates during the recession, it is of interest to include an indicator of employment protection legislation.

Among the discarded items we find wage bargaining centralization, wage bargaining coordination, government involvement in bargaining, and public sector employment size. While these are certainly important for several outcomes of interest related to inequality, they did not conform as well to the guiding principles above as did other items. Seven indicators were finally chosen, as shown in Table 2.2. For each item, its correlation (factor loading) with the underlying scale (principal component) is shown. The highest loading is for low wage dispersion, measured as the ratio between decile 1 and the median (decile 5) of the earnings distribution. Of the purely institutional indicators, collective bargaining coverage is most strongly correlated with the scale. Active labour market policies, union density, welfare state redistribution, and left party cabinet share all have substantial loadings. In contrast, employment protection legislation (EPL) correlates only weakly with the equality scale, reflecting the well-known fact that EPL is strictest not in the most equal countries (such as in Scandinavia), but rather in Southern Europe, in turn showing that legislation is sometimes a substitute for bargaining power.

Table 2.2. Items of scale measuring equality-promoting labour market institutions. Loadings on primary principal component, unrotated

Low wage dispersion (d1/d5)	0.93
Collective bargaining coverage	0.91
Active labour market policies	0.73
Union density	0.69
Welfare state redistribution	0.67
Left party cabinet share	0.58
Employment protection legislation	0.28

Sources: Wage dispersion (d1/d5), Active labour market policies (share of GDP) and Employment protection legislation (general scale), OECD; Collective bargaining coverage and Union density, ICTWSS Database version 3.0 (AIAS, University of Amsterdam, J. Visser, variables adjcov and ud); Welfare state redistribution, Dolls et al. (2011), table 3, col. 4; Left party cabinet share, Comparative Political Data Set III (Institute of Political Science, Bern University, K. Armingeon et al.), weighted average of variables gov_right2, gov_cent2 and gov_left2, weights = 0, 1, 2 resp.). All data refer to 2007 except Left party cabinet share which refers to average values for 1990–2007.

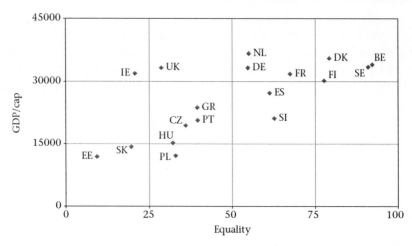

Figure 2.5. Equality-promoting institutions and economic wealth

Sources: Equality scale, see Table 2.2; GDP/capita (average 1990–2007), see Figure 2.2.

The values on this equality index for each of the eighteen countries are shown in Figure 2.5, cross-classified with economic wealth level (GDP/capita). As indicated earlier in this chapter, it is important to consider these two dimensions (equality and wealth, or distribution and growth) together, since they are interrelated in various ways which should be taken into account when attempting to examine the role they play in economic life. Accordingly, Figure 2.5 makes clear that equality and wealth are quite strongly associated with each other, an issue we will soon return to.

When combined with economic development level, the continuous equality scale orders the examined countries in a manner according well with established categorical groupings. The nine richest countries, half of the entire group of eighteen nations, are geographically located in the northwest of Europe. These nine can be subdivided into three categories dependent on their degree of institutionalized equality, with Ireland and the UK being least equal, Germany, France, and the Netherlands in a mid-level category, although somewhat closer to the equality than inequality pole, and finally the Nordic countries (Denmark, Finland, Sweden) and Belgium being most equal. The only slightly anomalous case here is Belgium, which usually is categorized with other Continental European countries rather than with the Nordics. But note that the equality dimension is exclusively tied to class-based criteria, meaning that gender inequality and family policies are not defining features of the scale. This sets it apart from Esping-Andersen's (1990) three worlds of welfare capitalism, for instance, in which the distinction between Scandinavia and Continental Europe is based in important part on gender relations.

The nine less wealthy countries are located to the south and east of Europe. In their case as well, a division into three subcategories can be made on the basis of their degree of equality. Estonia and Slovakia are the least equal countries, and rather close to Ireland along this dimension. A second category consists of Greece, Portugal, the Czech Republic, Hungary, and Poland, which are not far from the inequality level of the UK. Most equal of the less wealthy countries are Spain and Slovenia, rather close to the equality level of Continental Europe. Notably, there is no category among the Southern and Eastern countries that matches the high equality level of the Nordics and Belgium. Also notably, there is no case of a large or poor equal country. All highly equal countries are small and rich.

Among all eighteen countries there is a clear positive correlation between equality and wealth, since the richest nations are on average more equal than the less rich. But the association is hardly causal in any simple manner, at least not running from equality to wealth. The association comes about for historical and political reasons, with the older democracies of the north-west having had more time to develop their economies than those to the south and east. Among the older democracies, which are also the nine richest countries, the correlation between equality and wealth is close to zero as evident from Figure 2.5. This confirms the finding from earlier research (see e.g. Kenworthy 2010) that equality and efficiency are not incompatible with each other.

Since the correlation between equality and wealth is nonetheless substantial across all the eighteen countries, with more equal countries on average being much richer than others, the equality scale needs to be adjusted in order for its associations with other factors to be interpretable. A simple way to do this is to run a regression with equality as outcome and wealth as predictor and estimate the residual, which will accordingly be uncorrelated with wealth, and to use this residual as a purified measure of equality-promoting institutions. The country variation of this adjusted equality scale is shown in Figure 2.6.[3]

The main difference in country pattern between the first equality scale and its wealth-adjusted version is that Ireland, the UK, and the Netherlands have moved closer to the inequality pole of the scale, while especially Slovenia but also Finland have moved in the other direction. We now have a pattern where both Anglo countries are highly unequal, the Nordics are uniformly

---

[3] Most correlations between the equality scale and its constituent indicators remain of similar size to those reported in Table 2.2. There are two main exceptions. The correlation with employment protection legislation (EPL) is clearly higher with the wealth-adjusted scale (0.54 compared to 0.28 with the unadjusted scale) and the correlation with active labour market policies (ALMP) is clearly lower with the wealth-adjusted scale (0.38 compared to 0.73 with the unadjusted scale). These changes in correlations occur because EPL tends to be stronger in the less rich equal countries, while the rate of ALMP tends to be higher among the richer equal countries.

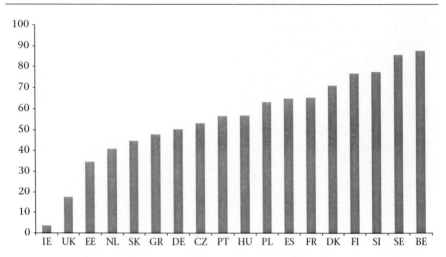

Figure 2.6. Equality-promoting institutional structure net of economic wealth
Sources: Equality scale, see Table 2.2; GDP/capita (average 2000–2007), see Figure 2.2.

equal (although with Sweden clearly higher on the scale than Denmark), while the Southerners draw towards the middle and both the Continental and Eastern countries are markedly heterogeneous with respect to equality. For example, Estonia and Slovenia are very far apart, and the same goes for the Netherlands and Belgium. It is also notable that all the large countries except the UK, i.e. Germany, Poland, Spain, and France, tend to be close to the middle of the scale. At least among the European nations examined here, then, it seems to take a small country to be extreme with respect to equality, in either direction.

Labour market inequality and general outcomes of the crisis

We are now prepared to empirically examine the expectation formulated earlier that countries with equality-promoting institutions have experienced a relatively small reduction of employment in the period of contraction. A natural starting point is to simply look at the association between these two factors—equality and employment fall—without any control variables involved (but recall that the equality scale is now purged of its correlation with wealth). The outcome is shown in Figure 2.7.

As expected, the association is negative (the regression line is sloping downward), implying that equal countries have experienced relatively small employment declines in the course of the crisis. The correlation is minus 0.41. There are six countries that are rather far from the regression line: The most severely struck trio—Ireland, Estonia, and Spain—are a good distance above the line, meaning that their employment fall has been much larger

46

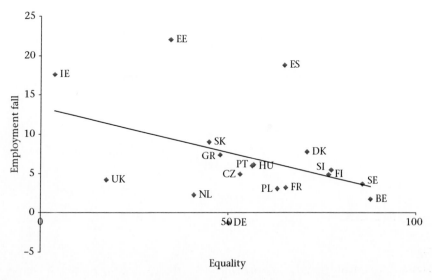

Figure 2.7. Employment fall 2007/8–2010 by equality-promoting institutions

than would be expected from their equality-related institutional structure alone. Conversely, the UK, the Netherlands, and Germany have a much better employment record in the contraction than their institutional structure would predict. Among the remaining twelve countries, which all lie fairly close to the regression line, the correlation between equality and employment decline is minus 0.64.

We have not yet taken a closer look at what mechanisms may be involved in producing the association in Figure 2.7. In the earlier discussion, two kinds of mechanisms were suggested to be important, with counteracting impacts. On the one hand, countries that institutionally promote equality should also attempt to dampen employment volatility, especially in order to minimize employment declines in economic downturns. On the other hand, these countries' relative lack of flexibility with regard to adjusting wages and working hours in the face of weakened general demand, as well as their reliance on temporary work contracts to mitigate insider–outsider problems, might exacerbate employment losses.

A convenient way to empirically isolate the importance of volatility in examining the association between equality and employment decline is to correlate equality with two different measures of employment fall: (a) the reduction in employment predicted by the volatility indicators used in the previous section (GDP fall in the crisis, construction industry size at the eve of the recession, and employment expansion pre-recession), and (b) the reduction in employment given (residual from) this volatility. According to the suggested mechanisms above, equality should be negatively associated with

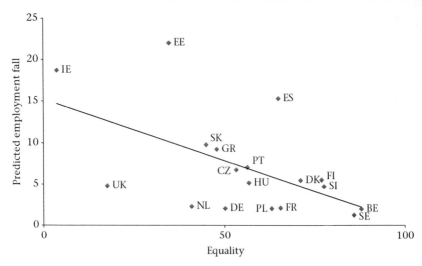

Figure 2.8. Volatility-predicted employment fall 2007/8–2010 by equality-promoting institutions

(press down) volatility-driven employment decline but positively associated with (push up) non-volatility-driven employment decline. The first of the two associations is displayed in Figure 2.8.

The association is indeed, as expected, clearly negative. Since the predictive power of the regression, as we saw in the previous section, is very strong (recall that more than 90 per cent of the variance in employment decline is accounted for; see Table 2.1), it is not surprising that the negative association from Figure 2.7 is largely reproduced here. But it is notable that the slope of the regression line is slightly steeper in Figure 2.8—the correlation between equality and volatility-predicted employment decline is minus 0.55 while the raw correlation was minus 0.41. This indicates, in line with the expectations formulated earlier, that the negative association between equality and employment fall is entirely—indeed more than entirely—due to volatility mechanisms, thus suggesting that employment decline given volatility has actually been larger in equal countries than in others.

To check whether this interpretation holds, the association between equality and non-volatility-driven employment reduction is displayed in Figure 2.9. The association is positive, just as expected, with a correlation of rather sizeable magnitude, 0.43. Still, this result must be seen as highly tentative. First, to repeat, since volatility is such a powerful predictor of employment decline, there is not very much left to explain given volatility. Second, as evident from the figure, several countries are located quite far from the regression line. At the high end, Spain has lost much more employment in the crisis than can be accounted for by equality-promoting institutions. Denmark and Sweden are similar to Spain in this regard, but with smaller numbers involved. At the

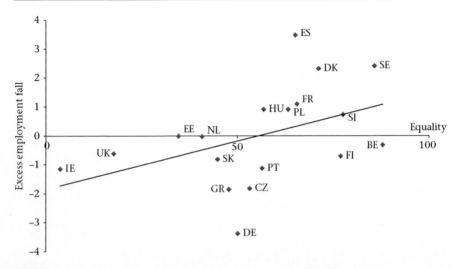

Figure 2.9. Excess (given volatility) employment fall 2007/8–2010 by equality-promoting institutions

other end, Germany is the single most successful case, with a clearly better employment evolution going through the downturn than predicted. But several other countries have performed above expectations, with a very wide 'regime' variation: two Southern countries (Greece, Portugal), one Eastern country (the Czech Republic), one Continental country (Belgium), and one Nordic (Finland). But their internal order tends to follow the line in the diagram, with less equal countries performing better.

To sum up our examination of the association between institutional structure and employment performance in the crisis, the expectations formulated earlier are essentially confirmed. More equal countries have seen smaller employment reductions than other countries have, and this is mainly or even entirely due to less volatility in labour markets where institutional structures promote equality. In short, the boom and bust pattern of economic expansion and contraction in the period leading into and through the downturn is primarily a characteristic of fairly unequal societies. Aside from these volatility-driven employment fluctuations, there is not very much employment change during the crisis to explain. Nonetheless, the limited residual variation across countries does to some extent appear to be tied to equality-related institutions, but in the opposite direction to the case of volatility, such that more equal societies have experienced relatively large employment reductions.

In the conceptual discussion above on the institutional structure of inequality, a distinction was made between prices and quantities, or between wages and employment. The scale of equality-promoting institutions that we just used in the empirical examination is primarily tied to the wage dimension of inequality, and we made a brief earlier remark on the apparent difficulty of constructing a parallel scale of the employment dimension of inequality. Before turning to the final section of the chapter, containing a summary and concluding discussion, we attempt below to at least partly fill the identified gap by looking at flows between labour market states. The purpose is to use data on individual mobility to estimate rates of job separations, job finding, and labour force entries and exits. These dynamic features are likely to reflect institutional characteristics of national labour markets that are not visible from the equality-related indicators used so far in the chapter. They might therefore provide clues to complementary structural dimensions of inequality that would help us understand how employment contractions evolve in institutionally different countries.

The Structure of Labour Market Flows

In the European Labour Force Surveys, respondents are asked about not only their current labour market activity but also what employment situation they were in twelve months earlier. The answers to these retrospective questions thus provide data on labour market dynamics—how individuals move between employment, unemployment, and other activities (such as education or child care). In this section, we make use of these flow data in order to complement the picture given above on how the labour market is structured in different countries and, in turn, how those differences have affected the employment record during the recession.[4] Of the eighteen countries examined above, dynamic data are available for fifteen; we lack data for France, Ireland, and the Netherlands.

We begin by estimating two fundamental dynamic characteristics of labour markets—the rates of job separation and job finding. The separation rate is measured as the number of employed workers at time-point 1 who have lost their job by time-point 2 (one year later) divided by all employed workers at time-point 1. Similarly, the job finding rate is the number of non-employed workers (either unemployed or outside the labour force) at time-point 1 who have become employed by time-point 2 (one year later) divided by all non-employed workers at time-point 1. Figure 2.10 shows these rates for the year prior to the start of the recession (2006–7 if the downturn started in 2007 and 2007–8 if the downturn started in 2008; see above).

The job finding rate is on average clearly higher than the job separation rate, around 16 per cent versus 6 per cent. This difference is due to the variation

---

[4] These data were skilfully prepared by Hande Inanc to whom we are most grateful.

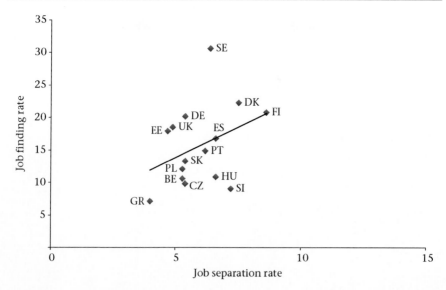

Figure 2.10. Rates of job separation and job finding one year prior to the start of recession

in group size: the employed are a larger category than the non-employed. As proportions of the whole population, job finders and losers tend to be equally numerous, between 4 and 5 per cent on average.

There are large differences across countries in both rates. Sweden had by far the highest job finding rate of all the examined countries: around 30 per cent of all non-employed individuals (age 20–64) in 2006 had found employment by 2007. At the other end we find Greece, where the job finding rate was only 7 per cent in the year preceding the recession. Job separations were most frequent in Slovenia, Finland, and Denmark, where between 8 and 10 per cent of all employed in 2007 had lost their job by 2008 (prior to the onset of the recession). Greece was again lowest, with a separation rate of around 4 per cent.

A modest positive association is evident between the rates of job finding and job separation. We will later make use of this pattern by constructing a measure of labour market flexibility. The correlation in Figure 2.10 is a moderate 0.36, but as can be noticed, Hungary and Slovenia tend to break the pattern and with those two countries excluded the positive correlation rises substantially to 0.55. The Nordic countries stand out as clearly more flexible than others with relatively high rates of both job finding and job separation.

In all countries, the most dramatic economic decline occurred from 2008 to 2009. It is therefore of interest to examine how the employment flow rates of entries and exits changed from the year just prior to recession (Figure 2.10) to the deep downturn. Figure 2.11 shows the rates of job finding and separation between 2008 and 2009.

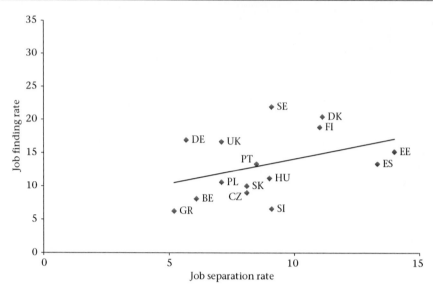

Figure 2.11. Rates of job separation and job finding between 2008 and 2009

Several things may be noted from this pattern. First, Estonia and Spain stand out from all others by having very high job separation rates. The special position of these two countries is of course not surprising given their extreme employment declines as documented in detail above (recall that the third hard-hit country, Ireland, is not included in this dynamic comparison due to its lack of flow data in the European Labour Force Surveys). Second, job finding rates are very far from zero even in this year of dramatic economic decline. As we will soon show more explicitly, employment entries fell in frequency almost everywhere from their pre-recession level to the economic trough in 2009, and in some cases markedly, but the average rate in Figure 2.11 is still as high as 13 per cent, down from 16 per cent in the earlier comparison year. Third, with Estonia and Spain as exceptions, the country pattern of entry and exit flows remained rather similar between the two time-points. Hence, the Nordics held their position as relatively flexible in this sense, and the same goes for Greece at the inflexible pole.

To sharpen the picture of how flow rates changed as the recession deepened, Figure 2.12 displays the difference in rates between the two comparison years. In the research literature on labour market cycles there has been an ongoing debate in recent years over whether fluctuations in employment and unemployment are mainly due to changes in job finding or job separation. So far, this literature has been inconclusive. Shimer (e.g. 2012) claims that shifts in the likelihood of job finding are the driver of aggregate unemployment numbers while others (e.g. Elsby et al. 2010) take the more agnostic view that job finding and job separation rates are both important, with a differing weight across time and place. We make a tentative contribution to this debate

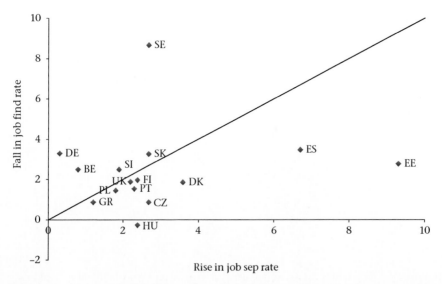

Figure 2.12. Changes in job finding and job separation rates from 2006–7/2007–8 to 2008–9

here by looking at how much job finding and job separation changed in frequency in the fifteen examined countries going into 2009.

For the majority of countries, job separations rose more than job finding fell from pre-recession to 2009, as can be seen from the fact that most nations are below the diagonal line in Figure 2.12. The relative importance of job separations is especially clear for Estonia and Spain. Sweden stands out as an exceptional case, with a much larger fall in job finding than a rise in job separations, but then Sweden's rate of job finding was extremely high in the year preceding the recession (see Figure 2.10), so regression to the mean is apparently involved in its outlier position here.

The main conclusion from the pattern in Figure 2.12 is that job separations played a dominant role for overall employment decline in the recession. Not only did most countries (ten out of the fifteen compared) experience larger changes from 2007/8 to 2009 in job separation rates than in job finding, but, as noted earlier, the number of individuals involved tends to be larger for employment exits than entries, since a majority of the population is employed in most countries (i.e. the base on which the flow rates is estimated is larger). Further, there is a strong correlation between the relative importance of job separation rise over job finding decline and the fall of aggregate employment during the recession. Among all fifteen countries this correlation is 0.75, which increases to 0.85 with the deviant case of Sweden omitted. (This correlation is not immediately apparent from Figure 2.12.) Even without the extreme cases of Estonia and Spain the correlation is 0.50, and with Sweden excluded 0.63.

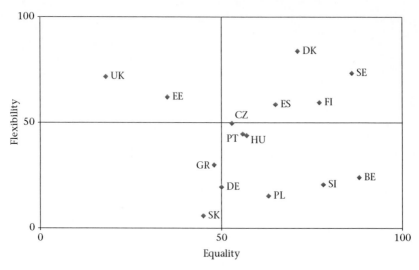

Figure 2.13. Two dimensions of labour market institutions: equality and flexibility

Returning now to the issue of flexibility, an important task is to construct an overall measure of how dynamic the labour market is with respect to flows across the employment border. Such a measure would provide a vital piece of the puzzle in revealing the institutional structure of inequality. We build a measure of flexibility by combining four rates of flows and retention: (a) job finding, (b) job separation, (c) unemployment retention (staying in unemployment from one year to the next), and (d) moves from unemployment to outside the labour force (a sign of giving up on job search). The construction is a ^ b minus (c + d), meaning the overlap (exchange) between job finding and separation, indicating flexibility, minus the proportion of the population trying but failing to achieve employment, indicating rigidity.[5] The failure to find employment is obviously not only a sign of labour market rigidity but is also, depending on the level of the business cycle, a result of low labour demand. In order to isolate the rigidity component, we measure the retention rate of unemployment at a neutral or high point of the cycle, in this case in the year preceding the recession.

Figure 2.13 shows how this measure of flexibility is associated with the scale of equality-promoting institutions used in the preceding section of the chapter. In combination, the two scales provide a more elaborate and useful characterization of labour market institutions than either one in isolation. The flexibility measure can be seen as one possible way of scaling the dimension of employment quantities discussed earlier, so that we now have

[5] Job finding and separation rates are estimated on the whole population (age 20–64) as a base in this construction, in order to more accurately measure the overlap (exchange) between them by using a common denominator.

a combination of the price (wages) and quantity (employment) sides of the institutional structure of inequality.

The figure has been divided into four quadrants by marking the midpoint lines of each dimension. The two right-hand boxes, with relatively high values of equality, are more densely populated than the two quadrants towards the inequality pole, partly reflecting that Ireland and the Netherlands are not included here (due to their lack of flow data), but neither is France (which would be on the equality side of the figure) present.

There are several interesting observations to be made from the overall pattern. The correlation between the two dimensions is close to zero (minus 0.03). There are three basic types of countries: unequal and flexible (primarily the UK but also Estonia), equal and inflexible (Belgium, Slovenia, and to some extent Poland), and equal and flexible (primarily the Nordics but also Spain to some extent). In addition, there are countries that are close to the average on equality and low on flexibility (Slovakia, Germany, Greece) and finally a group near the middle on both dimensions (Czech Republic, Hungary, Portugal). The empty part of the map is the lower left, the corner of low equality and low flexibility, which would appear to be a quite unattractive place.

In a standard economic view of how labour markets work, a negative association between equality and flexibility might be expected. The members of the upper left and lower right quadrants essentially conform to this orthodox expectation of a trade-off between distribution and growth. But it is well known that the Nordic countries tend to break this pattern in important ways, and their place to the upper right in Figure 2.13 supports this impression. More surprising, perhaps, is that Spain shows up as a fairly close neighbour to the Nordics. One particular feature that these countries have in common is the wide use of time-limited employment contracts, partially used as a device to climb north from the lower right of the figure. We do not have space here to pursue the detailed mechanisms (like the design and mix of employment contracts) that could account for each country's location on the institutional map, but leave that essential task to future work.

We conclude this section by revisiting the attempt to account for the cross-national variation in employment decline during the crisis. As shown above, to a very large extent this variation is associated with what can be called The Great Regression: the tendency that the magnitude of economic expansion before the recession is mirrored by the degree of economic contraction in the downturn, with large employment declines as a consequence. Given this cycle of boom and bust, equality-promoting institutions appeared to be associated with larger rather than smaller employment falls. Aided by the measure of flexibility we now have at our disposal we can probe somewhat deeper into this question. What is the relation between excess (i.e. residual

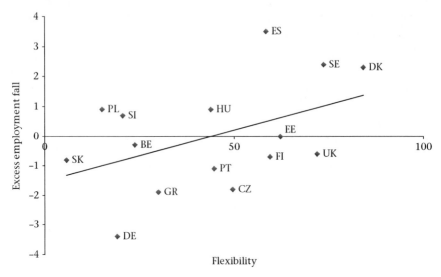

Figure 2.14. Excess (given volatility) employment fall in recession by labour market flexibility

to The Great Regression) fall in employment and the degree of labour market flexibility? Figure 2.14 gives the answer.

The association is clearly positive, implying that higher labour market flexibility contributed to a larger employment fall in the crisis. The correlation is 0.46, about the same order of magnitude as the positive relation shown above between equality and excess employment decline. Since equality and flexibility are basically uncorrelated, they should together account for a sizeable fraction of the employment outcome, which turns out to be the case. If the two dimensions are combined into a single scale, the association with excess employment decline increases to a correlation of 0.63 (this is not shown in figure form).

It is essentially not surprising that more dynamic (flexible) labour markets take a harder employment hit from economic downturns than more rigid labour markets do. It is to be expected that as the cycle eventually turns upward, flexibility will be an asset in terms of employment expansion. Still, as discussed earlier, volatility tends to be disliked by those who favour equitable distributions since the workers affected by employment downturns are often the same as the workers with low rewards in other respects. The benefits of flexibility may nonetheless be substantial. In the years preceding the recession, there was a clear positive connection between labour market flexibility as measured here and the level of aggregate employment. This relation is obviously much too complex to be sorted out further here, but there seems to be a rather close empirical association between high general employment levels and the size of labour market flows. In turn, this might indicate that employment losses in the contraction in countries with dynamic labour markets before the recession are likely to be more temporary than in other places.

Summary and Conclusions

We have examined labour market outcomes of the economic crisis in Europe through 2010. Among the eighteen countries considered, three were hit much harder than all others: Estonia, Ireland, and Spain. The main common trait of these three cases is their strong economic expansion in the years leading into the downturn of 2007–8. Estonia and Ireland had extremely high rates of economic growth prior to the crisis, while Spain's growth rate was only slightly above the EU average. All three, however, had strong construction booms in the pre-recession period. Estonia and Spain also saw large employment expansions in the years leading into the recession. The dramatic employment decline from 2007 to 2010 in all three nations, much larger than anywhere else in Europe, is almost completely accounted for by this pattern of initial expansion and subsequent contraction. At lower levels, the same kind of cyclical fluctuations tend to characterize much of the crisis experience of other countries as well. We refer to this general development of boom and bust across the downturn border as The Great Regression.

Most of the variation in labour market outcomes of the crisis is thus explained by economic factors such as growth rate volatility, industrial structure, and general demand. But institutional traits have also been important to some degree. In particular, countries characterized by equality-promoting labour market institutions have seen smaller employment reductions than other countries have. This is mainly or even entirely due to less volatility in more equal labour markets.

Aside from these volatility-driven employment fluctuations, the variation across countries in employment experience appears to be tied to equality-related institutions, but in the opposite direction to the case of volatility, such that more equal societies have experienced relatively large employment reductions. In addition, higher labour market flexibility—essentially uncorrelated with labour market equality—appears to have contributed to a larger employment fall in the crisis.

Acknowledgements

An earlier version of this chapter was presented at the ECSR/Equalsoc annual conference in Stockholm, 24–26 September 2012. Thanks to the conference session participants, to the co-authors of the present book, and to Robert Erikson, Ante Farm, and Walter Korpi for helpful comments.

3

Distribution in the Downturn

Michael Tåhlin

Introduction

The previous chapter was concerned with cross-national differences in the magnitude of general employment decline during the economic crisis. We found that the boom and bust pattern of initial expansion and subsequent contraction ('The Great Regression') accounts for a very large share of the variation in labour market developments in the downturn. Institutional factors appear to have played a secondary but still significant role, with mechanisms related to both equality promotion and flexibility likely to have been involved. This chapter examines changes in the distribution of employment by gender, age, education, and occupation. How have employment reductions affected different groups of the population? To what extent can these distributive patterns be accounted for by the depth of the general employment decline? How much of the variation in distributive outcomes is associated with the institutional structure of inequality? Changes in the distribution of education and occupation among the employed will also indicate shifts in the structure of skill demand. How have rates of skill upgrading and skill polarization been affected by the great recession?

A fundamental feature of labour markets in all economically advanced societies is that rates of employment and unemployment differ greatly across worker and population categories. In general, the distributional pattern of employment closely resembles the structure of wage inequality. The young and the less educated have lower rates of employment and higher rates of unemployment, as well as lower wages, than more experienced and well-educated workers. Further, women tend to have inferior labour market conditions relative to men, with regard to both employment (but not unemployment) and wages. This pattern of inequality is evident in all OECD countries, at all points over the business cycle, and across long stretches of time.

Aside from this very stable general structure, however, the *degree* of inequality in labour market conditions is highly variable. It is well known that labour market inequalities differ considerably in magnitude both across countries and between time periods. In addition, rates of inequality tend to differ over the business cycle, sometimes in rather complex ways.

In Europe, the economic crisis of recent years has hit some groups harder than others with regard to rates of unemployment: youth, men, immigrants, the low-skilled, and workers on short-term contracts (see e.g. European Commission 2010b). Generally, with the exception of gender (men rather than women tend to be over-represented in cyclically sensitive industries, like manufacturing and construction), traditionally vulnerable groups in the labour market thus tend to be hardest hit by economic downturns. A stylized fact is that there is a close correspondence between group-specific (by age, education, etc.) unemployment rates as observed in a cross-section and the cyclical volatility of unemployment for the same groups (see e.g. Elsby et al. 2010). Typically, group-specific rates are multiplied by a constant factor in economic downturns, so that absolute differences between groups increase in size. This pattern recurs across countries.

Retention of workers, while generally high in many European countries (although with adjustment in work hours in several cases), has been skill-biased, in line with the pattern of previous cyclical downturns. Short-term contracts tend to be used primarily in low-skill jobs, and even among more permanent contracts the incentive to keep high-skill workers is relatively strong, in order to avoid replacement costs as demand rebounds. Upgrading of the job structure, which is a strong long-term feature in most labour markets, hence tends to accelerate in recessions. Although job creation rates generally fall in recessions, especially in the early phase of the cyclical downturn, and job destruction rates rise, the negative development tends to be particularly strong for low-skill work.

The present chapter is organized as follows. We begin by sketching the employment profiles of the eighteen countries in the years prior to the onset of recession, before turning to the pattern of change in employment distribution during the economic downturn. After a descriptive overview of cross-national differences in the evolution of employment gaps by gender, age, and education, we evaluate two expectations of empirical regularities. First, we expect that crisis severity will magnify the changes in employment gaps. Second, we expect labour market institutions to modify the association between downturn magnitude and the distribution of employment decline. Aside from assessing the change in employment gaps between population categories, special attention will be given to shifts in the occupational structure reflecting skill upgrading and polarization. The final empirical section looks at changes in wage inequality. Here too, the cross-national pattern of change will be related to the crisis magnitude and institutional structure, as well as to shifts in the occupational composition of the employed population. A summary and brief discussion of the main findings concludes the chapter.

Comparative Employment Rates by Population Group before the Recession

Before turning to distributional developments during the crisis, it is useful to give a background picture of the pre-recession employment profiles of the countries involved in our comparison. We begin by providing some general numbers that complement the description given in the previous chapter. Figure 3.1 shows the labour market performance of the eighteen countries prior to the recession. (As in Chapter 2, all numbers in the following are based on aggregate data from the European Union Labour Force Surveys, EULFS, unless otherwise indicated.) The rates of employment and unemployment are averages for the period 2000 to 2007. Denmark was the top performer in these years, with a high employment rate, second only to Sweden, and a low unemployment rate, second only to the Netherlands and Ireland. The UK and Portugal also had relatively favourable labour market conditions. At the other end, Poland had the worst conditions, followed by Slovakia. The labour

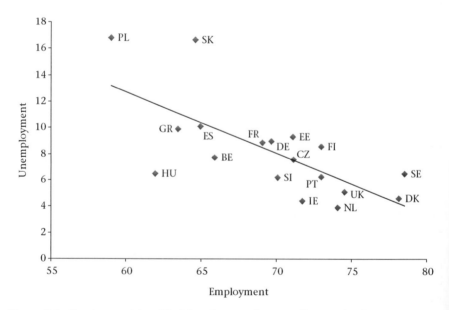

Figure 3.1. Employment (age 20–64) and unemployment (harmonized) rates, averages 2000–2007

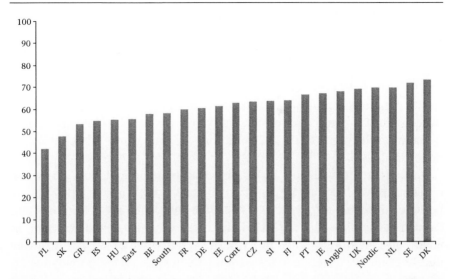

Figure 3.2. Employment index (employment rate minus unemployment rate) by country, average 2000–2007

markets of Greece, Spain, Hungary, and Belgium also showed relatively low participation levels and/or high jobless rates. In general, rates of employment and unemployment show a similar picture as indicated by the rather steep line of association between them, although there are a few outliers, mostly among the Eastern European countries.

Combining the employment and unemployment rates into one overall measure, by subtracting unemployment from employment (see Chapter 2), yields the country ranking shown in Figure 3.2. Aside from the eighteen individual countries, the chart indicates averages by country group. In order of appearance in the figure they are: 'East' for Eastern Europe (Poland, Slovakia, Hungary, Estonia, Czech Republic, Slovenia), 'South' for Southern Europe (Greece, Spain, Portugal), 'Cont' for Continental Europe (Belgium, Germany, the Netherlands), 'Anglo' for the Anglo countries (Ireland, the UK) and 'Nordic' for the Nordic countries (Finland, Sweden, Denmark).

The variation in total employment levels according to this index is rather strongly tied to GDP levels (the correlation is 0.66), which is not surprising since employment volumes and GDP are associated by construction. Still, as can be seen in Figure 3.2 there are several cases that deviate from a simple linear pattern. For example, Belgium, France, and Germany have lower employment levels than the size of their economic wealth would predict, while Portugal has an unexpectedly high employment level.

With regard to institutional structure (as measured by the scales of equality and flexibility described and used in Chapter 2), overall employment

levels tend to be unrelated to equality promoting institutions (the correlation is –0.08), but appear to be strongly and positively tied to labour market
flexibility (the correlation is 0.75). The strong association between employment and flexibility partly comes about through the connection of both factors with the level of economic wealth (GDP per capita). But even net of the
wealth link, the degree of labour market flexibility is clearly connected to
overall employment levels (the partial correlation is 0.52). Needless to say,
causal interpretations of these associations are far beyond the scope of the
present analysis.

Turning to the variation in employment across population categories,
differences by gender are displayed in Figure 3.3. Male and female rates are
positively interrelated, again with Poland at the low end and Denmark and
Sweden at the high end. Positive outliers regarding female employment, in
addition to the Nordics, are Estonia and Slovenia, while Greece and Spain are
negative outliers. Given their male employment rates, female employment is
also relatively low in Belgium, the Czech Republic, and Ireland.

Youth labour markets are strongly tied to general labour demand, to an
extent not always appreciated in the literature. As seen in Figure 3.4, youth
(age 20–29) unemployment is everywhere clearly higher than mid-age (30–
54) unemployment, typically by a factor of around 2, so the line of association is steep (only men are included here in order to isolate the age pattern).
Still, there is also a fair amount of deviation from the line. Greece and
Poland have relatively high jobless rates among their young given general
(prime-age) unemployment numbers, which is also true although to a lesser

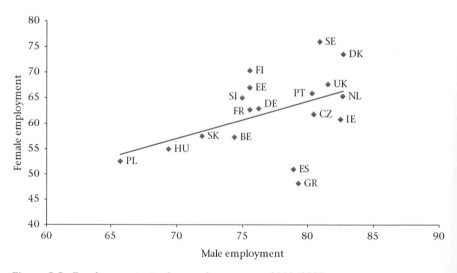

Figure 3.3. Employment rates by gender, averages 2000–2007

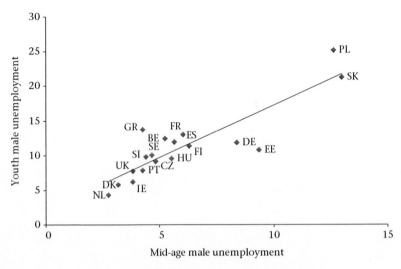

Figure 3.4. Male unemployment rates by age, averages 2000–2007

extent for Belgium, France, and Spain. Germany and Estonia have comparatively low relative rates of youth unemployment, and the same goes for the Netherlands, Ireland, and Denmark but less clearly. The case of Germany is notable, since it is often heralded as a success story in the policy debate on youth labour markets: while the German youth to mid-age unemployment ratio is indeed low, the rate of youth unemployment was in fact higher than in most other countries considered here in the period 2000–7. A similar pattern is evident for Estonia.

Employment at older ages (55–64) varies a good deal across the eighteen countries; see Figure 3.5. Again, there is a positive association between employment rates across demographic categories, underlining the fundamental role of general labour demand (growth) rather than categorical trade-offs based on a fixed number of jobs (zero-sum distribution). Hence, labour market participation among older men tends to be more frequent in countries with a high prime-age male employment rate. However, the pattern is not entirely clear-cut: among the countries with the highest prime-age rate, the association with elderly activity rates tends to be negative. Of all considered countries, Sweden has the highest employment rate among older men, around 70 per cent, followed by the UK, Ireland, and Denmark. Given its prime-age rate, Estonia also has a high elderly employment rate. The lowest labour market participation rate among older men, below 40 per cent, is found in three Eastern European countries—Poland, Hungary, and Slovenia—and two Western European nations—Belgium and France.

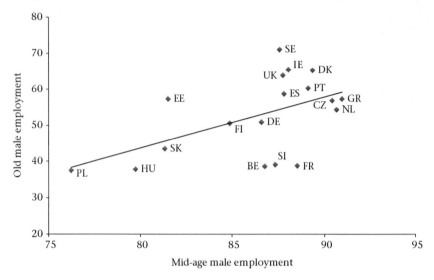

Figure 3.5. Male employment rates by age, averages 2000–2007

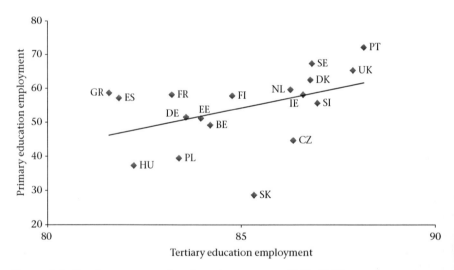

Figure 3.6. Employment rates by education, averages 2000–2007

The pattern of positively associated employment rates recurs with regard to education; see Figure 3.6. Employment rates among the highly educated are uniformly high, consistently above 80 per cent. The big variation across countries is among the low-educated (primary or lower secondary schooling); note that the horizontal and vertical scales in the figure differ greatly in range. Three Eastern European countries have very low activity rates in the low-educated group, below 40 per cent: Slovakia, Hungary, and Poland.

At the other end, Portugal has the highest rate, close to 70 per cent, and also has the highest rate among those with tertiary education. The position of Portugal is associated with its very low average education level: more than 70 per cent of the population has less than upper secondary schooling, by far the largest share of low-educated of all considered countries. Spain and Greece also have fairly low average education (close to 50 and 40 per cent with primary schooling, respectively), and consistent with this a fairly high employment rate of their low-educated.

Distribution in the Downturn: Employment Fall in Different Population Groups

We now turn to the main issue of the present chapter: how employment decline during the economic crisis has been distributed across different groups of the population. As explained in the previous chapter, the starting year of the contraction was 2007 in six of the examined countries (Estonia, Hungary, Ireland, Spain, Sweden, and the UK) and 2008 in the remaining twelve. In the following we compare the magnitude of employment reduction across countries and population groups by estimating the change in employment from the start of the recession to 2010. The measure of employment we use is the summary indicator defined and motivated earlier (see Figure 3.2 and Chapter 2): the employed share of the population minus the unemployed share of the labour force.

With regard to comparing changes in employment for different groups (e.g. women and men) we take the difference in percentage points between the employment levels for 2007 (or 2008) and 2010 for each group and then compare the group-specific changes. Alternatively, we could have estimated the ratio between group-specific levels at each time-point and then compared these ratios over time. The choice between comparing group-specific percentage point changes and comparing time-specific ratios can make a substantial difference. For example, if women's employment level declined from 60 to 50 per cent and men's from 84 to 70 per cent, the percentage point comparison would find that male employment fell more than female (14 versus 10 points) while the ratio comparison would find no change since the male to female ratio remained stable at 1.4.

There is no way to unequivocally decide which of the two methods gives the more accurate picture; there are good arguments for both. (See also the point made above in connection to Figure 3.4 on how to compare youth unemployment rates across countries.) We mainly use the percentage point comparison here because this method comes closest to counting real individuals rather than more abstract quantities; 14 per cent of a group of a given size reflects a larger number of individuals than 10 per cent does, regardless of the ratio involved. Nonetheless, the choice is also of a pragmatic kind. One method may simply provide a better fit to the available data than the other, and could be reasonably preferred on that ground. We will encounter such cases below, and will then temporarily switch to the more relative approach for purely statistical reasons.

Our empirical description of differential employment change across population groups begins with looking at the average development for all examined countries. As evident from Figure 3.7, there are large differences between population categories in how much employment has fallen. Men have seen larger losses than women, youth larger losses than prime-age workers, and there is a steep educational gradient in employment rate change. Older workers have fared much better than all other distinguished categories, with an overall change close to zero. With regard to education, the low-educated (individuals with primary or lower secondary schooling) have fared worst while workers with tertiary education have seen the smallest employment decline and individuals with secondary education falling in between, although on average somewhat closer to the low-educated than to the tertiary group.

Our next task is to examine how this population group variation in employment decline differs across countries. In doing so, we will be guided by two main expectations of empirical regularities. First, as discussed in the introductory section, economic downturns typically affect some worker categories more adversely than others, and the pattern we have showed above is largely in line with this tendency. Hence, we might expect that the more severe the downturn has been, i.e. the stronger the general decline of employment, the

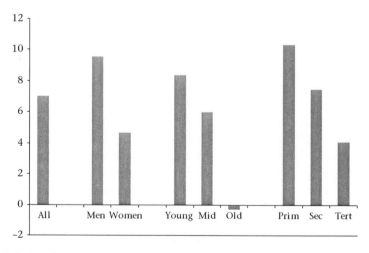

Figure 3.7. Employment fall 2007/8–2010 by gender, age, and education (percentage point differences between time-points); 18 countries, unweighted averages

more marked will be the differences across population groups. Second, an important issue is to determine the extent to which institutional factors modify the relation between crisis magnitude and the distribution of employment decline across worker categories. As in Chapter 2, we focus on two fundamental institutional traits that tend to be empirically independent (uncorrelated): equality promotion and labour market flexibility.

Stratification of employment change by regime

As a descriptive first step in assessing cross-national variation in distributive outcomes we compare changes in group-specific employment decline between the institutional clusters of countries used earlier (see Chapters 1 and 2 and Figure 3.2). The three countries with exceptionally large reductions of employment—Estonia, Ireland, and Spain—have been removed from their respective 'regimes' in the following charts, and form a joint separate category in order to clarify the cross-national comparison. Figure 3.8 shows the country variation in employment decline by gender.

In general, the distributional pattern of change is similar in all country categories. But the details differ, in some cases notably. Men have experienced larger employment losses than women in all cases, although the male–female percentage point difference has been exceptional in size in the hardest hit group of countries. However, women as well as men have seen much

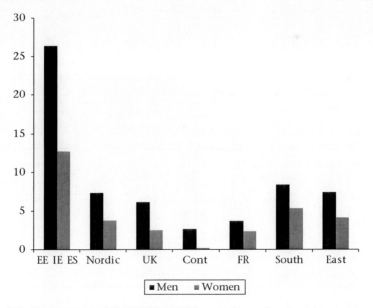

Figure 3.8. Employment fall 2007/8–2010 by gender and regime (percentage point differences between time-points)

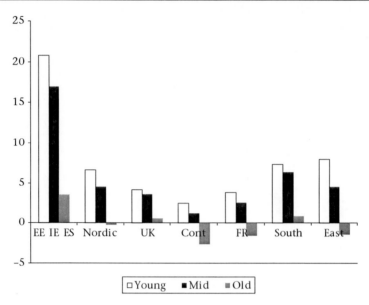

Figure 3.9. Employment fall 2007/8–2010 by age and regime (percentage point differences between time-points)

bigger losses there than anywhere else. In the Continental group (Belgium, Germany, and the Netherlands), by contrast, the average employment loss for women has been close to zero.

The country pattern of employment decline by age is displayed in Figure 3.9. Young people (age 20–29) have been hit hardest everywhere, but the difference relative to prime-age (30–54) workers is comparatively large in Eastern Europe and in the most severely struck country group, and smallest in the UK. Older workers (age 55–64) have lost significantly in employment only in the hard-hit country trio, and have actually made a notable gain—not only relatively—in Continental Europe and to some extent in France and in Eastern Europe as well.

As evident from Figure 3.10, educational inequality in employment loss during the crisis has a similar general pattern in all country groups, but the UK stands out as particularly unequal in this regard with a bigger difference in employment decline between workers with primary and secondary education than anywhere else. At the other end, the Continental European countries display fairly small educational differences, in line with their low overall rate of labour market deterioration.

Distributive Outcomes by Crisis Magnitude

As discussed earlier, we have two main expectations regarding the country variation in the distribution of employment decline across population

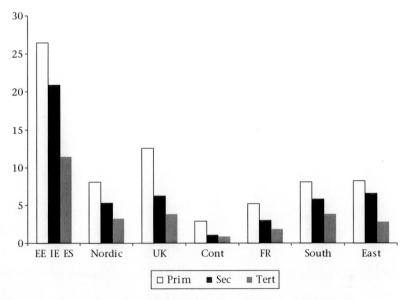

Figure 3.10. Employment fall 2007/8–2010 by education and regime (percentage point differences between time-points)

groups. In this section, we begin to empirically examine the first of these two expectations: that the magnitude of the downturn, indicated by the total size of employment reduction, tends to widen the differences in development across population groups. Figure 3.11 shows the association between total employment fall and the gender gap in employment change.

As can be seen, the association is very strong; the correlation is 0.88. Hence, the larger the total reduction of employment during the crisis, the bigger has been the closing of the gender gap in employment, due to disproportionately large losses for men relative to women. The association is mainly driven by the three hardest hit countries, but even among the less severely struck economies (fifteen countries) the correlation is substantial, at 0.48.

With regard to the evolution of employment gaps by age and education, there are similar country patterns concerning the link with downturn magnitude. To save space, these associations are not shown in figure form. Instead, the patterns are summarized in Table 3.1 by reporting correlations between total employment decline and the change in employment gaps.

In all cases, there are very strong associations in the expected direction. While all correlations are somewhat weaker when excluding Estonia, Ireland, and Spain, they remain substantial. A partial exception is the widening employment gap between workers with primary and secondary education, with a comparatively moderate connection to downturn magnitude.

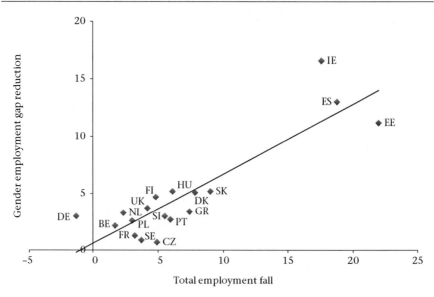

Figure 3.11. Fall in gender employment gap 2007/8–2010 by total employment decline

Table 3.1. Correlations between size of total employment decline 2007/8–2010 and changes in employment gaps by gender, age, and education

Category	Direction	Corr with rec magn	Excl EE ES IE
Gender	male emp loss vs. female	0.88	0.48
Youth	emp loss vs. mid-age	0.78	0.75
Old	emp gain vs. mid-age	0.91	0.70
Prim educ	emp loss vs. sec educ	0.59	0.23
Tert educ	emp gain vs. sec educ	0.92	0.69

Labour Market Institutions and Distributive Outcomes of the Crisis

We have just seen that the employment decline during the economic crisis has been very uneven across population categories, and that these differences by gender, age, and education tend to be larger the deeper the downturn. But how general is this pattern of inequality? It is reasonable to suppose that labour market institutions have affected the ways through which employment reductions are transmitted across different groups. In this section, we examine how the distribution of employment decline is associated with the scales of equality promotion and labour market flexibility that were constructed in Chapter 2.

In order to estimate these associations we first run a regression model with the change in each employment gap (by gender, age, or education) as outcome and three predictors: (a) crisis magnitude (total employment reduction), (b) institutional structure (equality promotion or labour market flexibility), and (c) the interaction between crisis magnitude and institutional structure. Based on this regression, we then compute the predicted change in inequality (population group employment gap) net of the main effect of employment decline. The correlation between this measure and the institutional scale indicates the extent to which equality promoting institutions and labour market flexibility, respectively, have affected the change in inequality by gender, age, and education during the crisis, given the size of general employment decline.

Note that it would be insufficient to simply control for employment decline in these regressions. Doing so would implicitly be based on the assumption that the size of the employment fall would affect all population groups in the same manner regardless of institutional context. But that assumption would contradict the main rationale underlying the expectation we formulated above: the major purpose of labour market institutions is precisely to modify market determined distributions, so interaction effects are to be strongly expected.

Figure 3.12 gives a summary overview of the results of the empirical examination carried out as just described. The five data points in the chart indicate the associations (correlations) between the five employment gaps (one by gender, two by age, and two by education) and the two dimensions of labour market institutions (equality and flexibility).

According to these results, both kinds of institution have been important for the distribution of the employment impact of the crisis, but in distinctly different ways. Men's employment decline relative to women has been moderately larger in more equal countries (the correlation is 0.39) and marginally larger in less flexible countries (–0.24). One institutional interpretation of these associations is that high wage floors and downwardly rigid working hours have had a more negative employment impact on male employment in the crisis than on female. Alternatively, the industrial and occupational structures of national labour markets are associated with labour market institutions in a manner that has put men and women at a differential disadvantage in the economic downturn. Although the detailed mechanisms at work cannot be distinguished here, the gender employment gap has apparently evolved somewhat differently across countries, with a pattern that at least to some extent seems tied to institutional variation.

Changes during the downturn in employment gaps by age have been rather strongly correlated with flexibility but uncorrelated with equality. Employment chances of the young (age 20–29) relative to prime-age (30–54)

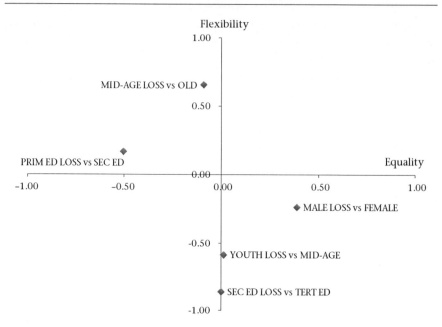

Figure 3.12. Residual employment loss 2007/8–2010 by institutional structure. Correlations between five employment gaps (by gender, age and education) and two dimensions of labour market institutions (equality and flexibility)

workers have declined particularly much in countries with a comparatively inflexible labour market; the negative correlation is 0.59. Conversely, mid-age workers have fared less well relative to older (55–64) workers in more flexible countries; the positive correlation is 0.65. In contrast, the associations between the change in employment gaps by age and equality promoting institutions are very weak, close to zero.

With regard to education, the pattern is mixed: excess employment losses for low-educated workers are moderately associated with high inequality (0.51) but less with flexibility (0.17), while relatively large employment reductions for workers with secondary (relative to tertiary) education are highly correlated with flexibility (–0.86) but not at all associated with equality (0.00).

Skill Change and Occupational Polarization

For several decades, labour markets in OECD countries have been in a general and long-term phase of skill upgrading. This upgrading has two sides: supply (workers) and demand (jobs). The relative pace of skill rise on the supply and demand sides differs over time and across countries, and is also an issue of discussion in the literature. Measurement of the relevant quantities is a crucial aspect of this debate. Labour economics has traditionally tended to measure only supply (education) and prices (wages), and then inferred demand (the skill requirements of jobs) from the relation between supply and price (see e.g. the analysis of long-run developments in the US labour market by Goldin and Katz 2007). In contrast, some recent economic research has attempted to measure skill demand explicitly by using data on job tasks (see e.g. Autor et al. 2003 for the US, Goos and Manning 2007 for Britain, and Spitz-Oener 2006 for Germany). This new economic research echoes a well-established, almost century-long tradition in occupational classification based on skill distinctions, assembled and used by statistical agencies in many countries and figuring prominently in large amounts of sociological research for many decades. The International Standard Classification of Occupations (ISCO), developed and updated by the International Labour Organization (ILO), is a prominent and widely used example.

A notable data innovation is the large-scale effort by Cedefop, the EU agency for vocational education and training, to put together internationally comparable time-series (including forecasts) of both skill supply and demand, with demand measured via ISCO; see Cedefop (2010). The trends revealed by these data, based on the European Labour Force Surveys, show strong upgrading of both education and job skill requirements in EU member countries, with the supply side typically ahead in pace. Available forecasts indicate that these trends, including their relative strength, will continue through 2020. While such predictions are obviously less than certain, the underlying forces tend to be highly robust since they reflect strong fundamentals, demographically, economically, and institutionally.

An important issue is the extent to which the long-term trends are affected by macro-economic conditions, with the great recession as a focal case. How have educational attainment and the skill structure of jobs changed due to the steep and widespread economic downturn, and how has the matching between workers and jobs evolved? In general, the EULFS data show that the low-skill share of all jobs declines significantly as the recession unfolds, thus raising the speed of occupational upgrading (Cedefop 2010). On the supply side, recessions usually lead to a rise in educational enrolment, as individuals turn to schooling as an apparently productive alternative to employment when jobs are scarce.

What are the potential implications for job–worker matching of these recession-induced shifts in skill demand and supply? In the short term, generally falling recruitment coupled with a relatively large loss in available low-skill jobs, may lead to bumping-down: the difficulty for well-educated workers to find a high-skill job increases due to the recession, leading them to take a low-skill jobs as a (hopefully) temporary substitute. This in turn may add to the already increased difficulty for low-educated workers to find (or keep) a low-skill job, which pushes them into unemployment or out of the labour force. In the longer term, some time into the post-recession period of increased hiring rates, the pace of skill upgrading on the demand side will probably slow down as compared to the recession years, but skill supply will have been raised in the meantime, while jobs were hard to find. The net outcome of these two shifts is hard to predict. An additional issue is how unemployment and general economic conditions early in the career affect future labour market prospects. Previous research has found substantial long-term negative outcomes; a recent example is Kahn (2010) who documents significant losses in long-run earnings growth for US college graduates who entered the labour force in economic downturns. One reason may be difficulties in escaping the consequences of early skill mismatch.

We now turn to empirically examining the structure and change of skill supply and demand in the eighteen countries under comparison. On the demand side, a continuous measure of occupational skill requirements has been constructed on the basis of the distribution of the employed population across 1-digit ISCO categories. Each category has been assigned a skill demand score from 0 to 2 depending on the typical educational requirements of its included occupations, with 0 meaning that no schooling beyond the primary or lower secondary level is normally required, 1 that upper secondary but not tertiary education is the normal requirement level, and 2 that the occupations typically require a tertiary education degree. Based on these criteria, professionals (ISCO 2) are assigned a score of 2, managers (ISCO 1) and semi-professionals (ISCO 3) a score of 1.5, craft workers (ISCO 7) a score of 1, clerical employees (ISCO 4), sales and service workers (ISCO 5), semi-skilled agricultural workers (ISCO 6), and factory workers (ISCO 8) a score of 0.5, and elementary workers (ISCO 9) are assigned a score of 0.

For education, a continuous measure has been constructed in the same manner as for occupational skill. Hence, education is scored 0 for primary schooling (including lower secondary) or less, 1 for completed upper secondary schooling, and 2 for a completed tertiary education degree.

On the basis of these measures, both transformed (simply multiplied by 50) to run from 0 to 100, Figure 3.13 shows average education levels of the population and average skill levels of the occupational structure in the eighteen countries. The numbers are averages for the years of the last decade prior to the start of the recession, 2000–7. A strong positive association is evident between the two skill dimensions, i.e. the skill levels of individuals and jobs, respectively. Still, the relation is far from perfect, and displays a fairly large amount of apparent excess supply of education: most countries are clearly above the flatter of the two lines in the figure which connects points of similar magnitude along the two dimensions. The steeper line is the regression

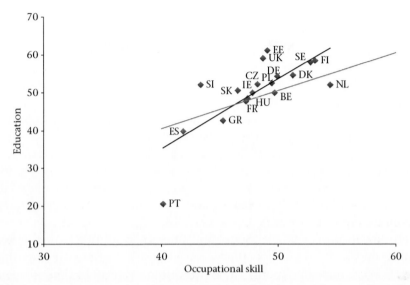

Figure 3.13. Levels of occupational skill and population education, averages 2000–2007 (scale 0–100)

line, and the fact that it is steeper confirms the systematic tendency of over-education: for each point increase in skill demand there is a consistently larger amount of increase in skill supply. In a sense, this is an underestimation of actual over-education rates, since (a) the employed relative to the full population are positively selected on education, and (b) there is mismatch at the individual level even when aggregate skill demand and supply are equal in size. On the other hand, all education is not useful in the labour market since not only levels but also fields of education are relevant, so some apparent over-education reflects horizontal rather than vertical mismatch.

There are exceptions to the pattern of educational over-supply. Portugal is an extreme case, with both a far less educated population than in all other countries under comparison and a large shortage of education relative to its occupational structure, despite its occupational skill level being the lowest of all. Greece, Spain, and the Netherlands are further cases of apparent education shortage relative to the skill level of their occupational structures. All other countries have a higher average education level of their populations than the average skill level of their occupational structures. Estonia, Slovenia, and the UK have the highest rates of structural (aggregate) over-education, while Belgium, France, and Hungary are close to balance.

In line with our parallel interest in distribution and growth (see the conceptual discussion in Chapter 2), the link between skill levels and economic wealth is important to examine. Both individual education and the skill level of occupations are positively related to wealth (measured by GDP per capita). The wealth association is clearly stronger with occupation than with education, in part reflecting that much education is not used in production: many of the population are not employed, many of the employed have more education than their job requires, and there is a fair degree of horizontal mismatch. In addition, the correlation between educational quantity and quality is far from perfect, and the wealth connection is much stronger with quality than with quantity (Hanushek and Woessmann 2008).

Figure 3.14 shows the association between average occupational skill level and wealth. There are three distinct groups of countries. The first consists of the nine richest countries, located in Europe's North West region, which also have the most highly skilled occupational structures. For the two other groups of countries, the rank orders of wealth and occupational skill, respectively, are inconsistent. The Southern European countries have the least skilled job structures but nonetheless have a clearly higher GDP level than the Eastern European nations. These two country categories thus appear to follow partly different developmental paths: The economic disadvantage of the South relative to the North West is mainly tied to its technological structure as reflected in its occupational distribution. In contrast, the Eastern economic disadvantage is both technologically (relative to the North West) and institutionally (relative to both the South and the North West) driven. The transition economies of Eastern Europe have so far had very limited time to catch up with more mature capitalist societies, and still suffer from relatively

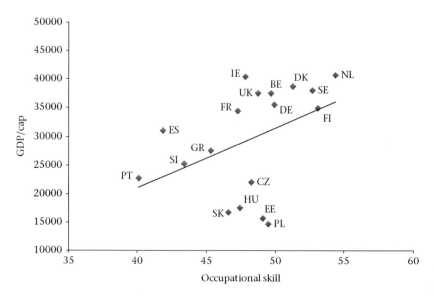

Figure 3.14. Occupational skill level (scale 0–100) and economic wealth (GDP/capita), averages 2000–2007

low levels of productive efficiency and governance quality. One indication of the efficiency lag problem is the strong correlation (0.66) between GDP per capita given the skill level of the occupational structure and a standard measure of governance quality, the corruption index assembled by Transparency International. When excluding the transition countries this correlation is almost eliminated (0.17).

Changes in skill distributions, part 1:
educational and occupational upgrading

After having sketched the skill supply and demand profiles of the eighteen compared countries in the years preceding the recession, we now move to examining how skill structures have changed during the economic downturn. As discussed earlier, economic downturns typically involve shifts in the skill distribution, both regarding education and occupation, since employment tends to be more reduced for low-skill than for high-skill categories.

Figures 3.15 and 3.16 are in line with this general pattern. The distributions of education as well as of occupational skill have shifted upward, and more strongly in countries with relatively large employment reductions. Average education has tended to increase more than average occupational skill. This implies that excess education has increased, raising the risk of skill mismatch, especially over-education.

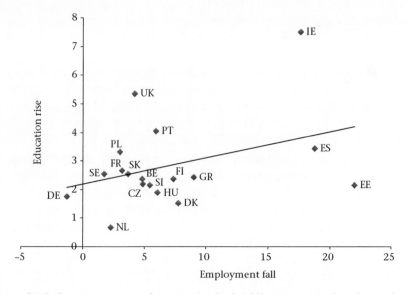

Figure 3.15. Rise in average education (scale 0–100) among employed population (age 25–64) from 2007/8 to 2010 by size of total employment decline

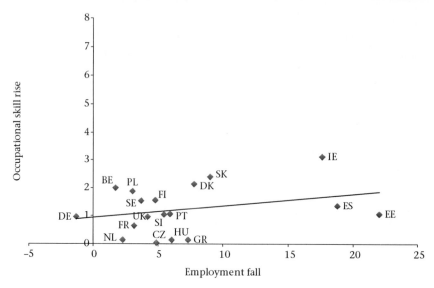

Figure 3.16. Rise in average occupational skill level (scale 0–100) from 2007/8 to 2010 by size of total employment decline

However, the associations involved are not very strong. Crisis magnitude correlates 0.37 with educational rise and 0.31 with occupational skill upgrading, but these correlations are not very systematic given the rather splintered country pattern. Apparently, other factors than employment decline determine changes in the skill structure, which should come as no surprise given the forceful long-term trends in skill supply and demand net of cyclical employment conditions.

An additional way to examine the association between crisis magnitude and occupational skill upgrading is to compare upgrading rates before and during the downturn. Figure 3.17 shows the difference in upgrading speed between two periods, the first running from 2004 to 2007 and the second from 2007 to 2010. If the economic decline increases skill upgrading, we should expect two things from the country pattern in the figure. First, most countries should lie above zero on the vertical axis, implying that average occupational upgrading has accelerated in the economic downturn. Second, the regression line (indicating the association between crisis magnitude and the change in the upgrading rate) should slope upward, reflecting that acceleration has been particularly sharp in countries where the employment downturn has been especially severe.

Both these expectations are met by the empirical outcome. However, the overall associations are not very strong. A majority of the countries have indeed seen a rise in their upgrading rates, but the increase in speed is not

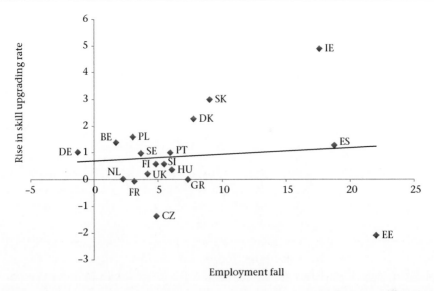

Figure 3.17. Change in occupational skill upgrading from 2004–2007 to 2007–2010 by total employment decline

dramatic: the average upgrading rate among all eighteen countries in the pre-recession period from 2004 to 2007 was 0.4 on the occupational 0–100 scale, increasing to 1.2 in the downturn (2007–10). The regression line does slope upward, but only barely; the correlation between general employment decline and the change in upgrading rate is only 0.10. The pattern of association is quite scattered, with some conspicuous outliers. Foremost among the latter is Estonia, where skill upgrading actually decelerated (from a rise of 3.2 in 2004–7 to a rise of 1.1 units in 2007–10). Excluding Estonia markedly raises the correlation between crisis magnitude and upgrading acceleration, to 0.55. The highest increase in upgrading speed occurred in the Irish labour market. In contrast to most other countries, and especially to Estonia, the pre-recession years (2004–7) in Ireland involved a fall in average occupational skill, by 1.8 units on the 0–100 scale, turning to a strong upgrading with 3.1 units in the course of the crisis, to produce a change across the two periods of almost 5, which is the highest upgrading acceleration rate of all.

In summary, the labour market downturn does appear to increase the rate of occupational skill upgrading, reflecting a concentration of the fall in employment opportunities to low-skill work. But the association is only moderate in strength and displays a quite scattered pattern across countries. A reasonable interpretation of these findings is that shifts in the occupational structure are mainly driven by fundamental economic and social factors that tend to influence skill demand through mechanisms operating in the longer run. Cyclical phenomena like the recent recession, while far from unimportant, are likely to be secondary drivers in this long-term development, not only because of the less than overwhelming empirical associations with downturn severity indicated above, but also due to their temporary character with upturns of demand eventually compensating for much of the impact of the foregoing decline.

Changes in skill distributions, part 2: occupational polarization

Shifts in the skill structure do not only involve unidirectional change in levels (mostly upward), but also changes in distributional shape. A prominent line of labour market research in recent years has explored tendencies of polarization of the occupational structure, with both high-skill and low-skill jobs expanding in number relative to mid-level jobs (see Autor 2010 for an overview). In theory, technological change (especially IT expansion) is the main driver of polarization, the mechanism being an imperfect correlation between the skill content of job tasks and their potential for being replaced by computer technology. Many low-skill jobs do not lend themselves easily to technological replacement because they require human capacities that are difficult to imitate by using computers or other machines, like eye–hand coordination. In contrast, some job tasks that are relatively skilled, like book-keeping, have a structure and content more conducive to technological replacement, like IT-based accounting. This technological development is called task-biased rather than skill-biased labour demand change, and is assumed to have repercussions across all industries. In practice, the main mechanism behind polarization appears to be the decline in manufacturing employment, especially in skilled manual occupations.

There seems to be a good deal of variation across countries in the degree of polarization over time. The first empirical evidence (Autor et al. 2003) came from the United States and the UK (Goos and Manning 2007) and showed tendencies of a relative decline in the number of jobs at medium skill and wage levels. Despite some claims to the contrary (e.g. Goos et al. 2009), for most European countries evidence of job polarization during recent years seems rather weak, at least until the recession; see Cedefop (2011). Importantly, technological factors—crucial in the standard explanatory model—seem to have had only a minor impact on the evolution of the relative number of low-skill jobs.

How might occupational polarization have been affected by the economic crisis? There has been a particularly large fall in manufacturing and construction employment in most countries. If this decline has tended to primarily affect skilled manual work, then polarization is likely to have increased since

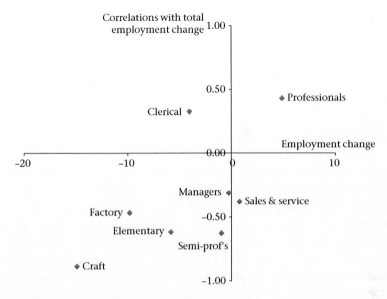

Figure 3.18. Changes in employment size by occupation (per cent) and correlations with total employment change 2007/8–2010

craft occupations are perhaps the major instance of mid-level jobs in the skill structure. Figure 3.18 shows changes during the downturn in the number of jobs at the 1-digit ISCO level together with the correlation between these changes and crisis magnitude (total employment decline).

Changes in occupational employment size are indicated on the horizontal axis. The clearly largest change is the steep decline (around 15 per cent on average) in the number of craft workers (ISCO 7), i.e. skilled manual workers mainly in manufacturing and construction. Relatively large falls in employment have also occurred for factory workers (ISCO 8) and elementary workers (ISCO 9), while the number of clerical employees (ISCO 4) has fallen somewhat. In stark contrast, employment of professionals (ISCO 2) has actually increased even in the economic downturn (around 5 per cent on average). Finally, the employment of managers (ISCO 1), semi-professionals (ISCO 3), and sales and service workers (ISCO 5) has not changed much in the course of the economic crisis.

Correlations between downturn magnitude (total employment decline) and changes in the size of different occupational categories are indicated on the vertical axis. The occupations showing the largest fall in size (craft, factory, and elementary workers) are also the ones that correlate strongest with economic downturn severity. At the other end, the change in employment size of professional occupations is positive and also correlates positively with crisis magnitude.

Altogether, this pattern of shifts in occupational structure confirms the tendency shown in the previous section that the economic crisis has been associated with skill upgrading, with some nuance provided by the disaggregation of the continuous skill measure used above into the occupational categories displayed in Figure 3.18.

Tendencies of polarization are also clearly evident. In particular, the large decline in the number of craft workers relative to all others, both high-skill and low-skill occupations, implies that the contraction of employment has increased polarization of the job structure. Overall, there has apparently not been a unidirectional change in occupational skill level during the downturn, but rather a combination of upgrading and polarization.

Figure 3.19 gives the country pattern of change in occupational polarization by crisis magnitude. All countries show an increase in polarization, although in some cases very slight. On average, the rise is 1.5 units on the 0–100 scale, with Estonia showing the largest increase (4.0) and Sweden the smallest (0.1). The association with total employment decline is strong; the regression line in the figure reflects a correlation of 0.85. Evidently, an important reason for this tight link is the large decline in employment of skilled manual workers during the downturn (see Figure 3.18).

Skill upgrading, occupational polarization, and institutional structure

We end this section by examining how changes in the occupational structure during the economic crisis have been associated with the structure of labour

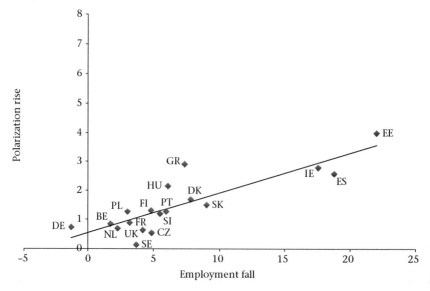

Figure 3.19. Change in occupational polarization (scale 0–100) 2007/8–2010 by total employment decline

market institutions. Figure 3.20 displays correlations between the change in size of different occupational categories and the institutional scales of equality promotion and labour market flexibility used earlier. In addition to the occupational groups, the continuous measure of occupational skill is indicated in the figure together with a continuous measure of polarization. The latter is constructed in a similar manner as the skill level scale, but in the polarization case mid-level occupations (craft) are scored lowest, high-skill occupations (professions) and low-skill occupations (elementary) are both scored highest, and the remaining occupations are scored in between. All correlations shown in the figure are estimated net of crisis magnitude, following the same procedure as in the section above on the distribution of employment decline by gender, age, and education.

According to the results, labour market institutions have been important for the pattern of change in the occupational structure during the downturn. In countries with strong equality-promoting institutions, the employment of professionals and semi-professionals, as well as of craft workers and factory workers, has been maintained at relatively high levels compared to less equal countries. In contrast, the number of clerical employees and sales and service workers has declined relatively little in unequal countries. With regard to labour market flexibility, employment levels of elementary workers have

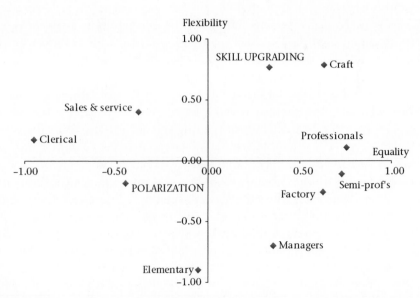

Figure 3.20. Changes in occupational structure (skill rise, polarization, and occupational category size) 2007/8–2010 by labour market institutions (equality and flexibility)

fallen more sharply than elsewhere in flexible countries, while sales and service workers to some extent show the opposite tendency.

Overall, skill upgrading has apparently been stronger in equal and flexible countries, with the Nordics being a prime example (see Chapter 2 for the full country pattern with regard to institutional structure in this respect). Occupational polarization, on the other hand, has been particularly sharp in unequal countries, and to some extent also in countries with less labour market flexibility.

Changes in Wage Inequality

A central issue closely tied to skill supply and demand is economic inequality. We close the present chapter by briefly assessing how the structure of wages has changed in different countries during the downturn. As shown above, the labour market has changed its composition of jobs and workers during the economic crisis, with tendencies of both upgrading and polarization. While these tendencies have been rather moderate and uneven, they are likely to have affected the wage structure. Compositional shifts need to be taken into account in examining the cyclical evolution of wages (see e.g. Solon et al. 1994).

In general, predictions of how recessions affect economic inequality are not straightforward. While it is clear that job loss and unemployment disproportionately hit traditionally vulnerable groups, there are several counteracting mechanisms involved. For instance, an important driver of wage growth among high-skill workers is job-to-job mobility, often across firms. The opportunities for this kind of mobility are strongly reduced in economic downturns, thus weakening high-skill wage growth.

Previous research has not arrived at a clear set of findings regarding the overall relation between business cycles and economic inequality. For example, a study of the Nordic countries during the deep recession of the early 1990s (Aaberge et al. 2000) shows that, as a net outcome of complex mechanisms, 'income distributions were remarkably stable' (Aaberge et al. 2000: 95). For the US, Barlevy and Tsiddon (2006) find that the impact of recessions on earnings inequality resembles the general trend of the time period: in times of increasing inequality, recessions tend to raise the rate of increase, and vice versa. A recent overview of the literature (Fiorio and Saget 2010) concludes that overall income inequality commonly falls somewhat following financial crises, while the impact on earnings inequality is more uncertain.

Descriptive international trends of wage inequality are regularly published (see e.g. ILO 2010; OECD 2010), and the latest available information is used below to assess the downturn's consequences for the distribution of earnings. At the time of writing (November 2012), there are relevant data for thirteen

Table 3.2. Change in earnings inequality during the recession and correlations of inequality change with recession magnitude, shifts in occupational structure, and labour market institutions (n = 13, except last column where n = 11)

Decile ratio	Average change	recession	rec net	skill change	polar ch	equality	flexibility
				Correlations with:			
d9/d1	−0.11	−0.19	0.02	−0.04	−0.15	0.18	0.78
d9/d5	−0.03	−0.42	−0.68	−0.11	0.34	−0.51	0.48
d5/d1	−0.03	0.16	0.67	−0.01	−0.46	0.91	0.64
d avg	−0.06	−0.21	−0.01	−0.06	−0.12	0.10	0.82

Source (decile ratios): OECD Earnings Structure database.

of the eighteen countries in our comparison, i.e. data extending through 2010 (or in one case, the Czech Republic, through 2009). For five countries—Belgium, Estonia, the Netherlands, Slovakia, and Slovenia—there are as yet no published comparative data on changes in wage inequality beyond 2008.

Table 3.2 shows how economic inequality, in the form of ratios between earnings levels at deciles 1, 5, and 9 among full-time employees, has changed during the crisis as well as correlations between inequality change and a number of factors of interest including downturn magnitude, shifts in occupational distributions, and the structure of labour market institutions.[1]

Changes in the rate of inequality are shown in the first column of the table. All changes are negative, implying that wage inequality has decreased during the employment downturn. The size of the fall in inequality is just above 3 per cent in the case of the ratio between deciles 9 and 1 (where the average ratio is around 3) and a little less than 2 per cent in the d9/d5 and d5/d1 cases (where the average ratios are around 1.9 and 1.7, respectively). This indicates that the economic downturn on average across the thirteen countries with available information has had a slight dampening impact on wage inequality. Consistent with such an interpretation, the correlations between inequality change and downturn magnitude (see column 2 of the table) are mostly negative, with the exception of the ratio between median and low earnings (d5/d1).

As discussed above, some of the change in economic inequality is likely due to shifts in the job structure. As a way of indicating the importance of

---

[1] Deciles indicate points in a percentage distribution (of wages, for example), with decile 9 indicating a high point where the (wage) level is higher than 90 per cent of all individuals and lower than 10 per cent of all individuals. Correspondingly, decile 5 is at the median of the distribution, with 50 per cent of all individuals earning more and 50 per cent earning less; finally, decile 1 indicates a low point where the (wage) level is below 90 per cent of all individuals and above 10 per cent of all individuals.

the composition mechanism, the third column of Table 3.2 (labelled 'rec net') shows the correlations between inequality change and total employment decline given occupational skill upgrading and polarization. The strong correlations in this case emerge when median earnings are involved in the ratio: net of compositional shifts in the occupational structure, the economic downturn appears to have increased relative earnings more at the middle level than at the high and low levels. This difference is mirrored by the associations between occupational structure change and inequality change, given crisis magnitude (see columns 4 and 5 of the table). While the correlations with skill level change are generally weak, the correlations with polarization that involve median earnings are fairly strong. In line with the decline in demand at the middle of the skill structure, primarily reflected by falling employment of skilled manual workers and being especially large in countries with a strong increase in occupational polarization, wages at the median level appear to have fallen relative to both tails of the distribution.

Finally, the last two columns of Table 3.2 display the associations between the change in wage inequality and the structure of labour market institutions. (As in the earlier analyses in this chapter, the institutional associations are estimated net of downturn magnitude.) In the case of equality-promoting institutions, it seems that wages at the median level have held up better relative to both high and low earnings in relatively equal countries. This pattern is consistent with the comparatively small loss in employment of craft workers in more equal countries; see Figure 3.20. In contrast, the correlations between labour market flexibility and the change in wage inequality rates are generally positive and fairly strong, implying that economic inequality has increased more (or decreased less) in relatively flexible than in more inflexible countries.

We end this section on a cautionary note: since the wage data used above are only available for thirteen of the eighteen countries involved in the larger comparison, the conclusions based on them must be seen as preliminary. This is especially the case with regard to the correlation analyses; with such a small number of cases, and with the rather limited variation across the available countries, any interpretation of the findings must be quite careful. While clearly suggestive, the results just reported concerning economic inequality will obviously need further empirical investigation as the amount of useful information expands.

Summary and Conclusions

In this chapter, we have examined distribution in the downturn: (a) how employment decline during the economic crisis has affected different population groups as defined by gender, age, education, and occupation, (b) how wage inequality has changed, and (c) how these patterns are associated with downturn magnitude and the structure of labour market institutions.

Aside from the sharp contrast in crisis magnitude between the three extreme national cases (Estonia, Ireland, Spain) and the remaining fifteen countries, labour market outcomes have been strongly uneven along social and demographic lines. Youth, men, and low-skilled workers have seen their job prospects deteriorate significantly in most countries, while labour market conditions for older, female, and high-skilled workers have changed much less. The skill-biased employment change during the downturn has slightly enhanced the continuous upgrading of the occupational structure but has also contributed to its polarization, with comparatively large job losses occurring among skilled manual workers in manufacturing and construction.

Regarding changes in the distribution of earnings, the available information suggests that inequality has fallen somewhat, or at least not increased. To the extent that any impact of the economic downturn is discernible, the distribution of earnings has become slightly more compressed. Based on the limited data available, median earnings might have been more affected than either high or low earnings have. While the increase in occupational polarization would seem to have reduced relative wages at the middle of the skill distribution, the magnitude of the downturn net of compositional shifts appears to have counteracted this decline of median earnings.

In general, then, the impact of the economic crisis on labour market inequality has been mixed and multi-faceted rather than unidirectional and simple. Gender inequality has decreased, class inequality has increased in employment but not in earnings, while the change in age inequality has been mixed, with youth losing more than prime-age workers and older employees coming through largely unscathed.

4

Continuing Training in Times of Economic Crisis

Martina Dieckhoff

Introduction

Continuing labour market training has received much attention in recent years. Not only are opportunities for continuing training considered to be central for the quality of work (Gallie 2003: 65), they are also seen as becoming increasingly important in preventing the widening of socio-economic disparities in European labour markets (e.g. OECD 2004). Opportunities for continuing training are particularly important for older and lower-skilled workers as they face higher risks of skill obsolescence (OECD 2004). Continuing training participation has been shown to reduce workers' unemployment risk (OECD 2004), and increase their promotion opportunities (e.g. Melero 2010) as well as their job satisfaction (Jones et al. 2009). This chapter addresses the question of whether economic downturn negatively affects the volume of continuing training and hence impedes processes of skill development in the employed population. It undertakes a comparative empirical analysis of nineteen European countries which not only differ in the extent to which they have been affected by the recent economic recession but which also exhibit very distinct institutional contexts. A central aim of the chapter is to examine whether and how institutional contexts mediate the implications of the economic recession for training participation.

It has long been 'conventional wisdom' that firms cut down their training investments during economic recession as they have fewer economic resources (Felstead and Green 1994: 219). At the same time, however, opportunity costs for training are lowered during times of slack demand (DeJong and Ingram 2001; Caponi et al. 2010). Considering further the costs involved in firing incumbent workers during downturns and hiring new ones when the economy recovers, it can be efficient for employers to 'hoard' labour during recession and invest in their employees' training so as to be equipped with highly productive staff once demand recuperates (e.g. Brunello 2009; Möller 2010; Felstead et al. 2011). If such conjoint labour hoarding and increased training investment strategy were mainly constrained to skilled employees, one would expect that stratification in access to training becomes even more pronounced during recession with already disadvantaged workers—the low-skilled—being further penalized. However, given that training during recession is 'cheaper', economic downturns may be times when firms also invest in workers that are normally left out, e.g. their lower-skilled workforce.

Existing empirical evidence is scarce and mixed. Felstead and Green (1994) as well as Felstead et al. (2011) suggest no or only a small fall in training incidence for the UK, while findings by Mason and Bishop (2010) suggest that the recent recession has induced training cuts in the UK. Analysing US data, Majumdar (2007) comes to the conclusion that training is clearly pro-cyclical. By contrast, Caponi et al. (2010) find on the basis of Canadian data that firms' training provision is counter-cyclical. To date, our knowledge about the effect of recession on training provision is thus still limited. Moreover, existing work has focused on single countries and we still lack a comparative account. Repeated measures on continuing training incidence in the ESS for 2004 and 2010 make it possible to examine the consequences of economic downturn on training volume in a cross-nationally comparative perspective.

Theory and Comparative Context

Training investment in times of economic crisis

POTENTIAL IMPLICATIONS FOR TRAINING VOLUME
Becker's human capital theory (Becker 1964) remains the central approach to explain the rationale underlying training participation and provision. Even though some of the central assumptions of this model have been challenged, the general idea that the expected returns to training relative to its costs are the most important aspect of any training investment decision for both workers and employers continues to be the starting point of most theoretical and empirical work on this topic. Given that the vast majority of continuing training is employer-funded or employer-organized, accounts of training investment rationales have often focused on the perspective of the employer (e.g. Majumdar 2007). Economic downturns imply increased uncertainties for employers as to when and whether the returns to any training they provide can be recouped. Moreover, the financial constraints firms experience during recession could also make them reluctant to invest in training

(Majumdar 2007; Felstead et al. 2011). Both theoretical considerations would lead to the expectation that recession brings about training cuts. Of course, reduced hiring rates during recession also entail reduced levels of induction training, which is another potential mechanism leading to a decline in the overall rates of training (Felstead et al. 2011).

At the same time, however, there are also a number of arguments as to why employers may train more during recession: the costs of training are lower during recession as lost productivity during the actual training period is less problematic when demand is slack (Caponi et al. 2010; Felstead et al. 2011). Moreover, it is costly to fire incumbent workers and then hire and train new ones when the economy recovers—employers may thus decide to hold on to their labour, especially the highly skilled (labour hoarding rationale). Holding on to labour and training it in times of downturn can thus be an economically viable option which equips the company with productive staff once demand recuperates (Brunello 2009; Möller 2010; Felstead et al. 2011). Also, as argued by Felstead et al. (2011: 5), slack demand increases competition and firms are—more than usually—forced to compete on the basis of quality. Alternatively, they may need to diversify their services and products. Both of these scenarios are likely to require more rather than less training efforts (Felstead et al. 2011: 5).

As most continuing training is employer-funded and since recession affects the resources available to the employer as well as the cost of training, the theoretical focus in this chapter is on employers' 'training investment rationale' and how this is affected by economic downturn. Nevertheless, in the empirical analyses we observe actual training participation, i.e. the joint probability of training opportunities being offered to and being taken up by the worker. Therefore, the 'worker perspective' is also briefly reviewed. Even though the vast majority of all continuing training is financed by firms, workers may have to accept lower wages in return for training receipt (e.g. Acemoglu and Pischke 1999, 2003). And while it is generally assumed that most employer training is not purely firm-specific but also imparts a fair amount of general (transferable) skills, it has been argued by some authors that firms differ in terms of the 'mix of skills' most relevant for their productivity, so that the skills package workers develop at the training firm is more valuable to their current employer than to other employers (Bishop 1996). If workers are worried that they may lose their job due to economic downturn, this could make them reluctant to invest in employer training if they anticipate that the skills they would obtain are predominantly firm-specific. At the same time, however, participating in employer training increases workers' productivity and value within the firm, and hence reduces their risk of lay-off. Moreover, training offers during economically difficult times can be understood as a signal that the employer wants to retain the worker and should thus increase the worker's confidence of having a longer-term perspective within the organization. By contrast, refusing a training offer may signal low commitment to the employer which could increase the risk of job loss. Adopting this logic would lead to the prediction that employees' likelihood of taking up training opportunities offered by their firm is not negatively affected by economic downturn. Moreover, it has be to be borne in mind that workers' training decisions are likely to be less exclusively conditioned on economic rationality than those of firms, as training can also elicit intrinsic job rewards by providing opportunities for further self-realization and development (e.g. Burgard and Görlitz 2011). In sum, then, there are reasons to believe that recession is more likely to have implications for employers' than for employees' training investment rationales and therefore, in the remainder of the chapter the focus will be exclusively on the former.

POTENTIAL IMPLICATIONS FOR STRATIFICATION OF TRAINING
Existing work on continuing training participation has shown that training is very stratified: highly skilled workers have substantially higher participation rates than the lower-skilled, and younger and mid-career workers have higher participation rates than old workers (e.g. OECD 1999; Gelderblom and De Koning 2002; O'Connell and Byrne 2012). Again the theoretical premise of the human capital model (Becker 1964) that the anticipated returns to training (in terms of higher productivity) relative to the costs involved are at the core of any training investment decision is frequently cited in order to explain the observed pattern. Training costs are considered to be substantially lower for workers with higher levels of education as they require fewer hours of training than their counterparts with lower levels of education. This makes it more likely that employers invest in the training of their high-skilled staff, while neglecting investment in their lower-skilled employees. Older workers are disadvantaged because the time during which any benefits to the training investment can be recouped is shorter than for younger workers (see also Schils 2005). In addition, older workers are often considered to be less trainable than younger ones (e.g. Taylor and Walker 1998), leading to the expectation of more training hours and increased training costs.

The different ways in which recession can affect training investment decisions may also have important implications for the degree of stratification in continuing training participation. During times of economic downturn firms tend to have fewer economic resources which could make them adhere even more strictly to cost–benefit estimations. This is likely to shift their training efforts even further towards their most productive workers and lead to increased 'training stratification'. A 'recession strategy' of labour hoarding with intensified training efforts also could work in the direction of increased skill-based training stratification. This is because the labour hoarding rationale is held to be most pertinent for highly skilled workers as these are assumed to be the ones most needed for the firm to be competitive when the economy recovers (Dietz et al. 2010). Moreover, the medium- or even longer-term perspective of such strategy could also disadvantage older workers. Counter to this, actual training costs are lower during recession because there is less demand and hence lost productivity during the actual training period is far less consequential. This may lead employers during recession to rely less strictly on cost–benefit estimations in their training decision than during 'normal' times. Economic downturn could hence be the ideal time for employers to invest in the competencies of the lower-skilled segments of their workforce or to update the skills of their older workers.

Comparative institutional context

Economic downturn, then, may affect the training investment rationales of employers, but the implications of 'recessionary effects' for training provision are theoretically unclear: it can be economically efficient to invest more heavily in training during times of economic downturn, but it can also be rational to cut training investment. The answer to the question of which strategy is most feasible may depend on institutional context. Existing work has theoretically argued and empirically shown that labour market institutions are central in understanding cross-national differences in processes of skill formation and vocational learning. In the following—after briefly reviewing these theoretical perspectives—it will be outlined how such differences could also lead to different 'training responses' to recession.

In analysing cross-national differences in skill formation, attempts have been made to group countries into ideal-typical clusters, or regimes. Countries are grouped according to their similarity in those institutions (or combinations thereof) that are deemed most relevant in shaping different skill formation systems. Two such 'categorizations' are production regime (Soskice 1999; Estevez-Abe et al. 2001; Hall and Soskice 2001) and employment regime theories (Gallie 2007b, 2011). In a nutshell, production regime theory emphasizes the role of 'non-market' coordination for vocational learning. Coordinated economies encourage 'long-term cooperative relations, between one company and another, between companies and employees, and between companies and their owners' (Soskice 1999: 106). Such cooperative relations, it is argued, are conducive to long-term investments in high-level specific skills. By contrast, the lack of coordination capacity and the inherent economic short-termism prevalent in liberal, uncoordinated, market economies inhibits serious development of vocationally specific skills (e.g. Hall and Soskice 2001). While production regime theory has emphasized the importance of coordination for *initial* vocational training at labour market entry (Estevez-Abe et al.

2001), it is generally understood to also be central for understanding cross-national differences in the provision of *continuing* labour market training (e.g. Dieckhoff 2007). Of the countries analysed in this chapter, this perspective classifies Germany, Belgium, the Netherlands, Sweden, Norway, Denmark, and Finland as coordinated regimes, Britain and Ireland as Liberal regimes, while classifying France, Spain, Portugal, and Greece as more unclear cases representing another type of capitalism (Hall and Soskice 2001: 21).

The production regime approach has been criticized, inter alia, for its emphasis on coordination while neglecting the question of the 'inclusiveness of the regulative system' (Gallie 2011: 14). The employment regime approach, by contrast, emphasizes the *inclusiveness* of bargaining coordination which can be most immediately measured by means of its 'scope' and its 'depth'. The scope of the inclusiveness of a regulative system can be best proxied by the level of collective bargaining coverage, while its depth can be proxied by union density (Gallie 2011: 14). Besides coordination, the actual strength of organized labour and its possibilities to influence training policies have been argued to be crucial in determining the volume and the distribution of continuing training opportunities as well as the portability of the skills provided (Ok and Tergeist 2003; Dieckhoff 2007; Edlund and Grönlund 2008; Gallie 2011). The employment regime approach differentiates—based on the strength and involvement of organized labour—inclusive, dualistic, and market (or Liberal) employment regimes (Gallie 2011). Compared to the dichotomous categorization originally proposed by production regime theory, the employment regime approach groups Northern Continental and Scandinavian countries into separate categories, the former being classified as dualistic, the latter as inclusive employment systems (Gallie 2011). The classification of the Southern European countries and the new member states remains an open question, however, and is to date theoretically underdeveloped. The Mediterranean countries can provisionally be classified as dualistic, though with particularly strong insider protection, and the new member states as market or Liberal employment regimes (Gallie 2007b: 10, 2011: 11; Edlund and Grönlund 2008: 251).

While both the production regime and employment regime theory give important insights into cross-national differences in training provision, they are also crucial in developing predictions on training behaviour in times of economic downturn. The financial system and cooperative relations in coordinated systems allow for more long-term solutions and outlooks, making current profitability less crucial than in Liberal production regimes (Hall and Soskice 2001: 22–3). Therefore, it should be easier for coordinated economies to hold on to skilled labour and their core workforce throughout periods of economic downturn (Hall and Soskice 2001: 22) and the strategy of increased training efforts during recession is thus likely to be more feasible and consequently more prevalent in these systems. Moreover, besides the level of coordination, the actual strength of organized labour, which is held to vary by employment regime, should be central in shaping training behaviour during recession. Union strength—collective bargaining coverage in particular—is associated with greater wage compression (e.g. Card et al. 2003) and wage compression provides incentives for employers to invest *equitably* and *sufficiently* in the continuous training and upskilling of their workers, thereby reducing the gap between (high, collectively agreed) wages and actual productivity (Streeck 1992; Acemoglu and Pischke 1999)—this mechanism could possibly even be reinforced during recession which lowers training costs but seldom wages (Bewley 1999). Strong employment protection—which is more prevalent in inclusive and dualistic than in Liberal regimes—can be expected to exert rather similar effects as it increases the costs of hiring and firing and should thus encourage employers to invest in training during recession and to do so equitably in order to raise the productivity of their workforce when opportunity costs of training are comparatively low.

Given the influence of organized labour in the inclusive regimes it is expected that economic downturn will have the least negative effects on training provision in these regimes and may even lead to increased training investments. It is also predicted that the institutional set-up of dualistic regimes will prevent training cuts during recession. By contrast, in Liberal regimes training provision should be negatively affected by recession. Moreover, it could be expected that increased stratification in training participation is less likely to occur in inclusive and dualistic regimes than in Liberal ones.

In light of these theoretical considerations, a central concern of this chapter is to examine whether recessionary effects vary by regime type. Combining insights from both the production and the employment regime perspectives, it distinguishes between the inclusive-coordinated regime which is represented by the Scandinavian countries, the dualistic-coordinated regime consisting of Germany, the Netherlands, and Belgium, as well as the Liberal regime comprising the UK and Ireland. As noted before, the Mediterranean countries could be seen as having proximity to the dualistic regime, while the Transition countries share similarities with the Liberal regime. Given that these categorizations still lack thorough theoretical grounding, however, in the presentation and discussion of results these two country groups will be treated as separate categories. Note also, that for reasons discussed in the introductory chapter of this edited volume (Gallie, chapter 1), France is treated as a further special case which is not included in the Mediterranean country grouping. More generally, given that regimes are ideal-types, there is still a substantial degree of within-regime heterogeneity in terms of the central institutional features. The chapter will therefore also aim to account and test for direct institutional effects (e.g. employment protection, collective bargaining coverage, coordination) as central crisis mediators by employing multi-level regression models.

Data and Methods

The analyses are based on the European Social Survey (ESS) *Round 2* fielded in 2004/5 and *Round 5* fielded in 2010/11, using data from nineteen countries: Belgium, the Czech Republic, Denmark, Estonia, Finland, France, Germany, Greece, Hungary, Ireland, the Netherlands, Norway, Poland, Portugal, Slovenia, Slovakia, Spain, Sweden, and the UK. They are restricted to dependently employed workers between 25 and 64 years of age.

Continuing training is understood here to include any training or education that is *work-related*, but does not represent initial vocational training at labour market entry or any participation in active labour market policies (see also Arulampalam et al. 2004; Dieckhoff 2007; Dieckhoff and Steiber 2011). Moreover, the aim is to measure *formal* employer training (i.e. course or workshop participation) rather than any *informal* learning or training activities (e.g. 'job-shadowing'). Unfortunately, it is not possible in the analyses conducted here to distinguish whether training is employer-funded or not as this information is not available in the 2004 survey. However, we know that the vast majority of all training undertaken by employed individuals is employer-funded (e.g. O'Connell 1999; O'Connell and Byrne 2012). This is also shown by Round 5 of the ESS survey where this additional information exists: 84 per cent of all workers in our 2010 sample who participated in continuing training stated that this was fully or mostly funded by their employer. The ESS question which constitutes the basis of our measure of formal employer training reads: 'During the last twelve months, have you taken any course or attended any lecture or conference to improve your knowledge or skills for work?' Responses to this survey question could also include initial vocational training or activation training undertaken during an unemployment spell. In order to ensure that only *continuing* training is measured, the analyses in this chapter exclude young workers under the age of 25 years as well as workers who have been with their current employer for *less* than one full year.[1]

---

[1] Unfortunately, the tenure measure that one can construct on the basis of the ESS data is not very precise: 'time of interview—*year first started to work for current employer*'. A difference of 2 is hence required to ensure that only workers with a minimum of one full year of tenure are included, but this restriction can in the 'worst case' also entail the exclusion of workers who have been with their employer for two full years.

To examine the impact of economic downturn on *continuing training* incidence (both measured as the change between 2004 and 2010), the central *explanatory* variable is time (captured by a dummy variable *Year 2010*). While 2004 represents pre-recessionary times, in 2010 most countries were still in economic crisis (see Tåhlin, Chapter 2 of this volume). In these analyses, the focus is on cross-national differences in the association between economic downturn and training provision and whether these can be accounted for by regime-type explanations. Controlling for compositional change is crucial here, as those individuals who remained in employment throughout the recession may be a selective group. The analyses—using logistic regression models[2] –control for age, education (ISCED), occupational class (based on the Eurosec schema), working time, tenure, tenure squared, health, intrinsic motivation, union membership, and firm size.[3]

Further analyses undertake more direct tests of institutional and recessionary effects by means of two-step multi-level models (see Franzese 2005; Primo et al. 2007). Here the estimated parameters of interest from the country-by-country logistic regression models described above (*step-1 analyses*)—that is, the effects for the variable *Year 2010* which captures the change in training odds—are used as the dependent variable and countries become the unit of analysis (*step-2 analyses*). Besides change in GDP growth (used here as an indicator of crisis *severity*), these analyses investigate the importance of institutional mediators in shaping training behaviour in recession, namely employment protection legislation, collective bargaining coverage, and wage-setting coordination (cf. Table A4.2 in the appendix for details on these macro-level variables).[4]

---

[2] The comparison of standard logit coefficients across groups within samples, across samples, and over time is not unproblematic (e.g. Allison 1999; Mood 2010), 'because the unobserved heterogeneity can vary across the compared samples, groups, or points in time' (Mood 2010: 68). Given that, to date, there exists no consensus on what reasonable solutions to these problems may be, the analyses in this chapter apply standard logistic regression models and show standard logit coefficients. These are presented on the understanding that even though we have to be careful about causal interpretation of log odds ratios, they do represent an accurate 'description' of how the odds of receiving training differ across time, across countries, and across groups within countries.

[3] The tenure restriction also means that many workers on short-term contracts are excluded and the analyses hence ran into sample-size issues regarding fixed-term employees in a number of countries. The analyses could therefore not control for contract type (even though contract type has been shown to determine training opportunities, see e.g. Arulampalam and Booth 1998; O'Connell and Byrne 2012).

[4] Given that the dependent variable in the *step-2 analyses* is *estimated*, the analyses should account for the fact that the uncertainty of these estimates varies across observations. To correct for this, Lewis and Linzer (2005) propose a feasible generalized least square (FGLS) approach, which is applied here (using the EDVREG routine for Stata: see <http://svn.cluelessresearch.com/twostep/trunk/edvreg.ado>).

Participation in Continuing Training 2004–2010

How have training incidence rates developed in Europe at large? Table 4.1 presents the results from a logistic regression model based on the pooled sample of nineteen countries. This analysis has been weighted so that each country is represented equally irrespective of its actual sample size. The variable *Year 2010* measures the net effect of temporal change between 2004 and 2010. It shows that the log odds of training have significantly declined: exponentiating the logit coefficient, we obtain an odds ratio of 0.81 which shows

Table 4.1. Logistic regression: continuing training amongst the dependently employed, pooled model

Variables	Logit Coefficient	Sig.
Year 2010 (ref.: 2004)	−0.211	***
Male	−0.104	*
Age (ref.: > 50 years)		
< = 35 years	0.377	***
> 35 & < = 50 years	0.294	***
Education (ref.: less than lower secondary)		
Upper Secondary	0.414	***
Tertiary	1.005	***
Occupational Class (ref.: Routine)		
Lower Technical	0.138	
Lower Sales & Service	0.797	***
Lower Supervisors & Technicians	1.080	***
Intermediate Occupations	0.916	***
Lower Mgrs & Professionals	1.472	***
Higher Mgrs & Professionals	1.511	***
Union Member	0.430	***
Firm size (ref.: <25 employees)		
25–99 employees	0.336	***
100–499	0.383	***
500 or more	0.573	***
Good Health (ref.: ≤ fair health)	0.107	*
Intrinsic Motivation (ref: high)		
Medium/Low	−0.223	***
Very High	0.103	*
Tenure	0.000	
Tenure Squared	0.000	
Working Hours	0.002	
N	21,422	

Note: (*) $p<0.1$, * $p<0.05$, ** $p<0.01$, ***$p<0.001$.

Source & sample: ESS 2004–2010 (weighted). Dependently employed aged 25–64 with tenure ≥ 1 year. Country dummies included but not shown here.

that the odds of training in 2010 were almost 20 per cent lower compared to 2004 after controlling for compositional change in the workforce.

The results for the other factors that were controlled in the model are consonant with the theoretical expectations of the human capital model on training investment rationales as well as with already existing empirical work concerned with distributional patterns of training participation. The odds of training participation significantly and substantially increase with level of education and occupational class. The results also indicate that both young workers under the age of 35 and mid-career workers aged between 35 and 49 have substantially higher training odds than older workers aged 50 years and above. High levels of intrinsic job motivation are also positively associated with continuing training participation. The same holds for good health.

We further observe that men in this pooled country sample are significantly less likely to train than women, but this effect is comparatively small. The results also indicate that the odds of training participation increase with firm size (again corroborating the findings of prior work on the determinants of continuing training). In accordance with the theoretical arguments on institutional 'drivers' of training participation, we find that union members have significantly higher odds of participating in training than comparable non-union members.

While we find a clear decline in training incidence between 2004 and 2010 in the pooled ESS data for all nineteen countries, there are reasons to expect important variance between countries due to differences in institutional context as well as in the severity of the economic downturn. The comparative pattern of temporal change will be investigated next.

Comparative patterns

Figure 4.1 displays the training volume in 2004 and 2010 by country (cf. also Table A4.1 in the appendix). If we look at average training volume by regime in 2004, we see—in line with theoretical expectation as well existing empirical evidence—that the inclusive-coordinated regime comprising the Nordic countries takes a clear lead with a training volume of 70 per cent. It also exhibits the highest degree of within-regime homogeneity by far. This country group is followed at some remove by the Continental group (average training volume of 49 per cent), which in turn is closely followed by the Liberal regime (47 per cent). The Transition countries (42 per cent) and France (41 per cent) come next, and the Southern group stands out with the lowest training rate by far (25 per cent). Interestingly, this overall 'regime ranking' persists even after the recession as can be seen when examining the 2010 incidence rates. But different training responses to the recession have led to more pronounced inter-regime differences. The gap between the

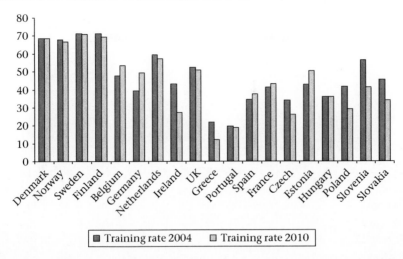

Figure 4.1. Time trends 2004–2010: continuing training amongst the dependently employed by country

Source & sample: ESS 2004–2010 (weighted). Dependently employed aged 25–64 with tenure≥ 1 year. See also Table A4.1 in the appendix.

Continental and the Liberal group as well as the gap between the Continental and the Transition group have grown substantially.

This purely descriptive analysis of change in training volume between 2004 and 2010 shows rather diverse patterns across countries. Training reductions were more frequent than training increases. The most drastic declines in training volume—ranging between eight and sixteen percentage points— are observed for Ireland, Greece, Slovenia, Poland, Slovakia, and the Czech Republic. The Netherlands, the UK, and Finland experienced small declines of around two percentage points. Finally, Norway experienced a negligible decline by one percentage point. Increases in training are observed for five countries. These were most pronounced in Germany, Belgium, and Estonia where the training volume grew by between six and ten percentage points. A small growth between two and three percentage points was observed for France and Spain. The remaining countries—Denmark, Sweden, Portugal, and Hungary—show no change in training volume over time.

While Figure 4.1 presented the gross within-country change in continuing training between 2004 and 2010, Table 4.2 accounts for compositional differences between the two years. It thus presents the net average change. These multivariate models confirm the picture of diverse time trends across countries, and broadly replicate the patterns of gross change. Even after accounting for compositional effects, the strong negative association between recession

Table 4.2. Net average difference *2010 versus 2004*: logit model predicting continuing training amongst the dependently employed by country

Country	Logit Coefficients (*Year 2010*)	Sig	N
Nordic			
Denmark	−0.061		1,083
Norway	−0.031		1,381
Sweden	−0.039		1,286
Finland	−0.131		1,274
Continental			
Belgium	0.245	(*)	1,104
Germany	0.372	**	1,829
Netherlands	−0.123		1,240
Liberal			
Ireland	−0.829	***	1,162
UK	−0.259	(*)	1,171
Southern			
Greece	−0.487	*	952
Portugal	−0.155		873
Spain	−0.021		984
France	0.082		1,216
Transition			
Czech	−0.464	**	1,424
Estonia	0.300	*	1,179
Hungary	−0.181		847
Poland	−0.727	***	848
Slovenia	−0.894	***	719
Slovakia	−0.808	***	850

Note: (*) $p<0.1$, * $p<0.05$, ** $p<0.01$, ***$p<0.001$. Controlling for: education, occupational class (Eurosec), sex, firm-size (grouped), age (grouped), working time in hours, tenure, tenure squared, health, intrinsic job orientation, union membership. Due to sample size limitations education was dichotomized for the country analyses, differentiating workers with tertiary education from those with secondary education or less. For the same reason, the Eurosec occupational class schema was aggregated into three categories (1) Routine, lower technical, lower sales and service; (2) Technicians and intermediate occupations; (3) Managers and professionals.

Source & sample: ESS 2004–2010 (weighted). Dependently employed aged 25–64 with tenure ≥ 1 year.

and training incidence is significant in Ireland, Greece, the Czech Republic, Poland, Slovenia, and Slovakia.

The positive temporal trend for Germany, Belgium, and Estonia is also confirmed. The small positive trends observed for Spain and France no longer show in the multivariate models. The small decline observed for the UK is significant and becomes more pronounced once compositional change is accounted for, while this is not the case for the small declines previously observed for Finland and Norway. In sum, the multivariate analyses broadly mirror the descriptive evidence of diverse time trends across the countries analysed. The analyses thus far have shown that there exists a lot of variance in terms of training trends even in the case of countries falling into the same country group. Nevertheless, there is some indication that institutions may have affected how countries responded to the recent recession. Both countries belonging to the Liberal group have experienced a significant negative net change in training incidence. The same is true for most countries of the Transition group. The Nordic countries of the inclusive-coordinated regime have not experienced any significant change either way. The dualistic-coordinated regime reveals a significant positive change for two out of three countries. However, one of these countries is Germany where the GDP growth rate in 2010 was actually higher than in 2004, so we should probably be careful to interpret the evidence of increased training investment over time as a homogeneous recession response of countries belonging to this group. Finally, the pattern within the Southern group is rather mixed. In sum, the results would then provide some support to the prediction that different regime types respond differently to recession. Specifically, within three of the country groups we find a 'homogeneous' pattern. While we do not find, as was hypothesized, that countries of the inclusive regime increase their training efforts during recession we observe that they—in contrast to the Liberal regime—do not react to the crisis by training cuts. Finally, the Transition countries—which in the literature have been *provisionally* ascribed to the Liberal regime—behave accordingly: a majority experienced significant declines in their training volumes (the exceptions being Estonia and Hungary).

As has been shown earlier in this edited volume (cf. Chapter 1 by Gallie; as well as Chapter 2 by Tåhlin) most of the countries under study have been affected by the latest recession, but there have been differences both in its severity and in its timing. Felstead et al. (2011) have argued that training behaviour may vary by recession severity and that during weak or moderate downturns it can be economically feasible to increase training efforts while severe recessions are likely to lead to training cuts. Do we find any evidence that different levels of crisis severity elicit different training responses? It can be seen in Figure 4.2, in which the changes in the odds of receiving training between 2004 and 2010 are regressed against GDP change between 2004 and 2010, that overall there was a reasonably strong positive linear relationship. But, many countries deviate from this general trend.[5] We see a lot of variation in the training responses amongst the countries which had been

---

[5] Note that additional tests have been conducted with an alternative indicator of crisis severity which measured change in unemployment growth rates based on Eurostat (2012b). This measure also suggested a linear relationship in the expected direction, but fitted the data less well than the GDP-based indicator used here in terms of explained variance.

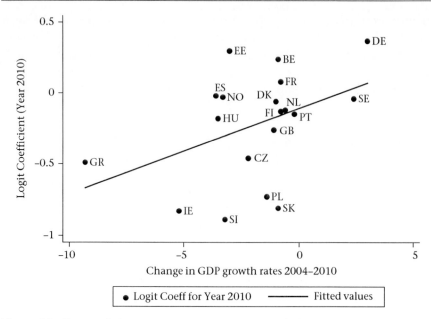

Figure 4.2. Temporal change in continuing training and change in GDP growth

Source & sample: ESS 2004–2010 (weighted). Dependently employed aged 25–64 with tenure ≥ 1 year.

most severely affected by the crisis in terms of the drop in their GDP growth rate between 2004 and 2010.[6] Estonia and Slovenia are a strong example of this: both have experienced similar declines in their GDP growth rates, yet Estonia responded with increased training efforts, while the typical worker in Slovenia had significantly lower training odds in 2010 compared to 2004. More generally, we find that at any given level of GDP decline most countries belonging to the Liberal or Transition regime tend to exhibit a fall in their training odds which is more severe than would have been predicted, while countries belonging to the other regimes more frequently exhibit a change in the odds that is more positive than—or in line with—the predicted values.

A direct test of institutional effects

In a next step, we investigate *directly* by means of two-step multi-level models (as described above in the section on Data and Methods) how the

---

[6] Change in GDP growth rates based on Eurostat (2012a). Growth rate in 2004 subtracted from growth rate in 2010 (growth rates are measured as percentage change over the previous year).

institutional variables emphasized by the literature as well as our indicator of the *severity* of the crisis (change in GDP growth) affect the trends in
training participation. Table 4.3 presents these estimations. Model 1 confirms that the positive relationship between change in GDP growth and
changes in the odds of training participation is (marginally) significant.
Put differently, this means the larger the drop in the GDP growth between
2004 and 2010, the lower the training odds in 2010 compared to 2004.
Model 2a shows that a variable measuring collective bargaining coverage
(*CBC*, see Table A4.2 in the appendix for details) has a positive but non-
significant effect. The interaction between *CBC* and change in GDP growth
is also insignificant (Model 2b) (and moreover does not have the expected
direction). In the case of employment protection legislation (*EPL*) the coefficient would suggest—the expected—positive relationship and reaches statistical significance at the 10 per cent level (Model 3a). This means that
the stricter the employment protection regulations, the less severe were the
training losses between 2004 and 2010. We find no confirmation, however,

Table 4.3. Macro-level determinants of change in training log odds between 2004 and
2010—Two-step estimation results (OLS)

	Model 1	Model 2a	Model 2b	Model 3a	Model 3b	Model 4a	Model 4b
Change_GDPgrowth	0.064(*)	0.059(*)	0.054	0.068**	0.071*	0.062*	0.038
	(2.01)	(1.79)	(1.27)	(3.12)	(2.47)	(2.39)	(0.44)
Collective Bargaining Coverage (CBC)		0.023	0.048				
		(0.47)	(0.75)				
Employment Protection Legislation (EPL)				0.220(*)	0.166		
				(1.81)	(1.05)		
Coordination of Wage- Setting (COORD)						0.070	0.139
						(0.68)	(0.96)
Change_GDPgrowth* CBC			0.014				
			(0.41)				
Change_GDPgrowth* EPL					−0.022		
					(−0.41)		
Change_GDPgrowth* COORD							0.033
							(0.40)
R-squared	0.1897	0.2118	0.2324	0.2856	0.2901	0.2306	0.2611
N	19	19	19	19	19	19	19

Note: (*) p<0.1, * p<0.05, ** p<0.010, t-values are shown in parentheses.

Source & sample: Dependent variables estimated based on ESS 2004–2010 (weighted) and obtained from country
by country logit models (Table 4.2). *Change_GDPgrowth*: Change in GDP growth rates based on Eurostat (2012a).
Growth rate in 2004 subtracted from growth rate in 2010 (growth rates are measured as percentage change over the
previous year). *CBC*: Collective Bargaining Coverage rate, divided by 10, the values of this indicator range from 1 to
10. The variable is centred at the mean. Measures pertain to 2008/2009, which were the most recent figures available
at the time of writing. Obtained from Visser (2011). *EPL*: Employment protection legislation measured on a scale from
0 (weak) to 6 (strict protection/regulation). The variable is centred at the mean. Measures pertain to 2008, which
were the most recent figures available at the time of writing. Obtained from OECD (2012). *COORD*: Coordination
of wage-setting measured on a scale from 1 (fragmented bargaining, mostly at company-level) to 5 (economy-wide
bargaining). Measures pertain to 2009. The variable is centred at the mean. Obtained from Visser (2011).

that the effect of change of GDP growth is significantly mediated by level of employment protection (Model 3b), although the interaction has the expected negative sign.

Finally, the coefficient for level of bargaining coordination (*COORD*) would suggest a positive but non-significant effect on the continuing training trend (Model 4a).[7] The interaction of bargaining coordination with change of GDP growth (Model 4b) is also not significant.

In sum, with the indicators used here, we find some limited support that institutions have shaped training trends between 2004 and 2010. Our measures of employment protection legislation, collective bargaining coverage, and coordination all showed the expected positive effects in this regard suggesting that training falls less when these variables have higher values. However, only in the case of employment protection did the estimate reach statistical significance (at the 10 per cent level). If we work on the assumption that most of the countries in our sample were still in economic crisis in 2010 we could thus conclude that high levels of employment protection do mediate whether economic recession leads to training reductions. A separate—but related issue—was whether the effect of the *severity* of the crisis (measured by the change in GDP drop between 2004 and 2010) on training provision could be mitigated by institutional variables. Here we found no evidence that institutions significantly mitigate the impact of GDP drop on training provision. It has to be borne in mind, though, that these macro-level analyses have the serious limitation that they are based on a very small number of cases (nineteen countries).

Increase or decrease of stratification in access to training?

What were the consequences of downturn for socio-demographic stratification in access to continuing training? As has been outlined in the theory section, there are arguments which would predict that economic downturn may increase stratification in training participation as well as arguments which lead to the expectation of declining inequality. On the one hand, firms have fewer resources which is likely to increase their adherence to cost–benefit calculations and to consequently focus exclusively on their highly educated young and mid-career workforce. On the other hand, actual training costs are lower during periods of economic crisis as demand is contracting and the cost of lost productivity during the training spell is hence less substantial.

---

[7] Note that additional analyses working with dichotomized measures of coordination (where countries with values 1–2 were categorized as having low levels of coordination and countries with values 3 and higher as having high levels of coordination), yielded substantively similar results (suggesting that high levels of coordination show positive effects) but did not reach statistical significance either.

This line of reasoning would suggest that employers may be more inclined to invest in workers that usually miss out on training resulting in a decline in stratification.

The inequality trends with regard to education are shown in Table 4.4a. The education variable had to be simplified due to sample size limitations. This meant collapsing those with higher secondary education and those with lower levels of education into one category. This risks underestimating the disadvantage of the low-skilled, as we only observe the contrast between

Table 4.4a. Time trends 2004–2010: net trends in educational inequality in continuing training participation amongst the dependently employed by country

Country	Logit Coefficient for Education (Tertiary vs. Secondary or Less)	Sig	Logit Coefficient Education* Year 2010	Sig	Trend
Nordic					
Denmark	1.124	***	−0.702	*	↓
Norway	0.647	**	−0.596	*	↓
Sweden	0.229		−0.132		
Finland	0.828	***	−0.555	(*)	↓
Continental					
Belgium	1.210	***	−0.073		
Germany	0.514	**	−0.356		
Netherlands	0.821	**	−0.784	*	↓
Liberal					
Ireland	0.746	**	0.037		
UK	0.544	(*)	−0.227		
Southern					
Greece	0.300		0.302		
Portugal	0.848	*	−1.538	**	↓
Spain	0.942	**	−0.569	(*)	↓
France	0.260		0.122		
Transition					
Czech	1.372	***	−0.991	*	↓
Estonia	0.905	***	−0.116		
Hungary	0.168		0.618		
Poland	1.420	***	−0.503		
Slovenia	2.655	***	−1.005	(*)	↓
Slovakia	0.987	*	−0.181		

Note: (*) $p<0.1$, * $p<0.05$, ** $p<0.01$, *** $p<0.001$. Controlling for: occupational class (Eurosec), sex, firm size (grouped), age (grouped), working time in hours, tenure, tenure squared, health, intrinsic job orientation, union membership, year of survey. Due to sample size limitations education was dichotomized for the country analyses, differentiating workers with tertiary education from those with secondary education or less. For the same reason, the Eurosec occupational class schema was aggregated into three categories (1) Routine, lower technical, lower sales and service; (2) Technicians and intermediate occupations; (3) Managers and professionals.

Source & sample: ESS 2004–2010 (weighted). Dependently employed aged 25–64 with tenure ≥ 1 year.

workers with tertiary levels of education and those with secondary education or less. To investigate whether the positive association between education and training has increased or decreased an interaction has been fitted between the education variable and survey year (i.e. the indicator of recession effects which takes a value of 1 for 2010).

We see that in 2004 in almost all of the countries under study the highly educated have significantly higher odds of participating in training than those with low or medium levels of education (Table 4.4a). Interestingly, we do not find any clear patterns in terms of employment regimes. Employment regime theory would have predicted, for example, that stratification in the inclusive (Scandinavian) but also in the dualistic (Continental) regimes would be less pronounced than in the Liberal regime.

Do we find any evidence of increased or decreased inequality trends over time? The findings suggest that in the majority of countries there has been no significant time trend in either direction. In these countries recession does not appear to be associated with increased or decreased education-based inequality in continuing training participation. In eight of the countries, however, a significant time trend emerged. This time trend is negative in the sense that it suggests a *decrease* of inequality, that is, a weakened association between education and continuing training participation. This decrease has been quite substantial in some cases. We observe a reduction in the differential by education in all of the Scandinavian countries (except in Sweden where there exists no significant educational stratification), the Netherlands, Spain, Portugal, the Czech Republic, and Slovenia. In fact in the case of two countries (Norway and Portugal), inequalities have not just declined but reversed, with the higher-educated having a training disadvantage in 2010.

Do these findings provide support to the thesis that lowered training costs during recession make employers more inclined to invest more than usual in their lower-skilled workers? Or is the decrease in inequality mainly driven by reduced investments in the higher-educated workers? Or, another possibility, has training decreased for both groups, just more drastically so for the higher-educated? The fact that none of the countries in which stratification declined experienced an increase in overall training volume makes it impossible that training of the highly educated remained constant while training for the lower-skilled increased at the same time. To investigate the question of what exactly drives the decline in inequality, the adjusted predicted probabilities of training for those with tertiary education and those with secondary education or less can be compared for 2004 and 2010 (the results of this are provided in Table A4.3a in the appendix). In all of the eight countries in which there was a reduction of differentials, the predicted probabilities of training for those with tertiary education declined. So declining training probabilities of the highly educated are an important part of the story, but there are still substantial differences across countries. In Denmark, Norway, Finland, and Spain the lower-educated experienced a clear training growth between five and eight percentage points, while the decline for the higher-educated ranged between nine and eleven percentage points. In Portugal and the Netherlands, the lower-educated have also experienced an increase in their training probabilities, but the declines for the highly educated were far more pronounced and the time trend we observed in Table 4.4a seems to be solely driven by the decrease of training probabilities of the higher-educated. Finally, in the Czech Republic and Slovenia training probabilities of both the lower-educated and the higher-educated declined substantially (which was to be expected given the aggregate time trends), but the decline of the higher-educated appears to have outweighed by far that of the lower-educated resulting in decreased inequalities.

Overall, then, we observe a decline in training inequalities between the higher- and the lower-educated in some of the countries under study. But in half of these countries this was mainly driven by reduced training probabilities of the highly educated. In four of the countries (Denmark, Norway, Finland, and Spain), however, the observed decline can be explained by a concomitant increase of training probabilities of the lower-educated and decline of the higher-educated, suggesting that employers in these countries may have re-shifted their training efforts during recessionary times.

Another important inequality dimension in access to training is age. Research concerned with determinants of training participation has frequently shown that older workers are less likely to receive or participate in training than younger ones (e.g. Schils 2005). Have such age-based inequality patterns increased or decreased during economic downturn? Table 4.4b presents the coefficients for the age gap in training participation, examining the gap between mid-career (35–49 years) and older workers (50–64 years). The results confirm that age is an important inequality dimension in access to continuing training with older workers having substantially and significantly lower training odds than mid-career ones in nine of the countries under study. While there appear to be some cross-national differences in the extent of training inequality these are—again—not structured according to a 'regime logic'. However, it does seem as though age is not a significant source of stratification of training participation in the transition countries, and that age-based stratification is particularly pronounced in the countries belonging to the Southern group. Turning to the central issue of inequality trends, we find—as was the case for education-based inequalities—that the degree of age-based stratification has not changed significantly between 2004 and 2010 in the majority of countries under study. In those five countries where change is observed—Denmark, Belgium, the Netherlands, Ireland, and Slovakia, there was decline in inequality. However, in the case of Slovakia,

Table 4.4b. Time trends 2004–2010: net trends in age inequality in continuing training participation amongst the dependently employed by country

Country	Logit Coefficient for Age (Mid-career vs. Old)	Sig	Logit Coefficient Age* Year 2010	Sig	Trend
Nordic					
Denmark	0.566	*	−0.645	(*)	↓
Norway	0.162		0.130		
Sweden	0.146		−0.075		
Finland	0.405	(*)	0.188		
Continental					
Belgium	1.271	***	−0.983	*	↓
Germany	0.537	**	−0.139		
Netherlands	0.480	(*)	−0.625	(*)	↓
Liberal					
Ireland	0.631	*	−0.885	*	↓
UK	0.501	(*)	−0.254		
Southern					
Greece	0.731		0.651		
Portugal	1.821	**	−0.998		
Spain	0.901	*	0.375		
France	0.632	*	0.069		
Transition					
Czech	0.191		−0.308		
Estonia	0.071		0.277		
Hungary	0.427		0.069		
Poland	0.328		−0.057		
Slovenia	0.530		−0.631		
Slovakia	0.128		−1.158	*	↓

Note: (*) $p<0.1$, * $p<0.05$, ** $p<0.01$, ***$p<0.001$. Controlling for: education, occupational class (Eurosec), sex, firm-size (grouped), working time in hours, tenure, tenure squared, health, intrinsic job orientation, union membership, year of survey. Due to sample size limitations education was dichotomized for the country analyses, differentiating workers with tertiary education from those with secondary education or less. For the same reason, the Eurosec occupational class schema was aggregated into three categories (1) Routine, lower technical, lower sales and service; (2) Technicians and intermediate occupations; (3) Managers and professionals.

Source & sample: ESS 2004–2010 (weighted). Dependently employed aged 25–64 with tenure ≥ 1 year.

the main effect shows only a small and statistically insignificant advantage of mid-career workers, so that the interaction effect suggests less a decline in inequality than a clear development to the disfavour of mid-career workers.

Again, adjusted predicted probabilities were estimated in order to understand what drove the time trend in these five countries (see Table A4.3b in the appendix). These reveal a rather heterogeneous picture. In Belgium, the only country among the five which experienced an increase in overall training between 2004 and 2010, old workers have experienced a marked increase in their training probabilities (by around eighteen percentage points), while mid-career workers have suffered from a very small decline (of two percentage points). In this country the decrease in inequality was thus clearly driven by increased investment in the older workforce. In the Netherlands as well as in the Denmark—two countries where overall training rates were stable over time—older workers have experienced an increase in their training probabilities by around six percentage points, while at the same time mid-career workers have experienced a decline in their training probabilities (by around ten percentage points). Here the decrease in inequality was thus driven by negative trends for mid-career workers as well as positive ones for the older ones. In Ireland and Slovakia, the two countries which experienced severe reductions in their overall training volumes, we find that the observed trend was driven solely by the decreased training probabilities of the mid-career workforce.

Concluding Discussion

This chapter has sought to explore how the recent recession has affected training provision in Europe and whether cross-national differences exist. It was argued that recession could lead to increased or to reduced training investments and that institutional settings are likely to determine which 'training response' will be observed at the national level. Another aim was to explore the implications of recession for training stratification. Do reduced resources, the labour hoarding of highly skilled workers, and heightened uncertainties about future returns lead to increased inequality in training provision to the disadvantage of lower-educated and older workers? Or does the fact that training investments are cheaper during recession lead to a more equitable distribution of training opportunities? Again, it was expected that the likelihood of either scenario would critically depend on institutional context. These issues were investigated on the basis of two ESS rounds, 2004 and 2010, with the former representing pre-recessionary times and the latter being a year in which most of the nineteen countries under study were still in economic crisis.

The analyses showed first that in Europe at large, training participation has declined significantly with the typical worker in 2010 being 20 per cent less likely than the typical worker in 2004 to have participated in any continuing training. Investigating training patterns in a comparative perspective it became clear, however, that cross-national differences exist. After controlling for compositional change in the ESS samples between the two years, we observed significant declines in training participation in seven out of the nineteen countries, three countries increased their training efforts, and the remainder revealed no significant trend. Crisis severity (here measured as change in the GDP growth rate between 2004 and 2010) offered some, but not too consistent an explanation of these cross-national differences. In line with the expectations formulated at the outset of this chapter, the results provided some indication of a regime-specific pattern of decline. Both countries belonging to the Liberal employment regime (UK and Ireland) and four out of the six Transition countries (Czech Republic, Poland, Slovenia, and Slovakia) experienced substantial decreases in continuing training participation. While the categorization of the Transition countries still lacks theoretical grounding, it has been argued elsewhere (Edlund and Grönlund 2008) that they approximate the Liberal employment regime. In terms of their training trends in recession, the findings of this chapter would indeed suggest that they 'behave' according to a 'liberal logic' where employers' training investment decisions are driven by immediate constraints and profitability. By contrast, the odds of training for the average worker did not change significantly in any of the Scandinavian countries representing the inclusive-coordinated regime (Denmark, Finland, Norway, Sweden). The evidence for the dualistic-coordinated regime (Belgium, Germany, the Netherlands) suggested training growth for two countries and stability in one, which was in line with predictions that—like the inclusive regime—the coordination capacity in these systems would prevent training cuts and could even make training provision during crisis times an efficient strategy. Finally, the pattern within the Southern country group (Spain, Portugal, and Greece) was mixed. Greece experienced a decline in training, while there was no significant time trend in Spain or Portugal.

Given that regimes are ideal-types, additional analyses using two-step multilevel models have been conducted to directly test the role of those labour market institutions considered relevant for shaping employers' training action during recession. These results offered some support to the assumption that employment protection makes training reductions less likely. We found no evidence that the other institutional variables examined here (collective bargaining coverage and coordination of wage-setting) significantly shape training trends. Moreover, none of the institutional predictors tested here appeared to significantly mediate the direct impact of GDP drop on training. It has to be emphasized, however, that these macro-level analyses were constrained by a small sample size and results have to be understood in the context of these limitations.

Finally, the results showed that in a number of countries (education- and age-based) inequality in access to training opportunities has decreased over time. Interpreting this time trend as a recession effect would then suggest that economic crisis is more likely to lead to more rather than less equitably distributed training opportunities. It is striking that we find no evidence of increased stratification in any of the countries, not even in the Liberal regimes where training cuts in response to recession were expected to go hand-in-hand with increased stratification in access to training. It was shown, though, that the observed decline in inequality was in many cases driven by reduced training probabilities of highly educated or young workers rather than increased participation of the lower-educated and older workers. But for some countries—Denmark, Norway, Finland, Belgium, the Netherlands, and Spain—the results suggested that the
110

reduction in inequality was really due to an increase of training for the lower-educated and older workers. These findings provided support to the expectation that lower training costs during recession could encourage employers to invest in training more equitably or re-shift their training efforts. With the exception of Spain, all of the countries where this was the case fell into either the inclusive-coordinated or the dualistic-coordinated employment regime for which it had been predicted that their institutional settings are likely to prevent increased stratification (or even lead to reduced stratification).

In sum this chapter has provided some important insights into the implications of recession for training participation. The severe training cuts observed in some of the countries are worrisome given the centrality of continuing training and learning for the quality of work and for cohesive labour markets. At the same time it was reassuring that even in those countries which experienced substantial declines in their overall training volume, this was not associated with increased stratification in training opportunities.

Appendix

Table A4.1. Time trends 2004–2010: overall volume of continuing training amongst the dependently employed by country

Country	2004	2010	Difference	N
Nordic				
Denmark	68.67	68.59	−0.08	1117
Norway	67.92	66.67	−1.25	1411
Sweden	71.17	71.08	−0.09	1313
Finland	71.14	69.43	−1.71	1296
Continental				
Belgium	47.82	53.42	+5.6	1136
Germany	39.48	49.14	+9.66	1890
Netherlands	59.50	57.30	−2.2	1279
Liberal				
Ireland	43.08	27.25	−15.83	1269
UK	52.14	50.63	−1.51	1272
Southern				
Greece	22.13	12.30	−9.83	1023
Portugal	19.59	18.89	−0.07	939
Spain	34.48	37.52	+3.04	1064
France	41.32	43.14	+1.82	1280
Transition				
Czech	34.12	26.30	−7.82	1617
Estonia	42.66	50.36	+7.70	1216
Hungary	36.01	35.92	−0.09	901
Poland	41.66	29.07	−12.59	902
Slovenia	56.55	41.50	−15.05	848
Slovakia	45.56	34.11	−11.45	940

Note: ESS 2004–2010 (weighted). Sample: Dependently employed aged 25–64 with tenure ≥ = 1 year.

Table A4.2. Macro-level variables

Country	Change in GDP growth rate 2004–2010	EPL: Employment Protection Legislation	CBC:Collective Bargaining Coverage	COORD:Wage-Setting Coordination
Nordic				
Denmark	−1.0	1.91	8.00	3
Norway	−3.3	2.65	7.40	4
Sweden	+2.4	2.06	9.10	3
Finland	−0.8	2.29	9.00	3
Continental				
Belgium	−0.9	2.61	9.60	4
Germany	+3.0	2.63	6.20	4
Netherlands	−0.6	2.23	8.23	4
Liberal				
Ireland	−5.2	1.39	4.40	2
UK	−1.1	1.09	3.27	1
Southern				
Greece	−9.3	2.97	6.50	4
Portugal	−0.2	3.05	4.50	3
Spain	−3.6	3.11	8.45	3
France	−0.8	3.00	9.00	2
Transition				
Czech	−2.2	2.32	4.25	2
Estonia	−3.0	2.39	1.90	1
Hungary	−3.5	2.11	3.35	2
Poland	−1.4	2.41	3.80	1
Slovenia	−3.2	2.76	9.20	4
Slovakia	−0.9	2.13	4.00	2

Note: Change in GDP growth rates: based on Eurostat (2012a). Growth rate in 2004 subtracted from growth rate in 2010 (growth rates are measured as percentage change over the previous year).

Source: Eurostat Real GDP growth rates (Eurostat, 2012a). Figures presented here pertain to change over time and were calculated by the author. *CBC:* Collective Bargaining Coverage. This indicator has been divided by 10, so that values range from 0 to10. Measures pertain to 2009 where these figures were already available, otherwise 2008 (NO, SE, BE, NL, GR, IE, ES, FR, PL) or 2007 (DK, FI). Obtained from ICTWSS Database on Institutional Characteristics of Trade Unions, Wage Setting, State Intervention and Social Pacts (version 3.0) by Jelle Visser (2011); Subject Code: AdjCov. *COORD:* Coordination of wage-setting measured on a scale from 1 to 5 where (1) = fragmented bargaining, mostly at company-level; (2) = mixed industry and firm-level bargaining; (3) = industry-level bargaining; (4) = mixed industry and economy-wide bargaining; (5) = economy-wide bargaining (level 5 does not exist in our country sample). These measures pertain to 2009. Obtained from ICTWSS Database on Institutional Characteristics of Trade Unions, Wage Setting, State Intervention and Social Pacts (version 3.0) by Jelle Visser (2011); Subject Code: WCOORD. *EPL:* Employment protection legislation measured on a scale from 0 (weak) to 6 (strict protection/regulation). Version 3 of the 'overall' indicator which is the weighted sum of sub-indicators for regular employment (weight of 5/12), temporary employment (5/12), and collective dismissals (2/12) (see Venn, 2009). Measures pertain to 2008 which were the most recent figures available at the time of writing. Obtained from OECD (2012).

Table A4.3a. Predicted probabilities of training by education group and survey year

Denmark	Secondary or Less	Tertiary Education
2004	.434***	.702***
2010	.483***	.588***

Norway	Secondary or Less	Tertiary Education
2004	.560***	.709***
2010	.611***	.623***

Finland	Secondary or Less	Tertiary Education
2004	.619***	.788***
2010	.694***	.694***

Netherlands	Secondary or Less	Tertiary Education
2004	.529***	.719***
2010	.555***	.564***

Portugal	Secondary or Less	Tertiary Education
2004	.217**	.393**
2010	.277***	.161*

Spain	Secondary or Less	Tertiary Education
2004	.357***	.588***
2010	.403***	.495***

Czech Republic	Secondary or Less	Tertiary Education
2004	.323***	.653***
2010	.263***	.343***

Slovenia	Secondary or Less	Tertiary Education
2004	.376***	.896***
2010	.230***	.608***

Note: (*) $p<0.1$, * $p<0.05$, ** $p<0.01$, ***$p<0.001$.

Predicted probabilities adjusted for: men aged between 35 and 49 years of age, who are working in intermediate or technical occupations, are employed by a medium-size firm (with 100–499 employees), are not members of a union, with good or very good health, high levels of intrinsic motivation, mean tenure and working hours.

Source & sample: ESS 2004–2010 (weighted). Dependently employed aged 25–64 with tenure ≥ 1 year.

Table A4.3b. Predicted probabilities of training by age group and survey year

Denmark	Age >50	Age >36 & ≤ 50
2004	.363***	.501***
2010	.422***	.403***
Belgium	**Age >50**	**Age >36 & ≤ 50**
2004	.188**	.453***
2010	.363***	.432***
Netherlands	**Age >50**	**Age >36 & ≤ 50**
2004	.473***	.592***
2010	.531***	.494***
Ireland	**Age >50**	**Age >36 & ≤ 50**
2004	.174**	.284***
2010	.156*	.126**
Slovakia	**Age >50**	**Age >36 & ≤ 50**
2004	.630***	.659***
2010	.647***	.395***

Note: (*) $p<0.1$, * $p<0.05$, ** $p<0.01$, ***$p<0.001$.

Predicted probabilities adjusted for: men with higher secondary education or less, who are working in intermediate or technical occupations, are employed by a medium-size firm (with 100–499 employees), are not members of a union, with good or very good health, high levels of intrinsic motivation, mean tenure and working hours.

Source & sample: ESS 2004–2010 (weighted). Dependently employed aged 25–64 with tenure ≥ 1 year.

5

Job Control, Work Intensity, and Work Stress

Duncan Gallie and Ying Zhou

Introduction

The scope that employees have for control over their work tasks, variously termed their job control or 'autonomy', has been a central dimension of the quality of work in quite diverse sociological perspectives on the transformation of work. It was at the core of both neo-Marxian accounts of the degradation of work (Braverman 1974; Durand and Hatzfeld 2003) and of neo-liberal accounts of the upgrading of work (Blauner 1964; Bell 1974; Walton 1985). It has been seen as critical for opportunities for self-realization and self-development through work. Research has confirmed empirically its implications for both work motivation and well-being in work (Zhou 2009). A wide range of studies have shown that it is strongly associated with job involvement and organizational commitment (Gallie et al. 1998) and that it is an important predictor of job satisfaction. Indeed, Kalleberg and Vaisey (2005) concluded that 'autonomy' is a necessary condition for workers to consider their jobs to be of high quality.

In recent decades, the argument for the importance of individual control has been reinforced by research by social psychologists and epidemiologists (Karasek and Theorell 1990; Johnson and Johansson 1991; Theorell and Karasek 1996; Marmot 2004; Theorell 2007). They have underlined the central role of job control in moderating the negative effects of work intensity for work stress. This has been shown to have significant implications not only for psychological well-being but also for physical health, in particular the risk of cardiovascular disease.

The onset of the most severe economic crisis since the 1930s thus raises vital issues about developments both in employee job control and in work intensity. Did it lead to a decrease in job control or did employers extend the responsibilities of employees? Did it raise levels of work intensity and, if so, how did these interact with changes in job control? The chapter first assesses how the level of job control of European employees has changed over the period 2004 to 2010. It then turns to consider the factors have helped to account for change and stability in the pattern. Finally, it addresses the implications of changes that have occurred for work intensity and work stress.

Economic Crisis and Job Control

As was seen in Chapter 1, there is remarkably little theory or evidence to directly guide us about the implications of the economic cycle, let alone major economic crises, for the quality of work. But the logic of different general perspectives on the factors determining work quality would lead to very diverse expectations. For those who emphasize the inherently conflictual nature of relations between employers and employees and the importance of power resources in determining patterns of work organization, economic crisis should lead to a radical shift in the balance of power in favour of employers and provide an opportunity for a significant increase in their ability to control the work process and to intensify work. In contrast, for advocates of crisis as a source of creative destruction, the expectation would be that the recession would decimate the technologically most backward sectors of industry, eliminating many of the lowest quality jobs. As a consequence, the expectation would be that the average level of job quality among those who remained in work should rise. Third, a number of arguments point to a long-term process of polarization within the workforce, with a growing divergence between those in a core sector of more skilled work and relatively highly protected employment and those in a periphery of less skilled and insecure work. If these are correct then the implications of the crisis may have been less in terms of some trend to increased or decreased job control, than to increased differentiation between employees. Finally, writers that have stressed the importance of institutional factors in structuring patterns of work organization would anticipate strong path dependency and relatively little change in underlying patterns across the period—at least in countries where the institutional system had been embedded for a significant period of time. Rather, there should be relatively stable differences between countries or groups of countries.

In examining change in job control we focus initially on changes in the average differences between country groups and then turn to examine changes in internal differentiation (or polarization) between employees within countries.

Trends in job control 2004–10

There are three items in the European Social Survey of 2004 that provide a measure of job control. They ask respondents respectively how much 'the management at your work allows you (a) to decide how your own daily work is organized; (b) to influence policy decisions about the activities of the organization; and (c) to choose or change your pace of work'. The items then cover not only immediate control over the work task (sometimes referred to as task discretion), but also people's perceptions of wider influence over organizational decisions. Responses were given on a ten-point scale, ranging from 0 = 'I have no influence' to 10 = 'I have complete control'. As these have a scale alpha of over 0.80, a summary score has been created by averaging the responses to the three items.

Taking the pattern in 2004 (Figure 5.1) there were marked variations between countries in the amount of control that employees felt that they had over their jobs. Job control was highest in the Nordic countries—Norway, Denmark, Finland, and Sweden—followed at some remove by France, the Netherlands, and Great Britain. In contrast, most of the East European countries had levels of job control that were below the average, although they were joined in this by Ireland and the Southern European countries—Greece, Spain, and Portugal.

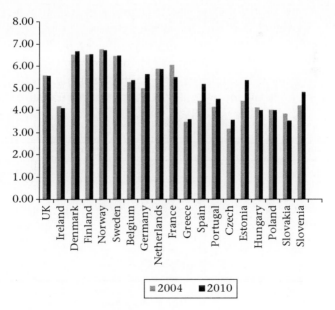

Figure 5.1. Employees' job control 2004–2010

Turning to the picture in 2010, perhaps the most striking point is the very high level of stability of pattern across the different countries. There was no evidence of change in the level of job control in any of the Nordic countries, nor in the Liberal countries the UK and Ireland. Among the Continental countries, there was a rise in job control in Germany, but not in either Belgium or the Netherlands. However, there was evidence of an increase in the level of job control among employees in Spain and Portugal and in three of the Transition countries—the Czech Republic, Estonia, and Slovenia. In contrast, there were only two countries in which there was a statistically significant reduction of employees' control over their jobs—France and Slovakia.

What were the implications of these country patterns for the relative positions of the country groups? In Table 5.1 the level of job control in each country group is compared with that in the Nordic countries. In both years, the Nordic countries stood out very clearly as having significantly higher job control than any other country group, while the Southern and Transition countries had the lowest levels. Comparing 2004 and 2010, it can be seen that the very distinctive position of the Nordic countries still remains very evident. There also has been no significant change in the relative position of the Liberal or Continental countries. These examples largely confirm the emphasis on stability of the neo-institutional theories, particularly supporting the expectation of the employment regime perspective that there would be a persisting significant difference between the Nordic and the Continental countries.

However, there are three cases where change has been more substantial: France, the Southern, and the Transition countries, although their paths have been rather different. France has moved away from being relatively close to the pattern of the Nordic countries to a position similar to the other Continental countries. In contrast, there has been a marked reduction in the relative disadvantage of employees in the Southern and Transition countries.

Table 5.1. Changes in job control 2004–2010 by country group

	2004		2010		Sig of Year Change with controls
Liberal	−1.68	***	−1.79	***	n.s.
Nordic	ref		ref		ref
Continental	−1.17	***	−0.99	***	n.s.
France	−0.78	***	−1.12	***	***
Southern	−2.53	***	−2.17	***	***
Transition	−2.60	***	−2.39	***	***

Note: Year coefficients for 2004 and 2010 are without controls. The final column reporting significance of year change is based on models with controls for age, sex, industry (nace_rev1.1), and establishment size. Sig = *** = <0.001.

Can these changes be accounted for by broad structural changes in the composition of the workforce? The last column of Table 5.1 shows the significance of the change in job control between 2004 and 2010 relative to the Nordic countries once controls have been introduced for sex, age, industry, and workplace size. The pattern remains basically the same. It shows that there has been some improvement in the relative position of both the Southern and Transition groups. France, however, has seen a relative decline in job control compared to the Nordic countries over the same period.

Polarization between employees?

Changes in the relative position of countries are only one indicator of whether work conditions deteriorated particularly sharply. The averages may conceal the fact that the period saw a marked increase of polarization within specific countries between different types of employee. Concern about polarization has focused primarily on differences between employees in terms of skill (reflected in occupational class) and of contract status.

A first point to note is that there is a very steep class hierarchy with respect to job control.[1] Figure 5.2 gives the job control scores for each occupational class taking all countries together. There is a rather clear break point, with

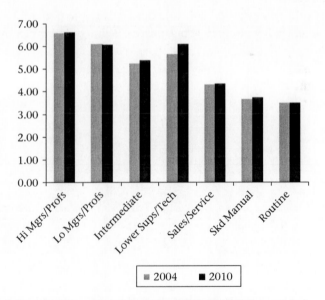

Figure 5.2. Job control by occupational class 2004–2010 (All countries)

[1] Class is defined in terms of the first digit groups of the Eurosec classification.

those in lower service, and particularly in skilled manual and routine occupations having much less job control than any of the occupational groups higher in the skill structure. It is notable that the overall pattern is very stable across the two periods, but with some evidence of an increase in the job control of those in intermediate occupational classes and more notably among those in lower supervisory and technical jobs.

But at the same time it is clear that the extent of the class differential differs very considerably depending on the specific country group. Figure 5.3 shows the ratio of the job control scores of higher professionals and managers compared to routine workers in the different country groups. This can be considered a measure of hierarchical distance between occupational classes.

It is notable that class inequality was much lower in the Nordic countries than in any of the other country groups. By far the most hierarchical are the Transition countries, followed by the Southern countries. As anticipated in employment regime theory, even the Continental countries are considerably more hierarchical than the Nordic—indeed their degree of class stratification is very similar in pattern to the Liberal group. The same broad pattern emerged when controls were introduced for differences in workforce structure with respect to age, sex, industry, and establishment size. The main difference was that the Continental countries now emerged as even more hierarchical than the Liberal.

Did class differences in job control change over the period? The expectation from an employment regime perspective is that, in relatively deregulated

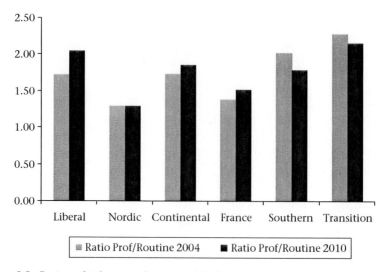

Figure 5.3. Ratios of job control scores of higher managers and professionals compared to routine employees by country group

Liberal systems, market power will be the main determinant of employee outcomes and one would expect the least skilled to be particularly disadvantaged in a period of economic difficulty.

The coefficients in Table 5.2 show the direction and significance of change over the period for each occupational class compared to the change experienced by higher managers and professionals, controlling for sex, age, industry, and establishment size. As can be seen, this confirms that in the case of the Liberal countries, routine (semi and non-skilled) employees saw their relative position sharply deteriorate over the period. There is no strong evidence for a similar pattern in any of the other regional groupings. However, there may have been some deterioration (at a marginal level of significance) of the position of the routine semi-skilled and non-skilled in the Continental countries. Further, there was a marked deterioration of the relative position of lower sales/service employees in France and (at a marginal level of significance) of skilled manual employees. In the Southern countries, the notable finding is that there was an increase in job control particularly among intermediary employees and supervisors and technicians, while in the Transition countries there was an increase among supervisors and technicians and (more marginally) among skilled manual employees.

Table 5.3 shows the patterns with respect to differentials and change in differentials in job control between men and women and between employees with different types of employment contract. Women generally had lower job control than men, with the exception of the Liberal countries and France. The pattern for part-time workers was more diverse—they had less job control in the Nordic and Continental countries and France, but higher discretion in the Southern and Transition countries. The most consistent

Table 5.2. Job control: year changes by class

	Liberal	Nordic	Continent	France	Southern	Transition
Class Year Interactions						
Hi Mgr-Prof	ref	ref	ref	ref	ref	ref
Lo Mgr-Prof	−.12	−.22	.07	−.05	−.10	.20
Intermediate	−.26	.18	−.03	.19	.70*	.16
Low Sup-Tech	.31	−.03	−.06	−.69	.71*	.89**
Sales/service	.08	−.04	.13	−1.00**	.35	.35
Skd Manual	−.08	−.35(*)	−.15	−.81(*)	.41	.41(*)
Routine	−.73**	.15	−.42 (*)	−.38	.11	.20

Note: Class is measured in terms of the first digit groups of the Eurosec class classification. Changes in differentials are based on the pooled data for 2004 and 2010, introducing interaction terms between each class and year 2010. Controls are for sex, age, industry, and establishment size.

Table 5.3. Year changes in differentials by sex and contract status

	Liberal	Nordic	Continent	France	Southern	Transition
Sex and Contract Differentials (2004+2010)						
Female	−.02	−.20***	−.21**	−.17	−.19**	−.22***
Part-time work	.01	−.47***	−.20**	−.51**	.20 (*)	.32**
Temporary work	−.59***	−.62***	−.25**	−.43*	−.26**	−.37***
Sex and Contract Year Interactions						
Female	−.04	.11	.18	.23	.15	−.12
Part-time work	.39(*)	.07	−.17	−.40	−.33	−.04
Temporary work	.27	−.11	−.34*	.01	.16	.61***

Note: Estimates are based on the pooled data for 2004 and 2010. Change is estimated by introducing interaction terms between type of employee and year 2010. Controls are for age, class, industry, and size of establishment. Sig *** = p<0.001; ** p<0.01; *p<0.05; (*) P<0.10.

finding was that temporary workers were disadvantaged in all country groups. In general the pattern does not support the assumption of employment regime theory that the differentials in employment conditions associated with atypical contracts are particularly severe in the dualist Continental group. Rather the disadvantages associated with temporary work appear to be very pervasive.

But did the pattern of change over time confirm the greater vulnerability of such employees in times of severe economic crisis, particularly in the case of the countries with more dualistic forms of employment regulation? To begin with there is no support for the expectation of a relative decline in the quality of women's jobs in any of the country groups. But, as predicted, there was indeed a marked deterioration of the position of temporary workers in the Continental countries. There was no significant change in the position of either type of non-standard worker in the Southern countries. In contrast, the relative position of part-time employees improved in the Liberal group, as did that of temporary employees in the Transition group.

Overall, the evidence supports the view that there has been a high level of stability over the period in relative country group positions. However, there has also been a limited measure of convergence—with the least developed areas of the EU to some degree catching up in terms of the involvement of employees in decision-making about their jobs. There is only clear evidence of class polarization in the Liberal group and of contract status polarization in the Continental group.

Sources of Change and Stability in Employees' Job Control

Economic crisis and employment restructuring

The most significant change over the period was the relative improvement in employees' job control in the Southern and the Transition countries. The scenarios predicting change related this to employers' responses to the pressures of economic crisis. There are two processes that may have contributed to the pattern. Economic crisis may have improved work quality due to changes in the composition of the workforce as a result of the selective nature of workforce reductions involving the disproportionate destruction of low-skilled, low-control jobs. Alternatively it may have led to changes in the working conditions of those that remained employed, as employers sought to enhance the commitment to change of their employees. A number of studies have argued for the benefits of employee involvement for dealing with uncertain environments and the need for rapid organizational change (Burns and Stalker 1961; Wall et al. 2002).

An approach to the issue of selective workforce reductions is to look at the nature of the inflow into unemployment in the central year of the economic crisis—2009. The European Labour Force Surveys provide a source of evidence for most of the countries in question, although unfortunately no relevant data are available for either France or Ireland. They give the employment status twelve months earlier of those unemployed in 2009, and, for those who were employed in the previous year, it is possible to distinguish the occupational level of the jobs that they occupied. This makes it possible to assess the class distribution for each country of those who lost their jobs in the course of the recession.

It can be seen in Table 5.4 that there were very substantial differences between country groups in the extent to which the unemployment inflow consisted of those from manual occupational classes, which typically had the lowest level of job control. Whereas less than half of the unemployment inflow consisted of manual workers in the Liberal, Nordic, and Continental countries, the proportion rose to 57 per cent in the Southern countries and was highest of all (63 per cent) in the Transition countries.

The extent of loss of certain types of jobs will depend partly on the severity of the unemployment crisis. The two were very closely related: the countries that were most severely affected by unemployment were also those that had the highest levels of inflow from lower occupational classes. The effect of this in accounting for changes in job control over the period can be assessed by introducing into the regression an interaction term combining the proportion of the lower-skilled in the unemployment flow with the level of unemployment in 2010. It substantially reduces the coefficient, and eliminates the

123

Table 5.4. Unemployment inflow in 2009 from the manual working classes and job control

	Liberal	Nordic	Continental	Southern	Transition
% of unemployed inflow in 2009 from manual occupational classes	45%	49%	45%	57%	63%
Initial change in job control	−0.11	ref	0.18	0.37***	0.21**
Change in job control taking account of unemployment inflow from manual classes	−0.10	ref	0.15	0.34**	0.15

Note: Unemployment inflow figures were estimated from the EULFS by Hande Inanc. Job control effects are based on ESS 2010. Sig *** = p<0.001; ** p<0.01.

significance, of the job control increase in the Transition countries (an initial coefficient of 0.21 at the p = <0.001 level becomes a non-significant 0.15). But, although the coefficient for the Southern country group diminishes a little and reduces in significance, it still remains statistically significant (changing from 0.37 at p = <0.001 to 0.34 at p = <0.01). There is some support then for the view that, at least in the Transition countries, the increase in job control partly reflected the fact that a particularly high proportion of employees in the types of jobs where job control was typically low were eliminated from the workforce.

But how did the pressures of the economic crisis affect the jobs of those that remained in the workforce? As was seen in Chapter 1, some arguments would lead to an expectation of employers increasing employee job control in a situation of crisis, either because of a greater emphasis on innovation or in order to enhance employee commitment in a situation of organizational change. Other arguments would point to a reduction of employee influence, due to a concern to ensure numerical flexibility or to intensify work.

We compare first the job control of those who were in organizations that had experienced a deterioration in their economic prospects with those in organizations that had not experienced financial difficulty (Table 5.5). The patterns are quite diverse between the different country groups. In France and the Nordic countries those with employers in great financial difficulty had lower control over their jobs than other employees, whereas in the Liberal, Continental, Southern, and Transition countries they had higher levels of control.

These patterns, however, may reflect differences in the types of organizations that were affected by the crisis in different countries. To discount this, we introduced controls for class, industry, age, sex, and firm size to assess the effects for broadly similar types of employees. This showed that it was only in the Continental and in the Transition countries that severe economic

Table 5.5. Job control by financial difficulty of the firm in 2010

	Lib	Nordic	Cont	France	South	Transition
No financial difficulty	4.83	6.77	5.50	5.49	4.58	4.16
Some financial difficulty	4.81	6.63	5.95	5.60	4.48	4.37
Great deal of financial difficulty	5.55	6.53	6.28	5.32	4.71	4.77

Table 5.6. Job control in organizations experiencing financial difficulty in previous three years compared to those without financial difficulty (with controls for workforce characteristics)

	Lib	Nordic	Cont	France	South	Transition
Employer with financial difficulty	0.13	−0.04	0.26**	−0.05	0.15	0.25***
–some financial difficulty	0.08	−0.01	0.19	0.01	0.12	0.16
–great deal of fin. difficulty	0.29	−0.10	0.44**	−0.29	0.27	0.54***

Note: reference category: employers not in financial difficulty. Note: Sig *** = $p<0.001$; ** $p<0.01$.

difficulty was significantly associated with higher levels of job control once other factors had been taken into account (Table 5.6). Moreover, this only occurred in conditions of severe economic difficulty. In the other country groups the financial position of the firm made no significant difference, although the coefficients were positive in the Southern and Liberal countries, while they were negative in the Nordic countries and above all in France (tentatively suggesting that employers reduced employee job control in conditions of economic difficulty).

In short, at least for the Transition countries, there is some support both for displacement and for upgrading effects of economic crisis. These countries experienced a very strong outflow of the types of workers that had relatively low levels of job control, while remaining employees in firms experiencing economic difficulty appear to have benefited from policies of greater involvement.

Sources of stability: job control and institutional systems

The most notable feature of the pattern over time was the high level of stability in the relative positions of the different country groups with respect to job control, despite such a severe period of economic turbulence. Arguments predicting stability have tended to emphasize the mutually reinforcing characteristics of institutional structures. Individual level control is anchored in broader structures of industrial relations that are more strongly institutional-ized and hence are relatively well protected from the pressures of shorter-term economic change. We turn then to address the issue of the way employee job control related to wider forms of employee influence in the workplace. We begin by examining indicators of the extent and influence of workplace par-ticipatory mechanisms and then turn to their implications for employees' immediate control over their job tasks. Finally, we consider how far workplace representation is itself anchored in a broader macro-institutional context.

WORKPLACE REPRESENTATION AND JOB CONTROL

European industrial relations systems differ widely in terms of formal insti-tutional regulations supporting employee workplace representation. While some countries have legal requirements for employers to establish works councils in firms above a certain size threshold, others leave the provisions for social dialogue to informal agreements with workforce representatives or simply to unilateral employer decision. The ICTWSS Database provides an indicator of works councils prevalence (Visser 2011). It combines the extent to which works councils or equivalent bodies are mandatory or voluntary with a distinction in terms of the proportion of eligible firms that are cov-ered. A score of 2 reflects that they are mandatory (either because of law or agreement between the peak social partners) and that they cover 75 per cent of eligible firms. A score of 1 indicates that they are mandatory but fall below 75 per cent coverage, while a score of 0 denotes that they are volun-tary (or absent) and cover less than 25 per cent of firms with 50 or more employees. Works councils may also have different formal rights of control over decision-making. The prevalence measure then is accompanied by a measure of works council rights that gives a score of 3 for co-decision rights, 2 for major consultation rights, 1 for information rights, and 0 where there is no representation.

It can be seen from the first two rows of Table 5.7 that there was a relatively high presence of works councils in the Nordic and the Continental country groups and in France and also a relatively substantial presence in the Transition countries. Works council representation was much weaker in the Southern countries and particularly in the Liberal country group. Among the countries with high prevalence, the Nordic and Continental countries, as well as France, also had works councils with relatively strong rights. In contrast, works coun-cils in the Transition countries had much weaker powers. Works council rights were particularly low in the Liberal and Southern country groups. If these indicators are compared across time, they show a remarkably stability both in the absolute scores and in the pattern of relative differences between country groups over the whole period from 2000 to 2009.

Table 5.7. Strength of workplace representation (mean scores) 2010

	Nordic	Liberal	Continental	France	South	Transition
Formal Institutions						
Works Council Score 09–10	2.00	1.25	2.00	2.00	1.33	1.75
Rights of Works Councils Score 09–10	2.00	.50	2.67	2.00	.33	1.33
Employee Reports						
Meetings with Representatives	74.3	61.3	55.3	60.7	34.8	54.0
Influence of Representatives Score	1.83	1.38	1.26	1.19	0.75	1.26

Note: Works council indicators, based on the countries in the 2010 ESS, derived from ICTWS, Visser (2011). Scores for representative influence range from 0 = no representation to 4 = quite a lot/ a great deal of influence.

However, an issue that has rarely been addressed is how far the presence of works councils provides employees with a sense that there is effective voice in the workplace. There might well be a discrepancy either because formal institutional provisions are not properly implemented by employers or because employee representatives may become increasingly aligned with management perspectives over time. This can be assessed by comparing the formal institutional provisions with employees' perceptions of the influence that their representatives have over work decisions. The ESS asked 'At your workplace are there regular meetings between representatives of the employer and employees, in which working conditions and practices can be discussed?' If there were such meetings, this was followed up by a question about how much influence such discussions generally had on working conditions and practices, with answers ranging from 'not much or no influence' to 'a great deal of influence'. A scale of representative influence has been constructed combining the two questions, with 0 indicating no representation, 1 the existence of meetings that had not much or no influence, 2 meetings with some influence, and 3 meetings with quite a lot or a great deal of influence.[2]

The picture that emerges from employees' reports has both important similarities and striking differences from that provided by formal institutional structure (see the last two rows of Table 5.7). The Nordic countries have particularly strong and the Southern countries particularly weak representation whichever measure is taken. But the influence of representatives appears to be rather stronger in the Liberal countries than is indicated by the formal institutional provisions. In contrast, the Continental countries and in particular

---

[2] As the proportions reporting 'a great deal' of influence for representatives were very small (under 3 per cent), this category has been combined with that of 'quite a lot of influence'.

France, which were very similar to the Nordic countries in terms of formal provision, have notably weaker representation on the basis of employees' reports. Further, the Transition countries are more similar to the Continental countries than would be anticipated from the formal provisions.

Looking in more detail at the pattern by country (Figure 5.4), it can be seen that there was some variation within the regime types. Representational influence was considerably lower in Ireland than in the UK. While all of the Nordic countries were relatively high, this was particularly the case for Norway and Sweden. Further, while all of the Southern countries had relatively low levels of representative influence, this was particularly marked in Portugal. The most homogeneous of the country groups was that of the Continental countries. The most heterogeneous was that of the Transition countries. Both in Hungary (where experiments with employee representation had begun in the socialist period) and in Estonia, representative influence was substantially greater than in the other transition countries, which were more similar to the pattern of the Continental country group.

Comparing country scores with respect to works council rights and employees' reports on representatives' workplace influence, there was overall a moderately strong positive association (correlation 0.48, p = 0.06). In general, countries with stronger works councils had higher levels of effective representation. Greece and Portugal ranked very low on both measures and the Nordic countries and Hungary ranked highly on both. But there were also cases where the two measures diverged. Great Britain and Estonia were

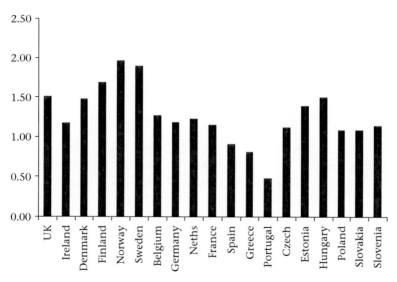

Figure 5.4. Influence of employee representatives by country (employee reports)

examples of countries where formal works council provision was very weak, but where representatives were thought to have considerable influence. In contrast, Germany and the Netherlands scored highest of all with respect to the formal rights of works councils but had only an intermediate score with respect to the actual influence of representatives.

At country level, the job control of employees was indeed clearly related to the wider control they could exercise in the workplace. The prevalence of formal works councils was positively associated with job control (correlation 0.43, p = 0.06). The association between the average country level of work-place representative influence and job control was even more evident, with a correlation of 0.66 (p = 0.002). Those countries with high levels of representative influence also tended to have higher levels of job control (Figure 5.5). The Nordic countries stand out as relatively high with respect to both, while Greece and Portugal are at the opposite extreme with both low representation and low job control.

Further, at individual level, employees who reported strong representative channels of influence were also much more likely to consider that they had personal control over their work decisions. Indeed, it can be seen that within each regime type employees who reported that there was strong representation in their workplace were more likely to have individual scope for taking decisions on their job (Table 5.8). This was the case even when controls were introduced to take account of differences between employees in age, sex, occupational class, industry, and the size of workplaces.

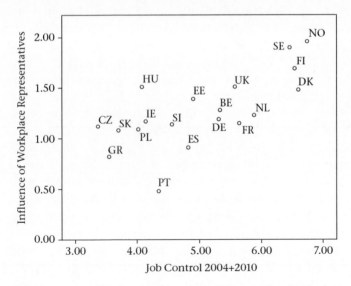

Figure 5.5. Influence of representatives in the workplace and individual job control
Note: Correlation 0.70, p = <0.001.

Table 5.8. Employee representation and job control (with controls)

	Liberal		Nordic		Continent		France		South		Transition	
Influence of representatives	.51	***	.31	***	.23	***	.24	***	.28	***	.39	***

Note: Controls include sex, age, industry, class, and size of establishment. Sig *** = p<0.001.

BARGAINING COORDINATION, TRADE UNION STRENGTH, AND WORKPLACE REPRESENTATIONAL INFLUENCE

If effective representation in the workplace was an important factor affecting the way jobs were designed, what in turn helped to account for the strength of representation? Production regime theory points primarily to a culture of employer coordination, while employment regime theory draws on a power resources model in which a central place is given to the strength of trade unions (Soskice 1999; Estevez et al. 2001; Hall and Soskice 2001; Gallie 2007b).

A measure of bargaining coordination, averaged over the period 2000–9, can be derived from the ICTWSS dataset. Table 5.9 shows that, consistently with the expectations of production regime theory, bargaining coordination was strongest in the Nordic and, to an even greater extent, the Continental countries. It was somewhat lower in the Southern countries and in France and lowest of all in the Liberal and the Transition countries. However, a country-level correlation of the degree of bargaining coordination with the influence of workplace representation showed no significant association, with a coefficient close to zero. As can be seen in Figure 5.6, this reflected the fact that some of the countries with the lowest levels of bargaining coordination, such as the UK and Estonia, had relatively influential workplace representation. In contrast, others which had very high levels of coordination—such as the Continental countries, Slovenia and Greece—had only intermediate or low levels of representational influence.

In contrast, it is notable that national union strength, as measured by trade union density, and the influence of workplace representatives were closely associated. Union density was (by far) the highest in the Nordic countries, it was intermediate in the Liberal and Continental countries, and relatively low in France and in the Southern and the Transition countries (Table 5.9). At country level the correlation between overall trade union density and employees' reports of the influence in the workplace of their representatives is 0.64 (p = 0.01).

As can be seen in Figure 5.7, at the extremes, the Nordic countries combined strong trade union density with strong workplace representation, whereas Portugal, Greece, and Spain combined weak trade unionism with low levels of workplace representation. There are grounds then for thinking

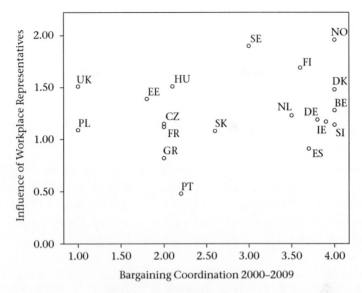

Figure 5.6. Bargaining coordination and influence of workplace representation

Note: Influence of workplace representation, ESS 2010; Bargaining coordination Visser ICTWSS V4. Correlation 0.23, p = 0.35.

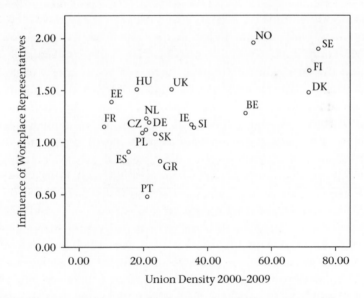

Figure 5.7. Trade union density and influence of workplace representatives

Note: Influence of workplace representation, ESS 2010; Union density Visser ICTWSS V4. Correlation 0.64, p = <0.01.

Table 5.9. Bargaining coordination and strength of trade unionism (mean scores) 2000–2009

	Nordic	Liberal	Continental	France	Southern	Transition
Bargaining Coordination Score	3.65	2.45	3.77	2.00	2.63	2.25
Union Density	68.1	33.8	31.5	7.8	20.5	21.3

Note: Data are from the ICTWSS dataset V4.

that union strength generally provides the framework for representational influence. However, three countries stand out somewhat from the generally close relationship between union strength and workplace influence—UK, Estonia, and Hungary—all of which have rather higher levels of representation than might be expected given their union strength.

Work Intensity, Job Control, and Work Stress

The final issue we address is whether economic crisis led to a change in the intensity of work and, if so, how far its implications for work stress were mediated by developments with respect to control. There is again a striking lack of theoretical literature on the relationship between the economic cycle and work intensity. There was a well-documented rise in work pressure following the major economic crisis in the 1990s (Capelli et al. 1997; Green 2001; Gallie 2005). But the factors underlying this increase are still poorly understood. There are again plausible arguments for quite different expectations about the effects of economic crisis per se. The need for cost reductions may lead employers to increase the pace of work reorganization, rationalizing work processes and increasing the intensity of work. But it is also possible that lower production demands reduce work pressure on employees. It could be that it is only when economies return to growth that work pressure increases, as employers try to increase output without additional recruitment.

It can also be questioned whether work intensity per se should be considered necessarily negative for the quality of work. Arguments emphasizing the negative effects of work intensity for employee well-being focus on 'constrained' work intensity, where employees have little choice about the effort they put into their work. But although work intensity may very often be the result of organizational policies, reflected in either supervisory pressures or machine pacing, it may also be the result of the individual's choice. Further, some would argue that some degree of work intensity is an inherent part of any serious creative effort, providing the challenge that enables people to develop their skills.

This has led to an attempt to distinguish between different types of work intensity. A particularly influential thesis has centred upon the way the impact of work intensity is related to the degree of control employees exercise at work. Karasek and Theorell's research, which developed the 'demand-control model', led to a wide range of Scandinavian and British research indicating that it was particularly the combination of high demands and low control that had severe implications for work stress and hence for employees' psychological and physical health.

We begin by looking at the trends with respect to a general measure of work intensity and then turn to a typology that takes into account levels of job control.

Rising work intensity?

The ESS contains two well-established measures of work intensity. They ask people how much they agree or disagree with the statements: 'My job requires that I work very hard' and 'I never seem to have enough time to get everything done in my job'. Responses to each are on a five-point scale running from 'agree strongly' to 'disagree strongly'. The average of the two items is taken to provide a summary measure of work intensity.

It is clear from Table 5.10 that there was a very general tendency for work intensity to have increased over the period. Indeed it rose in all of the country groups, with particularly marked increases in the Southern countries, France, and the Continental countries. This is similar to the picture for the early 1990s (in the aftermath of the previous European recession) when work intensity increased, but contrasts with the pattern in the late 1990s when research generally found that work intensity remained stable (Green 2001; Gallie 2005).

Was the rise in work intensity relatively general across the workforce or did it reflect a process of class polarization whereby the increase in work pressure was concentrated at one end of the class hierarchy, while remaining either stable or declining at the other? As can be seen in Figure 5.8, the rise in work

Table 5.10. Changes in work intensity 2004–2010

	2004	2010	Year Change	Sig Yr Change
Liberal	3.56	3.62	0.06	*
Nordic	3.35	3.39	0.04	*
Continental	3.26	3.35	0.09	***
France	3.24	3.35	0.11	*
Southern	3.31	3.50	0.19	***
Transition	3.28	3.33	0.05	***

Note: Sig *** = p<0.001; *p<0.05.

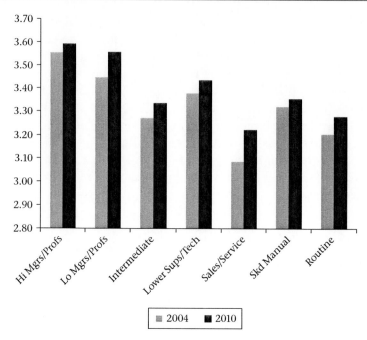

Figure 5.8. Work intensity and occupational class 2004–2010

Note: OLS regression showed that, with controls for age, sex, industry, and establishment size, relative to higher managers and professionals, work intensity rose significantly more among lower professionals and managers (coeff 0.05, $p = <0.05$) and among sales and service workers (coeff 0.10, $p = <0.01$).

pressure affected all occupational classes, but it was particularly evident in two: lower professionals and managers on the one hand and lower sales and services employees on the other. There is little evidence here of class polarization in work intensity.

Finally, was there any evidence of an effect of experience of the crisis on work intensity? Did pressure increase primarily in organizations that did relatively well in the crisis by expanding their markets or in firms that experienced financial difficulty or staffing reductions? We take two measures of organizational exposure to the economic crisis: the extent to which organizations had experienced financial difficulty in the previous five years and whether or not the number of people at the organization had increased or decreased over the same period.

Taking first the effect of financial difficulty, as can be seen in Figure 5.9, there was a clear linear impact of the extent of financial difficulty on work intensity, with work pressures rising the greater the level of difficulty. It is notable that the effect remains quite clear and at a high level of statistical significance even when account is taken of compositional differences in the

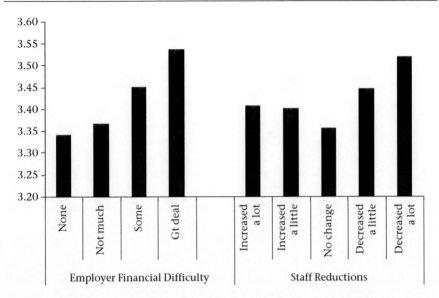

Figure 5.9. Work intensity, firm vulnerability, and individual change in job security

Note: Entered together in an OLS regression with controls for age, sex, class, industry, and establishment size, the coefficient for employer financial difficulty was 0.08, for staff reductions 0.05, and for a less secure job 0.07. All were significant at p<0.001.

workforce relating to sex, age, occupational class, industry, and size of establishment. The pattern is broadly similar with respect to the effect of staffing reductions. Increases in workforce numbers (and especially no change) were associated with relatively low levels of work pressure, but the organizations that experienced the highest levels of pressure were those which had experienced major decreases in staffing. Moreover, once account was taken of differences in workforce characteristics, there was still a significant effect of workforce reductions in raising levels of work pressure. Finally, it is notable that, even taking account of the general crisis pressures on the firm, there was a highly significant effect of whether the individual's own job had become less secure over the previous three years.

Work stress

Earlier research has shown that work intensity, as defined by these indicators, does appear to have important implications for people's lives; it is, for instance, strongly related to risks of work–family conflict (Gallie and Russell 2009; McGinnity and Russell, this volume). But Karasek and Theorell (1990) argue that, with respect to psychological and physical health, job control mediates between work demands (or work pressure) and subjective distress. When work demands are high, people with control over their work situation

135

will experience less severe psychological and physical health consequences than those who have low levels of control over their work.

They classify jobs into four broad types. Jobs that combine high demand and high control are 'active' jobs which allow for self-development. Jobs that are low on both control and demand are passive jobs that may have negative consequences because of the low levels of stimulation they provide. But by far the most problematic pattern, they argue, is the combination of high demand and low control. This is associated with higher psychological distress, heightened blood pressure, and increased risk of cardiovascular disease. Later work has confirmed that such work conditions lead to a 50 per cent increase in the risk of heart disease (Chandola 2010). Such jobs also come closest to the notion of 'constrained work intensity' that underlies most arguments about the implications of work intensity for the quality of work.

We estimated the proportion of employees in the different job strain types by creating four categories based on those above or below the median scores on the job control and work intensity scales respectively. For instance, those above the median score on both control and intensity are classified as being in active jobs; those below the median score for job control but above the median for work intensity are classified as being in high strain jobs.

The relationship between the different job types and psychological well-being can be shown by comparing the life satisfaction levels of employees in the different job categories. As can be seen in Figure 5.10, employees had highest life satisfaction when they were in jobs that offered relatively high

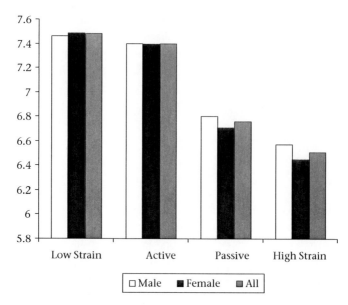

Figure 5.10. Job strain types and life satisfaction

levels of control but low work intensity (low strain jobs). However, life satis-faction was nearly as high among those who experienced high work intensity but could exercise control at work (active jobs). Those who were in 'passive' jobs (low control and low work intensity) had considerably lower levels of well-being, while those in high job strain jobs (high work intensity, but low control) had the lowest life satisfaction of all. The picture is very similar for men and women. The differences in life satisfaction of employees in the dif-ferent job types were at a high level of statistical significance. Overall, the pattern is consistent with the expectations of demand-control theory about the negative effects of passive and particularly high strain jobs on psychologi-cal well-being.

What was the prevalence of the different job types in the various country groups? Taking the picture in 2004, it is clear that the country groups had very different profiles in terms of the distributions of the four job types (Figure 5.11). There were particularly high proportions of high strain jobs in the Liberal and in the Southern countries, of active jobs in the Nordic countries, and of passive jobs in the Southern and the Transition countries. Taking the two categories that were associated with the highest life satisfaction scores, the quality of jobs was by far the highest in the Nordic countries, followed at some remove by France and the Continental countries. It was lowest in the Liberal countries and especially in the Southern and Transition countries.

It is notable that, while it was seen earlier that work intensity increased very generally across the European countries between 2004 and 2010, the

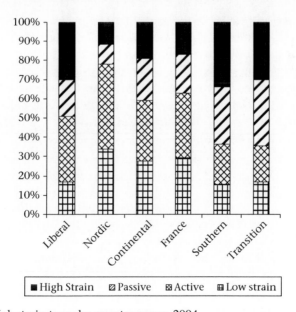

Figure 5.11. Job strain types by country group, 2004

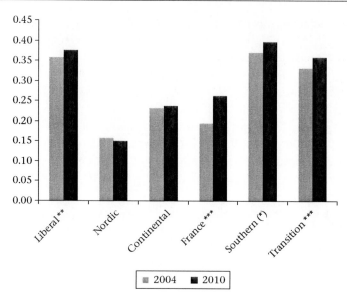

Figure 5.12. Change in proportion of high strain jobs 2004–2010
Note: Sig *** = p<0.001; ** p<0.01; (*) P<0.10.

proportion of high strain jobs—those that have been found to be most damaging to employees' psychological and physical health—increased only in
some of the country groups (Figure 5.12). There was a significant increase in
high strain jobs between 2004 and 2010 in the Liberal countries, France, and
the Transition countries (and in the Southern countries at a 10 per cent level
of significance). In contrast, there was no increase in high strain jobs in either
the Nordic or the Continental countries. In terms of the prevalence of jobs
potentially damaging for psychological and physical health, there was then
a growing divergence between the Nordic countries where the proportion
had been kept at a relatively low level over the period, and most of the other
country groups where there was an increase in what was already a higher
proportion of such jobs.

Polarization in job types?

Could it be that the relative stability in most countries in the prevalence of
high strain jobs concealed greater polarization in the distribution of such jobs
within countries?

The expectation was that class polarization would be most evident in
the Liberal group. This is precisely the pattern that is found (Table 5.11).
Compared to higher managers and professionals, there was a relative rise in
the prevalence of high strain jobs among routine semi-skilled and non-skilled

Table 5.11. Year changes in high strain jobs by class, sex, and contract status

	Liberal	Nordic	Continent	France	Southern	Transition
Class						
Hi Mgr-Prof	ref	ref	ref	ref	ref	ref
Lo Mgr-Prof	−.24	.20	−.10	−.54	.38	.13
Intermediate	.54(*)	−.69*	.50	−.80	.25	.25
Low Sup-Tech	−.35	.48	.18	.00	−.18	−.51*
Skd Manual	.35	−.09	.13	−.38	−.04	−.06
Sales/services	.31	.26	.28	.19	.19	.13
Routine	.88***	.00	.00	−1.13*	.07	.45+
Sex & Contract						
Female	.14	−.12	.00	−.18	.15	.05
Part-time work	−.11	−.40	.52**	−.29	.43(*)	−.18
Temporary work	−.61**	.04	.42(*)	.18	−.28(*)	−.31**

Note: Separate models for (a) class and (b) sex and contract status year interactions. Controls include sex, age, class, industry, and size of establishment. Sig *** = $p<0.001$; ** $p<0.01$; *$p<0.05$; (*) $P<0.10$.

workers. The only other country group where there was evidence of polarization was that of the Transition countries. In France, which had experienced the greatest increase in the prevalence of high strain jobs, the least skilled were more protected than all other employee categories. The rise in job strain in France was very general across the rest of the workforce.

The other lines of possible polarization were those of sex and contract status. These were expected to be strongest in the dualist Continental countries. There was no evidence that women were disproportionately affected by increases in job strain in these countries, but the Continental country group did see a rise in the relative prevalence of high strain jobs among both temporary and part-time employees.

Conclusion

Job control has been consistently shown to be a critical dimension of the quality of work, with vital implications for both employee motivation and well-being. Yet there has been little agreement about the long-term direction of change in the level of job control. Further, explanations of employer decisions about work design, which create the parameters for employees to exercise control in their work, have been very controversial. While some have seen employer decisions as primarily driven by economic conditions relating to the use of technologies or the pressures of competitiveness, others have emphasized the extent to which employer strategies are affected by cultural or political factors, with longer-term historical origins. Severe economic crisis provides an interesting test of these different views, since it places employers under exceptional levels of economic pressure in very diverse institutional settings.

The dominant picture that emerged from the comparison of the pre-crisis picture of 2004 with that of 2010 is of the basic stability of patterns both by country and by country region despite the very severe economic shock. The major differences between country groups in 2004, with the Nordic countries having exceptionally high levels of job control, the Liberal and Continental countries intermediate levels, and the Southern and Transition countries very low levels, still remained clearly evident in 2010. This testifies to the stability of institutional factors in the face of short-term change, reflecting their embeddedness in complex and interdependent formal rule systems. But, within this general pattern of stability, there was nonetheless also evidence of some degree of change. Most notably, there was a rise in the level of job control in the Southern and Transition countries, and a decline of job control in France. Similarly, while there were no general tendencies for economic crisis to lead to greater polarization within the workforce, it did increase class polarization in the Liberal countries and polarization by contract status in the Continental countries.

There are diverse ways in which economic crisis might lead to changes in the level of job control. It might lead to changes in the structure of the workforce, by eliminating disproportionately the worst jobs, which tended to give employees particularly low levels of control. But it might also lead to changes in employers' workforce strategies with respect to those that remained in employment, as they sought to enhance innovation and commitment to survive the crisis. Both arguments would lead to an expectation that change would be particularly marked in the Southern and Transition countries, since these were the most severely affected by the crisis over the longer term. There was some evidence for the Transition countries that job upgrading could have been affected by the selective nature of workforce cuts. Moreover, this may have been reinforced by the introduction of higher levels of workforce involvement among employees in firms in financial difficulty.

None of the economic explanations can provide a convincing explanation of the reduction of job control in France. France was not one of the countries most severely affected by the economic crisis and changes in the composition of its workforce also fell particularly heavily on the less skilled (which could have been expected to have raised the average level of job control). The nature of the evidence available did not allow further empirical investigation of this. But, speculatively, we would suggest that the introduction by the socialist government of the forty-hour week, which was fiercely opposed by employers, may have led to a reversion by employers to policies that emphasized the prerogatives of management over work organization and to the imposition of tighter control structures to try to recoup the economic costs of working hour reform through tighter monitoring of employee performance.

We also examined some of the institutional factors that might have accounted for the stability of relative differences between country groups. Institutional explanations generally assume that micro-level patterns are anchored by institutional structures at a higher level. Job control, as a phenomenon of power at micro-level, should therefore be affected by the structures of power affecting employees at workplace and national levels. This did indeed appear to be the case. There was a strong relationship between employees' sense of their personal scope for decision-making at work and the influence that was exercised over work conditions and practices. This was a finding that was compatible with both of the major institutional explanations we examined—production regime theory on the one hand and employment regime theory on the other. Where these different perspectives differed was in the emphasis they laid on higher level determinants of workplace representation. Production regime theory pointed to the importance of the strength of bargaining coordination between employers, employment regime theory to the power resources of organized labour. In the event, we found that workplace representation was unrelated to bargaining coordination, but was strongly associated with national-level union strength. The most plausible picture then is that employees' direct control over their jobs is to a significant degree dependent on the level of institutional protection provided by representative institutions at workplace level and trade union influence at national level.

Finally, we examined the implications of the trends in job control for employee well-being, in terms of their exposure to the types of jobs that have been found to be most detrimental to psychological and physical health. The period between 2004 and 2010 saw a very general rise in work intensity in all of the country groups. This was particularly the case in the Continental countries, in France, and in the Southern countries. Yet an influential strand of research has indicated that work intensity may not necessarily be damaging in itself, but does have negative effects for personal well-being when combined with low levels of control over the work process. Our evidence certainly confirmed that such 'high strain' jobs were associated with lower levels of psychological well-being. The implications of the growth of work intensity for the prevalence of high strain jobs differed considerably between country groups. There was no evidence that higher work intensity translated into a greater prevalence of high strain jobs in either the Nordic or the Continental countries. They increased most sharply in France, but also to some degree in the Liberal, Southern, and Transition countries. The fact that the increase was particularly high in France was linked to the specificity of that country in terms of the decline in job control over these years. It is consistent with the fact that this was the country that experienced the most pronounced crisis over the years with respect to work stress, with an exceptional wave of work-related suicides.

6

Insecurity and the Peripheral Workforce

Vanessa Gash and Hande Inanc

Introduction

Policies of labour market flexibilization, brought in by many European countries from the 1980s, have resulted in an increasing share of workers employed in non-standard employment contracts, particularly part-time and temporary work. Even during periods of economic growth, this led to a concern that such flexibilized employment relations were producing a polarized workforce, divided into a protected core and a disadvantaged periphery. The core workforce was described as highly skilled with higher pay, high job security, and favourable working conditions, while the peripheral workforce was described as holding non-standard employment contracts, with poor work conditions and considerable job insecurity.

Previous research has confirmed the poor quality of many atypical contracts (Kalleberg et al.; Polavieja 2001). Temporary employees are subject to lower pay, high risk of job loss, subsequent spells of precarious employment, and poorer opportunities for job-related training (for a review of findings see Inanc 2010). There have been contrasting views about the implications of temporary work for long-term career trajectories: whether it is a stepping-stone to better jobs or a source of entrapment. Some have argued that temporary jobs serve as entry ports to the labour market, which then enable the employee to get a stable job in the primary market. In contrast, others underline the negative effects of temporary work on future career outcomes, in particular due to the limited opportunities it provides for training and acquiring human capital.

Similarly, part-time work is also associated with poorer employment quality, as well as career outcomes. According to the OECD, part-time employees face a penalty compared with full-time workers in terms of pay, job security, training, and promotion. Part-time workers are also more likely to be poor and are less likely to have access to unemployment benefits or re-employment assistance if they become unemployed (OECD 2010). The bulk of part-time work is done by women, even though male shares have increased since the early 1980s. The difficulties faced by women in part-time work have been convincingly outlined in recent research (Gregory and Connolly 2008). Relative to women who work full-time, those employed part-time give up more than income in return for reduced hours. Part-time workers' hourly pay is less than both men's pay and women full-time workers' pay (e.g. Bardasi and Gornick 2008; Manning and Petrongolo 2008). Part-time employment tends to be concentrated in low-skilled occupations; this means women who switch to part-time jobs from full-time employment can often only do so if they accept a job of inferior occupational worth. This problem is aggravated by the fact that women in part-time jobs tend to get less training, with employers often reluctant to invest in a workforce regarded as peripheral (OECD 1999).

The current economic crisis accentuates concerns of a deepening labour market dualism between those on a standard employment contract (in full-time and permanent jobs) and those on atypical (reduced hours or temporary) contracts. Two essential questions emerge: Has the economic crisis resulted in an increase in the peripheral workforce? And have the inequalities between core and peripheral workers grown?

This chapter investigates these questions empirically to reveal the impact of the global economic crisis on the atypical workforce across Europe, inquiring whether or not those on non-standard contracts have disproportionately borne the cost of the crisis. It does so by first examining the changes in the workforce structure using the European Union Labour Force Survey (EULFS), which provides time series data on the changing shares of standard and atypical work, as well as on the extent to which this work is voluntary or involuntary. Second, the chapter aims to reveal whether peripheral workers have been disproportionately exposed to degradation in their working conditions in the form of increased employment insecurity. We conceptualize employment insecurity as a broad, multifaceted phenomenon. We examine (1) fear of job loss, (2) entrapment, that is working in positions that have no opportunities for advancement, as well as (3) changes in the financial security of workers. In this section we use the European Social Survey (ESS) which in 2010 asked a series of questions on job insecurity that replicate questions asked in its second round of data collection in 2004, allowing analyses of *changes* in job insecurity over the period. Third, we analyse variation by regime, since different countries had varying levels of exposure to the recession and diverged in policy response to macro-economic pressures. Therefore the insecurities experienced by workers, and in particular by peripheral workers, are expected to differ in severity between different types of regime.

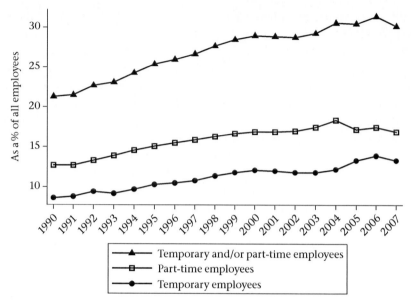

Figure 6.1. Growth of atypical work in Europe 1990–2007
Source: Eurostat Employment and Unemployment Database, covering 20–64 age group.

Growth of Atypical Work in Europe Prior to the Economic Crisis

The majority of EU countries have sought to deregulate components of their employment law allowing employers to hire workers on atypical contracts more easily. The share of atypical work in the EU has grown substantially. Between 1990 and the start of the economic recession of 2008, the share of temporary workers among all employees increased by five percentage points, constituting one-seventh of the workforce in 2007. Similarly, the proportion of part-time employees grew from 12.7 per cent to 17 per cent within the same period. By 2007 one-third of employees were working in at least one sort of atypical job (Figure 6.1).

There are, however, differences between European countries with respect to how labour market flexibilization took place. Southern countries such as Spain and Italy, as well as France, followed a 'partial and targeted deregulation' (Esping-Andersen and Regini 2000) which was age-targeted and deregulated the working conditions for new entrants and/or young individuals. Germany and other Continental European countries followed a 'partial reform strategy' (OECD 2006) which focused on the skill divide in the workforce (skilled-protected vs. unskilled-deregulated workers).[1] The

---

[1] For a detailed record of emergence and trends of non-standard employment in various EU countries see Barbieri (2007).

result of both of these strategies has been the creation of a dualistic and segmented workforce. Employees in the primary segment enjoy job protection and social benefits attached to their permanent contracts, whilst employees in the secondary segment hold temporary contracts which offer lower wages, lower training and skill-investment opportunity, as well as less social protection. In these countries, labour market flexibilization came at the cost of increasing social inequality between standard and non-standard workers as well as the risk of social and economic marginalization of the secondary segment.

Among the Nordic countries Denmark followed a 'flexicurity' strategy which allowed it to combine high degrees of flexibility in the labour market with high levels of social protection. Temporary work in the Danish system often takes the form of a job rotation system, with unemployed workers replacing employees who are on leave for training, further education, or to take care of children (Barbieri 2007). This scheme provides flexibility for employers, and provides unemployed workers with training opportunities, which, in turn, increases their employability. Denmark has become as productive as the liberal Anglo-Saxon countries, yet has been seen to minimize the social costs and negative externalities of flexibilization.

Finally in liberal regimes, such as the United Kingdom, while labour market flexibilization further deregulated an already weak system of employment protection, the share of temporary contracts increased only marginally and remained flat at around 4.6 per cent of all employment between 1984 and 1990 (Robinson 2000: 32). In the mid-1990s, the share of temporary work grew to a level of 6–7 per cent, affecting all industries.

Due to these different paths of deregulation and flexibilization there are significant dissimilarities across European countries regarding the size of the atypical workforce and the implications of atypical employment for job quality. Figures 6.2 and 6.3 show the proportion of temporary and part-time employees, respectively, in European countries between 2004 and 2010. The figures also reveal the share of those who are employed in atypical work *involuntarily*. There are remarkable differences among and within country groups in terms of the proportion of temporary employees. While in Liberal and most of the Transition countries the share of temporary workers is very small, the workforce in Spain, Portugal, and Poland has comparatively large shares of temporary workers making up over 20 per cent of the workforce. Almost universally, temporary contracts constitute a larger share of female employees than they do of male employees. In most of the Southern and Transitional countries, as well as in Belgium and Finland, a large proportion of temporary workers have these jobs involuntarily. Involuntary temporary workers are those who accepted a temporary job because they could not find a permanent job rather than through choice. Especially in Germany and Belgium, but also

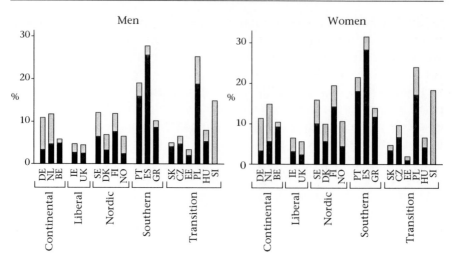

Figure 6.2. Temporary and involuntary temporary work among employees 2004–2010

Source: Authors' calculations from pooled EULFS, weighted frequencies for 20–64 age group.

Notes: 1. Temporary work is self-defined, referring to having a fixed-term contract or a job which will terminate after the completion of an objective. 2. Dark grey bars represent the proportion of involuntary temporary employees as of all employees. 3. Information on involuntary temporary work for Slovenia is not available.

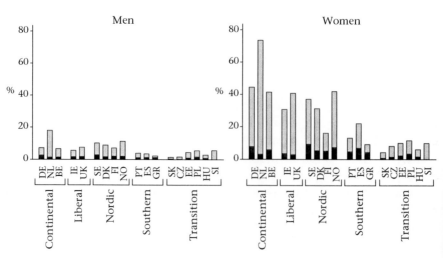

Figure 6.3. Part-time and involuntary part-time work among employees 2004–2010

Source: Authors' calculations from pooled EULFS, weighted frequencies for 20–64 age group.

Notes: 1. Part-time work is self-defined, with the exceptions of the Netherlands, Iceland, and Norway where part-time is determined based on actual working hours with the criterion of working fewer than 35 hours per week. 2. Dark grey bars represent the proportion of involuntary temporary employees as of all employees. 3. Information on involuntary temporary work for Slovenia is not available.

in Liberal countries and Norway and Denmark, temporary jobs do not take a predominantly involuntary form, reflecting the integrative nature of temporary work in these countries.

There are also differences between countries in terms of incidence of part-time work, with Southern and Transitional regimes situated at the lower end of the distribution and the Continental regime at the upper end. The most notable feature of part-time work, however, is its gendered nature. In all countries combined, the share of part-timers among the female workforce is considerably higher than it is among the male workforce, with an average of 34 per cent of female and 7 per cent of male employees (Figure 6.3). Additionally, there are fewer part-time workers than temporary workers who self-describe as involuntary, suggesting that many part-time workers are content with the reduced hours they work. Involuntary part-time work is defined as working part-time because one cannot find a full-time job, as opposed to working part-time due to reasons such as education, disability, and caring for dependants. Around a third of male part-timers in Germany, Spain, Ireland, Poland, and Portugal work in their jobs involuntarily, whereas 60 per cent of male Greek part-timers state that they could not find a full-time job. Among women, only in the Southern countries and Finland are over a third of them involuntary part-time employees.

Atypical Work and Economic Crisis

Issues

A central question is whether the economic crisis led to an increase in structural insecurity in the workforce, by increasing the relative size of the atypical sector. Temporary employment has long been recognized as a means for employers to manage cyclical and seasonal fluctuations in demand whilst simultaneously liberalizing wage and labour costs. The generation of temporary employment has been presented as a means, for employers, of transferring the risks associated with volatile markets to employees. But there could be different expectations about the implications of this for the effects of the crisis for workforce structure. One possibility is that there would be an increase in inflow into temporary jobs. Employers may be more inclined to offer temporary contracts to new hires whereas labour market entrants, who lost bargaining power against employers due to uncertainty and high unemployment, are more likely to accept temporary contracts to avoid unemployment. Temporary employment is also a means of decreasing the costs of labour: temporary workers are 'cheaper' than standard contract workers as they tend not to be entitled to redundancy payments and they are likely to be more malleable than standard contract workers since they are less protected by trade unions. But, in contrast to such arguments, there is also a possibility that economic crisis reduced the size of the atypical workforce. Countervailing greater incentives for recruitment, temporary workers also may have borne disproportionately the burden of workforce reductions. The costs of firing temporary workers are clearly lower than they are for permanent workers. Thus, after the economic crisis a large outflow from the temporary workforce might be expected.

A second question is whether the economic crisis led employers to reduce employees' working hours involuntarily, encouraged by public and private initiatives to sustain labour demand. It has been suggested that this played an important role in preserving jobs in the crisis (OECD 2010). When employers and employees encounter a trade-off between reducing the numbers employed and reducing working hours, an increase in the proportion of part-timers could be expected.

Finally it is possible that the labour market outcomes of atypical workers as a result of the economic crisis varied by institutional context. There are several pivotal institutions that structure atypical workers' outcomes. The first of these is the extent to which employment protection legislation is applied equally to both standard contract and atypical workers. Countries which have engaged in so-called partial deregulation, that is allowing for the generation of atypical contracts whilst leaving legislation for standard contract workers untouched, are expected to have the highest rates of atypical employment and the greatest disparity in the quality of employment between standard contract workers and atypical contract workers. According to the OECD's 2008 Employment Protection Indicators, countries with higher rates of employment protection of standard contract workers and lower rates of regulation of atypical contract workers include Slovakia, the Czech Republic, Sweden, and the Netherlands (Figure 6.4). We expect segmentation between typical and atypical employees to grow greater in these countries after the economic crisis. In contrast, in countries where a low level of protection of permanent workers is combined with lower levels of regulation of temporary employment, such as in the UK and in Ireland, we predict little change in the level of polarization between the core and periphery, since hiring and firing of permanent and temporary employees are equally easy.

Other expectations can be drawn from the literature on 'production regimes' (Soskice 1999; Hall and Soskice 2001) and 'employment regimes' (Gallie 2011). The production regimes literature distinguishes between liberal market economies and coordinated economies. Liberal economies (typified by the UK) have employers with preferences for low levels of employment protection (Wood 2001). In these economies we expect there to be lower

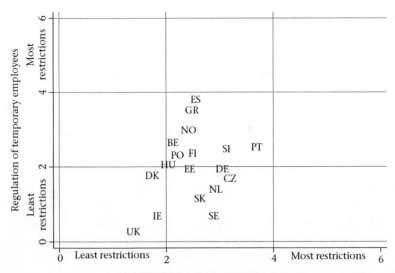

Figure 6.4. Level of employment protection in OECD and selected non-OECD countries 2008

Source: OECD www.oecd.org/employment/protection. Note: For France and Portugal, data refer to 2009. Scale from 0 (least restrictions) to 6 (most restrictions).

levels of segmentation between atypical and standard employees and little tendency to polarization. Coordinated economies (typified by Germany) tend to have more extensive employment protection, as a means of securing the commitment of employees who have invested in extensive skills training. We therefore expect the economic crisis to lead to greater polarization between the protected core and unprotected peripheral workforce in coordinated market economies. The employment regime literature distinguishes between employment systems in terms of their degree of inclusiveness. It would lead to the expectation that tendencies to dualism would be relatively weak in countries with an 'inclusive regime' (the Nordic countries) and particularly strong in those with dualistic employment structures (the Continental and Southern countries).

Economic crisis and polarization in workforce structure?

The period between 2008 and 2010 was marked by a reduction in the size of the 'core workforce' in Europe.[2] On average, the proportion of full-time permanent employees dropped from 69 per cent to 67 per cent, with

---

[2] Authors' calculations from EULFS.

notable variation across individual countries. Estonia experienced the sharpest decline, with seven percentage points, in its core workforce, followed by Ireland, Denmark, Hungary, and the UK. Conversely, in some countries there has been a slight growth in core workforce size, namely in Spain, Sweden, and Norway.

The proportion of temporary employees and involuntary temporary employees in the springs of 2008 and 2010 are shown in Figure 6.5, providing a snapshot of the situation at the start and (for most countries) after the recession. The average share of temporary employees in the overall groups of selected European countries has barely changed, but there were remarkable differences in the trend across countries. In Liberal and Transition countries (except for Poland), the share of temporary employees increased between 1 and 3 per cent and also to a lesser extent in Germany, the Netherlands, Denmark, and Norway. In contrast, in Sweden, Finland, Portugal, and particularly in Spain, there has been a decline in the share of temporary employment. Among temporary employees in most countries the share of those who work in these jobs involuntarily, or out of constraint, changed proportionately, with a few exceptions. For example, in the Netherlands and Norway, even though temporary employees constituted a larger part of employment in 2010 than in 2008, the level of involuntariness decreased. Conversely, in

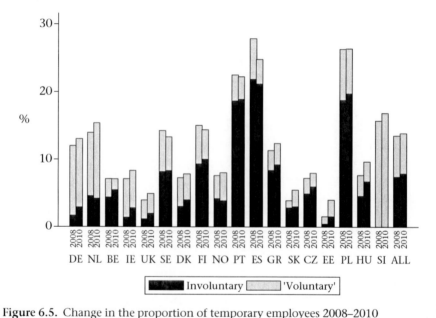

Figure 6.5. Change in the proportion of temporary employees 2008–2010

Source: Authors' calculations from pooled EULFS, weighted frequencies for 20–64 age group.

Notes: 1. Temporary work is self-defined, referring to having a fixed-term contract or a job which will terminate after the completion of an objective. 2. Information on involuntary temporary work for Slovenia is not available.

Finland and Portugal, despite the drop in temporary employment, the level of involuntariness increased.

On average, part-time work amongst employees also increased 2 per cent between 2008 and 2010, but there were fewer cross-national differences (Figure 6.6). Except for Germany, Sweden, Norway, and Portugal, where the part-time rate has either stayed constant or dropped 1 per cent, the share of part-time employees increased, with the Netherlands, Ireland, and especially Estonia exhibiting the largest increase. Involuntary part-time work also increased in most countries, parallel to the rise in part-time work.

Changes in the proportion of the atypical workforce at the country level might be a reflection of compositional changes within the workforce. For instance, the increase in part-timers could be a consequence of an inflow of women into the workforce. Therefore, it is important to investigate whether or not one's risk of working in atypical jobs has increased irrespective of demographic factors such as education level, occupational group, age, gender, partnership status, and migrant status. The results (see Table 6.1) indicate that workers in the Continental and the Transition regimes have experienced an increased risk of constraint in terms of contract type. In these regimes, except for Slovakia, the chances of working involuntarily as a temporary

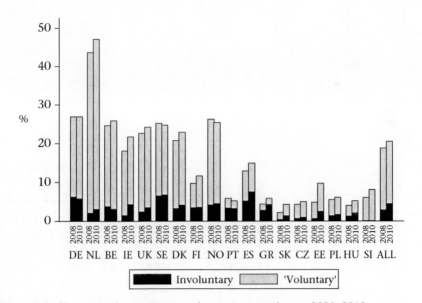

Figure 6.6. Change in the proportion of part-time employees 2008–2010

Source: Authors' calculations from pooled EULFS, weighted frequencies for 20–64 age group.

Notes: 1. Part-time work is self-defined, with the exceptions of the Netherlands, Iceland, and Norway where part-time is determined based on actual working hours with the criterion of working fewer than 35 hours per week. 2. Information on involuntary temporary work for Slovenia is not available.

Table 6.1. Recession and probability of involuntary atypical work (odds ratios)

	Reference year	Risk of involuntary temporary work vs. permanent work				Risk of involuntary part-time work vs. part time work			
		2008	2009	2010	N	2008	2009	2010	N
Continental									
Belgium	2008	–	1.11	1.31***	22883	–	0.84	0.93	21916
Germany	2008	–	2.42***	2.77***	9185	–	0.98	0.92	9144
Netherlands	2008	–	1.22**	1.02	24854	–	1.78***	1.84***	18440
Liberal									
Ireland	2007	1.80***	2.35***	3.67***	85233	0.78**	2.17***	2.76***	93069
UK	2007	0.69**	0.85	1.15	58718	N/A	1.53***	1.49***	48180
Nordic									
Denmark	2008	–	1.11	1.28**	29920	–	1.26*	1.38***	27659
Finland	2008	–	1.1	0.99	7000	–	0.98	1.24	7802
Norway	2008	–	0.99	0.98	7605	–	1	1.01	6661
Sweden	2007	0.98	0.96	0.99	115365	0.98	1.05	1.07	108709
Southern									
Spain	2007	1.03	0.94	1.03	28730	1.23*	1.48***	1.94***	34995
Greece	2008	–	0.99	1.10*	47915	–	1.26***	1.48***	77933
Portugal	2008	–	0.95	1.06	35779	–	0.9	1.01	44279
Transition									
Czech Rep.	2008	–	0.94	1.24***	53784	–	1.1	1.36*	63304
Estonia	2007	0.66	1.44	2.63**	6836	0.66	3.30***	2.26*	7114
Hungary	2007	1.02	1.1	1.51***	75629	1.06	1.49***	1.78***	86078
Poland	2008	–	1.03	1.11**	51277	–	1.12	1.17	68943
Slovakia	2008	–	0.99	1.01	24456	–	3.15***	5.56***	28614

Source: EULFS spring edition (weighted to control for bias in response rates and to ensure equal national proportions). Education level, occupational group, age, gender, partnership status, and migrant status are controlled for. Reasons for working part-time not available for UK in 2008. Sig = *** = <0.001.

employee increased significantly after the recession, although the risk only rose in Transition countries in 2010. The country where involuntary temporary work risk increased the most is Ireland: the odds of working with a temporary contract involuntarily in 2008 were 1.8 times as large as the odds in 2007, 2.4 times as large in 2009, and 3.7 times as large in 2010. Conversely, in the UK, the risk of involuntary temporary work declined. Among the Nordic countries there was no change in risk, except for an increase in Denmark.

The increase in the risk of involuntary part-time work is even more visible than for involuntary temporary work. With a few exceptions, in the Liberal, Southern, and the Transition regimes the probability of working part-time involuntarily increased remarkably. In the coordinated and Nordic countries (with the exception of an increase in the Netherlands and Denmark) the likelihood of involuntary part-time work remained stable over the period.

Upskilling or deskilling of the atypical workforce?

Two contradictory predictions can be made with respect to the changing skill structure of the atypical workforce after the economic crisis. It could be argued that an overall upskilling is likely to have taken place since employees from lower-skilled occupations are more vulnerable to lay-offs due to their low skill levels, leading to a change in the occupational distribution of atypical work. But there are also reasons why deskilling of the atypical workforce could be expected. As permanent and full-time jobs become scarce, the low-skilled will increasingly be concentrated in atypical jobs, resulting in deskilling of the atypical workforce.

Figures 6.7 and 6.8 display, within each occupational class, the share of temporary and part-time employees, respectively. There is a marginal increase in the proportion of temporary employees within 'Lower managerial/professional', 'Lower sales/services', 'Lower supervisory/technical', and 'Routine' occupations. This does not provide evidence for either an upskilling or deskilling of the temporary workforce. As for part-time employees, their share within each occupation increased slightly, except for the 'Lower technical' group, meaning that the skill structure of the part-time workforce also remained broadly the same after the recession.

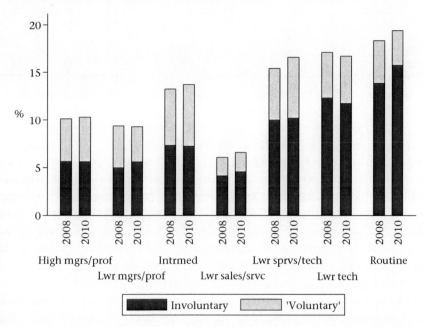

Figure 6.7. Share of temporary employees among occupational classes 2008–2010

Source: Authors' calculations from pooled EULFS for the 18 European countries, weighted frequencies for 20–64 age group. Note: Temporary work is self-defined, referring to having a fixed-term contract or a job which will terminate after the completion of an objective.

153

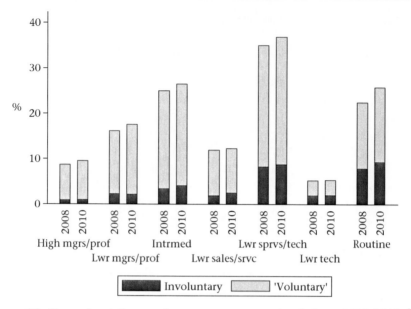

Figure 6.8. Share of part-time employees among occupational classes 2008–2010

Source: Authors' calculations from pooled EULFS, weighted frequencies for 20–64 age group. Note: Part-time work is self-defined, with the exceptions of the Netherlands, Iceland, and Norway where part-time is determined based on actual working hours with the criteria of working fewer than 35 hours per week.

Economic crisis and gender differences in atypical work

There might be different expectations about whether male or female atypical workers were most affected by the crisis. Since a larger share of females is in atypical work, one also might expect many more women finding themselves in non-standard jobs involuntarily. Counter to this, with standard jobs becoming scarcer, increasingly more men might have to accept temporary or part-time jobs out of constraint. Table 6.2 shows the results from a set of multivariate analyses where the period, gender, and the *interaction* of the two are included, as well as socio-demographic control variables. In Nordic, Southern, and Transition countries women are more likely than men to work involuntarily in temporary jobs (main effect). The interaction effect showing the change in the relative risks by sex over the period is only significant in the Transition countries, where women's risk of working involuntarily in temporary jobs was reduced relative to men's in 2009 and 2010.

As to part-time work, again, the probability of women working part-time involuntarily is greater than that of men (main effect). However, in the Nordic and Liberal countries, as well as in European countries considered together, men's risks of getting part-time jobs increased more than women's over the period of the crisis. The interaction effect indicates that, as a result of

Table 6.2. Involuntary atypical work: gender and period interactions (odds ratios)

	Involuntary temporary work vs. permanent work					
	Nordic	Continental	Liberal	Southern	Transition	ALL
2009 vs. 2008	1.01	1.73***	1.18	0.98	1.11**	1.11**
2010 vs. 2008	1.1	1.67***	1.71**	1.09	1.22***	1.20***
women	1.64***	0.91	0.71	1.16*	1.24***	1.27***
women*2009	1.04	0.81	1.07	0.88	0.88*	0.91
women*2010	0.91	0.99	0.96	0.87	0.90*	0.92
N	132864	56923	81517	105240	204708	581252

	Involuntary part-time work vs. full-time work					
	Nordic	Continental	Liberal	Southern	Transition	ALL
2009 vs. 2008	1.26*	1.2	12.66***	1.49*	1.48**	1.79***
2010 vs. 2008	1.23*	1.3	14.27***	1.78***	1.59***	2.01***
women	4.26***	6.86***	1.92***	5.49***	3.50***	4.81***
women*2009	0.79*	0.78	1.26	0.76	0.79	0.73**
women*2010	0.9	0.62*	0.95	0.81	0.84	0.67***
N	537046	112598	41914	69764	106053	206717

Source: EULFS data, spring edition (weighted to control for bias in response rates and to ensure equal national proportions). Education level, partnership status, age, and migrant status are controlled for. Sig = *** = <0.001.

economic crisis, men find it harder to find standard jobs, and take up atypical jobs in the absence of the availability of standard jobs.

Use of atypical work as a response to economic crisis

The economic crisis affected European countries to differing degrees. Moreover, in order to combat high unemployment, countries followed different strategies, partly due to the level of existing employment protection of the atypical workforce and partly due to the severity of the impact of the recession. Therefore, in this section we investigate further the relationship between unemployment and temporary work in each country setting, with the purpose of illuminating how atypical work has been used to buffer the potential unemployment shock.

The ideal analysis for this purpose would have been to compare the changes in job loss rates of standard and non-standard employees before and after the recession. This would have shown whether atypical workers moved into unemployment at a higher rate than did typical employees. However, neither of our datasets provides information on respondents' contract type the year before, which prevents us from constructing flow charts from standard and non-standard employment into unemployment. Thus, we use other available indicators to examine the extent to which temporary workers have been exposed to job losses in each country. We start with the distribution of reasons for job loss in each group of countries in the period between 2007 and

2010. EULFS asks non-employed respondents the reasons for leaving their last employment, with options such as dismissal, termination of job contract, illness, disability, family responsibilities, and retirement. We restrict the analysis to job losses that took place within the last twelve months. Table 6.3 shows that the percentage of job losses due to dismissals increased remarkably between the springs of 2007/8 and springs of 2008/9. On average only 20 per cent lost their jobs because of dismissals in 2008, whereas this figure jumped to 36 per cent in 2010. This pattern persists in each regime, with particularly remarkable increases in the Liberal, Nordic, and Transition countries.

The second part of the table presents the share of those who lost their jobs because their job contract ended. Note that these individuals are not employed at the time of the interview. Here, we potentially capture temporary employees whose contracts were not renewed, and since then remained jobless. On average, 25 per cent of job separations were caused by termination of job contract in 2008 and 2009, and this increased to 30 per cent in 2010. It is crucial to note that there is one-year gap between when dismissals and job terminations peak. Job separations due to dismissal increased suddenly in 2009 while separations due to ending of job contracts increased in 2010. The relative ease of dismissing temporary workers at the end of the contract may have made employers more willing to wait than in the case of permanent employees where the costs would not change. Also note that potentially some temporary workers were dismissed anyhow. Hence, the

Table 6.3. Job loss by reason 2008–2010

All job separations in the last 12 months because of...

	2007/8	2008/9	2009/10
	...dismissal or redundancy		
All countries	19.57	35.6	33.15
Continental	19.41	28.84	25.89
Liberal	21.96	59.14	55.1
Nordic	13.96	31.16	27.15
Southern	16.06	25.65	25.34
Transition	23.11	40.28	38.16
	...termination of a job of limited duration		
All countries	25.63	25.76	30.47
Continental	19.41	21.23	19.46
Liberal	14.51	10.69	12.48
Nordic	33.38	28.48	33.74
Southern	43.63	44.18	46.07
Transition	14.37	13.67	22.82

Source: Authors' calculations from EULFS spring edition, weighted frequencies.

increase in contract terminations is a conservative estimate of the increased flows from temporary work into joblessness.

Next, we look at the association between changes between 2008 and 2010 in the unemployment rate and in the share of temporary work for each country. There was no simple relationship between the severity of the crisis and the change in the proportion of temporary employees. As Figure 6.9 shows, almost all countries experienced an increase in unemployment—with the exception of Germany; however, this increase was not accompanied by a similar rise in the share of temporary employment. Moreover, in many countries, the share of temporary employees fell in 2010, which, again, suggests that temporary workers were particularly vulnerable in situations of economic crisis. Taking the countries where the crisis was the most severe, Spain experienced a 7 per cent decrease in the proportion of temporary employees, implying that Spanish atypical workers were disporportionately affected. But Ireland and Estonia also experienced a substantial enlargement in the share of the unemployed. However, there was an increase in the share of temporary workers in Estonia, while the proportion remained more or less stable in Ireland after the economic crisis.

Next we look at the changes in the employment rate in each country, decomposing it in terms of contract type as well as work hours. Figure 6.10 shows how much of the change in the employment rate in each country

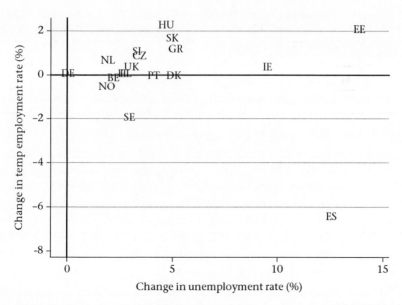

Figure 6.9. Change in unemployment and temporary employment 2008–2010

Source: Eurostat Employment and Unemployment Database. Note: For IE, UK, EE, SE, HU, ES spring 2007 data are used; for others spring 2008 data are used.

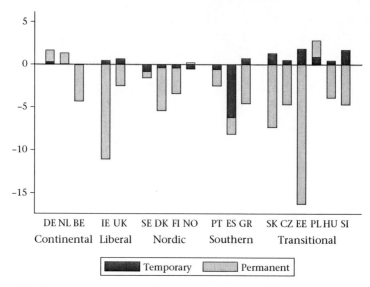

Figure 6.10. Decomposition of employment change by contract type 2008–2010
Source: Authors' calculations from Eurostat Employment and Unemployment Database.

resulted from the change in the share of temporary and permanent employees. The overall change in employment rate for each country is the sum of the changes in temporary and permanent jobs. For example, in Greece the percentage change in the employment rate attributable to permanent employees is –4.6, whereas for temporary employees it is 0.7, which means a 3.9 point fall in total employment rate.

In all countries, except for Germany, the Netherlands, and Poland, there has been a decline in employment rates between 2008 and 2010. Spain, Ireland, and Estonia again stand out as the countries experiencing the largest drops. In most countries, the largest share of the drop has been accounted for by the decline in permanent jobs. Only in Sweden and Spain did temporary jobs contribute a greater share to employment decline. Another striking pattern is that, in Liberal and Transition countries (except for Poland), the share of temporary employees grew during the economic crisis, whereas there was a sharp drop in permanent employment. This suggests that in these countries, temporary work has been increasingly used by employers in the context of increased uncertainty, as is partially expected from the low level of regulation of temporary employment in these countries.

Decomposition of employment growth/decline by part- and full-time jobs indicates that in most countries there was a growth in part-time jobs between 2008 and 2010 as opposed to a decline in full-time jobs (Figure 6.11). The dissimilarities between the trends in temporary and part-time work within

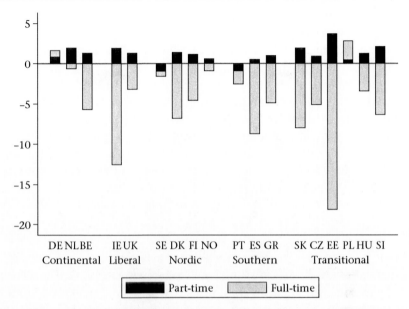

Figure 6.11. Decomposition employment change by work hours 2008–2010
Source: Authors' calculations from Eurostat Employment and Unemployment Database.

countries are noteworthy. For example, in the Netherlands, although there was no growth in temporary employment, the new jobs after the recession were mostly part-time. In Belgium, Denmark, Finland, Portugal, and Spain, where temporary employment dropped with the economic crisis, there was also an increase in part-time jobs. New jobs in Liberal and Transition countries have been in atypical forms, as the share of both temporary and part-time jobs increased as opposed to declining standard employment (with the exception of Poland). It can be summarized that, in general, a larger share of temporary employees in Europe experienced cuts than did part-time employees, whereas most of the employment growth was accounted for by the growth in part-time work.

Economic Crisis and Polarization in Insecurity

While attitudinal and other so-called 'soft' subjective data are frequently marginalized in empirical analysis of market dynamics there has been a recent resurgence of interest in these variables (e.g. Gash et al. 2012). Today an increasingly broad range of social scientists defend the analysis of subjective indicators as crucial for a holistic understanding of social phenomena (e.g. Veenhoven 2002b). This section reviews atypical workers' *experience* of their peripheralized status. It does so by examining whether they fear job loss as well as examining whether the insecurity of their position is mediated by the lure of career advancement, with atypical jobs often seen as a stepping-stone to a more secure employment contract. This section also reviews whether the working conditions of atypical workers have deteriorated during this economic crisis through an analysis of wage change and its implications. The empirical analyses compare the situation for temporary and part-time workers relative to workers in permanent and full-time employment (which is frequently understood to be the standard employment contract). Additionally, we make a distinction by gender to examine the extent to which labour markets are highly gendered in their structure.[3]

Subjective job insecurity

Previous research has underscored the strong relationship between workers' fears of job loss and both (1) national unemployment rates as well as (2) negative changes in their working conditions (Green 2003, 2009). This leads us to expect a strong increase in job insecurity for many workers as a result of the current economic crisis. We can also expect atypical workers to have a more pronounced fear of job loss as a result of their peripheralized status. Temporary workers' contracts are by their nature short-term, with the risk of unemployment a real possibility for many, and part-time workers may also feel at greater risk given their reduced hours. Research on insecurity has been consistent, revealing that *fears* of job loss can result in similar levels of stress as experienced by individuals who actually experience job loss (Burchell 1994; Dekker and Schaufeli 1995; Bohle et al. 2001; Paugam and Zhou 2007).

Moreover, it has been shown that threats to job security have adverse effects on health which are related neither to self-selection nor to health-related behaviour (Ferrie et al. 1998). In their Whitehall study, Marmot and Smith (1991) examined London-based office staff over time. During this period a subsample of workers were privatized which resulted in significant job losses. The study showed how the anticipated job losses due to privatization had a negative effect on employees' self-reported health status two to three years prior to the event. Gash et al. (2007) analysed the health effects of contract type in Germany and Spain. Adopting a change model, they examined the health effects of leaving unemployment for permanent and temporary work. They found that while returning to work restored health, those who obtained a temporary contract had much lower positive health effects suggesting that

---

[3] Note we focus our analysis on temporary workers in full-time positions, and only look at part-time employment for women. We do this because the number of men working in part-time jobs is quite low, making some of the multivariate analysis difficult to interpret.

the job insecurity surrounding the short-term nature of temporary contracts has notable negative effects. Burchell (1994) as well as Bohle et al. (2001) also find a negative relationship between job insecurity and physical and psychological well-being. They attribute the mechanism behind the relationship to people's need to plan and control their lives. If one is employed on a short-term contract or is fearful of job loss as a result of a struggling economy, it is clearly difficult to plan one's life in the longer term.

Nonetheless, the risks and fears associated with unstable positions are sometimes mediated by the lure of future career progression. Many researchers have identified a probationary element within temporary jobs, with some workers seen to progress to the standard employment contract with the same employer once they have proved their worth (e.g. Gash 2008a). We also know that while part-time workers tend to exhibit less subjective job insecurity, they also tend to have reduced opportunities for career progression (Gash 2008b). So it remains important to examine both the element of insecurity within atypical contracts as well as the possibility that these contracts act as a stepping-stone to the standard employment contract.

Financial insecurity

Insecurity is also associated with adverse outcomes for individuals' living standards and their job quality (Inanc 2012). Many workers kept their jobs in the economic crisis in exchange for inferior working conditions, one of the more problematic of these being decreased pay. Social scientific research has confirmed the negative relationship between financial insecurity and well-being (see Chapter 9). Both actual and anticipated financial insecurity have been found to decrease well-being (Jackson and Warr 1984). For instance, research from the US examined the financial implications of unemployment and found that financial strain (which was measured as difficulties in buying food, clothes, and medical care) explained a large part of the anxiety experienced by unemployed workers. Another study on living standards during unemployment showed that the well-being of the unemployed was affected by the ratio of savings to debt, with a decreasing ratio having adverse consequences on one's psychological well-being (Heady and Smyth 1989). The adverse consequences of financial problems are not limited to unemployed individuals. Inanc (2012) found that self-reported financial difficulty predicted decreased life satisfaction and well-being and an increase in the probability of depression among British couples. She also found that women who reported financial difficulties had decreased satisfaction in their personal relationships. An additional aim of this section will be to reveal the extent to which atypical workers have experienced degradation in working conditions as well as the extent to which these changes have led to financial difficulties.

We analyse trends in insecurity using the ESS and measure it using a combination of variables. We begin with an analysis of fear of job loss, with such fears expected to be exacerbated by the recent recession. Fear of job loss is proxied using a variable that asks respondents if their job is secure (in the sense of an actual or implied promise/likelihood of continued employment) with those who claim that their job is not at all secure classified as subjectively insecure. This variable was asked of respondents in both 2004 and 2010 allowing an assessment of change. We also examine whether atypical workers are trapped in their jobs, as well as the extent to which the recession may have increased their entrapment using a question asked in both the 2004 and 2010 ESS data. The question asks: 'Thinking about your current job, how much do you agree or disagree that [your] opportunities for advancement are good?', with respondents who disagreed or disagreed strongly classified as trapped in their jobs.

Our analysis of objective degradation in working conditions uses retrospective questions asked of respondents in the 2010 European Social Survey. Respondents were asked: 'Please tell me whether or not each of the following has happened to you in the last three years:...had to take a reduction in pay and...had to work shorter hours'. Finally, we supplement our analysis of degraded working conditions by an assessment of the implications of reduced pay for atypical workers' households. This section uses a variable which asked: 'Which of the descriptions comes closest to how you feel about your household's income nowadays? Living comfortably on present income, Coping on present income, Finding it difficult on present income, Finding it very difficult on present income', with the last two categories taken as evidence of financial insecurity.

Findings: employment security for peripheral workers

Previous work has revealed a strong relationship in the UK between poor macro-economic conditions and workers' fears of job loss (Green 2009). We could therefore expect an increase in subjective feelings of job insecurity for workers as a result of the recent recession. Table 6.4 reveals that regimes differ considerably from one another in job insecurity levels, with Nordic countries having the smallest share of insecure employees while Southern and Transition regimes have the largest share in both 2004 and 2010. It also indicates a marginal increase in the proportion of workers who are insecure in their jobs in 2010 relative to 2004. We find 15 per cent of employees claim to be insecure in their jobs in 2010 relative to 14 per cent in 2004. This small effect at the mean, however, masks strong differences between regimes. We find workers in Liberal, Southern, and to a lesser extent, Transition regimes to be significantly more insecure in 2010 relative to 2004, where almost one in four workers identify their jobs as insecure. Meanwhile we find a decrease in insecurity in Nordic and Continental regimes. Table 6.4 also reveals the extent to which the outcomes of atypical workers differ from those of standard contract workers; we have placed male permanent workers working full-time hours as the reference category. We find temporary workers, both male and female, to have considerably more job insecurity than permanent workers and also find workers in temporary jobs to be considerably more insecure. It is interesting to note that part-time working women in permanent positions tend to be less insecure than male standard contract workers, though this is only found to be the case in Liberal and Transition regimes. Finally, Table 6.4 examines whether temporary workers and part-time workers have become more exposed to insecurity in 2010 relative to standard contract workers. We find no evidence that this is the case, with the one exception of temporary workers in Liberal regimes. Here we find clear evidence that temporary workers have experienced a disproportionate increase in insecurity since the recession.

Table 6.4 also presents results that reveal changes in entrapment for atypical workers pre- and post-2008. Entrapment was operationalized using ESS data which asked respondents whether they have opportunities for advancement in their jobs, with those who claim not to have such opportunities classified as trapped in their jobs. This analysis is vital to any assessment of atypical jobs, as one of the qualifiers of these precarious positions is that they tend to be stepping-stones or stopgaps for workers on their way to more secure employment. We find our results to be very strongly gendered, that is that they are very different for men and women. We find no difference between male full-time workers by contract type, suggesting that many men regard their temporary positions as bridges to further and better employment. Women temporary workers, however, and indeed even women working in permanent but part-time jobs, regard their positions as dead-end jobs. We examined whether the recession increased workers' sense of entrapment, but find no evidence this was the case; additionally, we find no evidence that temporary and part-time workers faced an increased risk in 2010.

Table 6.5 reveals the proportions of workers who, rather than accept job loss, have accepted austerity measures that have brought in adverse changes to their working conditions. One of the more challenging changes in working conditions that has occurred has been a decrease in workers' take-home pay, with many workers accepting pay cuts in exchange for continued employment. The table makes a distinction between workers who have accepted an outright pay cut with no commensurate decrease in working time, and workers who have also experienced a decrease in working time in the face of their reduced pay. Table 6.5 uses retrospective questions from the European Social Survey which ask respondents whether their job content has changed in the

Table 6.4. Changes in subjective job insecurity and entrapment

	All	Nordic Regime	Continental Regime	Liberal Regime	Southern Regime	Transition Regime
JOB INSECURITY						
2004	0.14	0.1	0.14	0.09	0.16	0.19
2010	0.15	0.08	0.12	0.18	0.21	0.2
(ref: Male, Permanent Full-time)						
Temporary Full-time, Male	0.982***	1.428***	1.104***	1.074***	1.306***	0.464***
Temporary Full-time, Female	1.278***	2.103***	1.486***	1.180***	1.328***	0.806***
Temporary Part-time, Female	1.155***	2.084***	1.149***	1.069***	1.840***	
Permanent Part-time, Female	−0.290**			−0.467[*]		−0.566*
(ref: 2004)						
Increased Risk in 2010	0.140**	-0.274*	-0.206*	0.895***	0.434***	0.127[*]
Increased Risk for Temporary since 2004				0.630*		
Increased Risk for Part-time since 2004						
ENTRAPMENT						
2004	0.44	0.45	0.35	0.3	0.4	0.57
2010	0.4	0.42	0.33	0.33	0.37	0.45
(ref: Male, Permanent Full-time)						
Temporary Full-time, Male						
Temporary Full-time, Female	0.564***	0.749***	0.354[*]	0.804***		0.445***
Temporary Part-time, Female			0.557**	0.887***	1.390***	
Permanent Part-time, Female	0.254[*]	0.531***	0.717**	0.746***		
(ref: 2004)						
Increased Risk in 2010	−0.22***	−0.173**	−0.182*			−0.473***
Increased Risk for Temporary since 2004						
Increased Risk for Part-time since 2004						

Note: These logistic regressions use ESS data from 2004 and 2010 and are weighted. The regressions control for: working time, gender, partnership status, presence of children in the home, educational level, age, and occupational class. The regressions are weighted to control for bias in response rates and to ensure equal national proportions. The table only shows statistically significant coefficients. Sig = *** = <0.001.

Table 6.5. Changes in the working conditions of atypical workers. Dependent variable: Had to take a pay cut

During the last three years have you:	ALL	Nordic Regime	Continental Regime	Liberal Regime	Southern Regime	Transition Regime
...had to take a pay cut (with *no decrease* in hours)	17%	12%	9%	24%	21%	21%
...had to take a pay cut (with *a decrease* in hours)	8%	6%	6%	11%	7%	8%
...had to take a pay cut (with *no decrease* in hours)						
(Ref: Permanent Full-time, Male)						
Temporary Full-time, Male	0.508***	0.483[*]	1.077***		0.861***	
Temporary Full-time, Female	0.586***	1.012***	0.856**	0.439[*]	0.596*	
Temporary Part-time, Female				-0.771*		
Permanent Part-time, Female	-0.469***		-0.467[*]	-0.563*		-0.643[*]
...had to take a pay cut (with *a decrease* in hours)						
(Ref: Permanent Full-time, Male)						
Temporary Full-time, Male	0.783***	1.043**	0.803*	0.888**	0.926**	
Temporary Full-time, Female	0.747***	1.028**	1.754***			0.493[*]
Temporary Part-time, Female	1.442***	1.477**	1.271**	1.584***	1.773***	1.152*
Permanent Part-time, Female	0.690***	1.136***	0.549[*]		0.805[*]	0.732*

Note: These logistic regressions use ESS data from 2010 only and are weighted. The regressions also control for: partnership status, presence of children in the home, educational level, age, and occupational class. Weighted to control for bias in response rates and to ensure equal national proportions. The reference category is male employees in permanent jobs working full-time hours. The table only shows statistically significant associations. Sig = *** = <0.001.

past three years, providing a reference point similar to that used in the analyses using the EULFS data. We find that employees in the Liberal, Southern, and Transition regimes are most likely to have experienced pay cuts in the past three years, and note that the proportions that experience pay cuts are quite high: representing 24 per cent of all employees in Liberal countries and

21 per cent of all employees in Southern and Transition countries. Similarly, Liberal countries have the highest rates of decreased pay combined with a decrease in hours (11 per cent).

Table 6.5 also reveals whether temporary workers and part-time workers are disproportionately exposed to negative changes in their working conditions relative to a male standard contract worker, allowing us to examine whether concerns about atypical workers' polarization continue to have relevance. We find that temporary workers working full-time hours, both male and female, have been disproportionately exposed to outright pay cuts as well as pay cuts tempered by a decrease in hours. The situation for women in part-time posts is rather different, however. We find part-timers, irrespective of contract type, less exposed to outright pay cuts; they are, however, more exposed to wage cuts combined with reduced hours (echoing the rise in involuntary part-time work in earlier analyses). The tendencies are similar across regimes in general and broadly suggest that the current economic crisis has seen a degradation in the working conditions of workers and that non-standard contract workers have borne the brunt of these changes. It is worth noting nonetheless that full-time temporary workers in Southern, Continental, and to a lesser extent Nordic regimes, have experienced the brunt of outright pay cuts.

Given the extent to which workers have experienced a degradation in their working conditions in the form of outright pay cuts in all the regimes analysed, Table 6.6 tries to assess the implications of these pay cuts for workers. We do this by analysing the relationship between respondents who have experienced pay cuts and those who have found it difficult to live on their household income. Unsurprisingly, we find a strong relationship between pay cuts and the financial security of households. We find that workers who have experienced both outright pay cuts and pay cuts tempered by decreased hours are more likely to suffer from financial insecurity overall and for each regime (with the one exception of workers who have experienced an outright pay cut in Liberal regimes). We go on to examine whether workers employed outside of the standard employment contract remain more exposed to financial insecurity even after controlling for a degradation in wages. At an aggregate level, across all the countries analysed, we find all non-standard contract workers to suffer from financial insecurity in their households when compared to the standard contract worker. Nonetheless, we do note important differences between different types of worker. We find that male temporary workers on full-time contracts appear to fare better than women on similar contracts, being no different in their financial insecurity risk than the standard contract worker in Liberal, Southern, and Transition regimes. We also note that part-time workers in permanent contracts are also more exposed to financial insecurity than the male standard contract worker. These findings challenge a popular misconception that temporary and part-time workers'

Table 6.6. Risks of financial insecurity, national variations. Dependent variable: Difficult to live on household income nowadays

	ALL	Nordic Regime	Continental Regime	Liberal Regime	Southern Regime	Transition Regime
...had to take a pay cut (with *no decrease* in hours)	0.855***	0.800**	1.141***		0.600***	0.804***
...had to take a pay cut (with a *decrease* in hours)	0.996***	1.386***	0.508[*]	0.925***	0.908***	1.003***
Permanent Full-time, Male (reference)						
Temporary Full-time, Male	0.440***	0.681[*]	0.835**			
Temporary Full-time, Female	0.587***		0.849*	1.051**	0.732**	
Temporary Part-time, Female	0.570***	1.271*		1.011**		0.941**
Permanent Part-time, Female	0.245*		0.381[*]	0.626*		

Note: Logistic regressions use pooled ESS data from 2010 only, which are weighted. The regressions also control for: partnership status, presence of children in the home, educational level, as well as age. Weighted to control for bias in response rates and to ensure equal national proportions. Sig = *** = <0.001.

wages are predominantly of secondary importance to household income. The assumption is that many atypical workers accept their precarious positions in the knowledge that their wages are not an important source of household income. Were that the case temporary workers and part-time workers would not find themselves in households experiencing financial difficulties.

Conclusion

This chapter sought to examine the implications of the global economic crisis on atypical workers, that is, workers on temporary and/or part-time hour contracts, in a selected set of European countries. One of its aims was to reveal whether these workers were becoming further peripheralized in the labour market as has been predicted by earlier researchers in the field. The chapter looked at how the crisis may have changed the size and composition of the atypical workforce, as well as how it may have been disproportionately exposed to job and employment insecurity. It also sought to identify whether the institutional structure of different employment regimes shaped the outcomes of atypical workers. Based on the varying level of employment protection legislation in our countries, as well as on employment regime classifications outlined by Gallie (2011), we predicted an increased segmentation between the core and peripheral workers in the Continental and Southern regimes whereas we anticipated little polarization in the Liberal countries.

Our investigation of workforce changes since the recession revealed an increased exposure to involuntary atypical work between 2008 and 2010 in most countries. We found that men became more exposed to accepting temporary and part-time jobs out of constraint with full-time permanent jobs more scarce after the economic crisis. Our analysis revealed that countries responded to the macro-economic pressure differently. There was a remarkable reduction in temporary employment in Spain as well as in Portugal and the Nordic countries. While Liberal and Transition countries used temporary contracts more frequently after the recession, due to lower levels of regulation on temporary employment.

Our analysis of the working experience of atypical workers revealed conflicting results. While we found an increase in subjective feelings of insecurity overall and also found atypical workers to be disproportionately exposed to fears of job loss, we did not find atypical workers to be relatively more exposed to insecurity since the recession compared to those on standard contracts. We also found differences between atypical workers in their experience of insecurity. Women in part-time permanent contracts were generally less exposed to fears of job loss than men on the standard employment contract. Additionally, we examined whether atypical workers found themselves in dead-end jobs with few opportunities for advancement. We found atypical workers generally more likely to regard their positions to have reduced opportunities, but noted that men in temporary full-time jobs tended to regard their positions similarly to standard contract workers, underscoring the extent to which many temporary contracts are regarded as stepping-stones to better jobs by many workers.

Our analysis of the implications of the economic crisis for atypical workers' working conditions revealed a very clear and worrying tendency for a peripheralization of atypical workers' jobs relative to standard contract workers. We found atypical workers were much more likely to have experienced a pay cut, and these pay cuts in turn were found to have negative repercussions at the household level with many atypical workers finding it difficult to make ends meet even after we controlled for exposure to pay cuts.

We presented our analyses by regime type, with an expectation that Nordic countries would be more inclusive towards atypical workers while countries with dualistic employment structures (the Continental and Southern countries) would suffer greater inequalities between atypical and standard contract workers. What we actually found was a shared tendency across regime types in the peripheralization of atypical workers. That we also revealed an increased share in the workforce employed in atypical contracts suggests that early fears concerning the impact of flexibilization policies on market polarization remain relevant.

7

Work–Family Conflict and Economic Change

Frances McGinnity and Helen Russell

Introduction

In the past two decades, reconciling work and family life has become a critical issue for both academic and policy debates in Europe and the US, against
a backdrop of rising female participation and a concomitant rise in dual-
earning families, an ageing population, and falling fertility (McGinnity and
Whelan 2009). Under the traditional male breadwinner model, competing
demands in the paid work and family sphere were managed by a division
of labour between the sexes: men were primarily responsible for paid work,
women for caring. Now an increasing proportion of individuals are combining caring and paid work roles, and some struggle to do so, a phenomenon
known as 'work–family conflict'. Why is it important? It is important because
work–family conflict may have negative consequences for personal effectiveness, marital relations, child development, and life satisfaction (Gornick
and Meyers 2003; Kotowska et al. 2010). It has also been linked to decreased
job satisfaction, absenteeism, and stress-related outcomes such as anxiety,
depression, exhaustion, and alcohol abuse (Allen et al. 2000; Russell and
McGinnity 2011).

Much of the debate and research on work–family conflict has occurred
within the context of economic growth, when the problems facing individuals and households that were 'work rich' came to the fore. However, now
that many European countries have entered a phase of economic crisis, is the
issue of work–family conflict still salient? How does economic crisis influence
work–family conflict? By comparing in detail identical indicators from eighteen European countries in 2004 (a year of boom in many countries) and 2010
(a year of sluggish economic growth and higher unemployment in many
countries) we look at how work–family conflict experienced by individuals

and factors associated with it have changed over time. We examine variation between countries in how this has changed. We also explore in detail in what way changes in work and family circumstances in the three years preceding 2010 are associated with work–family conflict.

This chapter seeks to contribute to debates on work–family conflict, by considering the impact of economic crisis, as well as to debates on the impact of recession, by examining in depth how economic change can influence the reconciliation of work and family life.

Work–Family Conflict: Previous Research and Debates

In terms of theoretical perspectives, research on the work–life interface has been heavily dominated by the idea of role strain and conflict between roles, that is, that the time or energy devoted to one role is not available to another role (Goode 1960; Greenhaus and Beutell 1985). Linked to role theory, the demands–resources perspective distinguishes demands, or work-role requirements, and resources, which are assets used to cope with demands (Voydanoff 2005; Steiber 2009). *Demands* are aspects of jobs associated with sustained physical and/or mental effort. These include things like long working hours, working overtime at short notice, work pressure, responsibility, and job insecurity. *Resources* are factors that help people to reduce work–life conflict or cope with conflict, such as flexibility in assigning working hours, control or autonomy over one's work, and having supportive work colleagues. This perspective can be extended to family factors. Here, home demands are factors like the number and age of children, partner's long working hours, partner's unsocial hours, hours of housework, housework stress, and financial stress. Home resources are factors like having a supportive partner, a partner working shorter hours, having extended family close by, and financial resources like household income. Insights from border theory expand the demand–resource approach. Borders between work and family life are not fixed: people continually create and negotiate these borders (Clark 2000). If borders are flexible, demands may be accommodated by shifting borders.

Work–life conflict may be time-based conflict—where the amount of time devoted to one role makes it difficult to meet the demands of the other—or strain-based conflict—referring to physical tiredness or psychological stress resulting from the demands of work or home roles. Some authors distinguish time-based and strain-based conflict, though in practice this can be difficult and the two are often correlated.

Some authors investigating work–life conflict consider all employees, and broaden the concept to consider conflict between paid work and other aspects of life, not just family or partner. Others limit the focus to couples, for which the more accurate term is work–family conflict. This allows a fuller under-standing of how the partner's situation influences the individual's experience of conflict, and is the approach taken in this chapter. One appeal of the con-cept of work–life conflict for social research is that it allows a wider under-standing of non-work concerns to be encompassed in employment research. Yet this is also a crucial limitation of the concept: no matter how it is defined, work–life conflict is observed only for those in employment, and those with very high work–life/work–family conflict may have exited the labour market (McGinnity and Whelan 2009).[1]

Conflict can take two forms: work-to-family conflict or family-to-work conflict, though work tends to affect family more than vice versa, partly because of the greater permeability of the family domain (Frone et al. 1992), and most research has focused on work-to-life conflict. A small but growing body of literature meas-ures not work–life conflict or work–life balance but *satisfaction* with work–life balance (Drobnic 2011). In this chapter the primary focus is work-to-family con-flict, although family-to-work conflict is also briefly examined.

What has previous research found? In terms of work demands, the level of work–family conflict is related to work demands in terms of overall hours of paid work, scheduling, and control over hours. Long working hours have been found by many authors to be positively associated with work–fam-ily conflict (e.g. Crompton and Lyonette 2006; Van der Lippe et al. 2006). Unsocial hours such as regularly working weekends or evenings/nights typi-cally increases work–family conflict, as time that is usually 'family' time is devoted to paid work. Schedule flexibility which benefits employers, like working overtime at short notice, may also increase work–family conflict. Predictability is important to work–family balance: workers value jobs that are regular and somewhat flexible.

Work demands other than working time and its allocation may influence work–family conflict. If a job is very stressful and emotionally demanding, this may leave an individual with insufficient resources to engage in per-sonal life. Research has shown consistently that work pressure or work stress, typically combining time pressure and the demands of the job, has a strong influence on work–family conflict. This is true across Europe, and the marked rise in levels of work pressure in European countries since the early 1990s has contributed substantially to greater strain in managing work and family life (Gallie and Russell 2009).

Perceived job insecurity typically has a negative impact on work–family conflict (Voyandoff 2005). Linked to this, fixed-term employment has several negative effects on families and social relations, effects which are only partly

---

[1] Another limitation is that the focus here is on *current* work–family tensions and there may well be other current and future 'costs'—like limited family formation or career development.

explained by working conditions or subjective job insecurity. Temporary contracts do not seem to facilitate the reconciliation of work and family life, but rather exacerbate levels of conflict, dissatisfaction, and economic pressure (Scherer 2009).

In terms of job resources, having supportive work colleagues or a supportive boss does tend to reduce conflict (Byron 2005). Theoretical arguments suggest that job autonomy tends to reduce the pressures by giving workers some degree of control over the policy, pace, and organization of their work (Karasek 1979). Research on satisfaction with work–life balance has found that job control does reduce work–life conflict (Fagan and Walthery 2011). However, others who use the more typical measure of work–family conflict, which combines responses to a series of questions, find either that job control has no impact (Gallie and Russell 2009), or that job control increases work–family conflict (Schieman et al. 2009). Similarly, while some authors find that flexibility which allows employees to vary their schedule to accommodate their family lives tends to reduce work–life conflict (Fagan 2003), in some cases flexibility increases permeability and thus conflict between work and family life, particularly if employees are highly committed and work long hours (Schiemann et al. 2009). Professional social classes experience the highest work–life conflict, partly because they tend to have longer working hours and higher work pressure than other social classes, though the effect remains even after accounting for these factors (McGinnity and Calvert 2009; Schieman et al. 2009).

The level of work–family conflict also relates to demands and resources within the home. Jacobs and Gerson (2004) argue that a key factor to consider is not individual working hours, but the concentration of high hours within couples which is relevant for work–family conflict. Households are now supplying more labour to the market, and the feelings of time-pressure and work–family conflict are greater in dual-earner households struggling to manage the higher load of work, paid and unpaid, than that of earlier generations of male breadwinner households. Scherer and Steiber (2007) found that a high-level total (paid) work hours has also been shown to contribute to work–family conflict, though Gallie and Russell (2009) find little effect of partners' working hours per se. Previous research has found that the presence of children generally increases work–life conflict (Gallie and Russell 2009; Bianchi and Milkie 2010), though some studies find no effect of children (Schieman et al. 2009).[2] Bianchi and Milkie (2010) point to the potential support provided by partners as a family 'resource', though

---

[2] Note that the impact of age and number of children may be underestimated, as people who find it relatively easy to integrate work and family roles may decide to have more children, while those who experience conflict between their roles as workers and parents may not be employed when their children are small, or at least adapt their work situation in order to minimize conflict (Steiber 2009).

partners can also place demands on individuals and limit their time for other commitments. Crompton and Lyonette (2006) stress the importance of the gendered division of labour within the household for work–life conflict, as well as gender role attitudes and the consistency between attitudes and behaviour. Steiber (2009) suggests that egalitarian attitudes may actually increase conflict for women, and reduce conflict for men, though her findings only support the latter.

The effect of income is not straightforward, and in general there is less evidence. Those with higher incomes, high salaries, in professional and managerial jobs, tend to have higher work–life conflict (the 'yuppie qvetch hypothesis') even after controlling for job characteristics (McGinnity and Calvert 2009; Schieman et al. 2009). Yet Chung (2011) and Steiber (2009) both find that financial insecurity increases work–family conflict.

While work–family conflict is experienced by men and women, and for the most part similar factors are associated with it for men and women, research looking at gender differences has highlighted some salient differences (Steiber 2009). In particular, working hours have a stronger impact on work–family conflict for women than for men. In most countries, of course, women's working hours vary much more than men's hours. The presence of children is typically more salient for women than for men: so also is control over one's working time schedule (Steiber 2009). Authors have also found a stronger impact of job insecurity on work–family conflict for men than for women (Drobnic and Guillen Rodriguez 2011).

Comparative research has emphasized the importance of institutional-level factors, e.g. welfare regime or 'family friendly' policies such as parental leave and child care policy, which may explain variations in work–family conflict across countries (Strandh and Nordenmark 2006; Van der Lippe et al. 2006). Others have highlighted the role of labour market regulations and employment regimes, for example, collective control over working time and flexibility (McGinnity and Calvert 2009). However, cross-national findings on country effects are not consistent (McGinnity forthcoming). Some studies have found evidence that where the state gives greater support to families, work–family strain is reduced. For example Chung (2011), in an analysis of twenty-eight European countries, has found evidence that, after controlling for individual factors like working hours, higher spending on family and child policies reduces work–family conflict. Yet not all studies find this, arguing that the lack of well-developed reconciliation policies implies the reduction of women's working hours and the possibility of more traditional combinations of paid and unpaid work, thus potentially resulting in lower perceptions of work–family conflict, at least for women (Van der Lippe et al. 2006; Scherer and Steiber 2007). Some studies find that more affluent countries, with higher levels of GDP, have higher work–family conflict (Steiber

2009), yet others find the opposite (Chung 2011). Perhaps the clearest conclusion from comparative research is that work–family conflict is primarily an individual phenomenon, with much less variance at country level.

And of course while the relationship between the *level* of work–family conflict and national policy configurations at any given time may be contested, the same may not be true for change over time, the focus of this chapter. Policies—whether regulations, services, or cash payments—that support families and employees may protect them from the impact of economic change. This suggests that work–family conflict levels may be more stable in countries with well-developed policies relevant for combining work and family life.

Work–Family Conflict and Economic Crisis

How might work–family conflict be associated with economic crisis? There are a number of processes associated with economic change that may influence work–family conflict, which may work in opposite directions.

First, economic crisis may influence the volume of work at the individual or household level. Employers may introduce shorter working hours in response to a decline in demand (or decreased budgets in the public sector), which, based on previous research findings about the impact of working hours on work–family conflict, should result in lower conflict overall. However, some employees may experience pressure to work longer hours to keep businesses afloat, or in situations where other colleagues have been laid off.

Considering working hours in the household, in particular long working hours, any reduction in the propensity of partners to work long hours may also be associated with lower work–family conflict. Of course unemployment of one partner or non-employment and the consequent reduction in household working time, could also reduce work–family conflict, though this may also be offset by the financial pressures described below (see also Chapter 9).

Second, other working time issues may push work–family conflict upwards. The distribution of work hours has proved important for work–family conflict, with those working unsocial hours and overtime at short notice reporting higher levels of work–family conflict. Economic crisis may increase the number of employees facing such working conditions as their bargaining power decreases. The economic crisis may also reduce employees' opportunities to exercise their working time preferences. A second expectation is that changes in the scheduling of working hours, both for the individual and their partner, could increase work–family conflict.

Third, we expect that work pressure, another key determinant of work–family conflict (Gallie and Russell 2009), will increase during economic crisis.

This is likely to be especially true for those working in organizations that have experienced job losses or financial problems (for evidence on Ireland see Russell and McGinnity 2013). Of course job resources such as autonomy and support from work colleagues may help to alleviate pressures (see Chapter 5).

Fourth, job insecurity, often a feature of economic crisis (see also Chapter 6), may aggravate work–family conflict (Voyandoff 2005; Scherer 2009). Fifth, at a family level, money worries and financial difficulties may increase during economic crisis and exacerbate work–family conflict too.

Sixth, from a comparative perspective, the extent to which economic change influences work–family conflict may also be mediated by policy supports for reconciling work and family life. Alternatively, variation in economic change across countries may influence change in work–family conflict, rather than policy configurations. Thus countries where economic change was greatest would be expected to experience the greatest change in work–family conflict. These issues will be discussed in more detail when we consider how change over time in work–family conflict varies cross-nationally.

To examine these factors, we use data from the European Social Survey (ESS), which is an academically driven social survey designed to chart and explain the interaction between Europe's changing institutions and attitudes, beliefs, and behaviour patterns. The survey covers over thirty countries and employs rigorous survey methodologies. The ESS special modules on family, work, and well-being (2004) and work, family, and economic crisis (2010) were specifically designed to make possible an analysis of work–family conflict in a wide range of countries. Questions in the special modules cover topics such as work-to-family conflict and family-to-work conflict; work pressure, autonomy, and conditions of work; age and number of children; and gender role attitudes. By replicating a large range of relevant questions, the data offer a unique opportunity to examine work–family conflict in Europe, and how this has changed between 2004 and 2010

We investigate these issues in this chapter in the following way. In the next section we present details of how work and family factors have changed, on aggregate, for employees between the two years. Are our general expectations about change borne out by the data for eighteen countries? In the following section we pool both years, and estimate nested regression models to investigate the association between these changes with the change in work–family conflict. To what extent can we understand changes in work–family conflict in terms of changes in working hours and how working hours are allocated; changes in work pressure and other working conditions; changes in job insecurity and financial difficulties at family level? This follows a similar modelling strategy to Russell and McGinnity (2013) in their analysis of change over time in work pressure.

We then move to consider cross-country differences in work–family conflict and investigate our expectations about welfare regimes. We also exploit variation in the extent of economic crisis by considering how change in work–family conflict relates to changing economic circumstances, plotting the change in work–family conflict by the change in the unemployment rate.

The final section adopts a different approach to exploring the potential impact of economic crisis. Using variables unique to the 2010 survey about changes in families, firms, and jobs in the past three years associated with the crisis, we estimate a model of work–family conflict in 2010, to assess the impact of these changes.

Note that while these two surveys contain a rich range of indicators repeated for these countries at two points in time for a representative sample of individuals within countries, they are repeated cross-sections. We cannot infer anything about change over time for individuals, but rather aggregate patterns of change. In addition, while most countries in this sample experienced an economic downturn in the period, some, as discussed in Chapter 2, did not. Insofar as we use change over time to shed light on the impact of economic crisis, it is important to bear this in mind.

The core outcome of interest, the experience of work–family conflict, is measured as an index which takes the mean of four questions: 'How often do you keep worrying about work problems when you are not working?' 'How often do you feel too tired after work to enjoy the things you would like to do at home?' 'How often do you find that your job prevents you from giving the time you want to your partner or family?' 'How often do you find that your partner or family gets fed up with the pressure of your job?' The index varies from 1 (never) to 5 (always). The items are highly correlated.[3] All the analyses in this chapter are weighted to give countries a similar number of cases, and based on employees in couples, aged 20–64.

Change in Work and Family Factors among Couples in Economic Crisis

In this section we consider changes in work and family factors in economic crisis, measured for employees in couples in 2004 and 2010. Are the changes in the direction we might expect?

Table 7.1a compares the means of some key indicators and whether any change is statistically significant. We also look at family-to-work conflict in 2010. First, there is a modest but statistically significant rise in work-to-family

---

[3] This index has a Cronbach's alpha of 0.75 for the pooled sample.

Table 7.1a. Change over time in means, employees in couples, pooled across countries

Mean value	2004	2010	Sig. of change	Year diff. significant (p< = 0.05)?
4 item work to family conflict scale	2.53	2.61	0.00	YES
2 item family to work conflict scale		1.82	n/a	
Working hours (weekly)	39.61	39.52	n.s.	NO
Job Pressure Index	3.35	3.44	0.00	YES
Index of job control: work organization, policy and pace	5.23	5.40	0.00	YES

Source: European Social Surveys 2004 and 2010. Note: Chi-square test of significance. Employees in couples, 20–64, weighted to give each country the same number of cases. France excluded as there are no valid measures for 2004 on financial difficulties.

conflict, as described above, over the period.[4] Family-to-work conflict, just measured for 2010, is a two-item index of 'find that your family responsibilities prevent you from giving the time you should to your job?' and 'find it difficult to concentrate on work because of your family responsibilities?' While measured on the same scale, the mean of this scale is quite a bit lower than work-to-family conflict, as other authors have found. This suggests that this is not as salient for individuals as work-to-family conflict, the focus of this chapter.

As expected, mean weekly working hours have fallen slightly in these countries, from 39.6 hours in 2004 to 39.5 hours in 2010, though this difference is not statistically significant.[5] Job pressure or work intensity is measured as a combination of 'my job requires that I work very hard' and 'I never seem to have enough time to get everything done in my job' (ranging from 1, disagree strongly, to 5, agree strongly). The data indicate that it has risen in the period, and this change is statistically significant. This is a key theme of Chapter 5.

The job control index is a measure of how much an individual can influence the pace of their work and how they organize it, as well as policy decisions about the activities of the organization.[6] The scale ranges from 0 to 10 where 0 is no influence, 10 is complete control. Job control also rises in the period (see also Chapter 5), which may ameliorate the effect of the rise in work pressure, if the effect on work–family conflict is as anticipated.

---

[4] The direction of change in work–family conflict is consistent with the finding that a higher proportion of employees in couples would like to work fewer hours: 37 per cent in 2004, compared to 43 per cent in 2010.

[5] Working hours were top coded at 80 hours, following convention.

[6] Exact question is: 'Please say how much the management at your work allows/allowed you to: to decide how your own daily work is/was organized?/to influence policy decisions about the activities of the organization?/ to choose or change your pace of work?'

Table 7.1b presents the proportion saying 'yes' to selected work and family indicators shown by previous research to be associated with work–family conflict. Consistent with our expectations, Table 7.1b also shows a small but significant rise between 2004 and 2010 in the proportion of employees working evenings or nights at least once a week. There has also been a small rise in the proportion working weekends at least several times a month, though this fails to reach statistical significance. There has, however, been a rise in the proportion working overtime at short notice, from 13 per cent in 2004 to 15.5 per cent in 2010, consistent with an explanation that the incidence of these working conditions rises in economic crisis, as workers' bargaining power decreases.[7]

There has also been a fall in those reporting that they can decide start and finish times, consistent with our expectation that the economic crisis may also reduce employees' opportunities to exercise their working time preferences. There has been no change in the proportion reporting that their health or safety is at risk because of their work. Health and safety at work is more closely related to the physical work environment and self-reported risk is considerably higher in certain sectors such as construction, agriculture, and transport. The decline in employment in construction and agriculture over the period may therefore cancel out increases in perceived risk among those remaining in these sectors and in the wider economy. Interestingly there has been a rise in the proportion who say they have supportive work colleagues, which may counteract some of the negative changes in working conditions over the period. As expected, there is a significant rise in the proportion reporting that their job is insecure. [8]

One surprising indicator from Table 7.1b is the measure of financial strain in families: the proportion of employees reporting that they are finding it difficult or very difficult to live on current income has not changed.[9] This may be linked to the distribution of employment within households: the proportion of employees with partners not in the labour market has fallen by 3 per cent. The proportion whose partner is unemployed has risen, as we would expect, yet this is more than offset by the fall in labour force inactivity, so overall the proportion of partners not in employment has actually

---

[7] Detailed questions: 'How often does your work involve working evenings or nights/having to work overtime at short notice? (Response codes: Never/Less than once a month/Once a month/Several times a month/Once a month/Several times a week/Every day)'; 'How often does your work involve working at weekends? Never/Less than once a month/Once a month/Several times a month/Every week'.

[8] That is they responded to the statement 'My job is secure' with 'not at all true' or 'a little true'.

[9] Note this is based on a sample of employees in couples. 'Workless' households, where either both partners are unemployed, one partner is unemployed and the other inactive, or single adults who become unemployed will all tend to report higher levels of financial strain than employees in couples. Unemployment is also more prevalent among those with low skills and low income in the first place. The proportion of all adults finding it difficult or very difficult to live on current income has risen over the period (see Chapter 9).

Table 7.1b. Change over time in proportion saying 'yes' on selected work and family indicators, employees in couples, pooled across eighteen countries*

	2004	2010	Significance of change	Year diff significant (p< = 0.05)?
Work evenings or nights at least once a week	19.7%	21.0%	0.044	YES
Work weekends at least several times per month	29.0%	30.3%	0.078	NO
Work overtime at short notice at least once a week	13.1%	15.5%	0.000	YES
Can decide start and finish times (quite/very true)	26.4%	23.7%	0.000	YES
Health/safety at risk (quite or very true)	18.8%	19.0%	0.794	NO
Supportive work colleagues (quite or very true)	76.5%	78.2%	0.012	YES
Job insecurity (see text for details)	33.2%	35.2%	0.012	YES
Financial stress (difficult or very difficult to live on current income)	17.1%	16.4%	0.221	NO
Partner not in the labour market	20.4%	17.2%	0.000	YES
Partner unemployed	4.1%	5.1%	0.004	YES
Partner works over 40 hours	21.6%	18.9%	0.000	YES

Source: European Social Surveys 2004 and 2010. Note: Employees in couples, 20–64, weighted to give each country the same number of cases. Chi-square test of significance. *France excluded as there are no valid observations of financial stress for 2004. The pattern is not changed if France is included.

fallen slightly over the period. Note that to the extent that unemployment is concentrated in couples (e.g. Gregg et al. 2010), measuring the proportion of employees with unemployed partners will somewhat underestimate the extent of unemployment. The proportion of employees with partners working over 40 hours has also fallen. The fall in partners' inactivity and the fall in long working hours may be linked to longer-term trends in labour market participation and working hours in these countries that are not linked to economic crisis.[10]

[10] Given, as noted above, not all countries experienced recession between 2004 and 2010, in particular Poland, where the unemployment rate fell significantly between the years, we also investigate these changes over time without Poland, and this does not affect the pattern of results.

Work–Family Conflict: Investigating Change over Time 2004–2010

This section examines the relationship between the changes in working conditions and other factors, and changes in work–family conflict over time. First we discuss the association of these factors with work–family conflict for the whole sample, and where these associations differ for men and women.[11] The association between work–family conflict and working hours and scheduling are presented in Table 7.2a. Table 7.2b presents other job demands and resources and home and family factors. In these models the data are pooled by year and across countries: the focus is not on country differences, but rather a 'broad brush' picture of change in Europe.[12] In a second step we examine the explanations proposed about change in work–family conflict by presenting a series of nested models where various factors related to working hours, time flexibility and scheduling, other working conditions, other home factors, and occupational class are introduced successively. These results are presented in Table 7.3.

In Table 7.2a the 'Year 2010' coefficient indicates a small but significant rise in work–family conflict between 2004 and 2010, mirroring the figures in Table 7.1a. This is even after extensive controls for working hours, job demands and resources, and home and family factors. The rise was particularly pronounced for men, though not significant for women. Overall work–family conflict is higher for women, once we control for working hours (Table 7.2a).

Working hours has a very strong impact on work–family conflict, though to a greater extent for women than for men, consistent with previous findings. Having a partner who is unemployed increases work–family conflict, suggesting that financial strain and the negative impact of unemployment on well-being may outweigh any potential reduction in overall household working hours. This is also true of having a partner out of the labour market, which also increases conflict, though not to the same extent as unemployment. Having a partner working long hours is not associated with higher work–family conflict once unsocial hours are added to the model.

Control over working time and unsocial working hours of both the individual and their partner are also associated with work–family conflict. In particular, working overtime at short notice has a significant effect increasing work–family conflict. This is also true of working at weekends and in the

---

[11] Model estimates for men and women are presented separately but the statistical significance of these differences was formally tested in a pooled model with gender interactions.

[12] We estimated separate models for each year to confirm that pooling is a valid strategy, that is, that the impact of the covariates does not vary by year.

Table 7.2a. Work–family conflict for all employees in couples, 2004 and 2010, working time and scheduling

	All		Men		Women	
	Coef.	Sig.	Coef.	Sig.	Coef.	Sig.
Year 2010	0.037	**	0.060	***	0.009	n.s
Age	−0.001	n.s	−0.002	*	0.001	n.s
Female	0.086	***				
Working hours:						
Working hours (usual)	0.011	***	0.008	***	0.013	***
Partner inactive	0.099	***	0.116	***	0.108	**
Partner unemployed	0.179	***	0.239	***	0.105	*
Partner's long hours (over 40)	0.003	n.s	−0.042	n.s	0.039	n.s
Work time flexibility & scheduling:						
Work evenings or nights	0.109	***	0.085	***	0.140	***
Work overtime, short notice	0.222	***	0.246	***	0.204	***
Work weekends	0.179	***	0.160	***	0.206	***
Partner unsocial hours	0.031	***	0.048	***	0.018	*
Can decide start/ finish times	0.025	n.s	0.058	**	−0.020	n.s
R square	0.253		0.262	***	0.252	***
N of cases	15985		8379		7606	

Note: Models also include controls for work and family factors and social class (see Table 7.2b).

evening or at night. Having a partner work unsocial hours is also associated with higher work–family conflict. Thus as well as the volume of hours, the scheduling of working hours, particularly at short notice, impacts family life. Interestingly having control over one's working hours, typically seen as a work resource, does not reduce work–family conflict. In fact it has a small but significant impact in increasing work–family conflict for men, though not for women. Some authors have found control over working hours reduces work–family conflict for women, though not for men: others have found schedule control is an ambiguous resource, increasing conflict for those working long hours (Schiemann et al. 2009) or those in managerial/professional occupations (e.g. White et al. 2003). Schiemann et al. (2009) argue that to the extent that schedule control is associated with workplace expectations for dedication and engagement, it may increase role blurring and the permeability of border between work and family life.

Adding other job characteristics (Table 7.2b) we find that work pressure has a very strong, significant association with work–family conflict: higher pressure at work is associated with higher work–family conflict, as found in previous research. The model also shows that job control increases work–family conflict. While the effect is modest, it is statistically significant. Clearly control over one's work, while a resource, does not always function as a conflict-reducing resource.[13] Drobnic and Guillen Rodriguez (2011), who also find this, invoke a capability approach to argue that employees may not be able to convert job control into capability or agency. Having supportive colleagues is a resource which does reduce work–family conflict though.

The final job-related factor is job insecurity. Job insecurity, which has risen over the period, also increases work–family conflict, and partly explains the rise in work–family conflict over the period.

In terms of demands from home, the presence of children increases work–family conflict, particularly children under age 6. As expected, financial insecurity is associated with increased conflict. Gender role attitudes have no impact overall, though interestingly egalitarian attitudes tend to reduce conflict for men and increase conflict for women.[14] Men with egalitarian attitudes may be more likely to reduce paid work involvement to accommodate family demands. Women with egalitarian attitudes may be more likely to experience the current division of paid and unpaid work as unfair, which is likely to be associated with higher work–family conflict.

The model also includes occupational class, both to adjust for any change in the distribution of jobs, and to investigate whether any of the impact of work factors on work–family conflict is mediated by occupational class. Work–family conflict is significantly higher among professional/managerial workers, even after accounting for a range of other working conditions, as found by McGinnity and Calvert (2009). Work–family conflict is also somewhat higher among those from the intermediate occupations, compared to lower technical, sales, and routine occupational classes, the reference category for occupational class.

We now examine the role that each of these factors plays in accounting for the modest rise in work–family conflict over the period by estimating a series of nested models. For each successive model we look at whether the year coefficient has changed. The results are presented in Table 7.3: the models are labelled A to F for ease of presentation (see Table A7.2 for the full models). Model A shows a small but significant rise in work–family conflict over time,

[13] There is no evidence that autonomy ameliorates the impact of pressure: the interaction between work pressure and job control is not significant.

[14] Gender role attitudes are measured as a scale from 'strongly agree' to 'strongly disagree', combining responses to 'A woman should be prepared to cut down on her paid work for the sake of her family' and 'When jobs are scarce, men should have more right to a job than women'.

Table 7.2b. Work–family conflict for all employees in couples, 2004 and 2010, other work and family factors

	All		Men		Women	
	Coeff.	Sig.	Coeff.	Sig.	Coeff.	Sig.
Work demands and resources:						
Job Pressure Index	0.242	***	0.245	***	0.236	***
Health/safety at risk	0.178	***	0.170	***	0.204	***
Control over work organization, policy, and pace	0.014	***	0.015	***	0.013	***
Support from colleagues	−0.040	**	−0.038	n.s	−0.044	*
Insecure about job	0.080	***	0.090	***	0.070	***
Home demands and resources:						
Any child under 6	0.056	***	0.051	*	0.065	**
No. of children	0.014	*	0.016	*	0.016	n.s
Difficult or very difficult to live on current income	0.170	***	0.158	***	0.187	***
Egalitarian gender attitudes to work and family	0.001	n.s	−0.018	n.s	0.017	n.s
Occupational Class:						
Professional/ managerial class	0.204	***	0.209	***	0.194	***
Intermediate class	0.076	***	0.062	**	0.097	***
Constant	0.823	***	0.970	***	0.780	***
R square	0.253		0.262	***	0.252	***
N of cases	15985		8379		7606	

Note: Models also include controls for age, gender, working hours, and scheduling (see Table 7.2a).

mirroring the figures in Table 7.1a. Actually the addition of working hours of the individual and their partner (Model B) makes little difference to the differential: in fact the year coefficient is slightly larger. Mean working hours fell slightly during the period: if they had remained constant the rise in conflict would have been somewhat higher (see Table 7.1b).

Model C adds control over working time and unsocial working hours of both the individual and their partner, including working in the evenings/ at night, at weekends, and working overtime at short notice. These factors tend to be associated with higher work–family conflict, and accounting for these factors reduces the year coefficient (see Table 7.2a). Had these factors remained constant, instead of rising (Table 7.1b) the rise in work–family conflict between years would have been lower. These findings are consistent with our second broad expectation.

Table 7.3. Change over time in work–family conflict

	Model A Change over time		Model B Add working hours		Model C Add time flexibility/ schedule		Model D Add work pressure		Model E Add other work factors		Model F Add home factors and occupation	
	Coeff	Sig.	Coeff	Sig.	Coeff	Sig.	Coeff	Sig.	Coeff	Sig.	Coeff	Sig.
Year 2010	0.074	***	0.077	***	0.065	***	0.042	***	0.039	***	0.037	**
R square	0.005		0.075		0.137		0.223		0.236		0.253	

Note: This model successively includes the factors in Tables 7.2a and 7.2b. For the full six models see Table A7.1 in the Appendix.

Model D adds work pressure. The addition of work pressure alone reduces the year coefficient suggesting that the rise in work pressure partly explains the rise in work–family conflict (see expectation three). Individuals feel under more pressure at work on average in 2010, and this spills over into their family life.

Job insecurity is added with other work demands (Model E). While job insecurity has risen and does increase work–family conflict (our fourth expectation), the impact on change over time is modest—partly offset by the rise in the proportion of employees having supportive colleagues.

Model F introduces the impact of other home factors, namely the presence and age of children, as well as financial insecurity. While financial insecurity is associated with increased conflict, it did not rise in the period (Table 7.1b), so does not affect the change over time in work–family conflict. Model F also adds occupational class, here primarily to adjust for any change in the distribution of jobs. The addition of family factors and social class makes little difference to the overall year difference.

In summary, based on the eighteen countries pooled, we can say that the biggest single factor accounting for the change is work pressure. Other contributing factors are the rise in unsocial hours and working overtime at short notice and, to a lesser extent, job insecurity. Other work resources, like a rise in the proportion of employees with supportive work colleagues, counteract these changes somewhat, but play a much more minor role. The fact that there has been a very modest fall in working hours also counteracts this rise.

Work–Family Conflict, Change over Time: The Cross-National Perspective

The analysis so far has looked at patterns for all eighteen countries, yet these general figures may disguise cross-national variation. There is some reason

to expect differences between countries/regimes: the extent to which economic change influences work–family conflict may be mediated by policy
supports for reconciling work and family life. Such policy supports may also
come under threat during an economic downturn, particularly in countries
where reconciliation policies rely on employer provisions rather than on
statutory entitlements. Thus we expect those in Nordic, and to a lesser extent
in Continental regimes, to be better protected, given statutory entitlements,
both regarding supports for families and also protection of working conditions.[15] Here we expect less of a change in work–family conflict. We expect
Liberal regimes to be more exposed to financial pressures and insecurity,
which is also an issue within Transition countries, though scale of economic
crisis is rather different in these countries, which may be salient.

Alternatively, considering cross-national variation in the depth of economic crisis, one might expect that if crisis is associated with work–family
conflict, it will tend to rise more in countries that have experienced a sharper
economic downturn in the period and a greater rise in unemployment.
Conversely, work–family conflict should fall in countries like Poland, where
unemployment has fallen.

We estimate the model on eighteen countries first with only country differences, and country differences in change over time. Note the primary interest
is not in country differences per se, but country differences in change over
time. Figure 7.1a presents estimates of change over time in the work–family
conflict index by country first without any controls (gross) and then estimated from a model which includes all the work and family factors described
in the previous section. (See Appendix Table A7.2 for full models.)[16]

As was found in all countries together (in Table 7.1a), we see that in most
countries there was a modest rise in work–family conflict. For many countries
this rise was less than 0.1 in the index ranging from 1 to 5 (see Figure 7.1a),
and the differences are not statistically significant. Exceptions are Greece (rise
of 0.4), Portugal (rise of 0.26), the Czech Republic (rise of 0.25), and Estonia
(0.23). Conversely in Poland there was a fall of 0.17 in work–family conflict
experienced by employees in couples (Figure 7.1a). Looking at the effects
after taking account of other work and family factors, the first thing to note
is that country differences are much reduced. Many countries now have zero
change in work–family conflict. Examining the influence of different work

---

[15] The Nordic regime includes Norway, Denmark, Sweden, and Finland. The Continental
regime includes Germany, the Netherlands, and Belgium, the Liberal group includes UK and
Ireland. Spain, Greece, and Portugal are classified as Southern countries and the Czech Republic,
Hungary, Estonia, Poland, Slovenia, and Slovakia as Transition countries. See Chapter 1 for a
discussion of regimes.

[16] We also estimated separate country models and the estimates of change over time by country
are not different.

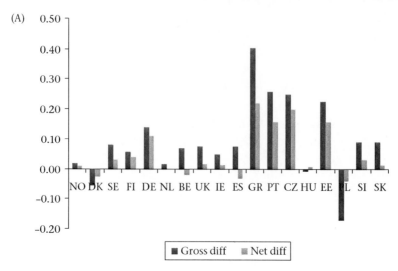

Figure 7.1a. Work–family conflict: change over time by country
Source: European Social Surveys 2004 and 2010.

and family demands and resources, the increase in work pressure plays a key role in understanding country differences in the change in work–family conflict.

In Figure 7.1a, the countries are grouped by regime type, and there are some interesting patterns. For example, two of the three Southern countries, Greece and Portugal, experience a much greater than average rise in work–family conflict and four of the Transition countries also experience a rise—though not Poland or Hungary. However, evidence to support the idea that those in Nordic, and to a lesser extent in Continental regimes, will be protected from change, while those in Liberal and Transition economies would be more exposed, is weak.

If it is not regime type then is there support for the idea that there an association at country level between countries that experience a sharper change in economic fortunes and change in work–family conflict? That is, in countries where the unemployment rate rose more strongly do we also see a more marked increase in work–family conflict? Figure 7.1b plots change in work–family conflict by unemployment rate change. We see a mild positive relationship: in those countries that saw an increase in unemployment, we tend to see a modest rise in work–family conflict. The correlation is 0.30.[17]

---

[17] If we were to plot change over time by an alternative economic change indicator, e.g. GDP change 2004–2010, we find a negative correlation, that is, individuals in countries where GDP has fallen tend to experience a rise in work–family conflict.

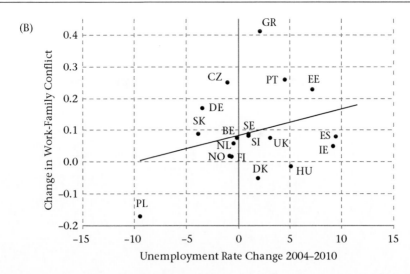

Figure 7.1b. Change in work–family conflict by unemployment rate change 2004–2010
Source: European Social Surveys 2004 and 2010.

We then look at how much of this difference remains when we adjust for the range of other work and family demands and resources shown to be associated with work–family conflict in the previous section. Is country variation in the change in work–family conflict driven by these changes—changes in working hours, scheduling, flexibility, working conditions, insecurity, family circumstances? Continuing to focus on country differences, Figure 7.1c plots the change in work–family conflict after controlling for these factors. Now the positive association between unemployment change and change in work–family conflict is much reduced (Figure 7.1c; correlation now 0.12).

In terms of the 'outliers', the differences between Greece and Poland and the other countries have been much reduced. This is less true of the Czech Republic, Portugal, and Estonia. Note that all five countries still differ significantly in terms of change in work–family conflict from the others. A more detailed explanation of why this is the case would require further individual country analysis which is beyond the scope of this chapter.

What we can conclude is that differences between countries in terms of change over time are modest. There is a tendency for work–family conflict to rise as unemployment rises: much of this can be understood in terms of changes in work and working conditions, particularly work pressure, though residual differences remain between a small number of countries. There are no clear regime patterns that help us understand the association between economic change and change in work–family conflict.

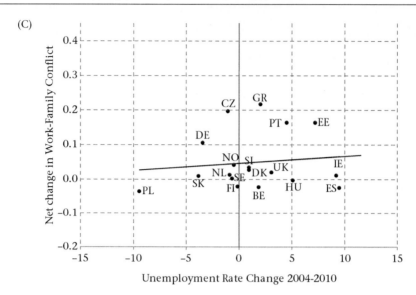

Figure 7.1c. Net change in work–family conflict, controlling for work and family factors, by unemployment rate change 2004–2010

Source: European Social Surveys 2004 and 2010.

Work–Family Conflict in 2010: The Impact of Recent Changes in Individual Circumstances

In this section we adopt a different approach to investigating the impact of economic crisis on work–family conflict. We use direct indicators of change in individual and family circumstances, in an attempt to understand how the economic crisis may impact individuals. We investigate crisis-driven change at three levels: family, firm/organization, and job.

Little previous research has been done on the impact of recent changes in either family situation or jobs on work–family conflict. Our expectations here are drawn from findings above. Firstly, given that financial stress is associated with higher work–family conflict, we might expect that negative change in family circumstances may lead to increased financial strain and increased work–family conflict.

Financial pressures at the workplace may generate greater strain-based conflict which spills over to family life. Given the strong association between working conditions and work–family conflict, changes at the job level are likely to be important.

The first measure of change is cutbacks at the level of the household. This measure focuses on deterioration in economic circumstances over the last three years and captures whether respondents have been exposed to economic pressures in the recent past. There were three statements: 'I have had to manage on a lower household income'; 'I have had to draw on my savings or get into debt to cover ordinary living expenses'; 'I have had to cut back on holidays or new household equipment'. Responses were measured on a six-point scale with 0 representing that this did not apply at all and 6 that it applied 'a great deal'. These responses were found to combine into a reliable scale with an alpha of 0.83.

Second, we measure difficulties at the firm or organization the individual works for, to see whether difficulties at firm level will influence work–family conflict. This is a combination of these two questions: 'During the last three years, would you say that the organization for which you work has experienced...a great deal of financial difficulty/some financial difficulty/ not much financial difficulty or no financial difficulty?' 'And during the last three years, would you say that the number of people employed at the organization for which you work for has 1 "decreased a lot" to 5 "increased a lot"?'[18]

Third, we measure negative job changes in the past three years. These are measured individually, as we wish to distinguish different potential associations. They are all measured as dummy variables in response to the following questions: 'Please tell me whether or not each of the following has happened to you in the last three years. Have you...had to take a reduction in pay/had to work shorter hours/had less security in your job/had to do less interesting work?'[19]

Table 7.4. The association of change in past three years with work–family conflict, 2010, accounting for other work and family factors

Model I	Coefficient	Significance
Other work and family factors (see Tables 7.2a and 7.2b) plus		
Changes in past 3 years:		
Cutbacks in family spending (index)	0.034	***
Firm difficulties (scale)	0.027	***
Job change: reduction in pay	−0.021	n.s
Job change: reduction in hours	0.017	n.s
Job change: reduction in security	0.092	***
Job change: job has become less interesting	0.111	***
_cons	0.577	***
R-squared	0.274	
N of cases	7810	

Note: Controls used are those from Tables 7.2a and 7.2b. See Appendix Table A7.3 for the full model.

[18] For those who changed job or employer in the past three years the reference period was 'since starting your current job'.
[19] Of course as Russell and McGinnity (2013) note in their analysis of Ireland, some of these changes may be independent of recession, and would also be reported in an economic boom.

Table 7.4 presents the impact of these changes, after controlling for the factors discussed above. We are thus interested in the impact of these changes, in addition to the factors we already know are associated with work–family conflict from the pooled model, including working hours, job insecurity, and financial stress. Here we see that even after controlling for current financial stress, having to make cutbacks in family spending has a positive and significant association with work–family conflict (Table 7.4). Consistent with expectations, firm difficulties in the past three years are also associated with higher work–family conflict. Difficulties at firm level are clearly associated with the individual experience of work–family conflict. The precise mechanism through which this operates would require further investigation.

In terms of changes to individual jobs, we find that neither a reduction in pay nor reduction in hours in the past three years impacts on work–family conflict.[20] There certainly is an impact of reduced security on work–family conflict though, even after controlling for current insecurity (which also increases conflict). It is very clear that subjective job insecurity is associated with work–family conflict.

An interesting finding is the particularly marked impact of doing a less interesting job. Those whose job has become less interesting in the past three years have higher work–family conflict.[21] This suggests that the trade-off between work and family life has shifted. Those whose job is less interesting may now feel the tension more keenly. This underlines the role that interest and motivation in paid work play in reducing work–family conflict—having an interesting job could be seen as a 'motivational resource' (Drobnic and Guillen Rodriguez 2011).

Summary and Conclusion

The overall picture is of a modest rise in the experience of work–family conflict between 2004 and 2010. Various factors play a role in explaining this—most noticeably the rise in work pressure between the two years, but also the rise in unsocial hours and working overtime at short notice, and the rise in job insecurity. Other factors—like a rise in the proportion of employees with supportive work colleagues and a fall in working hours—counteract these

---

[20] Even if the index of family spending cutbacks is excluded from this model, a reduction in pay is not significantly associated with work–family conflict.

[21] Given the relatively high proportion of respondents in Denmark, Norway, and Sweden reporting that their job had become less interesting, we also estimate this model without these countries. The result is not affected by the inclusion of these countries and potentially different interpretation of this question there.

changes somewhat, but play a much more minor role. Even after accounting for all of these changes, a small rise in work–family conflict remains between the two time periods.

In general cross-national differences in the change in average work–family conflict over time are small. No strong patterning of change over time by regime emerges, although changes are more pronounced in the Southern and Transition countries. If anything there is more support for the idea that it is countries experiencing sharper economic change, whether positive (Poland) or negative (Greece), where mean reports of work–family conflict change more dramatically. Though here too there are notable exceptions—Ireland and Spain, for example, where unemployment has risen sharply, but work–family conflict has not.

Finally, there is clear evidence of the aggravating effect of the economic crisis on work–family conflict from a detailed analysis of recent changes to individual circumstances preceding the 2010 survey. We find increased pressures associated with economic crisis from both the family—in terms of financial pressure—and from the workplace—both firm change, and also increased job insecurity in the past three years, are associated with higher work–family conflict for the individual. Moreover, negative changes in the nature of people's everyday work activities also had a effect: those whose jobs has become less interesting report higher levels of work–family conflict. A more detailed qualitative study on the mechanisms by which these changes impact on work–family conflict would be valuable in deepening our understanding of this. These findings extend our knowledge of the sources of work–family conflict. Aside from job insecurity, other factors associated with economic crisis such as cutbacks in family income, financial strain, and firm pressures have received much less attention in the analysis of the experience of work–family conflict.

Overall, the chapter shows that to understand change over time in work–family conflict, we need to look both at changes in the workplace, and at changes in family situations. It underlines the fact that many couples are struggling to find employment arrangements that are economically viable and beneficial to partners and children, and economic crisis can intensify that struggle.

Appendix

Table A7.1. Models of change over time in work–family conflict, showing all controls

	Model A Change over time		Model B Add working hours		Model C Add time flexibility schedule		Model D Add work pressure		Model E Add other work factors		Model F Add home factors and class	
	Coeff	Sig.	Coeff	Sig.	Coeff	Sig.	Coeff	Sig.	Coeff	Sig.	Coeff	
2010	0.074	***	0.077	***	0.065	***	0.042	***	0.039	***	0.037	**
Age	−0.004	***	−0.003	***	−0.002	**	−0.002	**	−0.002	***	−0.001	n.s
Female	−0.025	n.s	0.114	***	0.113	***	0.073	***	0.087	***	0.086	***
Working hours (usual)			0.020	***	0.015	***	0.011	***	0.011	***	0.011	***
Partner inactive			0.051	***	0.136	***	0.118	***	0.111	***	0.099	***
Partner unemployed			0.109	*	0.214	***	0.205	***	0.197	***	0.179	***
Partners' long hours (40+)					−0.002	n.s	0.006	n.s	0.009	n.s	0.003	n.s
Work evenings or nights					0.132	***	0.124	***	0.117	***	0.109	***
Overtime, short notice					0.334	***	0.236	***	0.221	***	0.222	***
Work weekends					0.171	***	0.175	***	0.166	***	0.179	***
Partner unsocial hours					0.040	***	0.033	***	0.032	***	0.031	***
Can decide start/finish times						***	0.069	***	0.047	***	0.025	n.s
Job Pressure Index							0.271	***	0.259	***	0.242	***
Safety at risk							0.991	***	0.173	***	0.178	***
Job Control index work organization, policy and pace									0.019	***	0.014	***
Support from colleagues									−0.039	**	−0.040	**
Insecure about job									0.083	***	0.080	***
Any child under age 6									0.000	***	0.056	***
No. of children									0.000	***	0.014	*
Difficult or very difficult to live on current income											0.170	***
Gender role attitudes											0.001	n.s
Professional class											0.204	***
Intermediate class											0.076	***
Const.	2.702	***	1.783	***	1.696	***	0.991	***	0.926	***	0.823	***
R sq.	0.005		0.074		0.136		0.234		0.241		0.251	
N.cases	15,985		15,985		15,985		15,985		15,985		15,985	

Table A7.2. Models of change over time in country differences, with and without controls

	Model G 'GROSS'(Just country diffs)		Model H 'NET' (With controls*)	
	Coeff	Sig	Coeff	Sig
Year 2010	0.080	n.s	−0.026	n.s
Belgium	0.102	n.s	0.129	*
Czech	0.069	n.s	0.024	n.s
Germany	0.114	n.s	0.069	n.s
Denmark	0.044	n.s	0.051	n.s
Estonia	0.136	*	0.134	*
Finland	0.216	***	0.192	***
UK	0.131	n.s	0.007	n.s
Greece	−0.146	*	−0.112	n.s
Hungary	0.021	n.s	−0.069	n.s
Ireland	−0.306	***	−0.314	***
Netherlands	−0.097	n.s	−0.066	n.s
Norway	−0.001	n.s	−0.031	n.s
Poland	0.235	***	0.069	n.s
Portugal	−0.410	***	−0.474	***
Sweden	0.071	n.s	0.040	n.s
Slovenia	−0.041	n.s	−0.132	n.s
Slovakia	0.293	***	0.015	n.s
Belgium 2010	−0.006	n.s	0.003	n.s
Czech 2010	0.168	*	0.223	**
Germany 2010	0.055	n.s	0.132	*
Denmark 2010	−0.133	n.s	0.001	n.s
Estonia 2010	0.146	n.s	0.191	**
Finland 2010	−0.022	n.s	0.066	n.s
UK 2010	−0.005	n.s	0.045	n.s
Greece 2010	0.330	***	0.243	**
Hungary 2010	−0.094	n.s	0.021	n.s
Ireland 2010	−0.032	n.s	0.036	n.s
Netherlands 2010	−0.064	n.s	0.027	n.s
Norway 2010	−0.061	n.s	0.038	n.s
Poland 2010	−0.252	**	−0.011	n.s
Portugal 2010	0.178	n.s	0.191	*
Sweden 2010	0.002	n.s	0.053	n.s
Slovenia 2010	0.007	n.s	0.060	n.s
Slovakia 2010	0.008	n.s	0.035	n.s
_cons	2.494	***	0.901	***
R square	0.048		0.292	

Note: Controls used are those from model F. N of cases is 15,985. For each country the difference between years is calculated as the year coefficient plus the country*year interaction term.

Table A7.3. Work–family conflict in 2010, including changes in work and family in past three years

	Model I Coeff	Sig
Age	0.002	*
Female	0.091	***
Working hours (usual)	0.013	***
Partner inactive	0.097	***
Partner unemployed	0.117	**
Partners' long hours (over 40)	0.020	n.s
Work evenings or nights	0.087	***
Work overtime, short notice	0.213	***
Work weekends	0.156	***
Partner unsocial hours	0.021	**
Can decide start/finish times	0.017	n.s
Job Pressure Index	0.245	***
Health/safety at risk	0.181	***
Job Control index work organization, policy and pace	0.013	***
Support from colleagues	−0.031	n.s
Insecure about job	0.029	n.s
Any child under age 6	0.061	**
No. of children	0.015	n.s
Difficult or very difficult to live on current income	0.093	***
Gender role attitudes	−0.010	n.s
Professional/managerial class	0.181	***
Intermediate class	0.033	n.s
Cutbacks in family spending (index)	0.034	***
Firm difficulties (scale)	0.027	***
Job change: reduction in pay	−0.021	n.s
Job change: reduction in hours	0.017	n.s
Job change: reduction in security	0.092	***
Job change: job has become less interesting	0.111	***
Constant	0.577	***
R square	0.274	
N of cases	7810	

8

Economic Downturn and Work Motivation

Nadia Steiber

Introduction

This chapter investigates the consequences of economic downturn for work motivation. A concern is that the experience of economic vulnerability during the economic crisis may have long-lasting repercussions for the population's employment commitment. This issue is of central relevance for the competitiveness of Europe that is increasingly dependent on a highly skilled and motivated workforce (Gallie 2007a). In knowledge-based economies the skilled and intrinsically motivated employee is an important asset. The growth of the service sector, rapid technological change, and the upskilling of the occupational structure are likely to extend the need for employers to give their workers greater discretion over the way they do their jobs (see Chapter 5 in this volume). Close supervisory control and tight performance monitoring become less effective, rendering employers more dependent on their workers' motivation.

For the purpose of the present study, the concept of employment commitment (EC) is particularly useful, because it allows for the analysis of work attitudes also among those not currently employed—as opposed to organizational commitment (OC).[1] Of central interest is the part of employee commitment that is not a function of the income that employment generates. This type of commitment has a long research tradition that goes back to the work of Marie Jahoda (1982) and the idea that employment offers manifest economic

[1] Whereas the latter refers to the commitment to a particular firm or organization ('loyalty'), the former refers to the commitment to employment per se ('to having a job'). Another reason for the focus on EC in this study is that the implications of a strong identification with a particular work organization are ambivalent. OC may increase employee moral dependence, while hampering the functioning of labour markets (when employees are prepared to continue working for a particular employer in the presence of more attractive alternatives).

rewards but also more latent ones (e.g. employment provides opportunities for social contacts, for identity building, and for personal development). Peter Warr (1982) coined the term 'non-financial employment commitment' for this classic concept that refers to the degree to which individuals find gratification in employment that goes beyond monetary compensation.[2] It taps the degree to which individuals see part of the value of having a job in the work itself, thus representing a measure of intrinsic work orientation. For brevity, we use the term 'employment commitment' to denote such non-financial employment commitment. Employment commitment has important implications for work-related behaviours. Warr and Lovatt (1977) found that more committed individuals re-enter employment more quickly after the closure of their workplaces than their peers with low commitment. Moreover, through its affinity with intrinsic work motivation, employment commitment is commonly assumed to be associated with greater work effort and performance (Dysvik and Kuvaas 2011).

The specific aim of the present study is to investigate the impact of the economic crisis on employment commitment, using cross-national comparative data from Round 5 of the European Social Survey for nineteen countries.[3] This involves the study of the consequences of unemployment but also of other 'correlates of economic crises' (Burchell 1992) such as widespread feelings of job insecurity among the employed. The empirical analysis presented covers the impact of involuntary job loss on the commitment of those affected as well as the impact of workforce reductions on 'surviving employees'. The central research aim is to test for potential variations across societal contexts in terms of economic crisis effects on non-financial employment commitment.

The Debates: Economic Crisis Effects on Employment Commitment

The latent deprivation model outlined by Jahoda (1982) has been widely used to explain the negative effects of unemployment in terms of psychological impairment. It suggests that individuals who lose their jobs are deprived of the social-psychological functions of employment with negative implications for their well-being (see also Chapter 9 in this volume). The classic 'deprivation theory' has also been used to explain unemployment effects on individuals'

---

[2] The concept has often been measured as individual responses to the 'lottery question', asking whether or not individuals would like to have a paid job even if they won the lottery—or whether they would stop working.

[3] These include Belgium, the Czech Republic, Denmark, Estonia, Finland, France, Germany, Greece, Hungary, Ireland, the Netherlands, Norway, Poland, Portugal, Slovakia, Slovenia, Spain, Sweden, and the United Kingdom.

work orientation. The experience of job loss is arguably an event that makes individuals more aware of the (lost) rewards in employment that go beyond monetary compensation.[4] Those losing their jobs are held to develop a less instrumental orientation to work. This contention receives support from various studies that find higher non-financial employment commitment among the unemployed than among those in paid work (e.g. Warr 1982; Gallie et al. 1994; Gallie and Alm 2000).

While most prior research finds greater employment commitment among the unemployed than among the employed and argues this to result from an increased salience and appreciation of the latent functions of work upon job loss (latent deprivation model) it has also been suggested that long spells of unemployment may have the opposite effect (e.g. Hyggen 2008). The long-term unemployed may start putting a lower value on paid work. They may adapt to their situation of joblessness and increasingly appreciate their non-work time (cf. Warr and Jackson 1984). In a similar vein, the literature on unemployment hysteresis as an aggregate phenomenon suggests that extended periods of high unemployment—at the regional level—lead to a weakening of the social norm of working or in other words to a 'culture of unemployment' (see Oesch and Lipps 2012 for a critical discussion of this perspective). Accounting for the large number of empirical studies that show the detrimental and long-lasting effects of unemployment for individuals in terms of economic welfare, physical and psychological health, and social integration (e.g. McKee-Ryan et al. 2005; Burgard et al. 2007; Dieckhoff and Gash 2012; see also Chapter 9 in this volume), however, the opposing view is that individuals do not adapt to unemployment. As unemployment continues, economic deprivation and social isolation grow and well-being continues to decline (Clark 2006; Gordo 2006; Oesch and Lipps 2012). The wish to re-enter employment for financial but also for non-financial reasons may thus not vanish at longer durations of unemployment (e.g. Warr and Jackson 1984).

Under the assumption that the anticipation of deprivation has similar effects as has actual job loss, the latent deprivation model has also been used to predict the well-being effects of job insecurity (e.g. Burchell 2009). It has been shown, for instance, that the negative consequences for well-being are of equal magnitude for those who 'merely' fear losing their job and those who actually do lose their job (e.g. De Witte 1999, 2005). Yet, whether this view is compatible with the mechanisms underlying the 'latent deprivation effect' of unemployment on individuals' work values can be questioned. Arguably, only the actual event of job loss triggers an increased salience of work's latent

---

[4] These 'latent functions of employment' pertain to the provision of a time structure, social contacts, status and identity, and regular activity and participation in collective purposes.

functions. The anticipation of job loss, by contrast, may trigger psychological processes aimed at reducing cognitive dissonance. This may lead to a devaluation of the job and its rewards in order to reduce the perceived costs of its potential loss.

An alternative framework for understanding the consequences of job insecurity is psychological contract theory. The perceptions of the employer and the employee about the mutual obligations implied in the employment relationship (in addition to the formal provisions) form part of an unwritten 'psychological contract' (Rousseau 1995). Such contracts have been argued to entail, among others, an expectation on the part of employees that their work effort will be reciprocated with a secure and stable work environment. A lack of job security may hence be perceived by employees as a breach of the psychological contract, with negative consequences for their work-related sentiments and behaviours (for review, see e.g. De Witte 2005). Also employee downsizing, i.e. the shedding of part of the workforce, has been argued to represent a violation of this contract (e.g. Morrison and Robinson 1997). In fact, available research shows that apart from the actual victims of lay-off also 'surviving' workers suffer from downsizing (Brockner et al. 1992). They tend to withdraw psychologically and reduce their work involvement and organizational commitment. The phenomenon has been labelled 'survivor syndrome' and has consistently been documented in a large number of studies (see Datta et al. 2010, for review). There is some evidence that the undesirable effects of downsizing on surviving workers' morale can be mitigated by employee perceptions of procedural fairness and the quality of social relations in downsizing enterprises (transparency, timely information of workforce, supervisor support, presence of cooperative unions), while they are accentuated by a perceived threat of future lay-offs and the level of job loss anxiety among the remaining employees (Armstrong-Stassen 1994; Sverke et al. 2005; van den Berg and Masi 2005; Cooper et al. 2012).

Institutional mediation

The consequences of job insecurity, job loss, and unemployment are likely to be mediated by socio-institutional contexts. Conceivably, the effects of job insecurity—i.e. a high subjective risk of job loss—are dependent on individuals' perception of the consequences of losing their job. The latter has been argued to be influenced by the access to alternative sources of income that are not dependent on re-employment and the perceived prospects of finding a new job (e.g. Anderson and Pontusson 2007). The costs of job loss defined in this way can be expected to be lower in countries that provide generous unemployment insurance and/or where the chances for a swift re-employment are high owing to a strong demand for labour and/or active labour market policies (ALMP) that help workers to quickly find a new and adequate job. It has been argued that 'job loss anxiety' (defined as the fear of the economic consequences of job loss) should be lower in countries that exhibit greater commitment and resources to ALMP, and/or that offer generous unemployment benefits for an extended period of time. Moreover, in terms of economic conditions, a low level of unemployment will generally increase individuals' chances of swift job replacement and may thus help contain the costs of job loss. Conversely, job loss anxiety may be particularly pronounced in *dual* labour markets that protect incumbent workers from job loss while reducing the chances of labour market entry for labour market outsiders. Job loss in *dual* labour markets can be characterized as less likely yet more costly.

With regard to work values, it has been argued that a lack of 'economic security'—a basic human need (Maslow 1954)—fosters the development of a more instrumental orientation to work (e.g. Alderfer 1969). Job loss anxiety for economic reasons would thus be expected to hamper intrinsic work motivation (e.g. Gallie 2007a).

Similar expectations can be formulated for the case of downsizing. The survivor syndrome may be less pronounced in countries that have established so-called 'flexicurity systems'(Wilthagen and Tros 2004), i.e. that offer income protection in case of job loss and that support those laid off with finding new jobs (e.g. van den Berg and Masi 2005). Such systems promote protected economic dynamism and mobility and may in fact have an influence on the psychological contract. They may arguably lower employees' expectations as regards the stability of jobs and mute their resistance and psychological reaction to mass redundancy.

The impact of unemployment is described by two rivalling perspectives. On the one hand, it is argued that the economic consequences of job loss pin individuals down at the lower end of the hierarchy of needs, making them unsusceptible to the intrinsic rewards of work (e.g. Gallie 2007a; Steiber 2008). The latent deprivation model, on the other hand, suggests that losing one's job is an event that makes us more susceptible to and appreciative of these rewards and the psycho-social functions of employment more generally. This latter model would also suggest that the loss of one's job will be all the more significant the higher the intrinsic quality of the lost job (e.g. challenging, interesting work that allowed for self-development).

Based on the needs-based model of job loss, the expectations as regards institutional mediation are similar to those spelled out above in terms of job insecurity. In countries where unemployment is more strongly associated with the risk of falling into poverty and where spells of unemployment tend to be long, a potential negative effect of unemployment on employment commitment would be expected to be stronger. Based on the latent deprivation model, by contrast, we would expect unemployment to have a positive impact on employment commitment, and more strongly so in countries where jobs tend to be of high intrinsic quality (e.g. in Scandinavia as shown by Gallie 2003, 2011; Chapter 5 in this volume). When employment tends to be precarious, involves irregular or unsocial time structures, and offers few rewards in terms of meaningful activity and status, by contrast, job loss may not be adequately described as latent deprivation. In other words, when employment offers few non-economic rewards, we may not expect to find significant differences between the employment commitment of those in paid work when compared to the unemployed.

The Great Recession: incidence of job insecurity and unemployment

It is of particular interest and timely to study the impact of job insecurity and unemployment in times of economic crisis and labour market recession. The impact of the Great Recession on European labour markets has been intense and its effects are likely to be long-lasting. The number of individuals unemployed in the EU-27 reached a new high of 25.5 million in summer 2012 (European Commission 2012), representing about 10.5 per cent of the labour force (Eurostat, seasonally adjusted). Moreover, in EU labour markets youth unemployment (below age 25) tends to be twice as high as unemployment for the total population.

High unemployment rates affect also those employed since they put pressure on wages and may generally exert a negative effect on the conditions of work (Chapter 5 in this volume). Moreover, high unemployment rates are likely to increase feelings of economic insecurity. Mau et al. (2012) examine the incidence of subjective insecurity using European Social Survey data from 2008/2009. Defining those who answered 'very likely' or 'likely' to the question 'How likely is it that during the next 12 months you will be unemployed and looking for work for at least four consecutive weeks?' as insecure, they find shares of insecurely employed individuals of more than 20 per cent in 10 out of 19 countries (and more than 30 per cent in the Czech Republic, Estonia, Greece, Hungary, Ireland, Portugal, and Spain).[5] Using the same source of data, Chung and van Oorschot (2011) identify rising unemployment rates as empirical correlates of high employment insecurity at the country level. Due to the tight link between rising unemployment and rising employment insecurity, an empirical relation between higher unemployment and lower well-being among the employed can be observed (Luechinger et al. 2010). Overall, we see that a large part of the workforce has been affected by the

[5] The lowest rates are found in Denmark, Finland, the Netherlands, Norway, and Sweden (less than 15 per cent).

Great Recession (and additional parts of the population have been affected indirectly via family and household contexts).[6] In Spain and Greece, for instance, about a quarter of the labour force was unemployed, while another third of employed persons strongly feared losing their jobs and not being able to find a replacement job swiftly.

Employment commitment, welfare and employment regimes

Employment commitment is likely to be shaped by individual circumstances and experiences throughout the life course (such as the experience of unemployment) but also by more stable values that have an institutional imprint (such as by the *work ethic* of a community). Regarding the latter, it has been argued that the Scandinavian welfare model embeds a system of norms that 'emphasises the non-financial values of having a job' (Hult and Stattin 2009: 109). Support for this perspective from available research appears fairly strong. Comparing the Nordic countries with Germany, Britain, and the United States, it is the Scandinavian countries that tend to stand out with exceptionally strong intrinsic work values and employment commitment (Hult and Svallfors 2002; Gallie 2007a; Esser 2009). *Universal welfare regimes* thus appear to be conducive to value placed on the intrinsic rewards of work. The underlying assumption of the welfare regime argument is that the characteristics of welfare regimes affect employment commitment via the provision of economic security (e.g. in case of job loss or illness). The classic Maslovian logic suggests that in countries that provide for citizens' basic security needs, providing encompassing social protection, individuals progress to higher-order needs and develop post-materialist values (including a non-financial motivation to work).

Welfare regimes differ in the degree to which a decent level of economic security is regarded as a social right and to which individuals can maintain a livelihood when they are not employed (conceptualized as *decommodification*, see Esping-Andersen 1990: 47). In terms of Esping-Andersen's typology the *social democratic regime* is characterized by the provision of security irrespective of employment status (universalistic, high decommodification). *Corporatist regimes* offer security—yet the level of protection varies rather strongly depending on individuals' employment history (modest decommodification). *Liberal regimes* provide only minimum, means-based protection and welfare is strongly dependent on employment status (low

---

[6] Mau et al. (2012) find that in 11 out of 18 EU countries, more than a quarter of respondents report that it is likely that during the next 12 months there will be some periods when they do not have enough money to cover their household necessities (with shares of above 40 per cent in Estonia, Greece, Hungary, and Portugal).

decommodification, 'workfare'). The *Southern European* countries have been grouped in a separate regime that features a fragmented system of income support and a high level of familialism, meaning that the family (and not the state) plays the central role in social protection and service provision (Leibfried 1992; Ferrera 1996; Bonoli 1997; Karamessini 2008; Tavora 2012). Welfare state development in post-communist Europe has initially been viewed as tending towards the liberal regime (see Aidukaite 2009 for review). The transition was in fact accompanied by wide-ranging welfare retrenchment. Yet, the historical legacy of comprehensive social policy during communist times may still play a role (as well as pre-communist influences of the Austrian-Hungarian Empire, cf. Aspalter et al. 2009). Authors who have attempted to define the unique characteristics of the welfare states that have emerged in post-communist, Eastern-Central Europe suggest that they feature low benefit levels and weak decommodification. Neesham and Tache (2010) suggest to divide the Eastern-Central European countries into two distinct groups: the Baltic states, Slovakia, Bulgaria, and Romania on the one side ('self-reliance' model displaying neo-liberal features) and the Czech Republic, Hungary, Poland, and Slovenia on the other ('welfare' model with similarities to the Continental model, see also Aspalter et al. 2009 for similar conclusions).

From a *welfare regime perspective*, the social-democratic welfare states of Scandinavia would be thought to be most conducive to the development of intrinsic work motivation as they cater for the basic security needs of all citizens irrespective of their employment status. Somewhat less favourable conditions are offered in corporatist regimes—for which Germany is the prime example—where security is insurance-based. Much less security is offered in the Liberal regimes (the United Kingdom tending to serve as the European prime example), in the residual welfare states of Southern Europe, and in the emerging welfare states of Eastern-Central Europe (especially in the 'self-reliance' model), where economic security is strongly related to employment status and where even those in employment are relatively weakly protected from poverty when compared to Continental and Northern Europe (e.g. Lohmann 2009: 494).

Departing from the welfare regime logic, *production regime theory* offers a second institutional account of cross-national variations in employment commitment (Soskice 1999). The argument is that employers in 'coordinated market economies' (CMEs) favour the 'high road' of capitalism, which aims for the production of high-quality goods and services. Therefore, firms are more strongly dependent on a highly skilled workforce able to work autonomously and willing to exert discretionary effort. The expectation would thus be that employers in CMEs—that theoretically include the ideal-typical corporatist regime of Germany as well as the social-democratic regimes of Scandinavia (Hall and Soskice 2001)—are more likely to create jobs and work environments that are conducive to work motivation than are employers in 'liberal market economies' (LMEs). A third theoretical perspective that allows for a differentiation within CMEs and hence accounts for the distinctiveness of Scandinavia is the *employment regimes perspective*, developed by Gallie (2007b). Based on a variety of institutional structures related to employment and industrial relations policies, three employment regimes are differentiated: the *inclusive* Nordic regime, the *dualist* Continental and Southern European regimes, and the *market-oriented*, Liberal regime. The upshot of this theoretical perspective for the purposes of this study is that we would expect the *inclusive regime* to be most conducive to the development of non-materialist work values. Ideal-typically, it aims at high levels of employment and features tight labour markets that can be argued to strengthen the power of labour. Stronger dependence of employers on employees due to skill scarcity would be expected to encourage employers to create favourable employment conditions in order to foster employees' work motivation. Moreover, *inclusive regimes* would be expected to foster employment commitment among all population groups, while *dualist* and *market regimes* provide protection only for part of the workforce, i.e. the more highly skilled core,[7] and may thus be expected to feature lower average levels of commitment as well as greater social inequality.

A related argument by Gallie (2007a) is that the Scandinavian countries stand out with regard to policies aimed at improving the quality of jobs, and that it may be for this reason that they have been shown to rank very high in terms of intrinsic work motivation. In fact, Scandinavia does stand out as providing exceptionally high levels of individual task discretion, job variety, opportunities for the use of initiative, participation in decision-making, continuing training, and subjective job security (e.g. Gallie 2003, 2007a, 2007b, 2009; Dieckhoff and Steiber 2011; Esser and Olsen 2012; Mau et al. 2012; see also Chapters 4 and 5 in this volume).

For the purposes of this study, typologies of *unemployment welfare regimes* are of central interest. The available literature (Gallie and Paugam 2000; Ferragina et al. 2012; Pfeifer 2012) pertains to the situation in the late 1990s or early 2000s and may thus not account for recent developments. Therefore, a rough classification of the countries covered in this study is developed,

---

[7] The Continental and the Mediterranean countries tend to be characterized as *dualist*, given employment systems that feature pronounced labour market segmentation (Gallie 2007b; Karamessini 2008). Employment regulation provides strong protection, good employment conditions, and generous welfare support only for the core workforce (and not for temporary workers, for instance). Regulation in *market* regimes is generally weak since institutional protection of employment is perceived as hindering the functioning of the market. The most vulnerable groups in market regimes tend to be the lower skilled who have least individual market power.

drawing on recent data pertaining to the universalism and generosity of unemployment protection systems and to the level of expenditure on active labour market policies (ALMP). To obtain a measure of how deteriorating labour market conditions during the crisis have related to benefit recipiency, the OECD (2011) compares the change in the number of benefit recipients with the change in the number of unemployed persons—relative to pre-crisis levels. The resulting measure of 'marginal coverage' (i.e. the extent to which expanding recipiency kept pace with growing unemployment) in the first year after crisis onset[8] is used as a first indicator. It covers regular and extended benefits as well as unemployment assistance. The second indicator is based on recent information about the level of income replacement offered by the system. Use is made of unemployment replacement rates for average workers who live in couples with two children (from Van Vliet and Caminada 2012). Following Allard (2005), the measures of universalism and generosity are combined in a single metric by multiplying the replacement with the coverage rate (see x-axis in Figure 8.1). Apart from the generosity of the unemployment system, it is also of central relevance to what extent the state supports the unemployed with finding new jobs that match their skills. To gauge the extent to which this is the case a third indicator measures the expenditure on ALMP per person wanting to work (see y-axis in Figure 8.1; see Appendix Table A8.5 for exact values).

Denmark and Belgium fit the classic description of *flexicurity regimes*, with very high expenditure on ALMP and medium levels of generosity. Norway and the Netherlands also feature high ALMP expenditures that are combined with more generous income replacement, however. The second 'tier' in terms of ALMP consists of Finland, France, Sweden, and Ireland. Yet, while Finland and Ireland offer benefits to most of the newly unemployed, this is less the case in France and Sweden.[9] The third 'tier' in terms of ALMP involves all of the Transition countries and Southern Europe. Within these, Hungary, Poland, Greece, Slovakia, and Estonia appear to form a *sub-protective* group, while medium levels of generosity are granted in Spain and the Czech Republic, and fairly high ones in Portugal and Slovenia.

---

[8] This refers to the 'trough' in the OECD harmonized unemployment rate, defined as the start of the longest spell of consecutive increase of the quarterly OECD harmonized unemployment rates since 2006Q1.

[9] The low figure for income replacement for Sweden derives from the OECD estimate of marginal coverage. Apparently the number of recipients of unemployment benefits in Sweden has not increased during the crisis despite a substantial increase in unemployment. This reflects recent trends in the Swedish unemployment insurance system (rising membership fees in 2007) that have encouraged substantial parts of the workforce to leave unemployment insurance before crisis onset. The system was again reformed in summer 2009 as a reaction to falling coverage. Yet, coverage rates continued to decline. The number of individuals receiving benefits divided by the number of unemployed (coverage) dropped from 77 per cent in 2006 to 32 per cent in 2010 (Anxo and Ericson 2011).

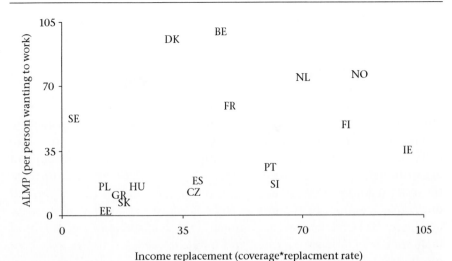

Figure 8.1. The characteristics of unemployment welfare systems after crisis onset

Sources: Coverage rate (OECD), replacement rate (Van Vliet and Caminada 2012), and ALMP expenditure (EUROSTAT). The original values (see Appendix Table A8.5) have been rescaled, the value of 100 being allocated to the country with the highest original value. Coverage not available for Germany—its ALMP value is 40.7; ALMP value not available for the UK—its replacement value is 38.6.

The expectation would be that job insecurity shows less of a negative effect on employment commitment in countries that exhibit greater commitment and resources to ALMP and/or that offer generous unemployment benefits for an extended period of time, while they may be particularly pronounced in the countries that feature sub-protective systems.

Assessing Employment Commitment

European Social Survey data (Round 5) from nineteen countries are used to investigate how individuals' non-financial motivation to be employed is shaped by job insecurity, redundancy, and unemployment. Non-financial employment commitment is measured by the question: 'To what extent do you agree or disagree with the following statement: I would enjoy having a paid job even if I did not need the money' (5-point scale). It has been asked of the general population including those not currently in paid work. In this study, the focus is on the population of 'core working age', i.e. between the ages of 20 and 64.

The investigation of the 'impact' of unemployment in this study is based on cross-sectional data. We do not observe the same individual's employment commitment before and after job loss. Instead, to gauge the extent to which unemployment makes a difference, those currently in paid work are compared with those currently unemployed, controlling for the differential composition of these two groups through regression analysis. The individual level ordinary least squares (OLS) regressions control for a range of individual characteristics: age, sex, years of education, years of work experience and its square term,[10] and subjective health (5-point scale). Moreover, in contrast to much of the previous work, the data at hand provide information on the type and quality of the job—either referring to the current or the last job. Hence controls can also be introduced for compositional differences in terms of occupational class (ESeC-scheme), firm size, type of work organization (central or local government, other public sector, state-owned enterprise, private firm, or self-employed), and level of discretion (used as a proxy for intrinsic job quality, see Chapter 5 in this volume).[11] The availability of detailed information on respondents' past jobs and their employment history allows for the attainment of a greater degree of comparability between the comparison groups. This mitigates potential problems of selectivity that may derive from otherwise unobserved differences between those currently unemployed and those employed. For instance, if the unemployed have a higher risk of unemployment due to weaker work morale (reverse causality), the analyses may underestimate potential positive effects of unemployment on employment commitment. Another possibility is that those currently unemployed tend to have lower-quality jobs and for this reason show a weaker work motivation. Again this would lead to an underestimation of a potential positive effect of unemployment on employment commitment, unless job quality is controlled for. Taking account of the characteristics of previous jobs implies that the analysis is restricted to persons who ever had a paid job. Our comparison group of unemployed persons thus consists of individuals who have had at least one job before they became unemployed, who report that their current main activity is being unemployed and who report wanting a job (irrespective of whether or not they are actively looking for a job).[12]

To investigate the impact of the duration of unemployment, the analyses are restricted to those currently unemployed. Duration effects are estimated as the difference in employment commitment between those who have recently

[10] This measure counts the number of years the respondent has been in paid work. To account for the possibility that experience and employment commitment are not related in a linear fashion, a squared term is included.

[11] An additive discretion index was formed using three indicators measuring how management at work allows/allowed the respondent 'to decide how your own daily work is/was organized, to influence policy decisions about the activities of the organization, and to choose or change your pace of work' (Cronbach's alpha: 0.85).

[12] Unemployment is identified based on the measure of current main activity, that differentiates between in paid work (including employees and self-employed), education, illness/disability, retirement, housework/care, unemployment involving active job search, and unemployment wanting a job but not actively looking for a job.

become unemployed (up to three months ago), with those who are unemployed for 4–11 months (long spell) or 12–36 months already (long-term unemployed). The analyses are based on cross-sectional comparisons, using OLS regression analyses that control for compositional differences between the three groups (age, sex, education, prior work experience, type and quality of the last job before unemployment). Selectivity bias may be an issue in the event that those with greater commitment are less likely to remain unemployed for extended periods of time (i.e. sample attrition). This would lead to an underestimation of the employment commitment of the long-term unemployed. Yet, the extensive list of controls used in the analyses should mitigate such biases.

Finally, the study investigates the impact of job insecurity and of employee downsizing. Job insecurity is defined as employees' perceptions of the risk of job loss. It is measured with a simple question that asks respondents how much they agree or disagree with the statement 'my job is secure' on a scale from 1 to 5.[13] The regression analyses apply a wide set of controls aiming to mitigate potential selection bias that may result from differences between those in secure and those in more insecure jobs that are not in fact related to job security. For instance, those in insecure jobs may tend to have less rewarding jobs and for this reason show lower commitment. To preclude the possibility that effects are driven by such mechanisms, extensive controls for *job quality* (i.e. discretion, learning requirements, advancement opportunities, time pressure, and subjective pay adequacy) are included (in addition to the standard controls for age, sex, health, education, years of experience, occupational class, firm size, type of work organization, and past experience of unemployment). Employees who experienced *downsizing* are identified as those who state that during the last three years the number of people employed at the organization for which they work has decreased 'a lot' (other answer possibilities: decreased a little, not changed, increased a little, increased a lot).

Non-financial employment commitment is measured on a 5-point scale and is reasonably well distributed. Therefore, linear regression analyses are carried out and their results reported. To test for the robustness of results also logit models are run using a binary measure of commitment (defining those who agree that they would enjoy having a paid job even if they did not need the money as 'committed'). In both versions, country dummies are included in all regressions that pool data for more than one country. Moreover, all of the regressions are weighted.[14]

With the aim to explain cross-national variations in the effect of unemployment and of job insecurity, a two-step strategy to modelling two-level

---

[13] The annotation in the questionnaire reads: 'Secure' in the sense of an actual or implied promise/likelihood of continued employment with that employer.

[14] These weights combine the design weights available in the European Social Survey with additional weights that account also for sample composition in terms of occupational class and rates of unemployment.

data is applied. In the first step, separate regression models for each country are estimated. In the second step, the estimated parameters from the first step (i.e. the country-specific unemployment and insecurity effects) are used as the dependent variable in country-level regressions. These step-two regressions are weighted using the weighting scheme proposed by Lewis and Linzer (2005). The advantage of this procedure is that it accounts for the differential precision with which unemployment/insecurity effects are estimated at country level. More precisely estimated effects receive a greater weight.

Country Differences in Employment Commitment

When comparing the share of the population who agree that they would enjoy having a paid job even if they did not need the money across countries (Table 8.1) little support for the *welfare regime perspective* can be discerned. In

Table 8.1 Share of non-financially committed population by country, age 20–64

	Total	Significance of country differences	Male	Female	Significance of gender gap	Sample sizes N (Total)
Nordic						
Norway	78%	higher ***	76%	80%	female (*)	1,127
Denmark	74%	higher ***	73%	74%	n.s.	1,083
Sweden	60%	(ref)	57%	63%	female (*)	995
Finland	53%	lower **	49%	57%	female **	1,294
Continental						
Netherlands	77%	higher ***	75%	79%	n.s.	1,320
Germany	70%	higher ***	67%	73%	female *	2,136
Belgium	66%	higher *	65%	67%	n.s.	1,242
France	55%	lower *	50%	60%	female **	1,251
Liberal						
Ireland	61%	n.s.	62%	60%	n.s.	1,882
UK	61%	n.s.	58%	64%	female *	1,668
South						
Greece	54%	lower**	58%	50%	male **	1,939
Portugal	49%	lower ***	52%	46%	male (*)	1,293
Spain	47%	lower ***	48%	46%	n.s.	1,425
Transition						
Hungary	56%	n.s.	54%	58%	n.s.	1,137
Slovakia	54%	lower*	53%	55%	n.s.	1,298
Poland	54%	lower **	50%	57%	female *	1,257
Estonia	47%	lower ***	41%	53%	female ***	1,205
Slovenia	39%	lower ***	34%	44%	female **	982
Czech	25%	lower ***	25%	25%	n.s.	1,760

Notes: ***difference to Sweden (ref) or difference between women and men sig at p<0.001; **p<0.01; *p<0.05; (*) p<0.10; n.s. not statistically significant. Source: ESS Round 5.

contrast to earlier findings, the Nordic countries do not generally stand out as those with the highest levels of commitment. The high-commitment countries are Norway (78 per cent) and the Netherlands (77 per cent), followed by Denmark (74 per cent) and Germany (70 per cent). There is little homogeneity within the regimes. Among the Nordic countries, Finland stands out as having exceptionally low levels of commitment (53 per cent).[15] Moreover, Sweden features similar levels of commitment as the UK and Ireland. In Continental Europe, France features comparatively low commitment (55 per cent). In summary, as shown in Figure 8.2, the Continental European countries (excluding France) feature equally high levels of employment commitment as the Scandinavian countries. The lowest levels of employment commitment are found for Southern Europe (50 per cent on average) and the Transition countries (46 per cent on average).

The lack of difference between Sweden and Finland (CMEs) on the one side and the UK and Ireland (LMEs) on the other suggests that the *production regime perspective* is also not of help for explaining differences employment commitment across countries. The alternative framework of explanation that

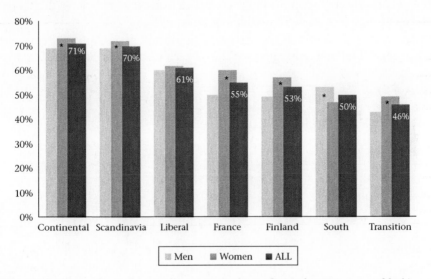

Figure 8.2. Share of non-financially committed population by regime, age 20–64

Notes: Continental: Belgium, Germany, and the Netherlands; *Scandinavia*: Denmark, Norway, and Sweden; *Liberal*: Ireland and the UK; *South*: Greece, Portugal, and Spain; *Transition*: Czech Republic, Estonia, Hungary, Poland, Slovakia, and Slovenia. * Statistically significant gender difference ($p<0.05$). See Appendix Table A8.1 for sex-specific values and sample sizes. Source: ESS Round 5.

[15] See also Turunen (2011) discussing the Finnish exceptionalism in terms of Nordic employment commitment.

puts the quality of jobs rather than the quality of social protection to the fore (Gallie 2007a) receives more support. As illustrated in Figure 8.3, a medium strong correlation (r = 0.62) is found between the average level of discretion in a country (a central indicator of job quality, see Chapter 5 in this volume) and the average level of employment commitment.

A prediction deriving from the *employment regimes perspective* is that average job quality and employment commitment will be lower in *dualist* and *market* regimes than in *inclusive* regimes, since the latter arguably provide employee rights and social protection to all. In *dualist* and *market* regimes, by contrast, only advantaged segments of the labour market and population are protected and able to negotiated favourable work conditions. As shown in Figure 8.4, empirical evidence would support such contentions insofar as higher ine-quality in employment commitment (measured by its variance) within the population is related to lower average levels of employment commitment (correlation of r = –0.68). Finland and France stand out with an exceptionally high variance in employment commitment, i.e. many respondents report a very low or very high level of commitment, while in many other countries a greater share of the population report medium levels of commitment, or in the case of the high-commitment countries (e.g. Norway, the Netherlands) cluster at high levels of employment commitment.

In the pooled sample (all countries), a significant gender difference to the advantage of women emerges (not shown). There are large variations across

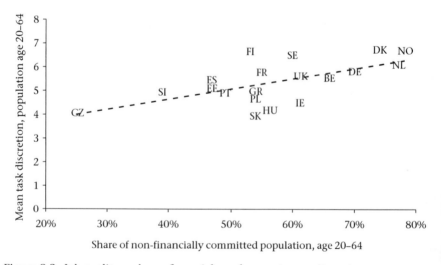

Figure 8.3. Job quality and non-financial employment commitment

Notes: For values shown in x-axis, see Table 8.1. Values on the y-axis pertain to the weighted average of task discretion (in current or last job). Correlation coefficient R = 0.62.

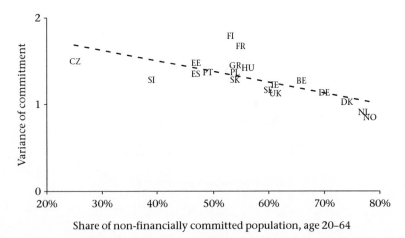

Figure 8.4. Level and variance of non-financial employment commitment

Notes: For values shown in x-axis, see Table 8.1. Values on the y-axis pertain to the variance in commitment (lower values signify a stronger social work norm). Correlation coefficient R = –0.68.

countries, however (Table 8.1). Women report significantly higher commitment than men in nine countries (Norway, Sweden, Finland, Germany, France, Poland, Estonia, Slovenia, UK), while it is the other way around in Greece and Portugal. No significant gender gap is found in the remaining eight countries.

Unemployment Effects

Unemployment effects are estimated by way of regression analysis. They pertain to the difference in employment commitment between those currently in paid work and those currently unemployed. The results for the pooled sample that includes all nineteen countries suggest that unemployed men and women have a higher average commitment than their counterparts in paid work (applying a rigorous set of controls, see Appendix Table A8.2 for detail on underlying regression model). There is great variation across countries, however, as summarized in Figure 8.5 for five country groups (Finland and France are analysed separately, accounting for their exceptionalism in terms of the *level* of commitment in the general population, see above).

The latent deprivation model that predicts positive unemployment effects appears to hold only in Southern Europe and the Transition countries. The predictions from the model show, for instance, that in Southern Europe, the

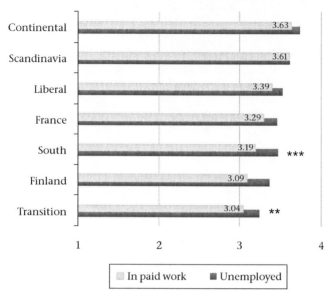

Figure 8.5 Unemployment effects on non-financial employment commitment

Notes: Population age 20–64; predicted margins from weighted OLS regressions. See Figure 8.2 for detail on country-groups; see Appendix Tables A8.2 and A8.3 for detail on underlying regression analyses and sex-specific results. ***sig at p<0.001; ** p<0.01.

unemployed show an average commitment of 3.19 (on a scale from 1 to 5) as compared to a value of 3.46 for the unemployed. Notably, this latter value is still far below the average levels of commitment found in Continental Europe and Scandinavia.

Closer inspection in terms of potential differences between women and men and between different age groups (Appendix Table A8.2) shows significant and positive unemployment effects also for Finish women and marginally significant positive effects for Continental European men. The Southern European cluster is the only one where positive effects can be found for both men and women. In the Transition countries, the effect is mainly visible for women. Quite interestingly, clear age differences in the strength of unemployment effects can be discerned. Significant positive effects are found for persons in their 20s and 30s, but not for their counterparts aged 40 and over (see Figure 8.6).

In a next step, it is tested whether the 'regime approach' masks important within-regime differences. To this end country-specific estimates of unemployment effects are obtained through country-by-country regression analyses on pooled samples of women and men (for sample size reasons, no gender-specific effects can be estimated at country level). These analyses show that the positive effect found for the South (Figure 8.5) is in fact driven by

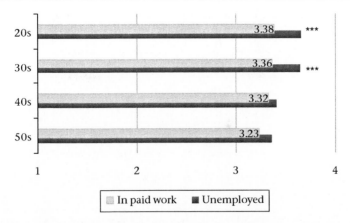

Figure 8.6. Unemployment effects on non-financial employment commitment, by age
Notes: Population age 20–59, divided into four groups. Values are predicted margins from weighted OLS regressions. For detail, see Appendix Tables A8.2 and A8.3. *** sig at p<0.001.

Greece and Spain, while no significant effect is found for Portugal. Significant positive effects of unemployment are furthermore found for Poland and Estonia (the latter marginally significant at the 90 per cent level). To explain the cross-country variation in effect strength, two-step multi-level models are estimated. The nineteen country-specific effect estimates are regressed on a set of country-level factors. The macro-level regressions use weights that give greater influence to more precisely estimated effects (that arise due to higher total samples and subsamples of unemployed persons).

Needs-based motivation theory holds that in countries where the economic costs of job loss are high, the unemployed are less likely to show intrinsic work motivation. The expectation would be that high/increasing unemployment and in particular a high incidence of long-term unemployment is associated with more negative—or less positive—effects of unemployment. Those who expect the development of a 'culture of unemployment' in countries characterized by a longer history of high unemployment would also predict extended periods of high unemployment to be associated with more negative effects of unemployment.

Yet, regressing the country-specific effect estimates on a set of macro-level characteristics related to unemployment (Table 8.2) suggests that the opposite is the case. Unemployment effects tend to be most strongly positive in countries that feature high rates of unemployment (M1). The share of long-term unemployment, however, does not show a significant association, either as a sole predictor (not shown) or when the unemployment rate is retained as a control (M2). The same is the case for a measure of unemployment growth as a result of the crisis (M3). All models control for the selectivity of the newly

Table 8.2. Country-level regressions modelling country-specific unemployment effects

	M1	M2	M3	M4	M5	M6	M7
Unemployment rate, year of survey	0.021*	0.023*					
Rate of long-term unemployment		−0.002					
Unemployment growth during crisis (through-peak)			0.014				
Mean unemployment rate 2000–2010				0.032	0.047**		
Income replacement (index)						−0.002	
ALMP (per person wanting to work)							−0.054(*)
Selectivity of newly unemployed	−0.029	−0.033	−0.022	−0.009	−0.019	−0.000	−0.023
R-squared	0.38	0.41	0.11	0.32	0.57	0.08	0.35
N	19	19	19	19	18	18	18

Notes: Coefficients from linear regression models for estimated dependent variables (using the EDVREG routine in STATA). The dependent variable consists of country-specific unemployment effects calculated using weighted OLS regression. The predictors are macro-level variables (see Appendix Tables A8.4 and A8.5 for detail). M5 excludes Slovakia; M6 excludes Germany; M7 excludes the UK for lack of data availability. **$p<0.01$; *$p<0.05$; (*) $p<0.10$.

unemployed in terms of their educational composition.[16] The negative coefficients support the expectation that smaller positive unemployment effects are found in countries where the newly unemployment are disproportionally low-skilled (although the effect does not reach statistical significance, the control unveils a slightly stronger main effect). Plotting the country-specific effects against the unemployment rate (Figure 8.7) shows a correlation of medium strength ($r = 0.43$) and a number of outliers. Poland, for instance, for which a positive unemployment effect is found, has a relatively low rate of unemployment and does thus not fit into this framework of explanation. M4 tests the impact of the average rate of unemployment during the period 2000–2010. No significant effect is found, the reason being that Slovakia represents a clear outlier. Removing Slovakia from the analysis (M5) reveals a rather strong and significant effect, suggesting that the positive effect of unemployment tends to be larger in countries where unemployment has been high throughout the 2000s. In fact, together with the selectivity control, M5 arrives at explaining 57 per cent of the variance in unemployment effects across countries. The gross association between estimated unemployment

---

[16] To account for the selective nature of workforce reductions in the sense that in many countries the lower skilled have been more affected by job loss than their more highly skilled counterparts, a control is introduced for the disproportionate increase in unemployment rates among the low skilled (cf. Appendix Table A8.4).

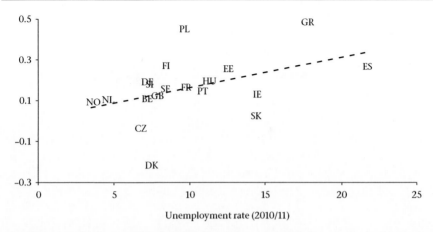

Figure 8.7. Unemployment effects, by unemployment rate

Notes: Relation between estimated unemployment effects and unemployment rates (see Appendix Table A8.4 for rates pertaining to the year in which the majority of the ESS interviews were collected within each country). Correlation coefficient R = 0.43.

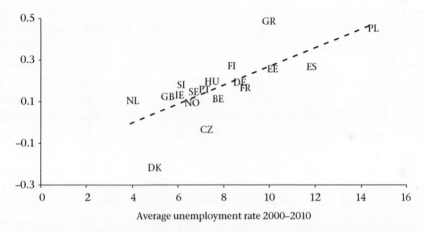

Figure 8.8. Unemployment effects, by average level of unemployment 2000–2010

Notes: Relation between estimated unemployment effects and the average unemployment rate in the years 2000–2010 (see Appendix Table A8.4). This figure excludes Slovakia as it represents a clear outlier with very high unemployment in the 2000s, yet a zero unemployment effect. R = 0.73.

effects and the average rate unemployment in the naught years is illustrated in Figure 8.8 (r = 0.73). In sum, the analyses so far suggest that the jobless are more likely to say that they would like to work irrespective of financial need in countries that are more used to the perils of high unemployment. It appears that in countries where unemployment has long been prevalent, the population is more aware of unemployment's damaging effects (from own or significant others' experience) and/or employment's latent functions.

A test of policy effects furthermore suggests that unemployment effects are more likely to be positive in countries that have weakly developed systems of ALMP (marginally significant, see M7). Neither the indicators measuring the universalism and generosity of the unemployment system (tested separately, not shown) nor the multiplicative combination of these two measures (M6) show an association with the strength of unemployment effects. The contention that latent deprivation effects of unemployment may be stronger in countries where jobs tend to be of high intrinsic quality (and where the average level of commitment thus tends to be high), is also not supported. Instead, the association of effect strength and the average level of task discretion is negative (but fails to reach statistical significance, not shown).

Unemployment duration

It has been argued that long spells of unemployment may have demotivating effects due to adaption processes at the individual or aggregate level. Testing this contention using regression analyses that apply rigorous controls for the composition of those in short unemployment spells when compared to the longer-term unemployed suggests that the duration of unemployment has no impact on employment commitment in the Nordic, Continental, and Southern European countries (see Appendix Table A8.6 for underlying regression analyses). The only significant effect is found for Ireland (which drives the effect for the Liberal countries shown in Figure 8.9) where commitment increases with unemployment

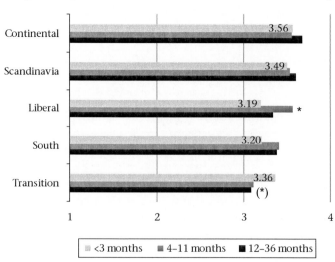

Figure 8.9. Non-financial employment commitment, by unemployment duration

Notes: Currently unemployed age 20–64. Values are predicted margins from weighted OLS regressions (see Appendix Table A8.6 for detail). *difference to short spell (<3 months) sig at p<0.05; (*) p<0.10.

duration. Finally, there is some indication (marginally significant) that in the Transition countries, commitment may in fact decline with the duration of unemployment.[17]

Combining the results for initial and longer-term unemployment, the following conclusions can be drawn: In Southern Europe unemployment tends to be associated with higher commitment—also at longer durations. In Ireland, it is only after some time that the unemployed increase their commitment to a significant degree. Finally, in the Transition countries, unemployment *per se* is associated with higher commitment when compared to those in paid work, but the level of commitment appears to decrease with the duration of unemployment. The latter result may either be interpreted in light of the dire economic situation of the unemployed in the Transition countries, while to some degree it may also derive from sample attrition that biases the long-term unemployed towards lower commitment. Conversely, an underestimation of the commitment of the long-term unemployed would render the positive effects found for Ireland (and in tendency also in Continental and Southern Europe and Scandinavia) even stronger.

Insecurity Effects

The implications of job insecurity are generally expected to be negative for commitment, based on motivation theory that assumes a hierarchy of needs, psychological contract theory, or a cognitive dissonance rationale (see above). Moreover, it has been argued that the impact of a perceived risk of job loss may be smaller in countries that provide generous income protection in case of unemployment and even more so in countries that have established flexicurity models that also involve the implementation of an extensive system of ALMP (Burchell 1992, 2011). The opposite would apply to dual labour markets. This general frame of theoretical expectation tends to be supported by the results shown in Figure 8.10 (see also Appendix Table A8.7 for underlying regression analyses). The most strongly negative effects of job insecurity are found in Southern Europe, where job insecurity is widespread (see also Chapter 6 in this volume) and where the economic consequences of job loss are pronounced. Marginally significant effects are found for the Continental European countries that have—along with Southern Europe—been characterized as *dualist* (Gallie 2007a) and for the Transition countries where income protection in case of job loss is minimal (see earlier in this chapter).

---

[17] Unfortunately the samples of those currently unemployed are too small to allow for country-by-country analyses (except for Ireland and Spain).

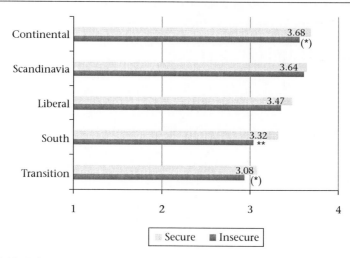

Figure 8.10. Job insecurity effects on non-financial employment commitment

Notes: Employees age 20–64. Values are predicted margins from weighted OLS regressions. See Appendix Table A8.7 for detail on regression analyses. **insecurity effect sig at p<0.01; (*) p<0.10.

As noted earlier, job insecurity tends to come along with other characteristics of jobs (e.g. lower pay, higher work pressure, less discretion, and fewer opportunities for advancement) that are likely to dampen employees' motivation. Models that include controls for these dimensions (which confirm a strong and significant impact of these variables on commitment, not shown) do in fact account for a substantial part of the lower average commitment found for the insecurely employed (cf. comparison of M1 and M2 in Appendix Table A8.7). The final results which control for job quality differences can thus be considered fairly conservative, rendering strong support to the notion that job insecurity has negative implications for commitment in some countries.

Attempts to explore socio-institutional mediators of the differential strength of insecurity effects across countries support the theoretical expectation that job insecurity is less likely to be associated with lower commitment in countries that have established strong systems of ALMP (see M2 and M3 in Table 8.3). Model M4 (which excludes Sweden for which the income replacement index may underestimate coverage of the newly unemployed) furthermore suggests that a tight safety net in terms of income protection in case of unemployment (replacement rate multiplied by coverage) also serves to reduce the impact of job insecurity. The contention that insecurity may have less of an impact on employment commitment in contexts of low unemployment does not receive empirical support (Table 8.3).

The youngest (i.e. those in their 20s) are found to suffer most strongly from job insecurity (Appendix Table A8.7). This reflects the specific situation of the

Table 8.3. Country-level regressions modelling country-specific insecurity effects

	M1	M2	M3	M4
Income replacement (index)	0.002		0.002	0.003(*)
ALMP (per person wanting to work)		0.048(*)	0.046(*)	0.047(*)
Unemployment rate, year of survey	−0.003	0.008	0.011	0.013
R-squared	0.12	0.21	0.29	0.38
N	18	18	17	16

Notes: Coefficients from linear regression models for estimated dependent variables (using the EDVREG routine in STATA). The dependent variable consists of country-specific insecurity effects calculated using weighted OLS regression. The predictors are macro-level variables (see Appendix Tables A8.4 and A8.5 for detail). M1 excludes Germany; M2 and M3 exclude the UK, M3 excludes both for lack of data availability. M4 excludes Sweden due to extremely low coverage rates from the OECD. (*) sig at p<0.10.

young who tend to be less well insured against unemployment than their older counterparts due to shorter employment histories (OECD 2011: 52). Moreover the young may be aware that unemployment early in the career has the most detrimental impact on future outcomes and is thus associated with especially high costs.

To get an idea of how job insecurity and actual job loss work together, the subsequent analyses are based on a sample that includes employees with job security, employees without job security, and the currently unemployed (Appendix Table A8.8 and Figure 8.11).[18] Comparing the unemployed with employees who do not think that their jobs are secure suggests a positive 'unemployment effect' in Southern Europe and in the Transition and Continental European countries. In the latter two country groups, the unemployed are also found to be more committed than the securely employed, while this is not the case for Southern Europe. Here, the unemployment effect is strongly dependent on whether it is viewed vis-à-vis the more or less securely employed.

Negative effects of job insecurity on commitment in Southern Europe and the Transition countries are of particular concern given the prevalence of job insecurity in these regions, i.e. 42 per cent of the Southern European and 38 per cent of the Eastern-Central European *labour force* (for methodological reasons, here somewhat narrowly defined as the sum of the dependently employed and the unemployed) are in insecure employment (e.g. as compared to 22 per cent in Scandinavia and 25 per cent in Continental Europe, see Appendix Table A8.8).

[18] These results for job insecurity are based on a dummy variable and not on the 4-point scale used in the analyses shown in Figure 8.10; hence the reason for lower statistical significance in Continental and Transition countries.

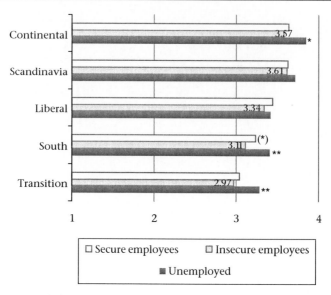

Figure 8.11. Effects of job insecurity and unemployment

Notes: Values are predicted margins from weighted OLS regressions. Insecure employees are those who say that the statement 'My job is secure'is not at all true or only a little true. See Appendix Table A8.8 for detail on underlying regressions. Significant difference to insecure employees (ref) **p<0.01; *p<0.05; (*) p<0.10.

Survivor syndrome?

The management literature argues that employee downsizing, i.e. shedding a substantial part of the workforce, may have negative implications also for those not affected by redundancy. The survivor syndrome has been described as including negative implications for work-related attitudes and motivation. Very little empirical support for this expectation can be found in terms of employment commitment (Appendix Table A8.9 and Figure 8.12).

No significant effects can be discerned for Scandinavia, the Southern European countries, or Liberal countries. For the Transition countries a negative effect is found, which is rendered smaller once a control is introduced for job insecurity (as would be expected). The effect eventually loses statistical significance when rigorous controls for the differential quality of jobs between those affected or unaffected by downsizing are added (M3). For Continental Europe, a positive effect of downsizing (M1) is found which increases in size once a control is introduced for job insecurity (since workers in downsizing enterprises tend to be less secure, see M2). Interestingly, the positive effect remains when rigorous job quality controls are added (M3)

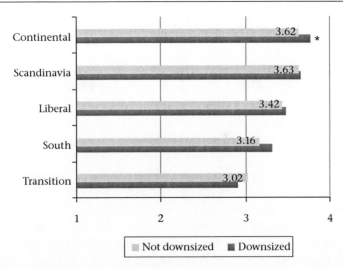

Figure 8.12. Employee downsizing and non-financial employment commitments

Notes: Employees age 20–64. Values are predicted margins from weighted OLS regressions. For detail on underlying regression analyses, see Appendix Table A8.9. *sig at p<0.001.

and also when a control for workers' achievement orientation[19] is introduced. The fact that the latter control is not able to explain away the positive effect of downsizing arguably suggests that it is not due to positive selection in the sense that more committed workers are more likely to 'survive' mass redundancies. An explanation for the non-observation of a survivor syndrome in terms of employment commitment may be that in times of economic crisis, downsizing is more likely to be perceived as 'legitimate' by employees, rather than as a violation of the psychological contract. Especially when surviving employees do not fear future lay-offs they may in fact be grateful for their situation and reappraise the value of being able to keep their jobs.

Conclusions

Non-financial employment commitment varies a great deal across Europe. The shares of the committed population range from highs of 70–80 per cent in Denmark, Germany, the Netherlands, and Norway to lows of below 50 per cent in some Southern and Eastern-Central European countries. Regime perspectives are deemed as being of limited help for explaining such cross-national differences. Instead it appears that economic affluence combined

---

[19] Computed as a summative index of two personality measures: 'important to show abilities and be admired' and 'important to be successful and that people recognize achievements' (6-point scales, Cronbach's alpha of 0.71).

with an institutionalized work ethic (i.e. low variance in employment commitment) and high levels of intrinsic job quality are characteristics of countries that are conducive to intrinsic work motivation.

Having established the 'baseline' of average commitment levels in the different countries, the study was then concerned with the potential consequences of the Great Recession on employment commitment in Europe. In the wake of the economic crisis in Europe, many workers fear losing their jobs and are left feeling economically vulnerable. In many cases this fear has led to actual job loss, with strongly rising rates of unemployment in some parts of Europe and for some population groups. The present study finds that these correlates of labour market recession—*unemployment* and *job insecurity*—have a differential impact on individuals' employment commitment across societal contexts. Some support for the latent deprivation model of unemployment is found insofar as the unemployed are found to be more committed than those in paid work in some parts of Southern and Eastern-Central Europe. As suggested by the results of two-step multi-level models, such 'unemployment effects' tend to be more strongly positive in regions of Europe that have been plagued by persistently high unemployment throughout the 2000s. Incidentally, these also tend to be the countries where perceptions of job insecurity are prevalent. In fact, a positive 'unemployment effect' is not observable in Southern Europe when the unemployed are compared only with those in secure jobs. It would thus be mistaken to expect a boost in work motivation in crisis-ridden countries. In some of the hardest hit countries, the unemployed appear to have higher employment commitment than the employed, which is, however, mostly due to the dismal levels of job quality in these countries which dampens workers' employment commitment to an alarmingly low level. On a more optimistic note, it is reassuring to see that long-term unemployment does not appear to damage individuals' work morale in most countries, despite its negative well-being implications. Although with cross-sectional data the direction of causality in the association between unemployment and commitment cannot be established, the finding that unemployment is not associated with lower commitment is relevant, especially since endogeneity issues would only lead to an underestimation of positive motivation effects.

A more worrisome pattern of results is found for job insecurity. A suspicion on the part of workers that their jobs may not be very secure is prevalent in Southern Europe. This is also where strong negative effects of such perceptions on employment commitment are found. Marginally significant negative effects are furthermore established for Continental Europe and the Transition countries. These effects pertain to the impact of subjective job insecurity, net of other (potentially demotivating) characteristics associated with insecure jobs. The results of two-step multi-level models suggest that negative insecurity effects tend to be more strongly pronounced where the economic costs of job loss are higher, i.e. in countries that offer low levels of income protection and that lack effective systems of ALMP. This finding corroborates the assumption that job insecurity is less likely to be a source of anxiety and demotivation in societal contexts where insecure workers can be more confident that, even if they do lose their job, they are unlikely to be unemployed for long and will not experience great financial loss.

In summary, negative implications for employees' intrinsic work motivation as a result of the crisis may be expected in those regions of Europe where job insecurity soars. The Great Recession has been deep and long; hence, widespread perceptions of insecurity are likely to remain a central feature of employment relations in Europe. There is evidence from longitudinal studies which shows that individuals do not get used to insecurity even when it lasts for a long time (see Burchell 2011). The impact of job insecurity can thus not be expected to fade with the duration of the crisis. The more likely scenario appears to be the one where intrinsic work motivation will further decline especially in those regions of Europe where it has already been comparatively low to start with. The share of the population affected by unemployment is in many countries relatively small compared to the one affected by job loss anxiety. The latter thus appears most relevant for judging the overall impact of the Great Recession on intrinsic work motivation. And it is the young generation that is most dramatically affected by the economic downturn and that—as suggested by the results of this study—also reacts most strongly to job insecurity.

Appendix

Table A8.1. Share of non-financially committed population by regime, age 20–64

	Total	Male	Female	N
Continental	71% n.s.	69% n.s.	73% n.s.	4,698
Scandinavia	70% (ref)	69% (ref)	72% (ref)	3,205
Liberal	61% ***	60% ***	62% ***	3,350
France	55% ***	50% ***	60% ***	1,251
Finland	53% ***	49% ***	57% ***	1,294
South	50% ***	53% ***	47% ***	4,657
Transition	46% ***	43% ***	49% ***	7,636

Notes: *** sig at $p<0.001$; n.s. not significant. Source: ESS Round 5.

Economic Crisis, Quality of Work, and Social Integration

Table A8.2. Unemployment effects, population age 20–64

	Total	Male	Female	N
Continental	0.11	0.24(*)	–0.05	4,322
Scandinavia	0.00	–0.08	0.09	3,077
Liberal	0.12	0.21*	–0.02	3,126
France	0.16	0.35	–0.10	1,190
Finland	0.27	0.13	0.55*	1,245
South	0.27***	0.26**	0.33***	3,720
Transition	0.19**	0.14	0.22*	6,567
ALL countries	0.17***	0.18***	0.15**	24,201
Age 20s	0.27***	0.31**	0.19*	4,092
Age 30s	0.27***	0.24*	0.33***	5,443
Age 40s	0.08	0.09	0.04	6,070
Age 50s	0.12	0.04	0.19(*)	5,767

Notes: Coefficients refer to the effect of current unemployment (ref: paid work), based on weighted OLS regressions of employment commitment on *main activity* (paid work, education, disabled, retired, *unemployed*, home-maker, or other). Control for age (5 groups), sex (in pooled models), health, years of education, years of work experience and its square term, and (either for current or last job) occupational class, firm size, type of work organization (public, private or self-employed), and *job quality (discretion)*. Country dummies are included in all regressions that pool data for more than one country. *** sig at p<0.001; **p<0.01; *p<0.05; (*) p<0.10. Source: ESS Round 5.

Table A8.3 Predicted margins for paid work and unemployment

	in paid work		unemployed		N
	mean	in %	mean	in %	
Continental	3.63	71%	3.73	73%	4,322
Scandinavia	3.61	71%	3.61	69%	3,077
Liberal	3.39	62%	3.51	66%	3,126
France	3.29	56%	3.45	60%	1,190
South	3.19	50%	3.46	60%	1,245
Finland	3.09	52%	3.36	57%	3,720
Transition	3.04	44%	3.23	51%	6,567
Age 20s	3.38	60%	3.65	68%	4,092
Age 30s	3.36	59%	3.64	67%	5,443
Age 40s	3.32	57%	3.40	60%	6,070
Age 50s	3.23	54%	3.35	58%	5,767

Notes: Predicted margins from weighted OLS regression as shown in Appendix Table A8.2. Predicted shares of non-financially committed population from logit regressions. Source: ESS Round 5.

Table A8.4. Macro-level characteristics pertaining to unemployment

	UR age 20–64 (survey year)	Long-term UR (survey year)	Average UR (2000–2010)	Increase in UR (through-peak)	Selectivity index
	[1]	[2]	[3]	[4]	[5]
Nordic					
Norway	3.5	22.9	6.5	1.2	2.0
Denmark	7.4	21.6	4.9	4.6	3.0
Sweden	8.4	20.6	6.8	2.9	3.5
Finland	8.4	25.2	8.3	2.6	2.4
Continental					
Netherlands	4.5	30.6	3.9	1.5	1.6
Germany	7.1	49.7	8.6	0.5	0.2
Belgium	7.2	49.5	7.7	1.3	-0.1
France	9.7	42.7	8.9	2.3	1.9
Liberal					
Ireland	14.4	59.4	6.1	10.4	4.9
UK	7.8	36.0	5.6	2.8	2.1
South					
Greece	17.7	49.5	9.9	6.6	1.0
Portugal	11.0	54.0	7.1	3.6	2.9
Spain	21.7	41.7	11.8	12.6	6.9
Transition					
Hungary	11.2	49.8	7.4	4.5	5.0
Slovakia	14.4	64.1	15.4	5.7	0.7
Poland	9.6	31.0	14.5	2.8	3.9
Estonia	12.5	57.3	10.1	14.9	3.0
Slovenia	7.3	45.4	6.1	3.9	4.5
Czech	6.7	40.0	7.2	3.4	4.8

Notes: [1] Unemployment rate (in %) for age group 20–64, pertaining to the year in which the majority of the ESS interviews were collected within each country (2010/2011); source: EUROSTAT. [2] Long-term unemployment (12 months or more) in age group 20–64 as a % of total unemployment in survey year (2010/211); source: EUROSTAT [lfsq_upgal]; [3] Mean of harmonized unemployment rate for the years 2000–2010; source: EUROSTAT; [4] Difference of unemployment rate between peak and through. Trough (peak) dates are defined as the start of the longest spell of consecutive increase (decrease) of the quarterly harmonized unemployment rates since 2006Q1; source: OECD *Economic Outlook 2011* <http://dx.doi.org/10.1787/888932479325>. [5] Index measuring the disproportionate increase in unemployment among the low skilled. It is computed by the author based on figures from EUROSTAT [lfsq_urgaed for age group 20–64] as follows: The change in the unemployment rate (UR) for the medium and high-skilled (ISCED 3–6) between 2008Q1 and 2010Q1 has been subtracted from the change in the UR for the low-skilled (ISCED 0–2) in the same period. The outcome pertains to the trend difference in UR expressed in % points. A higher value indicates that the increase in unemployment has disproportionally fallen on the low-skilled.

Table A8.5. Macro-level characteristics pertaining to unemployment systems

	Replacement rate (average worker)	Marginal coverage rate	Income replacement Index	ALMP (as % of GDP)	ALMP (per person wanting to work)
	[1]	[2]	[3]	[4]	[5]
Nordic					
Norway	0.71	107.9	76.6	0.510	5008.9
Denmark	0.64	44.1	28.2	1.407	6304.2
Sweden	0.53	5.8	3.1	0.812	3485.9
Finland	0.60	122.1	73.3	0.861	3249.5
Continental					
Netherlands	0.71	87.3	62.0	0.780	4911.5
Germany	0.71	n.a.	n.a.	0.558	2676.7
Belgium	0.56	73.3	41.1	1.268	6577.8
France	0.70	62.0	43.4	0.826	3899.8
Liberal					
Ireland	0.59	151.1	89.1	0.746	2327.9
UK	0.41	83.9	34.4	n.a.	n.a.
South					
Greece	0.42	34.5	14.5	0.216	746.6
Portugal	0.75	71.7	53.8	0.580	1710.5
Spain	0.68	51.6	35.1	0.673	1238.4
Transition					
Hungary	0.42	45.2	19.0	0.520	1033.5
Slovakia	0.57	28.1	16.0	0.232	457.9
Poland	0.26	41.8	10.9	0.603	1032.0
Estonia	0.51	21.8	11.1	0.142	175.8
Slovenia	0.64	86.0	55.0	0.339	1114.4
Czech	0.52	65.3	33.9	0.226	845.4

Notes: [1] Net unemployment replacement rate for an average worker, one earner couple with two children (RRAW); source: dataset assembled by Van Vliet and Caminada (2012). [2] Change in the number of unemployment benefit recipients as a percentage of the change in the number of unemployed persons (1st year, including extended benefits and unemployment assistance), reflecting the share of the newly unemployed covered; source: OECD *Employment Outlook 2011* <http://dx.doi.org/10.1787/888932479325>. [3] is the product of replacement rate and coverage. [4] and [5] Expenditure on ALMP referring to interventions that aim to provide people with new skills or experience of work in order to improve their *employability* or that encourage employers to create new jobs and take on unemployed people. Measures include various forms of intervention that 'activate' the unemployed by obliging them to participate in activities in addition to basic job search, with the aim of improving their chances of finding regular employment. The [4] indicator refers to PA3.S2 (sub-indicator) and pertains to the expenditure on ALMP as a % of GDP. The [5] indicator refers to PA3.S1 (sub-indicator) and pertains to the 'Expenditure on ALMP per person wanting to work' (in PPS). Source: EUROSTAT [lmp_ind_exp]; n.a. not available.

Table A8.6. Unemployment duration effects, unemployed age 20–64

	< 3 months	4–11 months	12–36 months	N
Scandinavia	ref	0.04	0.11	153
Continental	ref	–0.01	0.10	226
Liberal	ref	0.37*	0.14	416
South	ref	0.20	0.18	553
Transition	ref	–0.24	–0.27(*)	462
Ireland	ref	0.61*	0.43(*)	313
Spain	ref	0.19	–0.05	189
ALL countries	ref	0.04	0.02	1,988
Male	ref	0.04	0.09	1,091
Female	ref	0.07	–0.03	897

Notes: The sample includes the currently unemployed of age 20–64. Coefficients refer to the effect of the length of unemployment spells (less than 3 months, versus 4–11 months, or 12–36 months), based on weighted OLS regressions. Control for age (5 groups), sex, health, years of education, years of experience and its square term, occupational class, and job quality (last job). Country dummies included in all regressions that pool data for more than one country. *p<0.05; (*) p<0.10. Sample sizes across categories (<3, 4–11, 12–36): *Scandinavia* (61–40–52); *Scandinavia & Finland* (84–67–87); *Continental* (59–48–119); *Liberal* (88–72–256); *South* (128–157–268); *Transition* (96–122–244); *Ireland* (49–49–213); *Spain* (46–63–80). Source: ESS Round 5.

Table A8.7 Effects of job insecurity, employees age 20–64

	M1	M2	Predicted commitment from M2		N	mean insecure
			Very secure	Very insecure		
Continental	–0.07**	–0.04(*)	3.68	3.55	2,575	2.02
Scandinavia	–0.04	–0.01	3.64	3.61	2,115	1.89
Liberal	–0.07*	–0.04	3.47	3.35	1,520	2.33
Transition	–0.10***	–0.05(*)	3.08	2.93	3,452	2.41
South	–0.12***	–0.09**	3.32	3.03	1,772	2.54
ALL countries	–0.07***	–0.04**	3.37	3.26	13,521	2.22
Male	–0.07***	–0.04(*)	3.30	3.20	6,730	2.23
Female	–0.06***	–0.04*	3.44	3.33	6,791	2.21
Age 20s	–0.12***	–0.08*	3.49	3.26	2,248	2.30
Age 30s	–0.05(*)	–0.02	3.38	3.33	3,479	2.25
Age 40s	–0.07**	–0.04(*)	3.37	3.25	3,938	2.21
Age 50s	–0.07**	–0.03	3.27	3.17	3,155	2.18

Notes: The sample includes dependent employees of age 20–64. Coefficients from weighted OLS regressions refer to the effects of job insecurity measured on a 4-point scale. Controls for age (5 groups), sex, health, years of education, years of experience and its square term, occupational class, firm size and type of work organization (public or private or self-employed), and experience of unemployment within the past three years. M2 additionally controls for job quality (discretion, learning, advancement opportunities, time pressure, pay adequacy). Country dummies are included in all regressions. *** sig at p<0.001; **p<0.01; *p<0.05; (*) p<0.10. The predicted values pertain to the marginal effects for very high and very low security on the 4-point scale. Source: ESS Round 5.

Table A8.8. Effects of job insecurity and unemployment

A	secure	insecure	unemployed	secure	insecure	unemployed	N
Continental	ref	−0.06	0.21(*)	0.06	ref	0.27*	2,834
Scandinavia	ref	0.00	0.08	0.00	ref	0.09	2,275
Liberal	ref	−0.10	-0.03	0.10	ref	0.07	1,995
South	ref	−0.11(*)	0.17	0.11(*)	ref	0.29**	2,356
Transition	ref	−0.08	0.23*	0.08	ref	0.31**	4,173
B	secure	insecure	unemployed	secure	insecure	unemployed	
Continental	3.63	3.57	3.84	68.1%	25.4%	6.5%	2,834
Scandinavia	3.62	3.61	3.70	71.7%	22.2%	6.2%	2,275
Liberal	3.44	3.34	3.41	54.8%	33.0%	12.2%	1,995
South	3.23	3.11	3.40	39.0%	42.2%	18.8%	2,356
Transition	3.04	2.97	3.28	51.2%	37.9%	10.9%	4,173

Notes: Employees and currently unemployed age 20–64. A: coefficients from weighted OLS regressions refer to the difference between secure employees (ref in model 1), insecure employees (ref in model 2) and the unemployed. Controls for age (5 groups), sex, health, years of experience and its square term, years of education, unemployment experience in the past three years, and for current or last job occupational class, firm size and type of work organization (public or private or self-employed), and level of discretion. B: shows predicted values and the weighted shares of the sample in the three groups. **$p<0.01$; (*) $p<0.10$.

Table A8.9. Effects of employee downsizing, employees age 20–64

	M1	M2	M3	M4	N	% downsizing
Continental	0.13(*)	0.15*	0.15*	0.15*	2,486	10%
Scandinavia	−0.01	0.01	0.02	0.03	2,073	11%
Liberal	0.06	0.08	0.05	0.05	1,458	14%
South	0.09	0.12	0.14	0.15	1,691	8%
Transition	−0.18*	−0.15(*)	−0.13	−0.13	3,279	9%
ALL countries	−0.03	−0.01	0.00	0.01	12,954	10%
Male	−0.02	0.00	0.01	0.01	6,465	10%
Female	−0.03	−0.01	0.01	0.01	6,489	10%

Notes: Coefficients from weighted OLS regressions refer to the effect of downsizing (i.e. firms have decreased their number of employees *a lot* in the past three years). M1 controls for age (5 groups), sex, health, years of education, years of experience and its square term, experience of unemployment within the past three years, occupational class, firm size and type of work organization (public or private or self-employed). Country dummies included in all regressions that pool data for more than one country. M2 adds control for job insecurity. M3 adds controls for job quality. M4 adds control for achievement orientation (nested models). Source: ESS Round 5.

9

Unemployment and Subjective Well-Being

Helen Russell, Dorothy Watson, and Frances McGinnity

Introduction

The recent recession has seen a rising level of unemployment, falling national wealth, and fiscal crisis in many countries. While there has been much debate about the consequences of these events on financial systems, we consider here the impact on individuals: has the economic crash led to a corresponding decline in subjective well-being among European citizens?

Job loss and unemployment are likely to be a key route through which economic crisis leads to lower well-being. The link between unemployment and reduced subjective well-being has been demonstrated repeatedly in both longitudinal and cross-sectional research across a range of disciplines (see McKee-Ryan et al 2005; Paul and Moser 2009 for recent reviews). These studies have shown that while income loss and financial strain play an important and perhaps primary role in accounting for the distress experienced by the unemployed (Whelan 1992; Gallie et al. 1994) a range of other social and psychological factors are also important. These factors include uncertainty about the future, loss of status and identity, social isolation, and loss of time structure and meaningful purpose (Jahoda 1982; Warr 1987; Fryer 1992; Nordenmark and Strandh 1999). In her classic study Jahoda places a particular emphasis on the erosion of social and community relationships during unemployment due to the stigma of job loss (Jahoda et al. 1972).[1] Other studies have suggested that social support can moderate the negative impact of unemployment (see Kessler et al. 1988; McKee-Ryan et al. 2005). The balance of the evidence suggests that the impact of unemployment on subjective well-being goes beyond the effects of financial strain.

---

[1] For more recent research on sociability and unemployment see Russell (1999); Paugam and Russell (2000).

The effect of economic crisis is not limited to those who are currently unemployed. Increased insecurity among those who remain in employment can also reduce well-being, as can the unemployment and insecurity of other family members (Scherer 2009). Previous research has found lower levels of well-being among the partners of the unemployed, due to both financial and non-financial stresses such as role uncertainty (Liem and Liem 1988; Morris 1990; Inanc 2012). There may also be a scarring effect of previous unemployment on current well-being among those who have returned to work or have exited the labour market (e.g.Clark et al. 2001; Bell and Blanchflower 2011).

Wage cuts, tax increases, and cuts to welfare benefits may mean many individuals and families are suffering the financial effects of economic crisis, even though they are not unemployed or currently insecure (Russell et al. 2011). Previous research has found a robust association between income and subjective well-being at the individual level, but the relationship tends to be non-linear, with diminishing marginal utility as income increases in absolute terms (Frey and Stutzer 2001). In this sense it is important to consider the impact of financial strain on well-being, independently of employment status.

The primary aim of this chapter is to analyse the impact of economic crisis on individual well-being by considering the impact of unemployment, insecurity, and financial strain on life satisfaction. There is also speculation about whether economic crisis leads to a more general malaise, even among those not directly affected, for example due to pessimism about the future. While this is not the main focus of the chapter, we do consider whether the macro-economic situation has any influence on levels of well-being net of individual exposure to unemployment and financial strain.

Well-Being, Unemployment, and Economic Crisis: The Comparative Perspective

The impact of economic crisis on well-being may vary across countries, an issue the ESS is well designed to explore. The objective in this chapter is not to explain national differences in overall subjective well-being but rather to examine how individual effects (of unemployment, insecurity, and economic strain) might be mediated by macro-processes and institutions. Previous research has suggested that societal factors may influence the distress experienced by the unemployed (Gallie and Russell 1998). The most widely considered of these macro-level processes are the unemployment rate and the nature of welfare provision.

The influence of macro-level characteristics may not be confined to the well-being of the unemployed but may also influence well-being more widely across society. There has been a long-standing and growing literature on how the subjective well-being among the population is affected by state of the economy (as measured by factors such as GDP) either across time or across societies (e.g. Easterlin 1974; Ryan and Deci 2001; Frey and Stutzer 2002; Fahey and Smyth 2004; Fahey 2007).

Unemployment rate

There are a number of competing hypotheses regarding the influence of the unemployment rate on well-being. One possibility is that high unemployment will aggravate distress because it depletes the level of support in wider social networks and because the perceived opportunity to escape current circumstances is reduced (see Gallie and Russell 1998). Alternatively, high unemployment (and widespread insecurity) may reduce the stigma attached to unemployment or improve individuals' sense of their comparative well-being and so lead to an adaption to unemployment and reduced circumstances. This explanation fits into a broader theory that it is an individual's relative rather than absolute position that matters most for subjective well-being (Clark and Oswald 1996).

To date the empirical results on the effects of the unemployment level on the well-being of the unemployed are mixed. Clark (2003) found that the well-being of the unemployed was higher when the regional unemployment rate was higher. However, Oesch and Lipps (2011) find no evidence in panel data from Germany (1984–2009) or Switzerland (2000–2009) that high regional unemployment mitigates the effects of unemployment on life satisfaction. McKee-Ryan et al. (2005) in a meta-analytic review of research found that the unemployment rate at the time of the studies did not moderate the relationship between mental health and employment status.[2] An Australian study which considered a wide range of neighbourhood effects on life satisfaction (among the general population not just the unemployed) found no influence of unemployment rate (Shields et al. 2009). Nevertheless the study's finding that other neighbourhood factors explained a small amount of variance in life satisfaction over and above individual characteristics, indicates the potential influence of the wider social context.

Welfare regime

There is significant evidence that the type and level of social protection available within the welfare state influences the level of economic strain

---

[2] Note that the effect of the unemployment rate was not explicitly tested in the studies themselves. This conclusion was drawn from a comparison of the unemployment coefficients for studies with different unemployment rates.

experienced by those facing unemployment (Gallie and Paugam 2000; Hauser et al. 2000; Nordenmark et al. 2006; Avram et al. 2011). Given the importance of financial strain for subjective well-being it is therefore expected that the welfare regime will moderate the effect of employment across societies.

Five welfare regime groups are considered in this chapter: a Nordic group consisting of Norway, Sweden, Denmark, and Finland; a Southern group consisting of Spain, Greece, and Portugal; a Continental group comprising Germany, the Netherlands, and Belgium; and a Liberal group represented by Ireland and the UK. This classification follows Gallie and Paugam's (2000) taxonomy of 'unemployment welfare regimes'. The Gallie and Paugam study did not include the Transition regime group. Following Stovicek and Turrini's (2012) study of unemployment systems we identify a Transition group that includes the Czech Republic, Estonia, Slovenia, Slovakia, Hungary, and Poland. Stovicek and Turrini identify this group of countries (plus Greece) as having much less generous unemployment systems than the EU average (Stovicek and Turrini 2012: 15), replacement rates often drop sharply after the first year, and with the exception of the Czech Republic and Latvia entitlement conditions are strict. It is also noted that strict conditions on job search and availability often apply (Stovicek and Turrini 2012: 17).

The main distinguishing characteristics of the different regimes are the degree to which the systems rely on insurance-based or means-tested benefits for the unemployed, the generosity of benefits, coverage rates (which is a function of eligibility requirements and the make-up of the unemployed population), and spending on active labour market policies.

The differences in the social protection systems have consequences for the income replacement rates and the poverty status of the unemployed. The mean replacement rate for the short-term unemployed ranges from 74 per cent in the Continental regime, 71 per cent in the Nordic and Southern regime, 68 per cent in Transition regime, and 60 per cent in the Liberal Regime.[3]

The mean benefit coverage rate for the unemployed in 2009 ranges from 24 per cent in the Transition regime to 68 per cent in the Continental regime[4] (see Appendix Table A9.1). The level of coverage is also low in the Southern group standing at 31 per cent. The coverage rates in the Liberal and Nordic regimes both stand at 59 per cent. The traditionally high coverage rate for the Nordic countries is lowered by the rates in Norway and Sweden. In Sweden,

---

[3] Mean based on own calculations based on the OECD short-term (<1 yr) replacement rates: OECD Economic and Policy Reforms 2012. The OECD replacement rates are based on calculations for various household types and wage levels assuming full take-up of benefits.

[4] The coverage rate is based on the EU SILC data. We calculate the proportion of those unemployed (self-defined) for at least 6 months during the preceding 12 months who were in receipt of unemployment related payments during that 12-month period.

recent welfare reform has led to a dramatic drop in the proportion of the unemployed eligible for insurance-based benefits (Anxo and Ericson 2011).

EU figures suggest that the proportion of the unemployed who fall into poverty ranges from around one-third in the Nordic and Southern regimes to around a half in the Transition and Liberal regimes (see Appendix Table A9.1). The Continental regime falls between these two extremes with 42 per cent of the unemployed falling into income poverty. There are, however, a number of outliers within regime groupings: for example within the Transition group, Estonia has an extremely high poverty rate of 62 per cent while the Slovenian poverty rate (36 per cent) is closer to that recorded in the Southern and Nordic regimes.

These comparative poverty rates for the unemployed underline that it is not just the welfare system that is critical but also the demographic composition of the unemployed and the extent to which the unemployed can draw on economic support within the household. The employment status of other household members, be they partners or parents, is crucial in determining the financial strain experienced by the unemployed (Gallie et al. 2000; Immervoll and O'Donoghue 2004). The concentration of unemployment among younger people and the availability of familial support for this group have been identified as significant factors in preventing much higher rates of poverty among the unemployed in Southern Europe. The influence of the composition of the unemployed population is considered in the models below.

Assessing Subjective Well-Being

Subjective well-being (SWB) refers to positive feelings about one's life and one's self. The distinction between 'subjective' and 'objective' in this context is not a reference to methods of measurement (as in self-report or non-self-report), but to what is measured: whether personal feelings and evaluations or non-feelings/evaluations (Veenhoven 2002a; Gasper 2007).

Another important feature of the concept of subjective well-being is that it refers to relatively enduring, underlying states rather than brief emotional episodes. To be useful as an outcome measure, subjective well-being should not fluctuate wildly in response to fleeting occurrences, yet be responsive to changes in circumstances (Chamberlain and Zika 1992). Research has indicated that subjective-well being does have these desirable attributes (Chamberlain and Zika 1992; Steger and Kashdan 2007). Further, a meta-analysis and a number of original studies by Schimmack and Oishi (2005) demonstrated that measured subjective well-being is not unduly affected by situational factors such as survey context or response style. Objective conditions are not linked to subjective well-being in a straightforward manner and the discrepancies between the two have been extensively documented (for example Sen 1985; Veenhoven 1993; Diener and Suh 1997; Ryan and Deci 2001; Frey and Stutzer 2002). This divergence has been attributed both to processes of adaptation/reduced expectations (Sen 1985) and to the ability of SWB indicators to capture elements of quality of life that cannot be reduced to objective conditions and to reflect cultural differences in values and priorities which may not be captured in objective measures such as income, morbidity, and poverty rates (Diener and Suh 1997).

We adopt here one of the most widely used indicators of subjective well-being—overall life satisfaction. This indicator has a clear meaning and allows comparison over time as it has been widely used in other surveys. It allows individuals to assess their lives as a whole on their own terms in contrast to, for example, asking how satisfied they are with a limited set of specific life domains. Further, it captures both the affective/emotional dimension of SWB (sense of satisfaction) and the cognitive dimension (assessment of life, overall) (Veenhoven 2009). In the ESS, life satisfaction is measured on a ten-point scale. The first step in our analysis uses data from the 2010 ESS to consider the effects of individual exposure to economic crisis on life satisfaction. We examine the association with both current employment status and recent unemployment experience, which is thought to capture both insecurity and the potential scarring effects of unemployment. We also consider the unemployment experience of other household members. Based on previous research we anticipate that current unemployment will be associated with reduced life satisfaction. We also expect that life satisfaction will be lower among those, whether currently at work or not, who have experienced unemployment in the recent past, and where other household members are unemployed. For the currently employed, recent unemployment experience may also be an indicator of job insecurity, since the jobs entered from unemployment are often more unstable and recent unemployment can be a strong predictor of future unemployment risk (Arulampalam and Taylor 2000; Korpi and Levin 2001). Therefore the association between recent unemployment and satisfaction may also capture insecurity effects.

The analysis will also investigate the association between life satisfaction and financial difficulties, using subjective indicators of financial strain and having experienced deterioration in financial situation in the last three years. In the light of previous research we expect that financial hardship will significantly reduce life satisfaction. Moreover, we anticipate that the association between unemployment and satisfaction will be reduced when financial strain is controlled, but there will be a residual effect due to the non-financial effects of unemployment on well-being. A similar process is expected to occur for partner's unemployment.

The next step is to investigate regime variation in the association between unemployment and well-being. We expect that the association between unemployment and life satisfaction will be lower in regimes where the unemployed are protected by welfare system (Nordic) or by household support (Southern) and will be highest in regimes where exposure to financial strain among the unemployed is highest (Liberal and Transition).

Turning to the question posed by Clark et al. (2001) 'does unemployment hurt less when there is more of it about?' we test the alternative predictions that

(a) a higher unemployment rate will increase the satisfaction of the unemployed (or at least lessen the negative effect) because of reduced stigma, adaptation/reduced expectations or because the comparative situation of the unemployed is improved, or

(b) a higher unemployment rate in society will lower the life satisfaction among the unemployed because of reduced resources in networks and reduced prospects of exiting unemployment.

In the final section of the chapter we examine changes in subjective well-being between 2004 and 2010. This section addresses the puzzle of why the current economic crisis does not appear to have had a dampening effect on life satisfaction, despite the strong association between satisfaction, unemployment, and financial strain at the individual level.

In examining changes over time, it is possible that increasing unemployment has led to a weakening of the impact of unemployment on well-being, through a process of habituation (or reduced expectations). It is also possible that a change in the composition of the unemployed may have had an impact on the strength of the association between unemployment and life satisfaction. For instance, if more of the unemployed during an economic crisis are relatively well-educated individuals, they may have a more positive assessment of their prospects of escaping unemployment.

Employment Status, Financial Strain, Social Integration, and Subjective Well-Being in 2010

In Figure 9.1 we examine the association between life satisfaction and employment status, and the experience of unemployment and financial strain in 2010. As has been found in previous research, there is a strong association between employment status and life satisfaction in 2010. Those who are unemployed have a mean satisfaction score of 5.9 compared to a score of 6.8 for those of working age outside the labour market and rising to 7.2 for those in employment. Recent spells of unemployment are associated with an

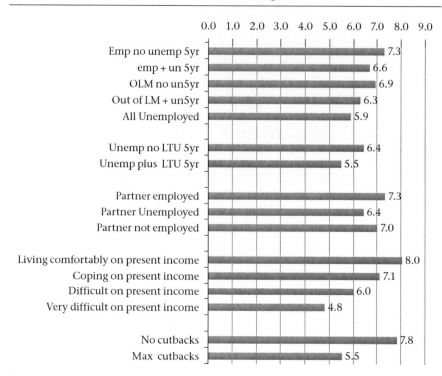

Figure 9.1. Life satisfaction scores by employment status and financial strain, 2010

additional decline in satisfaction among those currently employed and those outside the labour market, while the unemployed who have experienced a spell of unemployment of over a year record significantly lower levels of satisfaction than the short-term unemployed.[5]

While income has been widely used in the economic literature on subjective well-being this does not capture the differences in need that face households of different size and composition, nor does it reflect variations in the non-financial resources that a household can access.[6] Moreover previous research has found that measures of material deprivation and financial strain are more strongly associated with well-being than income (Whelan and McGinnity 2000). Therefore we adopt more direct measures of financial hardship and deteriorating finances.

---

[5] The ESS Round 5 does not contain a measure of unemployment duration. Information is collected from all respondents on whether they have been unemployed over the last 5 years and whether any of these spells lasted longer than 12 months. Therefore we cannot determine whether the duration of over 12 months applies to the current or previous spell of unemployment.

[6] There are a number of problems with the ESS income data: first, the measure changes between 2004 and 2010; second, the measure is not equivalized and would require returning to national currency codes to apply such corrections; and third, data are missing for Portugal in 2010.

The first financial stress measure assesses how respondents are coping on their current income. As anticipated, there is a very clear gradient in life satisfaction by level of financial strain: those living comfortably have a life-satisfaction score that is almost twice that of those who are finding it 'very difficult' (see Figure 9.1)

Our second measure focuses on deterioration in economic circumstances over the last three years and therefore captures the experience of change in respondents' financial situation in the recent past, rather than of current levels of deprivation:

- I have had to manage on a lower household income.
- I have had to draw on my savings or get into debt to cover ordinary living expenses.
- I have had to cut back on holidays or new household equipment.

Responses were measured on a six-point scale with 0 representing that this did not apply at all and 6 that it applied 'a great deal'. Just over half of respondents experienced deterioration on at least one of these items.[7] These responses were found to combine into a reliable scale with a Cronbach's alpha of 0.83. Taking the two extreme points on this 'cutbacks' scale we find that those who record no deterioration in financial situation on any of the three items have a satisfaction level of 7.8 while those who score the maximum on the cutbacks scale have a satisfaction level of 5.5.

Is financial stress higher among the unemployed? The distribution of the financial stress measures by employment status is as expected. Overall 60 per cent of the unemployed were experiencing financial strain in 2010 (difficult or very difficult to cope) compared to 19 per cent of the employed. The average score on the cutbacks scale was 3.6 for the unemployed and 2.2 for the employed. There was also a strong relationship by regime (see Figure 9.2 and Appendix Figure A9.1). However, here there are some differences from the pattern shown by the EU poverty figures. While the Nordic regime records the lowest financial stress among the unemployed and the Liberal and Transition regimes report a much higher level of financial hardship, as anticipated, the Southern countries score much worse on the subjective strain measure than on the European poverty figures in Appendix Table A9.1. The levels of financial strain are high for the employed as well as for the unemployed in Southern regimes, so that the gap between the two groups for this indicator is narrower than elsewhere.

The lower degree of social integration among the unemployed is also confirmed by the ESS data (Table 9.1). The unemployed are more likely than the employed to lack social support. Almost twice as many report that they do

[7] Those who placed themselves at 4 through 6 on any of the three scales.

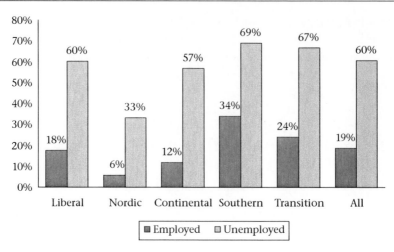

Figure 9.2. Percentage experiencing financial strain by regime and employment situation 2010

Note: Financial stress = Difficult or very difficult to cope on present income

not have someone to talk to about personal matters. The unemployed report somewhat lower levels of social contact than the employed and when asked to compare their levels of sociability with others of the same age, the unemployed fare even worse with 43 per cent reporting that they socialize less or much less than others in their age group. Finally the unemployed are significantly more likely to feel lonely.[8]

Experience of the economic crisis and life satisfaction

While the link between employment status and average life satisfaction is clear in Figure 9.1, these averages take no account of other sources of variation in well-being which might confound the relationship. We constructed a series of models including controls for a wide range of differences between individuals (such as age, gender, family status, education, health status, and social class) and examined the net effect of current unemployment and recent unemployment experience on life satisfaction.

Figure 9.3 shows the model-estimated life satisfaction based on exposure to unemployment. The dark bars present estimates from a model which just controls for personal characteristics. The lighter bars present estimates from a model which includes controls for both personal characteristics and financial

---

[8] These patterns are very similar across regime types with the exception that there is no difference in the level of social contact reported by the unemployed and employed in the Transition regime.

Table 9.1. Social integration and employment status

	Employed	Unemployed	Not in Labour Market
Meet socially with friends, etc. once a month or less	18.1%	21.5%	21.2%
Socialize less/much less than others of same age	33.2%	43.1%	41.2%
No one to discuss personal matters	6.5%	12.5%	9.4%
Feel lonely most/all the time	4.4%	11.7%	8.2%

Note: Except in the case of item 3, these percentages are taken from more detailed scales.

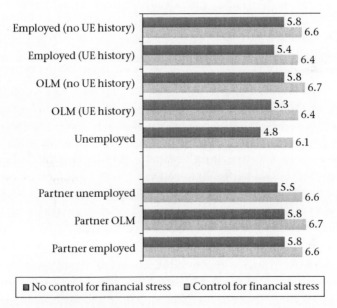

Figure 9.3. Relationship between unemployment and life satisfaction before and after controls for financial situation 2010

Note: Model predicted satisfaction scores controlling for gender, age, health and disability, family situation, partner economic situation, social class, and social support (estimated from Appendix Table A9.2 Models 2 and 3).

stress. The first thing to notice is that the effects of current and past unemployment remain strong even with other characteristics controlled.

Previous research on psychological distress among the unemployed led us to hypothesize that the effects of employment status on life satisfaction will be mediated through financial hardship. This hypothesis is supported by the model results. Once we control for financial strain and cutbacks the life satisfaction gap between employed and unemployed narrows. Before controls the range is from 4.8 (for the unemployed) to 5.8 (for the employed with no recent unemployment history) on the ten-point scale. After controlling for financial stress and the need to make cutbacks, the range between the employed and the unemployed narrows (from 6.1 to 6.6).

Despite the drop in the size of the unemployment coefficient, there is still a significant relationship between unemployment and life satisfaction net of economic hardship, suggesting a role for non-financial factors of the sort described above (such as loss of status and sense of purpose).

The wider effects of economic crisis within the household are also evident in the model results. Having a partner who is unemployed is associated with reduced life satisfaction even when the respondent's own status is controlled (see Figure 9.3). Subsequent models show that the effect of partner's unemployment on well-being operates through financial stress. When the financial variables are added, partner's unemployment is not significant (see Figure 9.3). Having a partner outside the labour market actually *enhances* life satisfaction but only in the absence of financial strain.

Apart from financial stress and cutbacks, it has been suggested that reduced social contacts may be another factor that mediates between unemployment and subjective well-being (McKee-Ryan et al. 2005). However, as can be seen by comparing Models 1, 2, and 3 in Appendix Table A9.2, while social integration is important for satisfaction in general it is much less consequential in accounting for the negative impact of unemployment on satisfaction.

Social contact and support are found to explain 5 per cent of variation in life satisfaction (R-squared increased from 0.126 to 0.172), compared to the 8 per cent of variance accounted for by financial strain and cutbacks. However, the main effect of current unemployment is reduced by 58 per cent when we add the control for financial stress and cutbacks (from –0.98 in Model 2 to –0.41 in Model 3). The corresponding decline in the impact of unemployment when the social support variables are added is only 7 per cent (–1.05 to –0.98, comparing models 1 and 2 in Appendix Table A9.2).

Regime variation

In order to test whether the effect of unemployment varies across the regimes we interact employment status and regime (Model 5 in Appendix Table A9.2). According to our hypothesis we expected the effect of unemployment on satisfaction to be lower in regimes where the unemployed are better protected through the welfare system (Nordic) or by household support (Southern) though our expectations about the Southern regime are tempered by the high financial strain noted in the ESS data. We expect that the effect of unemployment will be highest in regimes where financial strain among the unemployed is highest (Liberal and Transition).

The interactions (Model 5 in Appendix Table A9.2) suggest that the effect of unemployment on satisfaction is significantly weaker in the Southern regime, and to a lesser extent the Nordic regime, than in the Liberal, Transition, and Continental regimes. Figure 9.4 shows that, with other factors controlled, the expected gap between the unemployed and employed is markedly smaller in the Southern regime.

Controlling for financial situation reduces the satisfaction gap between the unemployed and the employed in all regimes. Before controlling for financial strain, the gap between employed and unemployed is largest in the Liberal, Transition, and Continental regimes. After controlling for financial strain, there is much less variation by regime in the size of the satisfaction gap between the employed and unemployed. Indeed the gap is now identical for all regimes except in the Southern regime, where the gap has closed.

When the measures of financial strain are added to the model the positive interaction between unemployment and the Nordic regime becomes non-significant. This suggests that the slightly weaker link between unemployment and life satisfaction in the Nordic regimes (compared to the Continental) could be due to the better financial circumstances of the unemployed in this regime.

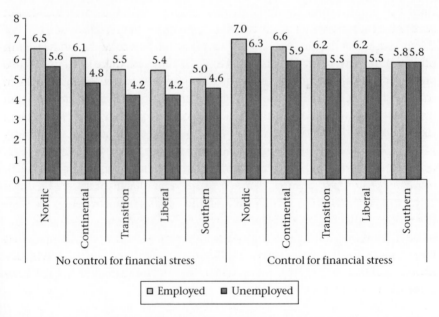

Figure 9.4. Model estimated life satisfaction by regime and unemployed vs. employed 2010

Note: Model predicted SAT controlling for gender, age, health and disability, family situation, partner economic situation, social class, and social support, (Appendix Table A9.2 Models 5 and 6).

The graph further illustrates the while the gap between the employed and unemployed in the Southern countries is very narrow, the level of life satisfaction of both groups, especially the employed, is comparatively low, while the satisfaction scores of the employed and unemployed in the Nordic regime are higher than elsewhere.

This raises the question: can the narrow gap between the unemployed and employed in Southern Europe be explained by the greater insecurity of the employed in this regime? It is worth recalling here that the reference group are the employed with no unemployment experience in the last five years, who are those most likely to be securely employed.[9] Therefore security is already at least partly taken into account. Further models confined to the employed showed that while past unemployment and perceived job insecurity were both strongly associated with life satisfaction, the higher levels of dissatisfaction among the Southern employed remained unchanged.[10]

The Macro-Social Context

Our final hypotheses for the 2010 cross-sectional analysis concerned the impact of the prevailing unemployment rate. Initial analysis suggested that there was a positive association between unemployment rate and well-being (with effect not varying by individual employment status). However, tests of the robustness of this finding showed that it was driven by Spain where unemployment rates were very high. When Spain is dropped, there is no significant association between satisfaction and unemployment rate. We also checked whether change in GDP in the previous two years had a significant effect on life satisfaction with individual characteristics controlled. Again, there was no significant association once Spain was dropped from the analysis or a dummy variable was included for Spain (see Appendix Table A9.2, Models 7b and 8a).

When macro-level characteristics alone were included as predictors, without controls for any personal characteristics, a significant negative relationship between unemployment rate and life satisfaction was observed, but the model explained little of the variation in life satisfaction (R-squared was 0.037). These results suggest that economic contraction and financial crisis have their impact on subjective well-being primarily through individuals' own experience of job loss, financial strain, and insecurity or that of their immediate family members.

---

[9] Overall, 34 per cent of the employed with no recent unemployment feel their job is insecure compared to 56 per cent of the employed with recent unemployment experience.

[10] Models available on request. Given the subjective nature of the dependent variable we opted for past unemployment as a more objective indicator of security in our main models; moreover we were interested in the potential scarring effects of past unemployment.

However, the results so far have been confined to one year of observation, and the influence of macro-level processes may be more apparent when subjective well-being is tracked over time. The availability of the 2004 module which predates the current economic crisis allows us to examine the hypotheses on unemployment levels in more detail. We turn to this issue in the next section.

Change in Subjective Well-Being 2004–2010

While the results for 2010 demonstrate a clear and strong association between individual experience of unemployment and financial hardship and life satisfaction, a range of previous research findings on well-being should caution us against expecting large changes in subjective well-being over the period in question. Several studies of long-term changes in satisfaction levels show that economic growth (as measured by GDP) has little effect on national levels of well-being (Easterlin 1974; Frey and Stutzer 2002). Fahey (2007) suggests that one reason for this apparent lack of response to economic growth is that in wealthier countries subjective well-being has stabilized at a high plateau and that there may be a natural limit to rising happiness beyond such a threshold.

The effect of the current economic crisis on subjective well-being has received only limited attention to date. In a recent US study Deaton (2012) found that the current economic crisis has had only a small and relatively short-lived effect on life satisfaction. Using Eurobarameter data, Walsh (2011) found that mean life satisfaction declined across the twenty-nine countries after 2009 although the decline was not uniform or as strong as anticipated on the basis of the macro-economic changes. The rising unemployment rate was found to explain a significant part of the change in satisfaction though this was offset by declining inflation which also had a significant positive impact; GDP also had a small but significant impact.[11] Walsh's methodology differs from ours in that it involves time series analyses of country-level data and no individual level characteristics are included.

Information on life satisfaction has been collected in each of the ESS rounds, therefore before focusing on the change between 2004 and 2010 we examine the broad trends in aggregate life satisfaction for between 2002 and 2010. The picture painted by the graphs in Figure 9.5 is predominantly one of stability. Very little change in life satisfaction is observed in the Nordic countries, the UK, and in most of the Southern and Continental countries. The most noticeable shifts seem to have occurred in the Transition countries,

---

[11] Walsh also found that corruption and income inequality had a significant impact.

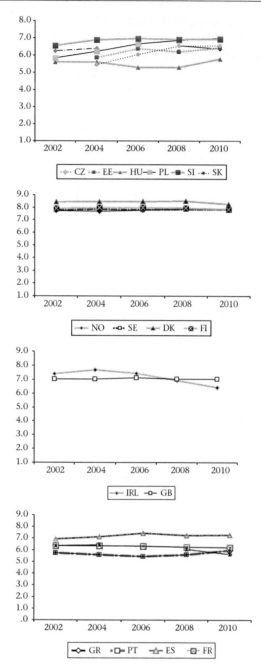

Figure 9.5. Change in life satisfaction 2002 to 2010 (ESS Round 1 to 5)
Source: ESS cumulative file 2002 to 2008; ESS 2010. Ages 20 to 64 years, with design weight.

particularly Poland, Estonia, Slovakia, and Hungary, where the average level of life satisfaction has increased over time, and in Ireland where there has been a downward trend since 2004.

This presents a puzzle: given that the effect of economic crisis at the individual level has such a strong relationship with satisfaction, why is there apparently so little change in well-being at the aggregate level?

A key question is whether the association between unemployment and life satisfaction changed over the period. And if so whether this was due to a change in the composition of the unemployed, a change in their financial position, or a change in the experience of unemployment related to the increasing prevalence of unemployment.

Figure 9.6 examines the changes in life satisfaction between 2004 and 2010 for each employment status category. While it is evident that there is a small increase in life satisfaction for all categories, the improvement was greatest for those who were unemployed. A greater than average increase in well-being was also noted among those who had an unemployed partner.

These changes in the effect of unemployment over time are not uniform but vary significantly across the five regimes (Figure 9.7). The increase in satisfaction has been particularly marked for the unemployed in the Transition regime and those in the Continental regime. In both cases the increase was more subdued for the employed leading to a narrowing in the satisfaction gap between the unemployed and employed over time. The Liberal regime is

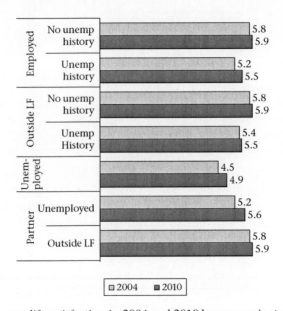

Figure 9.6. Average life satisfaction in 2004 and 2010 by economic status

Note: No controls for financial stress.

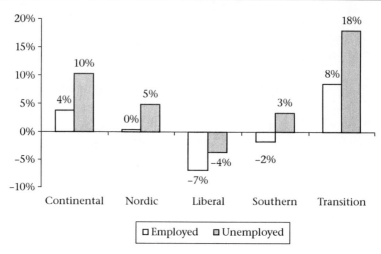

Figure 9.7. Life satisfaction changes 2004–2010 by regime and unemployment (before controls for financial stress)

Note: From model controlling for social and demographic characteristics; see Appendix Table A9.3, Model 9.

distinctive in recording a decline in life satisfaction between 2004 and 2010. The drop was larger for the employed than the unemployed meaning that here too there is a narrowing gap in the satisfaction scores of the two groups. The closing of the gap between the unemployed and employed is illustrated in Figure 9.8.

The narrowing gap between the unemployed and the employed between 2004 and 2010 is present in models that control for a wide range of social and demographic characteristics, therefore the trend does not appear to be due to the changes in the underlying composition of the employed or unemployed groups. Given the centrality of financial hardship in linking unemployment to lower life satisfaction we test whether reduced financial hardship among the unemployed may be a factor in explaining the time trend.

We find that changes in the level of financial strain accounts for *all* of the fall in satisfaction among the unemployed in Liberal countries and around a fifth of the improvement in life satisfaction of the unemployed in Transition regimes (comparing Figures 9.9 and 9.7). Rising financial strain also accounts for some of the decline in life satisfaction among the *employed* in the Liberal regimes. Underlying this pattern is the finding that the level of financial strain increased significantly in the Liberal regimes while it decreased for the Transition regimes (Figure A9.2). This decrease in financial strain is consistent with the economic figures which show a significant decline in unemployment levels in three of the six countries in the Transition group between 2004 and 2010 (see Chapter 2 this volume).

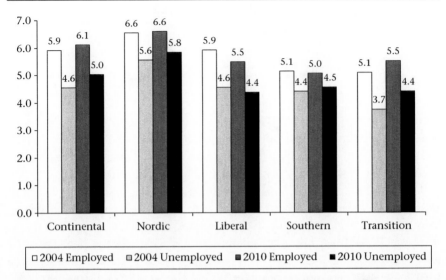

Figure 9.8. Model estimated life satisfaction rates 2004 and 2010 by regime and unemployment (before controls for financial stress, from Model 9 in Appendix Table A9.3)

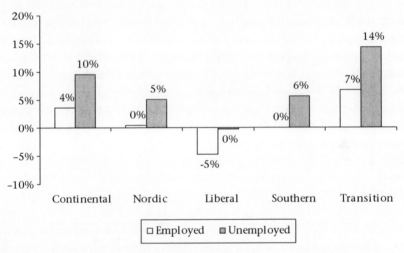

Figure 9.9. Life satisfaction changes 2004–2010 by regime and unemployment (controlling for financial stress)

Note: Estimated from Appendix Table A9.3 Model 8.

Again the Southern regime is distinctive: despite significant increases in financial strain between 2004 and 2010, the satisfaction of the unemployed increased while that for the employed remained unchanged.

In order to take account of this variation in the economic context within regime groupings we add country-level economic measures into the model.

This also allows a further test of our hypothesis on the potential impact of macro-level economic conditions on life satisfaction. We test the similar indicators to those used earlier, the unemployment rate and the change in GDP in the preceding two years; both figures vary for year and country.

The results support neither the argument that a high unemployment context will reduce the impact of unemployment on well-being (e.g. through reduced stigma or adaptation) nor that it will increase the impact (through decreased support and exit opportunities). We find that there is no significant influence of unemployment rate and well-being overall (once Spain is excluded) nor is there an effect specific to the unemployed.

We do find a significant positive relationship between change in GDP and satisfaction. This means that an increase in GDP is associated with higher satisfaction (and conversely a decline in GDP is associated with a decrease in satisfaction). Controlling for changes in GDP reduces the negative 2010 effect for the Liberal regimes which suggests the economic decline has contributed to the general lowering of subjective well-being in Ireland and the UK.[12]

These results suggest that the economic decline experienced in many countries has dampened down subjective well-being. This macro-level effect is over and above the direct impact through unemployment and financial strain. Where the economic situation has been improving this has increased life satisfaction in a general way. Given that the models control for such a wide range of individual level factors this result provides support for a real, though small, effect of the general economic context on life satisfaction. Controlling for change in GDP uniquely adds about 5 per cent to the explained variation in life satisfaction.[13] In the case of economic decline this may operate through increased pessimism even among those not directly affected by labour market failures and economic contraction.

Conclusions

The recent recession has seen rising levels of unemployment and increased insecurity in many countries, although some countries have been better sheltered from this crisis than others. The recession has also brought increased financial strain to many households: for example more than 51 per cent of people in 2010 reported deterioration in their financial situation of some sort.

---

[12] Model 8 in Appendix Table A9.3 shows that controlling for individual level characteristics, life satisfaction decreased in 2010 compared to 2004 in the Nordic and Liberal regimes, was unchanged in the Southern regime, and increased in the Transition and Continental regimes.

[13] This can be seen by comparing the R-squared of 0.281 for Model 10 when GDP change is added and the R-squared of 0.235 in the previous Model 9 in Appendix Table A9.3.

Drawing on a wide range of literature we hypothesize that exposure to economic crisis through the experience of unemployment and/or financial strain will have a detrimental effect on the subjective well-being of European citizens, as measured by life satisfaction. Our analysis shows that unemployment has a powerful effect on satisfaction, and that this effect is not limited to those who are currently unemployed but extends to those with unemployed partners and to those with a spell of unemployment in the recent past who have returned to work or have exited the labour market.

Our comparative analyses show that cross-regime variation in the relative impact of unemployment on satisfaction is modest. The main difference observed suggests that the impact of unemployment is lower in the Southern regime countries (Greece, Spain, and Portugal) and is marginally weaker in the Nordic regime.

Financial strain plays an important role in linking unemployment to life satisfaction, accounting for over half of the unemployment effect, and explaining all of the association between partner's unemployment and reduced satisfaction. However, the inclusion of measures of financial stress leaves the regime patterns unchanged, except that the weak Nordic effect disappears. Lower financial strain among the unemployed in the Nordic countries is consistent with a protective welfare regime.

Sociability and social support are positively linked to life satisfaction, and the unemployed are found to have lower access to support and have lower levels of social contact outside the home than those in employment. Nevertheless, social integration does not account for the lower life satisfaction of the unemployed; these factors play a much less prominent role than financial strain.

The results suggest that the Southern distinctiveness cannot be accounted for by a weaker link between unemployment and economic hardship in this regime. Indeed the unemployed here recorded some of the highest levels of financial stress and had scores on the cutback measures that were no lower than average. Some of the Southern distinctiveness may arise from the lower level of satisfaction among those *in employment* compared to other regimes. Job insecurity is particularly high among the employed in the Southern regime (e.g. Chapter 8 in this volume) and we find that insecurity is associated with lower life satisfaction, yet the distinctive Southern pattern remains even when perceived insecurity is controlled and when we compared the unemployed to the employed without recent unemployment experience, who are a relatively secure group. The narrow satisfaction gap between the unemployed and employed in Southern countries (which disappears when financial stress is controlled) suggests that the non-financial benefits of work (intrinsic rewards, social contact, etc.) are weaker in Southern countries. This is consistent with Steiber's findings (Chapter 8 this volume) that levels of non-financial employment commitment are significantly lower in the Southern regime. In a similar vein Marsh and Alvaro (1990) concluded that differences in the strength of the work ethic lay behind differences in the effect of unemployment on well-being in Spain and Britain. Some of the Southern distinctiveness may also be related to the important role played by family support (see Gallie and Paugam 2000), which may mitigate at least some of the effect of unemployment on life satisfaction.

We find no robust evidence that the prevailing level of unemployment moderates the effect of unemployment at the individual level, although the limited number of observations at the national level means that we cannot rule out the type of processes described above. The cross-sectional analysis for 2010 finds no effect for changes in national wealth (GDP). But our investigation of change over time between 2004 and 2010 suggests that falling GDP does play an independent role in reducing life satisfaction for the general population especially in the Liberal regime. The results nevertheless underline that the economic crisis influences subjective well-being primarily through the more concrete channels of unemployment and financial hardship. While we do not see an overall fall in average life satisfaction in Europe associated with economic crisis, for those who are exposed to unemployment and financial hardship, the detrimental effect on well-being is clear.

Appendix

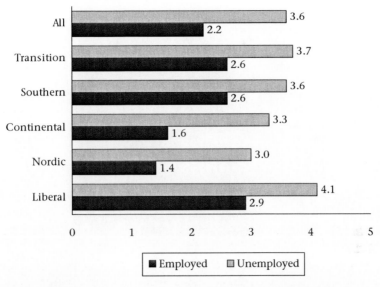

Figure A9.1. Mean cutbacks score by employment status and regime 2010

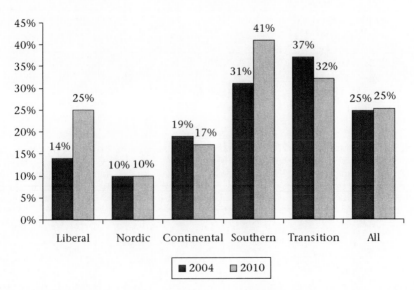

Figure A9.2. Proportion finding it difficult or very difficult to cope on their present income 2004 and 2010

Table A9.1. Poverty rates, replacement rates and benefit coverage among the unemployed

		Income Poverty Unemployed 2007	OECD Net replacement rate short-term u/e 2009	Coverage: % of u/e in receipt of unemp payments 2009
Transition	Czech Repub	48	73.5	20.9%
	Estonia	62	56.9	22.7%
	Slovenia	36	79.0	12.4%
	Slovakia	45	64.6	14.7%
	Hungary	46	70.1	54.7%
	Poland	43	61.4	17.8%
	Mean	46.7	67.6	23.9%
Continental	Belgium	56	72.6	93.9%
	Germany	51	73.0	87.7%
	Netherlands	27	69.0	27.2%
	France	33	79.5	62.8%
	Mean	41.8	73.5	67.9%
Liberal	UK	58	61.1	49.7%
	Ireland	43	58.6	67.9%
	Mean	50.5	59.9	58.8%
Southern	Greece	35	65.1	12.4%
	Spain	36	71.5	47.3%
	Portugal	32	77.4	33.1%
	Mean	34.3	71.3	30.9%
Nordic	Denmark	31	76.9	73.3%
	Finland	41	70.6	88.4%
	Norway	44	75.4	30.6%
	Sweden	26	65.0	45.4%
	Mean	35.5	72.0	59.4%

Note: see notes to Table 1.1 for sources.

Table A9.2. Life satisfaction 2010 (Ordinary Least Squares Regression Coefficients)

	Mod 1	Mod 2	Mod 3	Mod 4	Mod 5	Mod 6	Mod 7a	Mod 7b	Mod 8a
N cases	25120	25120	25120	25120	25120	25120	25120	25120	25120
R sq	0.126	0.172	0.249	0.222	0.223	0.276	0.276	0.279	0.289
Female	.08***	.08***	.14***	.09***	.09***	.13***	.13***	.13***	.14***
age2034	.30***	.20***	.21***	.23***	.23***	.23***	.23***	.23***	.24***
age4554	.08 *	.11 **	ns	ns	ns	ns	ns	ns	ns
age5564	.36***	.38***	.19***	.23***	.24***	.11 **	.11 **	.12 **	.12***
Formar	−.53***	−.48***	−.28***	−.48***	−.47***	−.30***	−.30***	−.31***	−.32***
Nevmar	ns	−.12***	−.12***	−.23***	−.23***	−.21***	−.20***	−.21***	−.22***
Lonep	−.56***	−.57***	−.33***	−.54***	−.53***	−.34***	−.34***	−.33***	−.31***
anykidun18	.39***	.40***	.38***	.18***	.18***	.22***	.22***	.24***	.22***

Table A9.2. (Continued)

	Mod 1	Mod 2	Mod 3	Mod 4	Mod 5	Mod 6	Mod 7a	Mod 7b	Mod 8a
N cases	25120	25120	25120	25120	25120	25120	25120	25120	25120
R sq	0.126	0.172	0.249	0.222	0.223	0.276	0.276	0.279	0.289
hh size	−.15***	−.15***	−.12***	.09 **	.09 **	ns	ns	ns	ns
isced01	−.36***	−.40***	−.25***	ns	ns	ns	ns	ns	ns
isced2	ns	ns	.07 *	.12***	.12***	.13***	.12***	.12***	.08 *
isced56	.19***	.15***	.06 *	.13***	.13***	.06 *	.06 *	ns	ns
fair/bad hlth	−.95***	−.82***	−.69***	−.72***	−.72***	−.63***	−.62***	−.64***	−.66***
Disability	−.15***	−.13***	−.10 **	−.35***	−.35***	−.27***	−.27***	−.26***	−.26***
Part unemp	−.36***	−.29***	ns	−.25***	−.24***	ns	ns	ns	ns
Part nonemp	ns	ns	.14***	ns	ns	.13***	.13***	.13***	.12***
prof/manag	ns	ns	ns	.07 *	.07 *	ns	ns	ns	.07 *
Self emp	−.44***	−.40***	−.25***	−.22***	−.21***	−.13 **	−.13 **	−.13 **	ns
Lowman/ serv	−.29***	−.21***	−.07 *	−.16***	−.16***	ns	ns	ns	ns
Dk occ	−.47***	−.38***	−.26***	−.19 **	−.17 **	ns	ns	ns	ns
Soc contact	−	.20***	.15***	.15***	.15***	.12***	.11***	.11***	.11***
Support	−	.59***	.48***	.55***	.55***	.46***	.46***	.48***	.46***
Social more	−	.23***	.19***	.23***	.23***	.19***	.19***	.20***	.20***
Emp& un5yr	−.48***	−.41***	−.18***	−.37***	−.36***	−.18***	−.18***	−.19***	−.20***
OLF& un5yr	−.63***	−.54***	−.16 **	−.52***	−.52***	−.20***	−.20 **	−.23***	−.23***
OLF & noun	ns	ns	.10 **	ns	ns	.09 **	.09 **	.09 **	.08 **
Unemployed	−1.05***	−.98***	−.41***	−.86***	−1.25***	−.70***	−.70***	−.73***	−.72***
Cutbacks	−	−	−.16***	−	−	−.13***	−.12***	−.13***	−.13***
Fin strain	−	−	−1.08***	−	−	−.97***	−.97***	−.95***	−.87***
Nordic	−	−	−	.47***	.45***	.39***	.40***	.40***	.40***
Liberal	−	−	−	−.62***	−.62***	−.38***	−.36***	−.47***	−.34***
Southern	−	−	−	−1.00***	−1.08***	−.78***	−.76***	−1.07***	−1.16***
Transition	−	−	−	−.59***	−.60***	−.41***	−.40***	−.55***	−.38***
Nordic unem	−	−	−	−	.37 *	ns	ns	ns	ns
Lib unem	−	−	−	−	ns	ns	ns	ns	−
South unem	−	−	−	−	−	.71***	.71***	.72***	.63***
Transi unem	−	−	−	−	−	ns	ns	ns	ns
GDPCh2Yr	−	−	−	−	−	−	.01 *	.02***	ns
Unemp rate	−	−	−	−	−	−	−	.04***	ns
Spain (dummy)	−	−	−	−	−	−	−	−	1.31***
_cons	7.61***	5.82***	6.55***	−	−	6.57***	6.59***	6.34***	6.66***

Note: * indicates statistical significance at p < = .10; ** statistical significance at p < .05 and *** statistical significance at p< .01.

Table A9.3. Life satisfaction, pooled 2004–2010 model

	Mod 1	Mod 2	Mod 3	Mod 4	Mod 5	Mod 6	Mod 7	Mod 8	Mod 9	Mod 10	Mod 11	Mod 12
N cases	50777	50777	50777	50777	50777	50777	50777	50777	50777	50777	50777	50777
R sq	0.001	0.044	0.045	0.178	0.241	0.277	0.277	0.28	0.235	0.281	0.281	0.288
2010	.13***	.14***	.10***	.09***	.11***	.12***	.12***	.22***	.23***	.30***	.32***	.29***
Emp & un5yr	–	–.68***	–.75***	–.59***	–.43***	–.38***	–.38***	–.35***	–.47***	–.35***	–.36***	–.37***
OLF & un5yr	–	–.88***	–.78***	–.41***	ns	–.14*	–.14*	–.35***	–.36***	ns	–.14*	–.13*
OLF & noun	–	–.33***	–.32***	ns	.07*	.10***	.10***	.11***	ns	.11***	.11***	.10***
Unemployed	–	–1.48***	–1.63***	–1.24***	–.80***	–.82***	–.98***	–.96***	–1.35***	–.97***	–.98***	–.98***
Partner unemp	–	–.59***	–.78***	–.59***	–.30***	–.34***	–.34***	–.31***	–.56***	–.31***	–.32***	–.32***
Part OLF	–	–.05*	ns	ns	.12***	.10**	.10**	.10**	ns	.10**	.10**	.09**
empun5 2010	–		ns	.19**	.17**	.15*	.15*	ns	ns	ns	ns	ns
OLM un5 2010	–		–.22*	ns	ns	ns	ns	ns	ns	ns	ns	ns
OLM noun 2010	–		ns	ns	ns	ns	ns	ns	ns	ns	ns	ns
Unemp 2010	–		.27***	.24***	.30***	.35***	.31***	.28***	.24***	.29***	.30***	.27***
Part unemp 2010	–		.34***	.31**	.26**	.30***	.30***	.27***	.31***	.28**	.29**	.25**
Part OLF 2010	–		ns	ns	ns	ns	ns	ns	ns	ns	ns	ns
female	–	–	–	.11***	.14***	.13***	.13***	.13***	.11***	.13***	.13***	.13***
age2034	–	–	–	.18***	.19***	.25***	.25***	.25***	.25***	.24***	.24***	.25***
age4554	–	–	–	.12***	.10***	ns	ns	ns	ns	ns	ns	ns
age5564	–	–	–	.42***	.30***	.20***	.20***	.19***	.27***	.19***	.19***	.19***
Former married	–	–	–	–.52***	–.38***	–.40***	–.39***	–.40***	–.52***	–.40***	–.40***	–.41***
Never married	–	–	–	–.11***	–.12***	–.22***	–.22***	–.23***	–.25***	–.23***	–.23***	–.25***
Lone parent	–	–	–	–.47***	–.28***	–.27***	–.27***	–.27***	–.42***	–.27***	–.27***	–.26***
Any kid <18yr	–	–	–	.36***	.37***	.18***	.18***	.16***	.12***	.16***	.17***	.16***
Hh size	–	–	–	–.17***	–.16***	.09***	.09***	.09***	.12***	.08**	.08**	.08***
isced01	–	–	–	–.27***	–.15***	ns	ns	ns	–.11**	ns	ns	ns

254

Table A9.3. (Continued)

	Mod 1	Mod 2	Mod 3	Mod 4	Mod 5	Mod 6	Mod 7	Mod 8	Mod 9	Mod 10	Mod 11	Mod 12
isced2	–	–	–	.10***	.12***	.12***	.12***	.09***	.06**	.08***	.09***	.05*
isced56	–	–	–	.19***	.11***	.07***	.07**	.05**	.10***	.05**	.05**	ns
fair2badhlth	–	–	–	-.90***	-.77***	-.66***	-.66***	-.65***	-.73***	-.65***	-.65***	-.67***
disability	–	–	–	-.17***	-.15***	-.33***	-.33***	-.33***	-.38***	-.33***	-.33***	-.33***
prof/manag	–	–	–	ns	ns	.05*	.05*	.06*	.07**	.05*	.05*	.07**
Self emp	–	–	–	-.30***	-.21***	-.09**	-.09**	-.09***	-.14***	-.10**	-.10**	ns
Lowman/serv	–	–	–	-.21***	-.08***	-.06**	-.06**	-.06**	-.15***	-.06**	-.06**	-.06**
Soc contact	–	–	–	.18***	.14***	.10***	.10***	.10***	.12***	.09***	.10***	.09***
Support	–	–	–	.60***	.51***	.48***	.48***	.48***	.54***	.48***	.49***	.48***
Socialize more	–	–	–	.25***	.22***	.22***	.21***	.22***	.24***	.22***	.22***	.22***
Fin. stress	–	–	–		-1.39***	-1.20***	-1.20***	-1.18***	–	-1.19***	-1.19***	-1.13***
Nordic	–	–	–			.50***	.48***	.58***	.65***	.53***	.54***	.53***
Liberal	–	–	–			-.31***	-.30***	ns	ns	-.16***	-.13**	-.17***
Southern	–	–	–			-.71***	-.75***	-.64***	-.76***	-.72***	-.75***	-1.05***
Transition	–	–	–			-.58***	-.58***	-.66***	-.82***	-.82***	-.88***	-.80***
Nordic unemp	–	–	–			–	.24*	.23*	.36***	.23*	.24*	.24*
Lib unemp	–	–	–			–	ns	ns	ns	ns	ns	ns
South unemp	–	–	–			–	.53***	.55***	.60***	.54***	.54***	.51***
Transition unemp	–	–	–			–	ns	ns	ns	ns	ns	ns
Nordic 2010	–	–	–			–	–	-.19***	-.20***	-.11**	-.12**	-.11**
Liberal 2010	–	–	–			–	–	-.52***	-.63***	-.32***	-.41***	-.32***
Southern 2010	–	–	–			–	–	-.21***	-.32***	ns	-.17**	ns
Transition 2010	–	–	–			–	–	.15***	.21***	.36***	.36***	.34***
GDPCh2Yr	–	–	–			–	–	–	–	.02***	.02***	.02***
Unemp rate	–	–	–			–	–	–	–	–	.01***	ns
Spain	–	–	–			–	–	–	–	–	–	1.01***
_cons	6.87***	7.17***	7.19***	5.78**	6.17***	6.22***	6.23***	6.20***	5.90***	6.16***	6.05***	6.22***

255

10

Economic Crisis, Political Legitimacy, and Social Cohesion

Javier Polavieja

Introduction

Between 2008 and 2009, the world's economy experienced a sharp downward turn. Although the epicentre of this global shock was located in the US sub-prime mortgage market, many European countries were amongst the hardest hit, suffering GDP losses unrecorded since the oil crisis of the early 1970s (see Chapter 1 in this book). The impact of recession has been particularly severe in Eurozone peripheral economies that experienced a real state bubble (i.e. Spain, Ireland, Greece), irresponsible banking practices (i.e. Iceland, Ireland, Spain), and/or decades-long governmental over-spending (i.e. Greece, Italy, Portugal). Unable to sustain their public finances, the governments of Greece, Ireland, and Portugal drew on IMF and EU full bailout packages in 2010 and 2011, whilst Spain requested a special Eurozone bailout to finance its tee-tering banking system in June 2012 (Spiegel and Mallet 2012). Exceptional actions to sustain national banking sectors were undertaken by many other governments across Europe. These actions have been followed by equally extraordinary measures to contain mounting public deficits.

Global economic crisis poses a major challenge to the so-called European model of social capitalism (Offe 2003). This model has historically been defined by the combination of national democratic institutions and exten-sive welfare provision. At its core lies the most advanced form of citizenship rights ever granted in political history (Marshall 1964).

This chapter analyses the impact of economic crisis on attitudes towards the political system and welfare-state redistribution across different European countries. Public support for the democratic institutions and the redistribu-tive policies that define European welfare states is crucial for the survival of the European social model. Specifically, I investigate how the experiences of economic vulnerability and economic crisis affect political trust, satisfaction with democracy, and attitudes towards income redistribution by exploiting the 2004 and 2010 rounds of the European Social Survey. These two data points provide an observation window to study the effects of the first wave of global recession. Analysing how this initial phase of the economic crisis affected attitudes towards the political system and welfare-state redistribution under different macro-level and individual-level conditions seems a highly relevant research question in a defining moment for Europe.

The Determinants of Support for Democratic Institutions and Redistribution

Support for democratic institutions

Political scientists have long argued that low levels of public support can pose serious problems for the working of existing democracies (see e.g. Lipset 1960, 1994). Hence a considerable amount of research has been devoted to understanding the determinants of public attitudes towards democratic institutions. Two classical theoretical perspectives have dominated the literature: the political culture perspective and the political economy perspective.

According to the former perspective, the stability of the existing democratic regimes would ultimately depend on the existence of a set of widely shared values, affects, and attachments through which citizens adhere to the principles and procedures of liberal democracy. Such core democratic values and attachments are transmitted from one generation to the next through powerful processes of political socialization, which take place mainly inside families and schools. Together, they compose a particular political culture. This culture, often called civic or democratic culture in the literature, acts as a cement for democracy, providing what Easton (1975) called 'diffuse support', that is, solid and largely stable attitudinal foundations for the existing democratic institutions (see also Almond and Verba 1963; Inglehart 1977, 1990; Hyman and Wright 1979; Barnes 1979; Putnam 1993; Kaase and Newton 1995). Although these sustaining democratic values are not seen as immutable, their pace of change is typically considered slow under this theoretical perspective (see Easton 1975; Clarke et al. 1993). Core democratic values would thus allow democracies to endure even through times of severe economic duress (see Bermeo 2003).

The claim that democratic legitimacy rests firmly on stable political values is challenged by the proponents of the political economy perspective. According to this perspective, the degree of legitimacy of the democratic

257

system would ultimately depend upon its capacity to meet and represent citizens' needs and demands, which are for the most part rooted in socio-economic interests (see e.g. Lipset 1960; Habermas 1973; Offe 1984; see also Macpherson 1977). Support for democratic institutions is therefore considered contingent upon institutional performance and hence much more changing and dynamic than the political culture perspective would concede.[1]

It follows from the political economy approach that the degree of support for the existing democratic institutions should be patterned by the class structure, as it is this structure that captures the main socio-economic interests of the population (e.g. Lipset 1960; Lipset and Rokkan 1967). In line with this prediction, accumulated evidence has shown that members of the working classes have higher levels of political disaffection, cynicism, and distrust than those placed in more privileged class positions (see e.g. Lockwood 1966; Goldthorpe et al. 1969; Hout et al. 1995; Goldthorpe 1996; Manza and Brooks 1996).

Classes capture the societal distribution of life-chances and hence they tap into the most stable drivers of social inequality. Yet more transient experiences of economic vulnerability also seem to have significant political consequences. Most research on the political effects of transitory economic vulnerability has focused on the study of unemployment. The existing evidence suggests that the experience of unemployment can also increase feelings of internal and external political inefficacy, discontent with the political system, distrust, and frustration (e.g. Leggett 1964; Jahoda et al. 1972; Schlozman and Verba 1979; Marshall et al. 1988; Gallie 1993; Polavieja 2003: Chap. 7).

In sum, there is abundant evidence showing that individual experiences of economic strain, whether lasting or transitory, can reduce citizens' degree of satisfaction with, and support for, the existing political institutions.[2] A less explored question is whether severe economic crisis shapes the political attitudes of individuals who are not directly affected by economic hardship. Awareness of the depth of the economic crisis is likely to spur fears about the future, leading many to feel increasingly unsafe (see Mughan and Lacy 2002). If increasingly anxious citizens believe that the existing political actors and institutions are incapable of pulling the country out of economic crisis, discontent with the political system could spread across the board. Note that the overall impact of economic crisis on public attitudes towards key democratic institutions would be much greater in this latter scenario.

---

[1] Although political culture and political economy perspectives may lead to different predictions about democratic stability, they are in many ways complementary approaches (see e.g. Clarke et al.1993; Green et al. 2002).
[2] This is precisely why extended social rights can be seen as having a crucial legitimizing impact on democratic institutions (see e.g. Clarke et al. 1993; Brooks and Manza 2007).

Whether or not economic crisis leads to an erosion of support for the political system beyond those directly affected by economic hardship is therefore a crucial question for the study of the economic determinants of political legitimacy. Following the terminology of the economic voting literature, I call attitudinal reactions that are triggered by individuals' own objective experiences of economic hardship *egocentric* reactions; whereas I call *sociotropic* reactions those reactions that are triggered by respondents' assessments of the economic situation of the country as a whole, regardless of their own economic conditions (see Kinder and Kiewiet 1981; Lewis-Beck and Stegmaier 2000).

Economic crisis effects and incomplete European integration

Sociotropic reactions to economic crisis in Europe could be especially intense under particular institutional conditions. Economic crisis has caught many European countries in the middle of an incomplete process of economic and political integration. Having renounced a great deal of economic sovereignty for the benefits of currency unification, national governments belonging to the European Monetary Union (EMU) currently find themselves lacking the standard monetary policy instruments to stimulate economic growth (e.g. devaluation). This makes national governments in the Eurozone objectively less efficacious than those outside, which can in turn lead to further economic deterioration. If citizens perceive that their governments are powerless to combat economic crisis, discontent with the economic situation of the country could soon spur widespread feelings of political distrust and disaffection. I therefore posit that the attitudinal impact of economic crisis on public support for the existing political institutions could be significantly stronger in Eurozone countries, as feelings of governmental inefficacy could be particularly marked inside the EMU.

Support for social cohesion through welfare policy

Socialization and political economy arguments can also be distinguished within the existing literature on attitudes towards social cohesion and the welfare state. Socialization approaches stress the key role that citizens' core values play in determining the degree of support for welfare policies. Again such values are seen as the product of political socialization in both families and schools (see e.g. Robinson and Bell 1978; Hyman and Wright 1979; Hasenfel and Rafferty 1989). Consonant with this literature, formal education, political ideology, party identification, and attitudes towards egalitarianism have been shown to have a significant effect on public support for welfare policies and the redistributive principles they embody (see e.g. Hasenfeld and Rafferty 1989; Feldman and Zaller 1992; Jacoby 1994; Kam and Nam 2008).

Advocates of the political economy argument stress the role of individual economic interests in shaping support for welfare policy (see e.g. Meltzer and Richard 1981). In line with this view, there is abundant empirical evidence showing that the most vulnerable citizens are consistently more likely to favour redistributive policies than those better off (see e.g. Hasenfeld and Rafferty 1989; Svallfors 1997; Edlund 1999; Andress and Heien 2001; Blekesaune 2007; Kam and Nam 2008). This evidence speaks clearly in favour of the existence of *egocentric* pro-distribution effects. But what about *sociotropic* effects? Does recession also affect the preferences for redistribution of those citizens who do not experience economic hardship directly? Are potential welfare contributors more or less inclined to support welfare policies in times of economic strain? Unfortunately, the existing literature does not allow us to make any clear prediction in this respect.

Authors such as Alt (1979) and Axinn and Stern (2005), for instance, have argued that the economic worries that recession brings should make potential contributors *less* inclined to support redistributive policies since redistribution runs against their own short-term economic interests. In contrast, Blekesaune (2007) and Blekesaune and Quadagno (2003) inter alia contend that both self-interest and altruistic motives should make contributors *more* willing to support welfare policies in time of economic duress (see also Kam and Nam 2008). According to these latter authors, altruistic motives could emerge if recession generates a genuine concern amongst potential contributors for those worse off; whereas self-interest motives would be triggered by contributors' perception that they might become potential recipients themselves.

Still a third argument could be made if we consider that economic crisis could reduce support for redistribution for altruistic reasons. As leaders across Europe repeat the mantra that today's austerity is a necessary precondition for tomorrow's growth, many truly altruistic Europeans could reduce their support to welfare spending for unselfish reasons. What is the overall sociotropic impact of economic crisis on public attitudes towards redistributive policies is thus an open empirical question.

To summarize, I have argued that economic crisis could have affected public attitudes about the political system both by eroding citizens' objective economic conditions (*egocentric* effect) as well as by spurring widespread anxiety about the country's future even amongst individuals who do not experience economic hardship directly (*sociotropic* effect). Both egocentric and sociotropic effects are likely to increase citizens' perception that the existing political institutions are incapable of meeting the pressing demands and needs of the people in times of economic strain. This should lead to an increase in political distrust and political dissatisfaction with the existing democratic institutions. These effects should be stronger the greater the depth of the crisis and possibly also stronger in countries belonging to the EMU, as in these countries governments lack standard monetary policy instruments to combat economic recession. Whether economic crisis enhances or erodes the degree of public support for redistribution through the welfare state is theoretically undetermined. Yet I expect to find higher support for redistribution amongst the most economically vulnerable respondents, as well as amongst those holding solidaristic and egaliatarian attitudes, values, and ideologies.

Data and Methods

I investigate the impact of economic vulnerability and economic crisis on political trust, satisfaction with democracy, and attitudes towards welfare-state redistribution using data from the 2004 and the 2010 European Social Survey datasets. The analysis is restricted to respondents aged between 20 and 64. The resulting analytical sample comprises over 53,200 individuals belonging to nineteen different European countries, namely: Belgium, the Czech Republic, Denmark, Estonia, Germany, Finland, France, Greece, Hungary, Ireland, the Netherlands, Norway, Poland, Portugal, Slovenia, Slovakia, Spain, Sweden, and the United Kingdom. For most—but not all—countries in this pooled dataset, 2004 is a pre-recession year, whilst 2010 is either a recession or a post-recession year.

I use a two-step regression approach: in the first step, I test for individual-level predictors of the three attitudes of interest and calculate country-level differences in the impact of time, measured as the change in net average attitudes between 2004 and 2010. These time effects are estimated by fitting nineteen different pooled regressions, one for each country in the dataset. If changes in the economic environment experienced in each country between 2004 and 2010 had any impact on the attitudes of their typical citizens, such impact should be captured by these fist-step time estimates. In a second stage, first-step estimates for the net impact of time are used as the outcome variable, whilst countries become the unit of analysis (N = 19). The fact that countries differ in the size of the economic contraction experienced between the two observation points provides a crucial source of variation for the identification of country-level economic crisis effects in this second step. I use two country-level predictors for the second-step regression: the change in GDP growth observed between 2004 and 2010 in each of the nineteen countries studied and a dummy variable capturing whether such countries were members of the Eurozone by 2010. Figures for GDP change are obtained from Eurostat (2012d). They measure the actual change in the economic environment experienced by each country between 2004 and 2010 (i.e. the size of economic contraction).[3] This second-step regression allows us to investigate what is the macro-level impact of economic crisis on net average political trust, satisfaction with democracy, and attitudes towards redistribution, as well as whether this impact is, as expected, stronger in countries inside the European Monetary Union, using a flexible and intuitive framework.

Indicators of political attitudes

The ESS pooled dataset includes three different questions that measure respectively respondents' degree of trust in party politics, trust in the national parliament, and trust in politicians using self-placement interval scales. Responses to these questions are highly correlated and hence they have been combined into one single trust index. The political trust index ranges from 0 to 10, is normally distributed, and shows very high levels of reliability (Kronbach's coefficient = 0.9). The political trust index is our first measure of support for national democratic institutions.

The ESS also includes an indicator of democratic satisfaction. Each respondent is asked 'How satisfied are you with the way democracy works in [your country]?' This is measured using a self-placement scale ranging from 0 to 10. Responses to this scale are again normally distributed. Traditionally, satisfaction with democracy has been interpreted as measuring Easton's conceptualization of diffuse support (Easton 1975).[4]

Our last dependent variable measures support for income redistribution through governmental action using a five-point interval scale that captures respondents' degree of agreement with the assertion 'the government should reduce differences in income levels'. Income redistribution is an essential policy instrument for the promotion of social cohesion as well as a defining element of European welfare states. Yet it is obviously not the only policy instrument governments use to combat social exclusion. Unfortunately, this is the only question tapping into citizens' support for welfare state principles that is present in both the 2004 and 2010 ESS rounds. Respondents are provided with five possible answers to this question, ranging from 'disagree strongly' to 'agree strongly'. Roughly 70 per cent of European respondents agree or strongly agree with this assertion. This already shows that support for redistributive principles is strong in Europe. In order to have a comparable

---

[3] In order to account for differences in sampling error across first-stage estimators, I use Feasible Generalized Least Squares estimation, as proposed by Lewis and Linzer (2005), using the program developed by Lewis (2000).

[4] A number of scholars have contested the validity of this scale as a measure of core democratic values (see e.g. Canache et al. 2001; Linde and Ekman 2003; Ruiz-Rufino 2013). They recommend interpreting the scale as measuring evaluations of democratic performance only. Note, however, that this latter form of democratic dissatisfaction could still pose a challenge to regime stability if it is widely spread across the population.

metrics with the previous two indices, responses to this question have been rescaled from 0 to 10.

Explanatory variables

Individual-level models for pooled data include estimates for respondents' age, years of schooling, marital status and number of children (not shown), together with class position, unemployment experience, and financial distress. The latter three variables capture *egocentric* effects. Class is measured using the Eurosec class schema;[5] unemployment experiences are captured using information about respondents' current employment status combined with retrospective information about past unemployment spells; financial distress is self-reported and refers to the household level.[6]

All individual-level models include estimates for political ideology, measured using the standard self-placement left–right scale, as well as for three core values: egalitarianism, altruism, and support for a strong state. Models also control for two personality characteristics possibly associated with the outcome variables: happiness and hedonism (not shown). Individuals' propensity to happiness could permeate their views about the political system, whilst hedonism is expected to reduce support for redistribution. Having such a rich set of values and traits as controls is rare in the study of political attitudes (further details about the construction of all attitudinal controls is provided in the appendix to this chapter).

A key attitudinal variable tested in all individual-level models is respondents' degree of satisfaction with the general situation of the economy in their respective countries. This is measured using a self-placement scale that ranges from 0 (maximum dissatisfaction) to 10 (maximum satisfaction). Respondents' views about the general shape of the national economy net of individual-level economic experiences capture *sociotropic* effects for the average citizen.

Political Culture, Economic Interests, and Political Attitudes

Political culture and political economy approaches disagree on the factors that most affect citizens' attitudes to political institutions (internalized values vs. economic interests). As a result, they make divergent predictions about

---

[5] For the sake of simplicity of presentation, tables below only show estimates for two particularly vulnerable occupational classes: lower technical workers and routine manual workers.

[6] Respondents reporting that it is 'difficult' or 'very difficult' to live on current household income are considered financially distressed. Those who claim to be 'living comfortably on', or 'coping with', current income are considered not distressed.

the degree of resilience of political attitudes to changes in the economic environment. The ESS data allow us to test for the effect of values and economic interests simultaneously, as well as to estimate the change in political attitudes observed between 2004 and 2010, a period that covers the first phase of global economic recession.

Table 10.1 presents the results of fitting an OLS regression model on each of the three scales measuring political attitudes: political trust, satisfaction with democracy, and attitudes towards redistribution. Several findings reported in this table are consonant with political culture explanations. First, we observe a positive and significant effect of years of education on all three political attitudes of interest. This is consistent with the so-called enlightening hypothesis, which links democratic culture and attitudes pro-redistribution to political socialization via schooling (but see Jackman and Muha 1984). We also observe a positive and significant effect of core egalitarian values on all three indicators. Unsurprisingly, this effect is particularly strong in the case of attitudes towards income redistribution.[7] Finally, we observe that right-wing respondents tend to be more trusting and more satisfied with the way democracy works in their respective countries than left-wing ones, but less supportive of redistributive policies.

The economic interest perspective also finds strong empirical support. As expected, class is significantly associated with all three dependent variables. Lower technical and routine workers show significantly lower levels of political trust and satisfaction with democracy, as well as higher levels of support for redistributive policies, than large employers, managers, and professionals, which is the reference category.[8] These findings are fully consistent with political economy arguments linking support for both political institutions and redistributive policies to stable socio-economic interests.

Transient experiences of unemployment also seem to leave a very visible trace on the three variables of interest. Currently unemployed respondents, as well as those employed respondents who have experienced unemployment in the last five years, show lower levels of trust and satisfaction with democracy and higher levels of support for income redistribution than employed respondents with no previous unemployment record. Interestingly, we also find the same significant differences, albeit roughly half as strong,

[7] Attitudes pro-redistribution are also significantly enhanced by altruistic values (coeff. = 0.04, p<0.001) and attitudes in favour of a strong government (coeff. = 0.06, p<0.001) (not shown). Personality characteristics also seem to have interesting effects: happiness-propensity increases political trust and satisfaction with democracy, but has no effect on attitudes to redistribution, whilst hedonism is associated with lower scores in all three political attitudes (available on request).

[8] Political trust and satisfaction with democracy is also low amongst small employers and self-employed respondents, whereas their support for welfare redistribution is only a little bit higher than that of large employers, managers, and professionals (available on request).

Table 10.1. OLS regressions on political attitudes: selected variables

VARIABLES	Political Trust	Satisfaction with Democracy	Attitudes towards Redistribution
	Model 1	Model 1	Model 1
Political socialization and ideology			
Years of schooling	0.04***	0.03***	−0.02***
Ideology (L–R)	0.07***	0.11***	−0.09***
Egalitarianism	0.04***	0.08***	0.11***
Class			
Large employer, higher managers & professionals	ref	ref	ref
Lower technical workers	−0.38***	−0.43***	0.36***
Routine workers	−0.31***	−0.41***	0.32***
Transient economic experiences			
Unemployment history			
Employed, no unemployment record	ref	ref	ref
Employed, unemployment spell more than 5 years back	−0.12***	−0.11**	0.06***
Employed, unemployment spell less than 5 years back	−0.20***	−0.26***	0.11***
Currently unemployed	−0.16***	−0.26***	0.08***
Experience of household financial distress	−0.46***	−0.65***	0.17***
CHANGE 2004–2010	−0.17***	−0.19***	0.01
Observations	46,169	45,466	45,963
R-squared	0.22	0.21	0.211

*** $p<0.001$, ** $p<0.01$, *$p<0.05$.

Notes: Models control for age, marital status, no. of children, and country dummies. Several class dummies are not shown. Models also control for altruism, attitudes pro-strong government, propensity to happiness and hedonism (not shown). Constant not shown. Weighted.

Source: Calculated by the author from Pooled ESS 2004–2010.

between employed respondents who experienced unemployment more than five years back and employed respondents who have never experienced unemployment. This suggests that the experience of unemployment could have long-lasting consequences on political attitudes.

Consonant with political economy approaches, we also find a very strong effect of household financial distress on the three outcome variables. As expected, individuals experiencing financial difficulties at home show significantly lower scores on political trust and satisfaction with democracy and significantly higher preferences for income redistribution. Finding that individuals' experiences of unemployment and financial distress affect their political attitudes constitutes clear evidence of 'egocentric' effects.

Change in political attitudes 2004–2010

In all the models in Table 10.1 the effects of time are estimated using the variable 'YEAR CHANGE 2004–2010'. This variable captures the difference in net average attitudes observed between the two observation years for the typical European citizen, net of all the variables in the model, including class and transient economic experiences. According to the regression estimates, this net coefficient shows an average decrease of roughly one-fifth of a point in political trust and satisfaction with democracy between 2004 and 2010. In contrast, the effect of time on attitudes towards redistribution for the typical European citizen is very close to zero and not significant. This already suggests that redistributive attitudes in Europe as a whole have remained mostly stable across the two observation points.

The change over time in political trust and satisfaction with democracy was very strongly affected by people's perceptions of the general economic situation of their respective countries (i.e. their sociotropic views about the economy). Table 10.2 shows that when such perceptions of the economy are introduced in the regression the effect of survey year on political trust and satisfaction with democracy is fully explained away. This indicates, first of all, that the change in net political attitudes observed between 2004 and 2010 is actually driven by economic crisis effects; and, second, that economic crisis (measured as time change) has not only egocentric but also sociotropic effects on political legitimacy, as it affects all types of citizens regardless of their own objective economic experiences. In other words, increasing distrust and dissatisfaction with democracy between 2004 and 2010 does not seem to be confined to the most vulnerable segments of society only. These are important findings.[9]

My estimates for the effect of economic crisis on attitudes towards redistribution offer a much less clear picture. First, as noted above, I find no significant changes between 2004 and 2005. Second, the estimated effect of sociotropic views on attitudes towards redistribution seems very small indeed: a full-range ten-point increase in satisfaction with the national economy would only yield a *reduction* in pro-redistribution views of less than half

---

[9] Introducing sociotropic views also yields a very significant reduction in the class, unemployment history, and financial distress coefficients for both political trust and satisfaction with democracy (available on request). This suggests that the experience of economic vulnerability shapes people's views about the general situation of the national economy which, in turn, affect political trust and democratic satisfaction.

Table 10.2. The effect of introducing perceptions of the economy on time change coefficients

VARIABLES	Political Trust		Satisfaction with Democracy		Attitudes towards Redistribution	
	Model 1	Model 2	Model 1	Model 2	Model 1	Model 2
Satisfaction with country's economy		0.40***		0.49***		−0.04***
CHANGE 2014-2010	−0.17***	−0.00	−0.19***	0.02	0.01	−0.01
Observations	46,169	45,796	45,466	45,196	45,963	45,604
R-squared	0.22	0.36	0.21	0.38	0.211	0.218

*** p<0.001, ** p<0.01, *p<0.05.

Notes: Model 1 as in Table 10.1. Model 2 adds perceptions of the economy. Weighted. Source: Calculated by the author from pooled ESS 2004–2010.

a point (see Table 10.2). The evidence on economic crisis effects on attitudes towards redistribution seems therefore very weak at the individual level.

Explaining country differences in the average change in political attitudes between 2004 and 2010

Let us now look at country differences in the effect of time. Table 10.3 shows the estimated time-change coefficients and the 2004 values for all three dependent variables and all the countries in the dataset. First-step estimates for the effect of time come from nineteen different country-specific regressions. These regressions include all the variables present in Model 1 in Table 10.1 with the exception of unemployment history and financial distress.[10]

The first thing to note is that there are very significant differences in the time effects found across different European societies. Cross-country variation is the largest in the case of attitudes towards redistribution,[11] although the size of these time effects is generally very small (with the exception of France, where we observe a one-point increase in support for redistribution between 2004 and 2010).

[10] Note that if these latter variables measuring transient economic experiences had been included in the country-level regressions, the resulting year-change coefficients would underestimate the total effect of recession on political attitudes, since recession increases the odds of experiencing both unemployment and financial distress.
[11] Note that eight countries show no significant change in attitudes to redistribution between 2004 and 2010 (Denmark, Estonia, Hungary, Slovakia, Slovenia, Spain, Sweden, and United Kingdom); in eight other countries we observe a significant increase in average support for redistribution (Belgium, Czech Republic, Finland, France, Germany, Ireland, Netherlands, and Portugal); whilst three other countries show a significant decrease (Greece, Norway, and Poland).

Table 10.3. GDP contraction, net coefficients for time change (2004–2010), and 2004 values for outcome variables by country

Country	Drop in GDP growth[a] 2004-2010	Political Trust			Satisfaction with Democracy			Attitudes towards Redistribution		
		2004 value[b]	Coef.	Sig.	2004 value	Coef.	Sig.	2004 value	Coef.	Sig
Greece	9.3	3.72	–2.16	***	5.84	–3.2	***	4.34	–0.22	***
Ireland	5.2	3.87	–0.67	***	5.56	–0.77	***	3.81	0.18	***
Spain	3.6	4.11	–0.87	***	6.03	–1.1	***	3.89	–0.02	
Hungary	3.5	2.83	0.31	*	3.9	0.08		4.23	0.09	
Norway	3.3	4.56	0.65	***	6.21	0.76	***	3.73	–0.23	***
Slovenia	3.2	3.5	–1.06	***	4.47	–1.31	***	4.2	–0.01	
Estonia	3	3.48	0.07		4.54	0.44	***	3.98	–0.05	
Czech Rep.	2.2	2.82	0.01		4.52	0.19	(*)	3.6	0.13	*
Poland	1.4	2.16	0.66	***	3.82	1.23	***	3.92	–0.14	**
UK	1.1	3.75	–0.26	**	5.2	–0.39	***	3.49	–0.01	
Denmark	1	5.78	–0.52	***	7.32	–0.42	***	3.17	–0.05	
Belgium	0.9	4.38	–0.4	***	5.41	–0.32	**	3.64	0.14	**
Slovakia	0.9	2.65	0.31	**	3.85	0.25	(*)	3.85	0.08	
France	0.8	4.78	–1.37	***	6.53	–2.38	***	3	1.08	***
Finland	0.8	5.18	–0.62	***	6.61	–0.5	**	3.89	0.25	**
Netherlands	0.6	4.5	0.59	***	5.66	0.46	***	3.36	0.09	(*)
Portugal	0.2	3.07	–0.35	***	3.77	0.08		4.22	0.17	***
Sweden	–2.4	4.71	0.65	***	6.09	0.66	***	3.69	0.04	
Germany	–3	3.44	0		5.24	–0.12		3.39	0.33	***

*** p<0.001, ** p<0.001, *p<0.05, (*) p<0.10.

Notes: [a] Real GDP growth drop is calculated as the rate of growth in 2004 less the rate of growth in 2010, where growth rates are measured as percentage change over the previous year. [b] Estimates for 2004 marginal values and for 2004–2010 change in coefficients are obtained from fitting 19 country-specific regression models identical to Model 1 in Table 10.1 but excluding transient economic experiences (i.e. unemployment history and financial distress)—all other variables constant at their means.

Source: Calculated by the author from pooled ESS 2004–2010 and Eurostat real GDP growth figures (Eurostat 2012d).

We also observe divergent patterns for the effect of time on both political trust and satisfaction with democracy. Greeks stand out as showing the largest erosion in political trust and democratic satisfaction of all respondents, with average decreases of two and three points respectively out of an 11-point scale. These are dramatic changes by all accounts. The erosion in political legitimacy, as measured by these two crucial indicators, is also very sizeable in France, Spain, Slovenia, and Ireland. France shows average drops of roughly one point in political trust and as much as two points in satisfaction with democracy. As we shall see, such drops are much larger than expected given the actual GDP losses experienced by France between 2004 and 2010. Drops in trust and satisfaction with democracy in Spain, Slovenia, and Ireland are roughly between two-thirds of a point and one point (see Table 10.3). Yet we find an increase in net average values of political trust and satisfaction with democracy between 2004 and 2010 in the Netherlands, Norway, Sweden, Poland, and Slovakia, whilst no change in either trust or satisfaction with democracy is observed in Germany. The rest of the countries show changes in one indicator but not the other. How can we explain these divergent patterns in time-change coefficients?

First of all, it must be noted that there is a high degree of variation in the way different countries experienced the first phase of global recession (see Chapters 1 and 2 of this book). I approximate these experiences by comparing the rate of GDP growth across the two observation windows, 2004 and 2010, in each country, using official figures (Eurostat 2012d). Greece stands out again as the country that has experienced by far the largest drop in GDP growth between 2004 and 2010, amounting to more than nine percentage points. Ireland, Hungary, Spain, Norway, Slovenia, and Estonia follow suit with GDP losses between five and three points. The observed change in GDP growth between the two observation years has been much more moderate in the Czech Republic, Belgium, Poland, France, Denmark, and Slovakia (with losses roughly between one and two points) and very small in Finland, the Netherlands, and Portugal. In Sweden and Germany the GDP growth rate was actually higher in 2010 than it was in 2004. Can country differences in the way public attitudes changed between 2004 and 2010 be explained by different experiences of the crisis?

Macro-level economic crisis effects

In order to answer this question, I next regress the first-step estimates for the effect of time on the typical citizen in each of the nineteen countries of the sample on the above-commented changes in GDP growth observed between 2004 and 2010. Note that the resulting estimate for changes in GDP growth will capture country-level economic crisis effects on attitudinal change between the two observation points *directly*. I further test whether this direct impact of economic crisis on political attitudes differs by membership in the European Monetary Union. Results are presented in Table 10.4.

Macro-level estimates yield significant economic crisis effects for all three attitudinal variables studied, although the effects for attitudes towards welfare redistribution are again very small. According to the estimates of a simple linear model (Model 1), a one-point reduction in GDP growth between the two observation years would reduce net average political trust and net average satisfaction with democracy by roughly one-sixth of a point in an 11-point interval scale. In the case of net average support for redistribution, the same drop in GDP would yield a reduction of as little as 1/25 of a point. Recall that the estimated coefficients for attitudinal change between 2004 and 2010 are net of individual-level predictors. In this sense, the GDP change coefficient

Table 10.4. Two-step regression estimates: the effect of GDP contraction and EMU membership on estimated changes in political trust, satisfaction with democracy, and attitudes towards redistribution[1] for the typical citizen

VARIABLES	Political Trust		Satisfaction with Democracy		Attitudes towards Redistribution	
	Model 1	Model 2	Model 1	Model 2	Model 1	Model 2
GDP contraction[2]	−0.16**	−0.02	−0.22**	−0.01	−0.04***	−0.01
EMU membership[3]		−0.75***		−1.07***		0.22**
EMU × GDP contract		−0.15(*)		−0.24**		−0.04
Constant	−0.26(*)	0.19	−0.33	0.32	0.09	−0.03
Observations	19	19	19	19	19	19
R-squared	0.30	0.59	0.29	0.59	0.14	0.34

*** $p<0.01$, ** $p<0.05$, (*) $p<0.1$.

Notes: [1] Estimates for change in dependent variables are obtained from fitting 19 country-specific regression models as explained in Table 10.3. [2] GDP contraction is calculated as the rate of GDP growth in 2004 less the rate of GDP growth in 2010, where growth rates are measured as percentage change over the previous year. [3] EMU membership status as in 2010. Slovenia adopted the euro in 2007 and Slovakia in 2009.

Source: Calculated by the author from pooled ESS 2004–2010 and Eurostat real GDP growth figures (Eurostat 2012d).

should be interpreted as the effect of economic crisis on the attitudes of the typical citizen in each country. It must therefore be noted that the estimated macro-level effect for attitudes to redistribution is not only very weak in size but, most importantly, runs in the exact opposite direction to the individual-level effect of sociotropic views presented in Table 10.2. Whilst the former effect suggests that economic crisis decreases average support for redistribution in Europe, the later indicated that citizens' awareness of economic crisis *increased* average support for redistribution. In light of these findings, our results for economic crisis effects on redistributive views must be considered both negligible and inconsistent.

Two-step regression estimates in Model 1 assume that the attitudinal effects for a given change in GDP are the same across the nineteen countries studied. Yet I have posited that the erosion of political legitimacy should be actually greater in countries belonging to the EMU, since the governments of Eurozone countries lack standard policy instruments to combat economic crisis, which should make their economic policies objectively less efficacious. I test this prediction by fitting an interaction term between membership in the Eurozone and GDP contraction (see Model 2). This interaction is significant at the 90 per cent level for political trust and at the 95 per cent level for satisfaction with democracy but insignificant in the case of attitudes towards redistribution.

This shows that the average levels of political trust and democratic satisfaction are lower on average in countries belonging to the EMU. Most importantly, it suggests that all of the impact of economic crisis on both indicators of political legitimacy could have been concentrated in Eurozone countries. Figure 10.1 graphs these observed effects. Note that France appears clearly as an outlier, with decreases in political trust and democratic satisfaction that are much larger than predicted given the actual change in GDP growth experienced between 2004 and 2010 in this country.[12]

Testing the robustness of the 'Eurozone effect'

Countries in the Eurozone might differ from those outside in many important institutional characteristics unrelated to the currency and which could also mediate the effect of economic crisis on political legitimacy. Two such characteristics are of particular concern. First, countries in the Eurozone subsample could provide less generous welfare benefits *on average* than countries outside. This could constitute an important source of estimation bias if welfare generosity cushions the impact of economic crisis on political attitudes. Second, there could be differences in the quality of democratic representation between the two subsamples contrasted. If countries with comparatively weaker political institutions happen to be over-represented in the Eurozone subsample, and if economic crisis effects on political views are significantly stronger in low-quality democracies, then our Eurozone effect could be again an artefact of omitted variable bias.

I have tested for differences between countries with high and low levels of net social expenditure[13] in the effect of GDP losses between 2004 and 2010 on political trust and democratic satisfaction. These are clearly non-significant (available on request). This suggests that the observed economic crisis effects on both political trust and satisfaction with democracy found in the Eurozone are not artificially driven by unobserved country differences in welfare generosity by EMU membership. I have also tested an interaction between the quality of democratic institutions, as assessed by external expert evaluations,[14] and GDP losses. This interaction is clearly not significant for

---

[12] France experienced escalating problems of highly visible political corruption during the analysed period, with major successive scandals involving first Jacques Chirac, president of France until 2007, and then Nicolas Sarkozy. Such scandals could have affected the observed change in political trust and satisfaction with democracy between 2004 and 2010.

[13] Social expenditure figures are for 2007 and have been obtained from the OECD database (see: <http://www.oecd.org/document/24/0,3746,en_2649_33933_2671576_1_1_1_1,00.html>). I have also tested an interaction between countries with high and low levels of social spending on the working-age population and GDP losses and results were again non-significant.

[14] Quality of democracy has been measured using the 2006 Quality of Democracy Index published by the Economist Intelligence Unit (*The Economist* 2007, pp. 3–6). I distinguish between high- and low-quality democracies.

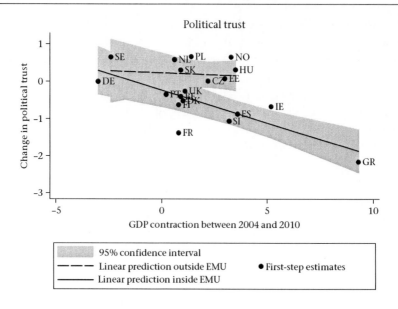

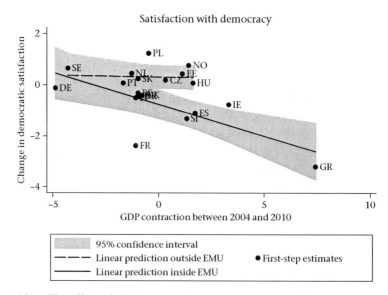

Figure 10.1. The effect of GDP contraction on net average political trust and democratic satisfaction for the typical citizen by EMU membership according to Model 2 in Table 10.4

Source: Calculated by the author from pooled ESS 2004–2010 and Eurostat real GDP growth figures (Eurostat 2012d).

political trust but is marginally significant (at the 90 per cent level) in the case of democratic satisfaction (available on request). This suggests that economic crisis effects on democratic satisfaction could indeed be higher in countries where levels of democratic quality are low. The key question to assess, however, is whether this statistical association is the real driver of the Eurozone interaction in the case of democratic satisfaction. Two further pieces of evidence suggest it is not: first, the Eurozone effect is a significantly better predictor than the quality-of-democracy;[15] second, and most importantly, the Eurozone interaction coefficient remains significant even after controlling for democratic quality (results available on request).

These robustness tests provide further support to the argument that there is something particular to Eurozone countries that makes the political attitudes of their citizens more reactive to economic crisis. I believe this peculiarity has to do with the objective economic policy limitations that Eurozone governments face in their fight against economic crisis. These limitations make Eurozone governments less responsive to the pressing demands and interests of their citizens in times of economic hardship. Moreover, they can aggravate the depth of recession itself, as the painful experiences of peripheral EU economies currently illustrate. Both effects combined could explain why we observe a much greater erosion of political trust and satisfaction with democracy in EMU countries.

Note, finally, that this explanation fully admits the possibility of economic crisis-threshold effects. According to this interpretation, citizens' support for democratic institutions could remain largely stable until a certain threshold of economic deterioration is surpassed, after which support could experience a precipitous decline. Greece is the country that experienced the largest deterioration in its economic environment between 2004 and 2010 (followed by Ireland). If we remove Greece from the data, neither the Eurozone interaction nor the direct effect of GDP contraction reaches statistical significance (albeit the coefficients for both parameters remain in the expected direction). This suggests that threshold effects could actually be part, perhaps an essential part, of the observed EMU interaction.

Summary and Discussion

This study has investigated the effects of economic vulnerability and economic crisis on political trust, satisfaction with democracy, and attitudes to welfare redistribution using the 2004 and 2010 European Social Survey

[15] The Eurozone interaction model explains 55 per cent more of the variance than the quality-of-democracy interaction.

datasets. I have argued that these attitudes express the degree of public support for the two essential elements of the European model of social capitalism, namely, national democratic institutions and extensive welfare provision.

The results have provided clear evidence that both political values and individual economic experiences play a key role in shaping citizens' support for democracy and welfare-state redistribution in Europe. Consonant with political culture approaches, I have found significant effects for schooling and ideology, as well as for several attitudes and values on all three indicators analysed. In line with political economy approaches, I have found that experiences of economic vulnerability are associated with lower levels of political trust and satisfaction with democracy and higher levels of support for redistributive policies. These latter findings show that public support for the democratic and redistributive principles of the welfare state has clear microlevel economic foundations.

However, net average support for national democratic institutions eroded fast in several European countries between 2004 and 2010. This erosion is less consistent with political culture explanations, as it shows that democratic legitimacy is to a considerable extent contingent upon economic performance. In many (but not all) of the nineteen countries analysed in this study both political trust and satisfaction with democracy decreased sharply. I have shown that such trends can be explained by a parallel increase in average levels of dissatisfaction with the economic situation of the country (i.e. *sociotropic* effects). This suggests that economic crisis decreases public support for the existing political institutions even amongst those citizens who do not experience economic hardship directly. I have also shown that the changes in average political trust and satisfaction with democracy in the nineteen countries studied are significantly correlated with the changes in GDP growth observed between 2004 and 2010, although this overall correlation seems mainly driven by the experiences of Eurozone countries.

The pattern of change in the case of attitudes to redistribution at the country level is, however, much less clear. Macro-level evidence seems to suggest that Europeans' net average support for income redistribution decreased with economic crisis in Europe. Yet the size of this effect is very small indeed. Furthermore, these macro-level estimates do not square well with the individual-level evidence, which shows that negative evaluations of the economic situation of the country's economy increase support for redistribution for the typical European citizen, although again the estimated effect of sociotropic views on attitudes to redistribution is very small. Overall, macro-level findings seem too negligible and inconsistent to grant any firm conclusion about the association between GDP and attitudes to redistribution. It appears that average attitudes towards redistribution for the typical European citizen have remained mostly stable in the face of economic crisis.

Economic Crisis, Monetary Union, and Political Legitimacy

I have argued that the erosion of political trust and satisfaction with democracy could have been particularly strong in countries inside the Eurozone because Eurozone governments no longer dispose of the standard monetary policy instruments to combat economic crisis (e.g. stimulating exports by devaluing their currency). In order to join the Monetary Union, national governments had to give up national sovereignty in exchange for supranational integration. But the process of European integration remains incomplete and this makes it inefficacious. Imperfect integration generates huge coordination problems, amplifies financial tensions, and opens up the door for speculative attacks on both the periphery's sovereign debts and the euro as a whole, which in turn pushes peripheral economies deeper into recession. This is the vicious circle that is currently endangering the European project.

The combination of global economic crisis and incomplete integration at the European level constitutes a particularly damaging cocktail for democratic legitimacy.[16] If economic crisis is deep and citizens perceive their elected representatives as largely incapable of pulling the country out of it, frustration, distrust, and disaffection might spread across the board. Discontent spills over from those directly affected by economic vulnerability to the median voter. The evidence presented in this study shows that this has already happened in several Eurozone countries. The erosion of democratic legitimacy is particularly sizeable in countries such as France, Ireland, Slovenia, and Spain. In the case of Greece, this erosion has reached most alarming proportions and deserves special comment.

Figure 10.2 shows the distribution of political trust and satisfaction with democracy in Greece in both 2004 and 2010. The change is dramatic. In 2010, 62 per cent of Greek respondents placed themselves within the four lower values of the democratic satisfaction scale and as much as 85 per cent of them placed themselves within the four lower values of the political trust scale. In both cases, value zero of the scale was the modal value, comprising 22 and 40 per cent of responses respectively. It is against this backdrop of huge political dissatisfaction that one should interpret recent political events in Greece, including the spectacular rise of the left-wing anti-bailout coalition SYRIZA, the crash of the Greek Socialist Party, PASOK, and the entrance

---

[16] To be sure, incomplete supranational integration poses serious problems for democratic theory on its own, as it reduces both political efficacy and democratic accountability at the national level, whilst providing no fully working substitute at the supranational level (see e.g. Scharpf 1997; Offe 2000; Follesdal and Hix 2006). Yet it is in times of economic crisis that the democratic deficiencies of incomplete integration become most apparent.

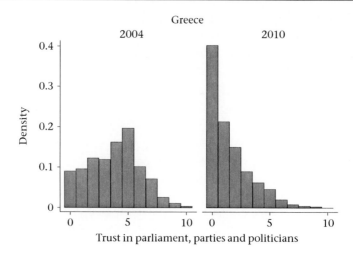

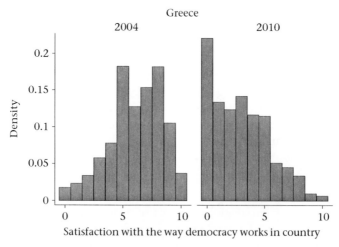

Figure 10.2. A Greek tragedy? Political trust and satisfaction with democracy in 2004 and 2010

Source: European Social Survey, 2004 and 2010.

of the anti-European neo-Nazi party, the Golden Dawn, in the Greek parliament.[17] Greece has also experienced increasing social unrest. Since 2010, a series of anti-bailout demonstrations have taken over the streets of the main

[17] SYRIZA is currently the second political force in Greece, after seeing its representation increase from only 1 MP (4.7 per cent of the vote) in the 2009 elections to 71 MPs (26.9 per cent of the vote) in the last elections of June 2012. In contrast, support for the socialist PASOK plummeted from 160 seats (43.9 per cent of the vote) in 2009 to only 33 seats (13 per cent of the vote). The neo-Nazi party the Golden Dawn advocates, amongst other things, the incarceration of illegal immigrants in labour camps. This party obtained 21 seats and 7 per cent of the popular vote in June 2012.

Greek cities. Many of these demonstrations turned into violent riots, some of which lasted for days.

The signs of growing political disaffection can also be read in many other peripheral countries across Europe. In 2009 mounting protests over the financial crisis in Iceland led to the Busahaldabyltingin, or Pots and Pans Revolution, which culminated in the prosecution of the former prime minister and the writing of a new constitution (Stjórnlagaráðs 2011). Peaceful mass protests have also swept across south-west Europe. In March 2011 rallies over the economic crisis were held in over ten Portuguese cities organized under the name of Geração à Rasca, Desperate Generation. Portuguese demonstrations were soon followed by the spectacular outbreak of the 15-M movement in Spain. Organized through web-based social networks without the involvement of any major union or political party, the 15-M movement's cry for 'real democracy' has attracted an unprecedented level of popular support.[18]

These new social movements illustrate well the growing chasm that separates many disaffected European citizens from their traditional political representatives. The data analysed in this study only cover the first phase of economic crisis. For many European countries things have only worsened since. Hence it is highly probable that the erosion of political legitimacy that the ESS data reveal has actually deepened, presenting serious potential risks that political crisis may compound economic crisis. This is indeed a momentous time for Europe. It seems that it is much more than the single currency that is currently at stake.

Appendix

All individual-level models include estimates for three core values: altruism, egalitarianism, and support for a strong state. Altruism is measured as the importance individuals assign to helping people and caring for others; egalitarianism measures respondents' degree of identification with the principle that people be treated equally and have equal opportunities; and support for the state is measured as the importance individuals assign to having a strong government that ensures safety. All core values are measured using six-point interval identification scales.

---

[18] According to a survey carried out in July 2011, between 6 and 8 million Spaniards would have participated directly in at least one public event organized by the 15-M movement, and as much as 76 per cent of Spanish citizens considered its claims as 'more than reasonable' (El Pais 2011, 3 August).

Models also include controls for two personality characteristics possibly associated with the outcome variables: happiness-propensity and hedonism. Respondents' propensity to happiness is estimated as the residual from a model where self-placement in a ten-point happiness scale is regressed against age and its squared term, schooling, self-reported family financial strain, subjective well-being, life satisfaction, country, and, crucially, observation year. The resulting happiness residual thus captures the individual propensity to happiness net of transient and contextual factors. Hedonism is measured using a six-point interval composite scale combining responses to four questions, which measure respectively the importance that respondents assign to: (1) trying new and different things in life; (2) seeking adventures and having an exciting life; (3) seeking fun and things that give pleasure; and (4) having a good time (Kronbach's coefficient = 0.76). Results for core values and personality characteristics have been commented on above (see footnote 7), and are available on request.

11

Economic Crisis, Country Variations, and Institutional Structures

Duncan Gallie

The central concern of this study has been to examine the implications of the economic crisis, during the period 2008 to 2010, for key dimensions of the quality of work and social integration in Europe. It has drawn on the evidence available for nineteen countries from two waves of the European Social Survey, carried out in 2004 and 2010. With respect to the quality of work, the chapters have focused on skill change, opportunities for training, job control and work intensity, job insecurity, and work–family conflict. In relation to social integration, they have examined the implications of the crisis for employment commitment, subjective well-being, and attitudes to political legitimacy. The analyses have revealed a number of general effects of the economic crisis, but at the same time considerable variation in patterns between countries and country groups. This chapter draws together the main findings with respect to both similarities and divergences and considers the usefulness for understanding them of the major current interpretative frameworks for the comparative analysis of employment and welfare systems.

The Effects of Economic Crisis

Economic crisis and the quality of work

How did the period of the economic crisis between 2004 and 2010 affect the quality of work in Europe? Our starting point was that there was little in the way of clear guidance from existing research, but that a number of scenarios were plausible. It could be that economic crisis led to deterioration in the quality of work due to its effects in changing the power balance between employers and employees to the disadvantage of employees. It could be that it improved the quality of work through a process of creative destruction in which low-quality jobs in more backward sectors of industry were dispropor-tionately eliminated or through employers adapting work organization in the face of reduced numbers of staff and the need to secure employee com-mitment to difficult measures of reorganization. Finally, it was possible that it led to sharper polarization between a relatively protected core workforce which retained good work conditions and a peripheral workforce character-ized by increasingly poor work conditions.

As was discussed in Chapters 1 and 2, an important point to bear in mind is that the timing, duration, and depth both of the initial recession and of the period of economic crisis (which we take as the period lasting from the onset of the recession to a return to the levels GDP and unemployment at the previ-ous peak of the economic cycle) varied very considerably between European countries. In terms of severity of the recession, over the period 2008 to 2010, all countries but one saw a drop in GDP per capita, but it declined to a low point of 84 per cent of its peak level in Estonia and 86 per cent in Ireland while Poland saw no decline and Belgium a decline to only 97 per cent of its pre-recession peak. In terms of unemployment rates, unemployment rose from 2007–2010 by 12.2 percentage points in Estonia, 11.8 in Spain, and 9.1 in Ireland. But there was no increase at all in Germany and only very small increases in the Netherlands, Finland, France, and Sweden. Any assessment of the effects of the economic crisis needs then to take account of its differential severity in the various parts of Europe.

SKILLS STRUCTURE AND SKILL POLARIZATION

The accumulating evidence of research prior to the economic crisis pointed primarily to a long-term trend of skill upgrading in most countries (Cedefop 2010). The link between computerization and higher skills was confirmed by a number of studies, although it was not uncontroversial (contrast Green et al. 2003 with Handel 2003). There was no evidence of a general tendency for skill polarization, but rather some indication of polarization in the spe-cific cases of the US, the UK, and Spain (Wright and Dwyer 2000, 2003; Autor et al. 2003; Goos and Manning 2007; Tåhlin 2007; Cedefop 2011; Oesch and Rodriguez Menes 2011; Kalleberg 2011). Even in these cases, the expansion of higher-skilled jobs was very much more marked than the expansion of lower-skilled. With respect to country differences, while there was evidence of quite marked differences in initial pre-labour market entry skill formation as a result of the importance attached to early vocational training, skill dif-ferences tended to even out over the life cycle with higher rates of post-entry skill development in countries with weaker initial vocational training sys-tems (Herrigel and Sabel 1999; Tåhlin, 2007). Overall, the commonalities in the process of long-term skill upgrading in advanced societies appeared to be greater than the dissimilarities, with countries using different means to attain broadly similar ends.

Much of the theoretical drive behind the expectation of upskilling was premised on the view that consumer purchasing power and expanding markets would provide the incentive for new technological development. Issues about the effects of a major recession simply had not been on the agenda and there was little grounded research that could inform them. However, earlier theories of change in work could be extended to lead to quite diverse expectations of the effects of economic crisis with respect to skills. By changing the balance of power between employers and employees, it might be expected to lead to the re-emergence of strategies of deskilling, even if these had been put into abeyance in a period of expansion. Alternatively, a view of economic crisis as a source of 'creative destruction' might lead to an anticipation of an accelerated process of skill upgrading as less competitive, technologically backward, industries with low-skilled employees were decimated. Finally, it was possible that economic crisis led to more extensive skill polarization, involving continuing upskilling of the already more highly skilled and a deskilling or elimination of those in intermediate-level jobs.

In Chapter 3, Michael Tåhlin examined the extent to which the economic crisis affected the employment fortunes of different types of employee in the labour market. As he emphasizes, the employment decline hit countries with very different initial patterns of employment and skill structure. But there were strong commonalities in the groups that were most affected by employment loss. With respect to skill as most commonly proxied by educational level, the low-skilled (those with primary or lower secondary schooling) suffered much more severe employment reduction than those who had secondary education, while the smallest employment decline occurred among those with tertiary education. There was some evidence of variation: the UK witnessed a greater difference in employment decline between workers with primary and secondary education than was the case in other countries, while there were relatively small educational differences in the Continental countries.

There are, however, limitations to the measurement of skill trends in terms of education. This fails to take into account changes in particular types of skills: for instance, men's jobs were typically hit harder by the economic crisis than women's as a result of their greater concentration in manufacturing. It may also lead to an underestimation of the decline in the skills required in jobs. There may be a process of 'bumping down' in which relatively well-educated workers are increasingly obliged to take less-skilled jobs.

A more reliable estimate of the effect of the economic crisis on the occupational skill distribution requires direct measures of the skill requirements of jobs. Tåhlin addresses this by constructing a measure of *job skill* which involves a ranking of occupations (taking the International Standard Classification of Occupations) in terms of the level of education or training required to enter them. He shows that countries more severely affected by the crisis saw a greater increase in occupational skill levels, although the effect was relatively modest and it was clear that other factors also played an important role in affecting skill change over the period. Similarly, over the period 2007/8 to 2010, there was a rise in the rate of skill increase in a majority of countries compared to the pre-recession period, but the change was relatively small and there were marked variations in pattern across countries. He concludes that the general process of skill upgrading was driven by relatively long-term economic and social factors and that, while economic crisis accelerated such long-term trends, it was very much a secondary driver.

There was stronger evidence that economic crisis had affected the structure of skills and the degree of skill polarization. The period of the economic crisis witnessed a particularly steep decline in skilled manual jobs in manufacturing and construction, in factory operatives, and in non-skilled elementary workers. In contrast, the employment of professionals increased. Further, the greater the overall decline in employment, the greater the reduction in these types of employee, while the less the fall in employment the greater the increase in the proportion of professionals. Taking an overall measure of the degree of polarization of the job structure, Tåhlin finds that all countries saw some increase in polarization. But there was a strong association with employment decline: the more severe the reduction of employment between 2007/8 and 2010, the greater the degree of polarization. Economic crisis then accelerated to some degree the overall process of upskilling, but at the same time it increased the polarization of the job structure.

TRAINING AND SKILL DEVELOPMENT

The changes in the skill structure discussed above resulted from the differential destruction of specific types of jobs. But the crisis may also have affected skill development through its impact on the provision of training to employees. This is examined by Martina Dieckhoff in Chapter 4. As she points out, there could be quite diverse expectations. Economic crisis could lead employers to cut training, as it increases the uncertainty as to whether they will see a return on their investment. Moreover, the financial difficulties firms experience during economic crisis could make it more difficult for them to invest in training, while lower levels of hiring would entail less need of induction training. But there are also reasons why employers may increase training: the costs of training are lower during economic crisis as the loss of productive time is less problematic when demand is slack. More difficult product conditions may lead employers to increase competition in terms of quality, which would increase the need for employee training. Finally, it is possible that economic crisis leads to polarization in the treatment of the workforce, with employers investing in the skill development of their highly skilled workers while cutting back on the training of their less-skilled or older employees.

Taking the overall pattern for the nineteen countries for which there are data for both years, there was a clear decline in training incidence. Indeed, the odds of training in 2010, even when a wide range of individual and work characteristics have been controlled for, were 20 per cent lower in 2010 than in 2004. But this pattern was not consistent across countries: in some training rose (the Continental), in some it remained very stable (the Nordic), and in yet others it fell heavily (above all the Liberal and East European). In analysing the factors that underlay the extent of change between the two years, Dieckhoff points to a significant relationship between the extent of change in GDP growth rates between 2004 and 2010 and change in training provision, with training provision falling most in countries that had experienced particularly sharp declines in growth rates. But the pattern was far from perfect. Countries such as Spain that had experienced very sharp declines in growth rates saw little change in training provision, while countries such as Poland and Slovakia which had seen relatively small changes in growth rates experienced quite substantial training reductions.

Finally, was there evidence of increased divergence over the period between the training provision for the advantaged and disadvantaged? In the majority of countries economic crisis neither increased nor decreased the differentials between the highly educated (those with tertiary education) and the less educated (those with secondary education or less). But in eight countries, there was a *decrease* in inequality. This was the case in all of the Nordic countries (with the exception of Sweden where educational inequality was already not significant). But it was also the case for the Netherlands, Spain, Portugal, the Czech Republic, and Slovenia. However, the reasons for declining inequality in training chances could be quite different between countries. In the two East European countries, it did not reflect an increase in training provision for the less educated, but a substantial decline among the higher educated. Similarly, although there was a small increase in provision for the less educated in Portugal and the Netherlands, the primary factor leading to greater equality were cuts in the provision for the higher educated. It was only in Denmark, Norway, Finland, and Spain that clear training growth among the less educated was an important source of reduced inequality. Further, insofar as there was change in age-based inequalities, this was also in the direction of decreased differentials—in five countries there was a decrease in age-based inequalities.

JOB CONTROL, WORK INTENSITY, AND WORK STRESS

How did the economic crisis affect intrinsic job quality? Job control has been widely considered to be the core factor in the intrinsic quality of work, as it is important both in itself, as a source of identity and creativity, and as an important determinant of other aspects of the work environment. In particular it has been seen as an important factor moderating the impact of work intensity. A number of studies have indicated that where employees have significant job control, work intensity has a less severe effect on both their psychological well-being and their physical health.

Different theoretical positions led to various expectations as to whether job control was likely to have risen or declined over the period. In examining the empirical trends, the evidence showed some striking continuities in pattern, despite the upheavals of the worst recession since the 1930s. In particular the marked differences between countries and country groups in levels of job control that existed in 2004 still remained very evident in 2010. But, insofar as there was change, this consisted predominantly in a rise of job control. This was the case particularly among the Southern and East European countries. (The major exception to this was France where employees experienced a sharp decline in job control.) In general there also was little evidence of increased polarization in the workforce. There were, however, two notable exceptions. In the Liberal countries, there was an increased divergence by class, with those in semi-skilled and non-skilled work seeing their position deteriorate relative to those in higher managerial and professional work. In the Continental countries, the relative position of temporary workers deteriorated compared to those in regular jobs.

There were two principal arguments for why economic crisis might have led to rising levels of job control. The first was that it led to a process of selective displacement from the workforce of those who were least skilled and who had least job control—namely manual employees. The second was that employers, confronted by difficult economic conditions and the need to restructure work, may seek to enhance the commitment of their employees by giving them higher levels of involvement. There was some evidence that both types of process were indeed at work and helped to account for some of the increase in job control. But, in both cases, the effects were only substantial in the case of the East European countries.

Turning to work intensity, research from the early 1990s indicated that it had increased more sharply in a period of economic crisis than in a period of economic growth. The principal expectation then was that the period 2004 to 2010 would have seen a further intensification of work. The evidence indeed confirmed that there was a widespread tendency for an increase in the level of work pressure, although rather less dramatically than the increases registered in the early 1990s. The increase was particularly marked in the

Southern countries, in France, and in the Continental countries. Moreover it was quite general across classes, revealing little sign of class polarization. The view that economic crisis was a significant source of the rise of work intensity was confirmed by the fact that it was higher in companies that had experienced financial difficulty and in those that had experienced staff reductions in the previous three years. But it was notable that increased work intensity was only associated with an increase in highly stressful jobs in a more limited set of countries—in particular the Liberal countries, France, and the Transition countries.

JOB INSECURITY AND LABOUR MARKET SEGMENTATION

The most evident effect of the economic crisis for work and employment conditions was the sharp increase in job loss and job insecurity. In all but one of the countries examined there was a sharp contraction of employment levels. But there is also the possibility that such cyclical effects (albeit of a particularly severe type) were accompanied by structural shifts in the work-force that were likely to lead to increased job insecurity for the longer term. An extensive literature since the 1990s has pointed to a growing divide in job security between employees on 'regular' or 'standard' contracts and those on atypical contracts—primarily temporary workers and part-time workers. A central issue then is whether the economic crisis accentuated tendencies to structural division in the workforce and whether the consequences of the economic crisis fell disproportionately on the peripheral workforce.

These questions are taken up in Chapter 6 by Vanessa Gash and Hande Inanc. They begin by examining whether the economic crisis led to an increase in the peripheral workforce. There was no general pattern with respect to temporary work; rather the trends proved to be very different between countries. In general the changes were relatively small. There was an increase in the share of temporary workers in the Anglo-Saxon 'Liberal' countries, in most of the Transition countries, and in two of the Continental countries (Germany and the Netherlands). In other countries—Belgium, Sweden, Finland, Portugal, and above all Spain—temporary work declined as a share of overall employment. In almost all countries, the overwhelming majority of the jobs that disappeared between 2008 and 2010 were 'permanent' jobs. Consistently, at the onset of the recession, dismissals rose much more rapidly as cause of job separations than the termination of fixed-term contracts (although there was also an increase in the latter from 2009 to 2010). The distinctive case was Spain, where temporary workers bore the main brunt of job cuts. In contrast to the lack of clear trend for temporary work, there was a very general tendency across countries for some increase in the proportion of jobs that were part-time and there were no countries in which there was a substantial decline. Full-time jobs declined, while there was a growth in part-time work.

The implications of atypical work are likely to be particularly negative where it is involuntary. It was primarily in the Continental and Transition countries that there was a rise in involuntary temporary work, although the single biggest increase was in Ireland. There were also increases in involuntary part-time work in the Liberal, two of the Southern (Greece and Spain), and most of the Transition countries. In contrast, with the exception of Denmark, there was no increase in either involuntary temporary or part-time work in the Nordic countries and there was no increase in involuntary part-time work in two of the three Continental countries (Belgium and Germany). A comparison of men and women showed that there was little difference in the pattern of change over time between the sexes in involuntary atypical work, apart from a greater increase of male involuntary temporary employees in the Transition countries and of male involuntary part-timers in the Continental countries.

Finally, was there evidence of increased polarization in employment insecurity between core and atypical employees? Gash and Inanc examine whether there was divergence in current job insecurity, perceived career opportunities, and financial insecurity. Taking the overall workforce, they found a marked contrast between countries in trends in current job insecurity. Insecurity rose between 2004 and 2010 in the Liberal, the Southern, and to a lesser extent the Transition countries. But, in sharp contrast, it *decreased* both in the Nordic and the Continental countries. Although temporary workers (and temporary part-time workers) had substantially higher levels of insecurity than those with standard contracts, there was no evidence that this grew worse between 2004 and 2010, except in the case of the Anglo-Saxon countries. Female permanent part-timers had very similar levels of security to men in permanent full-time work and there was no evidence that their situation deteriorated over the period.

A similar picture emerges with respect to career advancement. This was heavily gendered. Women temporary and part-time workers were much more likely than men on standard contracts to feel that their jobs were dead-end jobs, whereas male temporary employees had a similar view of their career chances to permanent employees (presumably reflecting the fact that for men temporary jobs were more likely to be seen as bridges to better work). But, again, there was no evidence that the period of the economic crisis increased the entrapment of either temporary or part-time workers.

The main source of increased insecurity among atypical workers was financial insecurity. In general, employees in the Liberal, Southern, and Transition countries were more likely to have experienced pay cuts in the previous three years—indeed this was the case for 24 per cent of employees in the Liberal countries and 21 per cent of all employees in the Southern and Transition countries. But full-time temporary workers, both male and female, were disproportionately exposed to pay cuts even when working the same hours. Female part-timers, however, were only disadvantaged with respect to wage cuts linked to reductions in hours.

WORK–FAMILY CONFLICT

A common expectation in the period of economic growth was that, with women's increased integration into employment, there would be rising levels of work–family conflict, at least in countries that had not introduced significant measures to increase work time flexibility and child care provision. But comparative research on trends in the period of economic expansion from the mid-1990s found instead a remarkably stable pattern over time (Scherer and Steiber 2007). The onset of economic crisis, however, clearly raised new potential threats to work–family balance, resulting from higher levels of job insecurity, greater work intensity, and reduced pay.

McGinnity and Russell examine this in Chapter 7. They focus on 'work-to-family' conflict, that is to say the impact of work pressures on family life, as past research has shown this to be a greater source of tension than the effects of family problems on work life. Taking the overall pattern, there was a small but significant rise in work–family conflict over the period 2004 to 2010. This was the case for most countries, with the notable exceptions of Denmark and Poland. But there were some countries that saw particularly sharp increases— namely two of the Southern countries (Greece and Portugal) and four of the Transition countries (the Czech Republic, Estonia, Slovakia, and Slovenia).

McGinnity and Russell explore the way that the potential risk factors had evolved over the period and their impact on the change in work–family conflict. Previous research had provided a quite consistent picture of the factors that underlay variations in work–family conflict. It is intensified by stronger work demands, whether in terms of working hours or work intensity. It is made worse by unsocial hours—for instance evening or night work and work involving overtime at short notice. Job insecurity, including employment on temporary contracts, places a major strain on work–family relations (partly because it is associated with other negative aspects of work conditions). While the principal pressures come from work, household financial insecurity also heightens the risks of conflict (Steiber 2009).

Several of the factors associated with greater work–family conflict became more salient with the economic crisis. As was seen in Chapter 5, there was a widespread rise in work intensity. There was also an increase in working overtime at short notice and in job insecurity. A development that potentially might have offset increased work pressure—a reduction in working hours—in practice did not occur. When changes in work conditions were controlled, the differences between countries in the growth of work–family conflict were sharply diminished. However, more detailed analysis showed that it was above all the rising level of work intensity that accounted for the increase in work–family conflict.

At macro-level, there was a significant effect of the severity of the experience of economic crisis, with a tendency for work–family conflict to be higher the greater the increase in unemployment. Much of this is accounted for by the link between the unemployment rate and changes in work and working conditions—particularly work pressure. At micro-level, there was a clear impact of people's personal experience of the crisis. There was a strong effect of the extent of household budget cuts on work–family conflict. With respect to work experiences, firm financial difficulty, a reduction in job security, and a reduction in intrinsic job interest all had significant effects in increasing pressures on family life.

Economic crisis and social integration

The last three substantive chapters of the book widen the focus to the implications of the economic crisis for social integration. There are objective and subjective dimensions of social integration. The objective dimension relates to patterns of individual involvement in work, community, and national life. The subjective dimension is people's sense of satisfaction with their everyday lives and their commitment to the prevailing institutions of their societies. The chapters focus on the subjective dimension and address this in terms of three key issues. The first is people's attachment to employment, given its increasingly central place in government views about the necessary conditions of social integration. The second is their degree of satisfaction with their personal life situation and the third is their attitude to the legitimacy of existing institutions of political governance and redistribution. While the harshest consequences of economic crisis are concentrated on those who lose their jobs and become unemployed, the chapters show that the implications of economic crisis for social integration can affect those in work and stretch even to those whose everyday lives are not directly affected by the economic crisis.

EMPLOYMENT COMMITMENT

For those of working age, commitment to employment can be taken as a core indicator of social integration. The importance of work for social integration has become a mantra of policy-makers in most European societies and the objective of maximizing the employment rate is viewed as one of the most important social and economic objectives of both national governments and the EU. Indeed, many of the changes introduced in welfare benefit policies since the 1990s were motivated by the perceived need to ensure high levels of employment commitment. Unemployment was thought to lead over time to an erosion of the work ethic and hence to an increased risk of long-term marginalization.

Among researchers, however, the implications of experiences of job loss and job insecurity for employment commitment are still a matter of considerable controversy. Many economists have been of the view that work is a disutility and consequently unemployment is likely to undermine the work ethic as people become habituated to a life of greater leisure. But, a contrary argument is that unemployment will tend to reinforce employment commitment because people will become aware of benefits of employment which they previously took for granted—for instance the time structure it gives to the day, their status and their ability to interact with other people on a regular basis. Similarly, there can be different arguments about the effects of insecurity on those who are still in employment. It is possible that employees become more committed to employment because of their awareness of their relatively privileged situation compared to employees who are losing their jobs. Alternatively job insecurity may undermine work motivation by leading to deterioration in the quality of jobs.

These issues are the focus of Nadia Steiber's analyses in Chapter 8. Her emphasis is on 'non-financial' employment commitment, as this is likely to be relatively stable and closely linked to motivation with respect to work performance. There were marked variations across different parts of Europe in the overall level of employment commitment. It was highest in some Continental and Scandinavian countries, where approximately 70 per cent of the population of working age was committed to employment, while the lowest levels of commitment were in the Southern European and the Transition countries.

Steiber's first approach to the impact of the economic crisis was to look at the effect of job loss. She found no support for the common belief that unemployment undermines the work ethic. This was the case even for those with relatively long spells of unemployment. The evidence was more consistent with the view that unemployment increases people's awareness of the advantages of employment, thereby increasing the motivation to be employed. Although there were higher levels of commitment among the unemployed in most country groups, these differences only reached statistical significance in the Southern and the Transition countries. Comparing countries, however, there is a broad trend whereby the higher the rate of unemployment, the greater the difference between the commitment of the unemployed and the employed. It was also the case that the higher commitment of the unemployed was particularly pronounced in countries that had experienced persistently high unemployment in the 2000s.

But the fact that employment commitment is higher among the unemployed than among the employed may reflect not just the experiences of the unemployed themselves, but also the experiences of those who are employed. A significant proportion of those in work experienced high levels of job insecurity. This was found to have a negative effect on employment commitment both directly and because it tends to be associated with generally worse working conditions, for instance lower levels of control at work and higher levels of work intensity.

There was considerable variation in the extent of job insecurity between different parts of Europe—it was particularly high in Southern Europe. The fact that the unemployed in the Southern and Transition countries have higher commitment turns out on closer analysis to be due to the difference compared to the insecure employed. There is no difference with those in secure employment. In short, the distinctiveness of these countries is not due to the nature of the experience of unemployment per se but rather to the impact of particularly high levels of job insecurity in reducing employment commitment among those in employment. This suggests that the main implications of economic crisis for employment commitment may be in the way it undermines the commitment of those most exposed to job insecurity. Given the importance of early attitude formation for longer-term orientations, it is notable that these effects were particularly marked among young adults under 30.

SUBJECTIVE WELL-BEING

A central aspect of social integration is people's subjective well-being. This can be taken as an overall indicator of the quality of their experience with the different spheres of social relations in which they are engaged. A good deal of past research has highlighted the adverse effects of labour market insecurity for people's well-being. There is consistent evidence that unemployment lowers sharply people's subjective well-being, that the relationship is causal, and that the negative effects endure for a significant amount of time. A German longitudinal study found the effect of unemployment in reducing life satisfaction was almost three times larger than that of bad health (Winkelmann and Winkelmann 1998). The effects of unemployment are not limited to those who have lost their jobs, but also lower the life satisfaction of other members of the household.

But there is little consensus about the way that personal experience of unemployment is affected by a substantial increase in the level of unemployment in an economic crisis. Some research has suggested that, where unemployment is generally high, the experience will be less distressing for the individual, as it will be less stigmatizing and destructive of identity where it is a fate shared by many others. However, higher unemployment also may aggravate the difficulties that people experience when unemployed. Support from unemployed people's social networks is likely to be undermined when other members of that network are themselves unemployed. Friends and relatives will have fewer financial resources to provide assistance, they may be less able to give emotional support when they are themselves confronting difficulties, and they are likely to have fewer links to the labour market that could help in the search for new jobs.

In Chapter 9, Helen Russell, Dorothy Watson, and Frances McGinnity assess the impact on subjective well-being of people's experiences of the economic crisis. They focus on differences in life satisfaction. Compared to measures of happiness which emphasize affect, life satisfaction includes the cognitive assessment of life situation as well as affective response. They find that unemployment had a very strong effect on life satisfaction and, indeed, that the effect was more acute for those who had been unemployed for over a year than for the shorter-term unemployed. Earlier researchers differed about the reasons why unemployment causes such distress—with some placing the emphasis on the financial deprivation that it entails and others on its non-pecuniary effects, such as weakening people's social support and leading to a loss of time structure, meaningful purpose, and identity. Russell et al. confirm both the much higher levels of financial deprivation of the unemployed and also their lower degree of social integration with respect to social networks and social support. But it is financial strain that is the main determinant of the lower well-being of the unemployed. It accounted for over half of the reduction of the unemployed individual's own life satisfaction and all of that of the partner of an unemployed person. While social support and contacts play a significant role in life satisfaction for people in general, they have a much less prominent role in explaining the lower well-being of the unemployed.

Did the higher level of unemployment associated with the economic crisis reduce or increase the distress experienced by unemployed people? In general the results both from a comparison of countries with different levels of unemployment at the same point in time and from an examination of change over time suggested that the overall level of unemployment makes little difference to how damaging unemployment is for people's well-being. It is the personal experience of the financial and non-financial consequences of unemployment that is critical for well-being and this seems to be relatively unaffected by the amount of unemployment in the local community or the wider society. The main cases of significant change over time were in the Eastern European countries, where life satisfaction among the unemployed had increased over time, and in the Anglo-Saxon countries where it decreased. This did not reflect change in the composition of the unemployed in these country groups. Rather the major factor affecting it was change in the degree of financial strain the unemployed experienced. In the Anglo-Saxon countries the financial deprivation of the unemployed had increased. In the Transition countries, despite the increase in unemployment with the recession, the unemployment rate was lower in 2010 in several countries than it had been in 2004 and the financial hardship experienced by unemployed people was less great.

ECONOMIC CRISIS AND POLITICAL LEGITIMACY

Arguably the effects of economic crisis on social integration may extend beyond their threat to individuals' personal well-being to affect broader attitudes to society. A spectre that was inevitably reawakened with the worst economic crisis since the 1930s was that of the potential erosion of commitment to democratic political institutions. The final issue then, examined in Chapter 10 by Javier Polavieja, was whether economic crisis had affected the bases of political legitimacy. He focuses on three key indicators: the extent of political trust, satisfaction with democracy, and finally attitudes to the prevailing system of redistribution.

His point of departure is the debate about the crucial factors that affect attitudes to political institutions. He contrasts the view that they are rooted in processes of early socialization and are hence very slow to change with the argument that they are influenced by the individual's more immediate economic interests and therefore will change with economic circumstances. But, in addition, he draws the distinction between the effect of immediate experiences of economic hardship as a result of the economic crisis (egocentric effects) and the effects of a more general awareness of the depth of the crisis that makes even those who have not yet experienced direct loss feel increasingly unsafe (sociotropic effects).

It is clear from the results that the effects of early socialization in creating specific forms of political culture are important in the formation of attitudes to political institutions. This was reflected in the strong effects of educational experience, people's broader values with respect to egalitarianism, and their political identification with respect to the left–right spectrum of politics. But at the same time, longer-term economic interests were also important, reflected in the impact of class position, as were more immediate experiences of the economic crisis in terms of recent unemployment. Those who were currently unemployed and those who had experienced unemployment less than five years back showed lower levels of trust and satisfaction with democracy than those without unemployment experience. At the same time they showed higher levels of support for redistribution. A similar effect is also found among those experienced financial distress. Interestingly, the effects of unemployment appeared to be enduring and were not eliminated by a later favourable change in the person's job situation. Even among those who were currently employed, people who had experienced unemployment in the previous five years showed the same pattern (although the effects were less strong).

Comparing the pattern of political attitudes in 2010 with that of 2004, attitudes to redistribution were relatively stable and there was little clear evidence of an effect of the severity of the economic crisis. But the picture was very different with respect to political trust and satisfaction with democracy. In the case of both indicators, there was a marked decline in political legitimacy over time. The most powerful factor affecting this proved to be people's views about the economic situation of the country. This showed that the effects of economic crisis on political legitimacy were not restricted to those who directly experienced economic loss, but had consequences even for those not directly affected. There were, however, very considerable differences in the size of these effects between countries.

The erosion of political legitimacy was particularly marked in France, Spain, Slovenia, and Ireland. But by far the strongest decline in both political trust and satisfaction with democracy was in Greece. A macro-level analysis of the relationship between the extent of decline in political legitimacy over the period 2004 to 2010 and the change in GDP growth over the same years showed a clear relationship. Political trust and satisfaction with democracy decreased more severely the greater the decline in economic growth rates.

Overall the picture that emerges from Polavieja's analysis is that the economic crisis had a substantial effect in eroding political legitimacy and that, given the enduring effect of experiences of unemployment, its consequences are likely to colour the political landscape for a significant period of time.

ECONOMIC CRISIS AND PATTERNS OF CHANGE: OVERVIEW
There were then a number of general effects of the economic crisis for work quality and social integration. But these were ambivalent with respect to the quality of work. In some respects, the period witnessed an improvement in the quality of work for those who retained their jobs. Economic crisis accelerated the tendency for skill upgrading and, insofar as there was change with respect to job control, it was primarily in the direction of increased influence at work for employees. But at the same time, there were clear negative effects: there was an overall reduction of employer training and this was greater the more severe the crisis. There was also a general rise in work intensity and this was the major source of higher levels of work–family conflict.

Economic crisis increased structural polarization in the distribution of skills, through the disproportionate destruction of intermediary level jobs. But there were few instances of polarization in the sense of a deterioration of the work conditions of the low-skilled relative to those in higher-skilled work (indeed, insofar as there was change, inequalities in training opportunities *decreased*). There was also no consistent evidence of an increase in the divide between a core workforce on regular contracts and a peripheral workforce on atypical contracts. There was no general tendency for a rise in the proportion of employees on temporary contracts, although there was a very general increase in the use of part-time workers. Moreover, there was no general increase in the relative disadvantage of those on non-standard contracts, whether temporary or part time, compared to those on regular contracts—with the exception of the greater vulnerability of atypical employees to pay cuts.

The picture was more consistent with respect to social integration. Countries that had particularly severe experiences of the economic crisis were those where job insecurity was associated with particularly low levels of employment commitment and where there was a strong growth of political distrust and dissatisfaction with democracy.

Country Variations and Institutional Structures

A neo-institutionalist approach would anticipate that the effects of economic crisis would be filtered by the nature of the institutions of employment regulation and welfare in particular countries or groups of countries. There have been two main approaches to classifying differences in the employment systems of advanced capitalist societies—the production regime (or varieties of capitalism) framework, which has emphasized the pivotal role in institutional structuring of employer coordination and skill formation policies, and the power resource perspective that has pointed to the differences between employment and welfare regimes with respect to equality and inclusiveness that result from stronger labour organization. These are ideal types and the relationship between specific country institutions and regime types is necessarily very approximate.

A notable shortcoming of both approaches has been their lack of clarity with respect to the classification of many countries. Within both perspectives there have been arguments for and against considering France and the Southern European countries as sharing a broadly similar institutional framework to the Continental countries. There have been few attempts to classify the East European countries, although on a number of indicators they appeared to be closest to the Liberal model.

Our approach has been to compare countries both at an individual level and in a relatively disaggregated number of groupings to assess the empirical pattern of differences and the potential relevance of the different institutional perspectives in accounting for these. In terms of country groups we distinguished between the Anglo-Saxon Liberal countries (the UK and Ireland), the Nordic countries (Denmark, Finland, Norway, and Sweden), the Continental countries (Belgium, Germany, and the Netherlands), France, the Southern countries (Greece, Portugal, and Spain), and the Transition countries (the Czech Republic, Estonia, Hungary, Poland, Slovenia, and Slovakia). The aim was to examine empirically the similarities or dissimilarities of pattern between these country groups to explore whether or not existing typologies could be usefully extended.

We consider first the variations in the effects of the crisis on the quality of work and social integration between countries and country groups and conclude with a consideration of their implications for some of the principal interpretative approaches.

Country variations in experiences of the economic crisis

THE SEVERITY OF THE EMPLOYMENT CRISIS

The initial severity of the recession of 2008 and 2009 in terms of loss of GDP was relatively independent of specific country clusters or types of regime. But there can be no simple distinction between the effects of the longer-term economic crisis (the period until recovery to the previous peak) and the effects of institutional structures, since the way in which countries with different institutional regimes handled the recession may have contributed to its duration and its implications for unemployment.

The issue of policies of economic management during the crisis lies outside the core agenda of this volume, although it has been treated in considerable detail by Nancy Bermeo, Jonas Pontusson, and their colleagues (Bermeo and Pontusson 2012). In accounting for the speed of recovery from the crisis, Cameron (2012) points to the role of the welfare and the fiscal system in providing 'automatic stabilizers' and to the importance of the level of budgetary surplus prior to the crisis for the capacity of governments to introduce discretionary fiscal measures (such as tax cuts and increased spending). Broadly speaking the countries of Northern and Continental Europe were able to meet the recession with stronger automatic stabilizers and higher budget surpluses than those in the Anglo-Saxon Liberal countries or in the Southern and East European countries. Institutional processes in the former countries were better adapted to ensuring relative stability across the economic cycle.

The importance of differences between countries in the volatility or stability of their longer-term pattern of economic development is also highlighted in Chapter 2 of this volume, where Michael Tåhlin analyses the extent of, and factors influencing, employment reduction. There was a high correlation between the rise in GDP between the 1990s and 2007/8 and the extent to which it fell during the economic crisis. Overall GDP fall was in turn a strong predictor of employment reduction, together with the degree of dependence of the economy on the construction industry. But, even when both of these factors had been taken into account, the rapidity with which employment rose between 2004 and 2007 was related to the extent to which it fell between

2007/8 and 2010. More rapidly expanding economies, Tåhlin suggests, are likely to have been more vulnerable to sharp declines after the onset of recession partly because of the phenomenon of regression to the mean, but also because of the inherent precariousness of forecasting and the greater risk taking that occurs with 'economic bubbles'. Their vulnerability is accentuated by the fact that they have a larger proportion both of new firms, which have not had the chance to mature their knowledge of products and methods, and of new recruits, who are less likely to benefit from the security that comes with seniority and long-term tenure.

There was an association between the degree of volatility and the nature of social institutions. The boom to bust pattern of economic development was primarily a characteristic of more unequal societies. Constructing a measure of 'equality-promoting labour market institutions' derived inter alia from indicators such as wage dispersion, collective bargaining coverage, active labour market policies, union density, and welfare state distribution, Tåhlin found that countries with equality-promoting institutions (most notably the Nordic countries) experienced relatively small employment declines and much of this institutional effect could be attributed to lower levels of economic volatility. But there was also some evidence of countervailing effects. Once its implications for volatility had been taken into account, higher levels of egalitarianism may have had negative effects for employment, possibly because it is less easy for employers in these countries to reduce costs in other ways, for instance through cutting wages or working hours. These effects, however, are very much weaker than the positive effects of higher control of volatility.

In contrast to the implications of egalitarianism, high labour market flexibility—measured in terms of rates of job acquisition and job separations, as well as exits from employment to work—appeared to be associated with larger rather than smaller employment falls. Such institutions made it much easier for employers to rapidly reduce the size of their workforces to offset declines in production.

Overall, both the Nordic countries and the Continental countries were distinctive in terms of their capacity to limit the extent to which recession turned into a long-term economic crisis in terms of reduced GDP and high unemployment. This fits well with the argument of production regime theory which stresses the benefits of well-established institutions of coordination for longer-term strategical thinking in economic policy, leading to greater stability in patterns of economic development.

THE QUALITY OF WORK
It has been seen that there was a relatively widespread effect of the economic crisis in accelerating the long-term trend to upgrading of the occupational

structure, while increasing occupational polarization. But as Michael Tåhlin shows in Chapter 3, an important factor that moderated the effects of the economic crisis on occupational structure was the nature of labour market institutions in specific countries. Controlling for the effects of the severity of the economic crisis, countries that had institutional frameworks that promoted class equality maintained the employment not only of professionals and semi-professionals but also of craft and factory workers better than those with institutions that allowed substantial class inequalities, such as the Anglo-Saxon countries, Greece, Portugal, and most of the East European countries. The extent to which the institutional framework encouraged labour market flexibility (in terms of rates of turnover and of transitions from unemployment to work) also affected economic crisis outcomes. Higher labour market flexibility was associated with larger employment falls in the economic crisis and with sharper falls (net of general economic crisis effects) in the employment of elementary employees. It is notable that institutional egalitarianism and labour market flexibility were uncorrelated. Overall, countries that combined equality with flexibility (the Nordic countries are the prime example) experienced overall skill upgrading, while unequal countries experienced sharper skill polarization.

Such effects on the skill structure were also reflected in inequalities in wages. While the period of the economic crisis was generally associated with a reduction of wage inequality, occupational polarization was associated with a decline of wages at the median level, reflecting the falling demand for skilled manual employees. But institutions also proved important for trends in wage differentials. The wages at median level held up better in countries with equality-promoting institutions, while a greater emphasis on labour market flexibility was associated with less favourable outcomes in terms of trends in income inequality.

Dieckhoff's analyses also showed that there were substantial country differences both in the level of continuing training provided and in the extent to which training provision was protected during the crisis. It is notable that in 2004 all of the Nordic countries had substantially higher levels of continuing training than the countries in any other country group (including the Continental countries). The lowest levels were to be found in two of the Southern countries—Greece and Portugal. Examining the trends over time, there was no significant change in the frequency of training between 2004 and 2010 in any of the Nordic countries and there was actually an increase in two of the Continental countries. In contrast there were decreases in the two Liberal countries (particularly in Ireland). The most negative development was in the East European countries, where training provision decreased substantially in four of the six countries and remained unchanged (at a low level) in one more. Of these countries, it is only in Estonia that there is evidence of a significant increase in training opportunities over the period. The institutional factor that proved to be most strongly related to trends in training during the economic crisis was the strength of employment protection. Stronger employment protection helped to prevent a decline in training provision even when the severity of economic change had been taken into account.

As with training, there were striking continuities in country differences with respect to job control, despite the severity of the economic crisis. Employees in the Nordic countries were the most likely to have a say in decisions about their work, while those in the Southern and East European countries had the least influence over their work. Indeed, in many countries, there was no evidence of a significant change over the period. This was the case for the Nordic countries, the Anglo-Saxon Liberal countries, and two of the three Continental countries. It was only in the Southern and Transition countries that there was evidence of a significant rise of job control, and only in France of a significant decline.

A probable source of this stability of pattern is that job control is embedded in wider institutional structures that are mutually reinforcing and consequently lead to a high degree of path dependency. Individual job control is likely to be easier to protect where there are well-developed institutions of workplace representation. In practice, workplace representation was stronger in the Nordic, the Anglo-Saxon, and (to a lesser degree) the Continental countries than in the Southern countries and several of the East European countries. Further workplace representation did indeed prove to be strongly related to individual job control both across countries and in all of the country groups. Finally, it was shown that the prevalence of workplace representation was itself closely related to the overall strength of trade unionism in a country, as reflected in trade union density. Since workplace and national level institutions are unlikely to be easily amenable to rapid change, the countries in which they were most developed were also the countries that showed a particularly high level of stability across time in the level of job control.

There was little country variation in the effects of the economic crisis on work intensity; it rose in all regions of Europe. While work intensification had serious negative consequences for employees' family lives, it was not, however, necessarily linked to an increase in the conditions that have been shown to create the greatest risks with respect to psychological and physical ill-health—namely jobs that combine high work intensity with low job control. There was a significant increase in such jobs only in the Liberal and Transition countries and above all in France.

Finally, with respect to job insecurity, it was notable that the Nordic and the Continental countries provided the greatest protection for their workforces. In contrast, the Liberal, Southern, and Transition countries saw a much sharper increase in insecurity. They experienced an increase in current job insecurity (while those in the Nordic and Continental countries experienced a decrease). They were also the most likely to have experienced pay cuts in the previous five years.

SOCIAL INTEGRATION

There were important country variations with respect to each of the key indicators of social integration. To begin with there was a significant difference between European countries in both the level of employment commitment and in the extent to which it was undermined by labour market insecurity. It was highest in the Continental countries and in the Scandinavian countries, while it was lowest in the Southern and the Transition countries. The countries that had high levels of employment commitment were distinctive in two respects. Attitudes to the importance of employment were very homogeneous across the population. They were also the countries that had the highest quality of jobs, supporting the view that more inclusive policies with respect to working conditions help strengthen people's preference to stay in work.

It has been seen that the main effects of the experience of economic crisis in reducing commitment to employment was with respect not to the unemployed, but to those in insecure jobs, whose commitment was reduced compared to those in more secure work. While the insecure had consistently lower levels of employment commitment than the secure, the difference was least pronounced in the Scandinavian countries. Steiber suggests that insecurity had a less severe effect in countries that protected the unemployed from falling into poverty through generous welfare provision and strong active labour market policies that supported swift reintegration into the labour market.

There were also notable differences between countries in the extent to which unemployment reduced personal well-being. Unemployment had a relatively weak effect on well-being in the Nordic countries, but a particularly severe effect in the Anglo-Saxon countries. There were very substantial differences in the extent to which different welfare systems protected the incomes of people who became unemployed, with the highest levels of support being in the Nordic countries. The unemployed in the Nordic countries were the least likely to experience financial strain. In contrast in the Anglo-Saxon Liberal countries, financial support for the unemployed was relatively low and financial deprivation among unemployed people had increased since 2004. Consistently, in these countries, not only was the effect of unemployment particularly severe, but life satisfaction among the unemployed had decreased over time. The differences between the experiences of unemployment could be largely accounted for by the different levels of financial hardship that the unemployed experienced. Indeed, once this was taken into account, there was little remaining difference in the effect of unemployment between country groups.

Strong welfare institutions were not, however, the only source of protection of the psychological well-being of the unemployed. The effect of unemployment was also relatively low in the Southern countries where welfare support is very infrequent. This was not due to the lower financial strain among the unemployed in these countries. But the family takes much of the responsibility for the support of the unemployed and this is likely to decrease risks of social isolation. The counterpart to this is that it adds a considerable burden on the financial resources of those in employment. The lower gap in life satisfaction between the unemployed and the employed in the Southern countries was in part due to the fact that the employed in Southern countries had lower levels of satisfaction than in other country groups.

The third aspect of social integration was people's commitment to their political institutions, as expressed in their levels of political trust, their satisfaction with democracy, and their attitudes to the prevailing system of redistribution. Polavieja found wide variations in the effects of the crisis on both political trust and satisfaction with democracy. While it collapsed catastrophically in Greece, political legitimacy rose in the Netherlands, Norway, and Sweden and also in two of the East European countries that were unscathed by the recession (Poland and Slovakia). While this was clearly related to people's personal experiences of insecurity in the crisis, it also had an institutional dimension, although in this case it relates to a supranational rather than national institutional framework. Membership of the European Monetary Union involved a substantial loss of sovereignty with respect to economic policy in particular as a result of the inability to stimulate exports by devaluing the currency. It represented then an objective restriction on the efficacy of governments in responding to the crisis. The effects of this appear to have marked public perceptions of their governments. Political trust and satisfaction with democracy were even lower in the Eurozone countries and, indeed, much of the effect of the economic crisis in undermining political legitimacy was due to the strength of its effects in these countries.

Country variation and institutional regimes

The considerable differences between country patterns and their relatively high stability across time, despite such a severe and prolonged economic crisis, suggest that both the quality of work and the level of social integration in a society are affected by institutional structures that are resistant to short-term pressures for change. There are, however, quite diverse views about the importance of specific institutional characteristics and the appropriate country groupings. What light do the patterns of continuity and change across the economic crisis cast on the usefulness of the main interpretative frameworks of institutional variation and their capacity to account for the wider set of European countries?

With respect to the quality of work both the 'production regime' and the 'employment regime' perspectives provide ideal type characterizations of different forms of employment regulation. Theoretically, the difference between the perspectives has centred on the relative importance of employer coordination and skill formation systems on the one hand and of the power resources available to organized labour on the other. Substantively the key issue has been the degree of similarity or difference between the Nordic countries on the one hand and the Continental countries on the other, relative to countries with more deregulated employment institutions. Production regime theory anticipates that they will be broadly similar (or are becoming more similar), employment regime theory that they will be distinctive with respect to the quality of work and employment.

It is clear from the analyses that, even after a period of prolonged economic crisis, the Nordic countries remain very different from the Continental countries in a number of ways. They have work conditions that offer better opportunities for employee self-development through continuing training, they provide employees with higher levels of influence over decisions that affect their work, the class gap in influence over work is less great, they have a lower proportion of 'high strain' jobs that pose risks for psychological and physical health, and they have lower levels of job insecurity. Overall, the quality of work would appear to be distinctly higher in the Nordic countries than in the Continental. In general these differences did not diminish over the period of the economic crisis, although there was some improvement in the overall amount of training provision in the Continental countries and some increase in class equality in training in the Nordic countries. The crisis also saw increased polarization in the Continental countries between core and non-standard employees with respect to job control and the risk of being in high strain work. But, in general, both the Nordic and the Continental countries appeared to have highly stable institutional patterns that changed little with economic crisis.

Both the production and employment regime perspectives predict that working conditions in the Anglo-Saxon Liberal countries could be expected to be considerably worse than in either the Nordic or the Continental countries, as a result of their relatively high level of deregulation. Similarly, by implication, these are the countries where it would be anticipated that the economic crisis would have had the most severe effects in reducing the quality of jobs. In practice there were striking differences between the UK and Ireland in work quality. Ireland in some ways fitted better than the UK the description of the work conditions of the Liberal model. Opportunities for training were very low, as was employee involvement in decision-making at work. In contrast, employees in the UK had levels of continuing training and job control as good as those in the Continental countries. The two countries, however, shared in common higher levels of work intensity than either the Nordic or the Continental countries, but, prior to the economic crisis, relatively low levels of job insecurity. With respect to change over the period of economic crisis, they had two similarities: unlike the Nordic and Continental countries, they experienced a decline in training and rising job insecurity (although both developments were much stronger in Ireland).

It was seen in Chapter 1 that there has been little agreement about how other European countries fit within these schemas. While often grouped with the Continental countries, France has tended to be regarded as a problematic case, with its rather specific pattern of conflictual industrial relations. Unlike Belgium, Germany, and the Netherlands it has a relatively low level of bargaining coordination. It is difficult then to classify it as a Coordinated Market Economy in the strict terms of the production regime schema, although it has been suggested that it may be a variant in which coordination is largely brought about by the state. It fits more easily within the dualistic category of the employment regime schema, given its high levels of bargaining coverage combined with its (exceptionally) low union density.

The coverage of our data on the quality of work in France is less good than with other countries, since information was either not collected or not made available on some key indicators. But, where comparison was possible, it came closest to the Continental countries, with intermediate levels of training and job control and very similar levels of work intensity.

It was more distinctive, however, with respect to the pattern of change between 2004 and 2010. Unlike the other Continental countries, there was a marked decline in employees' control over their jobs and this was associated with a particularly sharp rise in work stress. It is notable that France in this period experienced the most severe crisis in terms of work-related suicides. This led the French government in 2008 to order industry-wide collective negotiations on work stress and to launch a formal inquiry into the sources of stress at work and how they were to be monitored (Nassé and Legeron 2008; Gollac 2011). Any view on why French employers moved to more directive management practices in this period must be very speculative. But it seems plausible that it was a reaction to what was seen as the imposition by the government in 2000 of the 35-hour week, in the face of the objections of the main employers' organization MEDEF. French employers appear to have used the crisis to recoup productivity losses by tightening supervision and increasing workloads.

The Southern countries are also difficult to distinguish from the Continental in terms of the principal classifying criteria of both the production and employment regime perspectives. They have relatively high employer bargaining coordination, relatively high bargaining coverage, and relatively weak trade unions. But, on most of the key dimensions of the quality of work, these countries were distinct and offered much poorer quality work, even taking account of basic differences in occupational and industry structure. They offered employees fewer opportunities for training and less say in decision-making, while having a greater prevalence of high strain jobs associated with poorer psychological and physical health.

The case for regarding them, as Barbieri (2009) has suggested, as distinct variants of dualism seems a strong one. Much more research is needed on the characteristics of the Southern countries. It is clear, for instance, that there are some notable differences between them in employment structure. But, tentatively, while the Continental countries could be considered a form of corporatist dualism, where differences of employment privilege are primarily related to qualification, the Southern or Mediterranean countries may be closer to a form of paternalist dualism, where labour market divisions are more strongly defined by age and relational networks. Skill-based dualism is likely to have a greater concern for the development of employee competencies and involvement in decision-making than paternalist dualism, which is more attached to the preservation of traditional, hierarchical, patterns of work organization.

Practice in current institutional structures is likely to be influenced by the normative residue of past historical experience. The persistence of hierarchical and ascriptive norms in the Southern countries may relate to differences in post-war paths of political and religious development. The historical experience of three of the Southern countries stands out from that of the other regions of Europe in the relative recentness of experiences of authoritarian rule. Spain was controlled by the authoritarian dictatorship of Franco from 1936 to 1975. Portugal was ruled by a 'para-fascist' regime under Antonio de Oliveira Salazar from 1932 to 1968, continued by his close collaborator Marcello Caetano until it was overthrown by the 'Carnation' revolution in 1974. Greece experienced a military coup in 1967 and was controlled by a military junta until 1974. Even Italy, which has had a continuous democratic political tradition after the Second World War, has a culture heavily marked by the continuing institutional power of the Catholic Church, with strong political representation in a Christian Democratic Party that controlled the state until the 1990s.

The East European countries have rarely been classified in terms of such schemas but, as was seen in Chapter 1, they came closest in institutional terms to the Liberal countries in their relatively low levels of bargaining coordination and low levels of bargaining coverage. Slovenia was a clear exception to this with an institutional framework closer to the Continental model. Empirically, work conditions were not dissimilar from those in 'Liberal'

Ireland (although notably poorer than the UK) with respect both to job control and to the higher proportion of 'passive' jobs that offered few opportunities for self-development through work. But there were important variations within the East European countries. In particular, Estonia and Slovenia were distinctive from the other countries: they had levels of training and job control that were closer to the Continental countries, and levels of job insecurity that were closer to those of the Nordic countries. Although the East European countries were similar to the Anglo-Saxon Liberal countries in the substantial cuts they made to training over the period of the economic crisis (with the notable exception of Estonia), they had rather diverse experiences with respect to changes in patterns of job control and in job security.

In general, the degree of diversity in pattern of the countries closest to the Liberal model indicates that institutions of this type lead to rather undefined outcomes with respect to average work quality. In no case did they approach the quality of work prevalent in the Nordic countries, but in the best case they were comparable to the Continental and in the worst to the Southern countries. The initial regime theories tended to assume that employers in Liberal institutional contexts would operate with a common logic that gave priority to the protection of managerial prerogative, tight control over work performance, and a reliance on relatively low-skilled and insecure labour. This provides a rather inadequate account of the empirical patterns. But it also could be argued that diversity of employer strategies is precisely what is to be expected given the characteristics of this type of weakly institutionalized society.

As research has increasingly confirmed, a range of forms of work organization may be compatible with maximizing employer interests. While policies that emphasize managerial prerogative may be effective in traditional technological settings, employers may benefit from policies that provide higher commitment when they are able to draw on more highly skilled employees. Weakly institutionalized systems could be seen as offering a relatively high level of choice for employers to adapt their policies to local product, technological, and labour market conditions, without the constraints of the strong collective norms associated with more strongly institutionalized systems. In particular one could expect considerable differences of employer policy depending on the skill requirements of jobs.

From this perspective, there are likely to be two common features of countries of a Liberal type: first a relatively high level of internal inequality and second a greater flexibility (or volatility) in the face of new economic circumstances. The expectation of greater inequality within countries is consistent with the fact that it was in the Anglo-Saxon and Transition countries that there was the greatest class variation in levels of employee influence. With respect to flexibility, it is notable that, whereas the Nordic and Continental countries showed a high level of stability across the period, it was employees in the Liberal countries that experienced the most significant changes over the period in response to the crisis. The implications of such changes for the quality of work, however, were ambivalent. They involved reductions in work quality with respect to training, but in several of the East European countries employers responded to financial difficulty with changes in work organization that improved the quality of work.

Finally, the principal institutional perspective that was drawn upon with respect to social integration was that of welfare regime theory. The expectation was that the effects of the crisis on people's subjective well-being and commitment to social institutions would be filtered by the relative generosity of the welfare system in protecting those that were most vulnerable in the crisis—in particular the unemployed. With respect to employment commitment and subjective well-being, there was clear support for the view that the nature of welfare institutions can play a significant role in reducing the effect of economic crisis. The existence of more generous welfare provision helps to account for the lower impact of job insecurity on employment commitment. It also underlay the lower level of financial strain and the relatively high level of life satisfaction of the unemployed in the Nordic countries compared to those in the Continental and above all the Anglo-Saxon countries.

As in discussions of employment systems, there has been a sustained debate about the applicability of a common model of welfare regime to the Continental and Southern European countries. But again the evidence points to the distinctiveness of the patterns in the Southern countries rather their similarity with the Continental. It is likely that family structures play a more salient role in these countries and that, in situations of very low state welfare provision, strong family support may help to buffer the negative impact of unemployment.

Employment and welfare regime interpretations are consistent, then, with some of the patterns revealed by these analyses, but in their current form they have clear limitations. In particular, the assumption that the Southern European countries follow a similar institutional logic with respect to employment regulation to the Continental countries is untenable in the light of their sharp differences both in quality of work and in the pattern of change over the crisis. Welfare regime theories that assimilate the two groups of countries encounter similar difficulties. Further, the dynamic attributed to the Liberal model with respect to employment fails to account for the diversity of the experiences even of the Anglo-Saxon countries from which the model was initially derived. The problem only becomes more acute if the model is extended to cover the countries of Eastern Europe. This may reflect deficiencies in the theoretical elaboration of likely employer behaviour within a weakly regulated system.

It must be remembered that institutional models are ideal types that necessarily simplify greatly the detail of particular institutional configurations. Specific countries are classified in terms of relative proximity, but their institutional structures reflect the diverse influences of complex patterns of historical development. Similarly, the patterns that emerge from such institutional analysis are at a high level of aggregation—they indicate overall differences in tendency between different sets of countries. While the Nordic countries do appear to be very distinctive in pattern, with their high and stable level of both work quality and social integration, there is commonly a good deal of variation between the experiences of the countries within any 'regime' set. Specific national policies at any given period of time are likely to be only weakly determined by the broad institutional characteristics associated with regimes; they are also influenced by the distinctive characteristics of national institutional systems and their historical path of development. Even within such constraints, policy-makers retain significant scope for policy choice. An analysis of variations within such broad institutional types and of the implications of specific national patterns of employment regulation should retain then a central place on the research agenda.

References

Aaberge, R., Björklund, A., Jäntti, M., Pedersen, P. J., Smith, N., and Wennemo, T. (2000). Unemployment Shocks and Income Distribution: How Did the Nordic Countries Fare during their Crises? *Scandinavian Journal of Economics*, 102(1): 77–99.

Acemoglu, D. and Pischke, J.-S. (1999). The Structure of Wages and Investment in General Training. *Journal of Political Economy*, 107(3): 539–72.

—— (2003). Minimum Wages and On-the-Job Training. *Research in Labor Economics*, 22(2): 159–202.

Aidukaite, J. (2009). Old Welfare State Theories and New Welfare Regimes in Eastern Europe: Challenges and Implications. *Communist and Post-Communist Studies*, 42(1): 23–39.

Alderfer, C. P. (1969). An Empirical Test of a New Theory of Human Needs. *Organizational Behavior and Human Performance*, 4(2): 142–75.

Allard, G. J. (2005). *Measuring the Changing Generosity of Unemployment Benefits: Beyond Existing Indicators*. Instituto de Empresa Business School. Working Paper No. WP05-18.

Allen, T., Herst, D., Bruck, C., and Sutton, M. (2000). Consequences Associated with Work-to-Family Conflict: A Review and Agenda for Future Research. *Journal of Occupational Health Psychology*, 5(2): 278–308.

Allison, P. D. (1999). Comparing Logit and Probit Coefficients across Groups. *Sociological Methods and Research*, 28(2): 186–208.

Almond, G. and Verba S. (1963). *The Civic Culture: Political Culture and Democray in Five Nations*. Princeton: Princeton University Press.

Alt, J. E. (1979). *The Politics of Economic Decline: Economic Management and Political Behaviour in Britain since 1964*. Cambridge: Cambridge University Press.

Altindag, D. and Mocan, N. (2010). Joblessness and Perceptions about the Effectiveness of Democracy. *Journal of Labor Research*, 31: 99–123.

Amable, B. (2003). *The Diversity of Modern Capitalism*. Oxford: Oxford University Press.

Anderson, C. J. and Pontusson, J. (2007). Workers, Worries and Welfare States: Social Protection and Job Insecurity in 15 OECD Countries. *European Journal of Political Research*, 46(2): 211–35.

Andress, H.-J. and Heien, T. (2001). Four Worlds of Welfare State Attitudes? A Comparison of Germany, Norway, and the United States. *European Sociological Review*, 17(4): 337–56.

Anxo, D. and Ericson, T. (2011). *European Employment Observatory Review: Adapting Unemployment Benefit Systems to the Economic Cycle, Sweden*. European Employment Observatory.

References

Armstrong-Stassen, M. (1994). Coping with Transition: A Study of Layoff Survivors. *Journal of Organizational Behavior*, 15(7): 597–621.

Arulampalam, W. and Booth, A. L. (1998). Training and Labour Market Flexibility: Is there a Trade-Off? *British Journal of Industrial Relations*, 36(4): 521–36.

——and Stewart, M. B. (1995). The Determinants of Individual Unemployment Durations in an Era of High Unemployment. *The Economic Journal*, 105 (March): 321–32.

—— Booth, A. L. and Bryan, M. (2004). Training in Europe. *Journal of the European Economic Association*, 2(2–3): 346–60.

——and Taylor, M. P. (2000). Unemployment Persistence. *Oxford Economic Papers*, 52: 24–50.

Aspalter, C., Jinsoo, K., and Sojeung, P. (2009). Analysing the Welfare State in Poland, the Czech Republic, Hungary and Slovenia: An Ideal-Typical Perspective. *Social Policy & Administration*, 43(2): 170–85.

—— (1986). Employment Flexibility in Internal and External Labour Markets. In *New Forms of Work and Activity*. European Foundation for the Improvement of Living and Working Conditions. Luxembourg: Office for Official Publications of the European Commission.

Atkinson, A. B. and Micklewright, J. (1985). Unemployment Benefits and Unemployment Duration. London: Suntory-Toyota International Centre for Economics and Related Disciplines, London School of Economics.

Auer, P. and Cazes, S. (2003). *Employment Stability in an Age of Flexibility*. Geneva: International Labour Office.

Autor, D. (2010). *The Polarization of Job Opportunities in the U.S. Labor Market: Implications for Employment and Earnings*. Center for American Progress/The Hamilton Project. Washington, DC: Brookings Institution.

—— Levy, F., and Murnane, R. J. (2003). The Skill Content of Recent Technological Change: An Empirical Exploration. *Quarterly Journal of Economics*, 118(4): 1279–333.

Avram, S., Sutherland, H., Tasseva, I., and Tumino, A. (2011). *Income Protection and Poverty Risk for the Unemployed in Europe*. Research note 1/2011. European Commission Employment, Social Affairs and Inclusion Social Situation Observatory—Income Distribution and Living Conditions.

Axinn, J. and Stern, M. J. (2005). *Social Welfare: A History of the American Response to Need*. 6th edn. Boston: Allyn & Bacon.

Barbieri, P. (2007). *Atypical Employment and Welfare Regimes*. Equalsoc Policy Paper. Vol. 1, University of Antwerp.

—— (2009). Flexible Employment and Inequality in Europe. *European Sociological Review*, 25(6): 621–8.

Bardasi, E. and Gornick, J. C. (2008). Working for Less? Women's Part-time Wage Penalties across Countries. *Feminist Economics*, 14(1): 37–72.

Barker, K. and Christensen, K. (eds.) (1998). *Contingent Work: American Employment Relations in Transition*. Ithaca: Cornell University Press.

Barlevy, G. and Tsiddon, D. (2006). Earnings Inequality and the Business Cycle. *European Economic Review*, 50(1): 55–89.

Barnes, S. (1979). *Political Action: Mass Participation in Five Western Democracies*. Beverly Hills, CA: Sage.

Becker, G. S. (1964). *Human Capital: A Theoretical and Empirical Analysis with Special Reference to Education*. New York: Columbia University Press.

Bell, D. (1974). *The Coming of Post-Industrial Society: A Venture in Social Forecasting*. London: Heinemann.

—— and Blanchflower, D. (2011). Young People and the Great Recession. *Oxford Review of Economic Policy*, 27(2): 241–67.

Bermeo, N. (2003). *Ordinary People in Extraordinary Times: The Citizenry and the Breakdown of Democracy*. Princeton: Princeton University Press.

—— and Pontusson, J. (eds.) (2012). *Coping with Crisis: Government Reactions to the Great Recession*. New York: Russell Sage Foundation.

Bewley, T. F. (1999). *Why Wages Dont Fall During a Recession*. Cambridge, MA: Harvard University Press.

Bianchi, S. and Milkie, M. A. (2010). Work and Family Research in the First Decade of the 21st Century. *Journal of Marriage and Family*, 72(3): 705–25.

Bishop, J. H. (1996). *What We Know about Employer-Provided Training: A Review of Literature*. CAHRS Working Paper No. 96-09. Ithaca, NY: Cornell University, School of Industrial and Labor Relations, Center for Advanced Human Resource Studies.

Blauner, R. (1964). *Alienation and Freedom: The Factory Worker and his Industry*. Chicago: University of Chicago Press.

Blekesaune, M. (2007). Economic Conditions and Public Attitudes to Welfare Policies. *European Sociological Review*, 23(3): 393–403.

—— and Quadagno, J. (2003). Public Attitudes toward Welfare State Policies: A Comparative Analysis of 24 Nations. *European Sociological Review*, 19: 415–27.

Blumberg, P. (1968). *Industrial Democracy: The Sociology of Participation*. London: Constable.

Bohle, P., Quinlan, M. and Mayhew, C. (2001). The Health and Safety Effects of Job Insecurity: An Evaluation of the Evidence. *Economic and Labour Relations Review*, 12(1): 32–60.

Bonoli, G. (1997). Classifying Welfare States: A Two-dimension Approach. *Journal of Social Policy*, 26(3): 351–72.

Brannen, P. (1983). *Authority and Participation in Industry*. London: Batsford Academic.

Braverman, H. (1974). *Labor and Monopoly Capital: The Degradation of Work in the Twentieth Century*. New York: Monthly Review Press.

Brockner, J., Grover, S., Reed, T. F., and Lee Dewitt, R. (1992). Layoffs, Job Insecurity, and Survivors' Work Effort: Evidence of an Inverted-U Relationship. *Academy of Management Journal*, 35(2): 413–25.

Brooks, C. and Manza, J. (2007). *Why Welfare States Persist: The Importance of Public Opinion in Democracies*. Chicago: University of Chicago Press.

Brüderl, J., Preisendörfer, P., and Ziegler, R. (1992). Survival Chances of Newly Founded Business Organizations. *American Sociological Review*, 57: 227–42.

Brunello, G. (2009). The Effect of Economic Downturns on Apprenticeships and Initial Workplace Training: A Review of the Evidence. *Empirical Research in Vocational Education and Training*, 1(2): 145–71.

Burchell, B. (1992). Towards a Social Psychology of the Labour Market: Or Why We Need to Understand the Labour Market before We Can Understand Unemployment. *Journal of Occupational and Organizational Psychology*, 65(4): 345–54.

—— (1994). The Effects of Labour Market Position, Job Insecurity, and Unemployment on Psychological Health. In *Social Change and the Experience of Unemployment*, ed. D. Gallie, C. Marsh, and C. Vogler, pp. 188–212. Oxford: Oxford University Press.

—— (2009). Flexicurity as a Moderator of the Relationship between Job Insecurity and Psychological Well-Being. *Cambridge Journal of Regions, Economy and Society*, 2(3): 365–78.

—— (2011). A Temporal Comparison of the Effects of Unemployment and Job Insecurity on Wellbeing. *Sociological Research Online*, 16(1).

—— Lapido, D., and Wilkinson, F. (2002). *Job Insecurity and Work Intensification*. London: Routledge.

Burgard, C. and Görlitz, K. (2011). Continuous Training, Job-Satisfaction and Gender: An Empirical Analysis Using German Panel Data. *Ruhr Economics Papers*, No. 265. Rhine-Westphalia Institute for Economic Research (RWI).

Burgard, S. A., Brand, J. E., and House, J. S. (2007). Toward a Better Estimation of the Effect of Job Loss on Health. *Journal of Health and Social Behavior*, 48(4): 369–84.

Burns, T. and Stalker, G. M. (1961). *The Management of Innovation*. London: Tavistock.

Byron, K. (2005). A Meta-Analytic Review of Work–Family Conflict and Its Antecedents. *Journal of Vocational Behavior*, 67(2): 169–98.

Cameron, D. R. (2012). European Fiscal Responses to the Great Recession. In *Coping with Crisis: Government Reactions to the Great Recession*, ed. N. Bermeo and J. Pontusson, pp. 91–129. New York: Russell Sage Foundation.

Canache, D., Mondak, J. J., and Seligson, M. A. (2001). Meaning and Measurement in Cross-National Research on Satisfaction with Democracy. *Public Opinon Quarterly*, 65(4): 506–28.

Capelli, P., Bassi, L., Katz, H., Knoke, D., Osterman, P., and Useem, M. (1997). *Change at Work*. Oxford: Oxford University Press.

Caponi, V., Kayahan, B., and Plesca, M. (2010). The Impact of Aggregate and Sectoral Fluctuations on Training Decisions. *The B.E. Journal of Macroeconomics*, 10(1): 1–35.

Card, D., Lemieux, T., and Riddell, W. (2003). Unions and the Wage Structure. In *The International Handbook of Trade Unions*, ed. J. T. Addison and C. Schnabel, pp. 246–92. Cheltenham: Edward Elgar Publishers.

Castles, F. G. (1993). Social Security in Southern Europe: A Comparative Overview. Public Policy Discussion Paper No. 33. Canberra, ACT: Graduate Program in Public Policy, The Autstralian National University.

Cedefop (2010). *Skills Supply and Demand in Europe: Mid-Term Forecast up to 2020*. European Centre for the Development of Vocational Training (Cedefop). Luxembourg: Publications Office of the European Union.

—— (2011). *Labour-Market Polarisation and Elementary Occupations in Europe: Blip or Long-Term Trend?* Research Paper No. 9. European Centre for the Development of Vocational Training (Cedefop). Luxembourg: Publications Office of the European Union.

Chamberlain, K. and Zika, S. (1992). Stability and Change in Subjective Well-Being Over Short Time Periods. *Social Indicators Research*, 26(2): 101–17.

Chandola, T. (2010). *Stress at Work*. London: The British Academy.

Chung, H. (2011). Work–Family Conflict across 28 European Countires: A Multi-level Approach. In *Work–Life Balance in Europe: The Role of Job Quality*, ed. S. Drobnic and A. Guillen, pp. 42–68. Basingstoke: Palgrave Macmillan.

—— and Van Oorschot, W. (2011). Institutions versus Market Forces: Explaining the Employment Insecurity of European Individuals during (the beginning of) the Financial Crisis. *Journal of European Social Policy*, 21(4): 287–301.

Clark, A. E. (2006). A Note on Unhappiness and Unemployment Duration. *Applied Economics Quarterly*, 52(4): 291–308.

—— and Oswald, A. J. (1994). Unhappiness and Unemployment. *Economic Journal*, 104: 648–59.

—— (1996). Satisfaction and Comparison Income. *Journal of Public Economics*, 61(3): 359–81.

—— Georgellis, Y., and Sanfey, P. (2001). Scarring: The Psychological Impact of Past Unemployment. *Economica*, 68(270): 221–41.

Clark, S. C. (2000). Work/Family Border Theory: A New Theory of Work/Family Balance. *Human Relations*, 53(6): 747–70.

Clarke, H. D., Dutt, N., and Kornberg, A. (1993). The Political Economy of Attitudes toward Polity and Society in Western European Democracies. *The Journal of Politics*, 55(4): 998–1021.

Cooper, C. L., Pandey, A., and Quick, J. C. (eds.) (2012). *Downsizing: Is Less Still More?* Cambridge: Cambridge University Press.

Cressy, R. (2006). Why Do Most Firms Die Young? *Small Business Economics*, 26: 103–16.

Crompton, R. and Lyonette, C. (2006). Work–Life Balance in Europe. *Acta Sociologica*, 49(4): 379–93.

Datta, D. K., Guthrie, J. P., Basuil, D., and Pandey, A. (2010). Causes and Effects of Employee Downsizing: A Review and Synthesis. *Journal of Management*, 36(1): 281–348.

Deaton, A. (2012). The Financial Crisis and the Well-Being of Americans 2011: OEP Hicks Lecture. *Oxford Economic Papers* 64(1): 1–26.

DeJong, D. N. and Ingram, B. F. (2001). The Cyclical Behavior of Skill Acquisition. *Review of Economic Dynamics*, 4(3): 536–61.

Dekker, S. W. A. and Schaufeli, W. B. (1995). The Effects of Job Insecurity on Psychological Health and Withdrawal: A Longitudinal Study. *Australian Psychologist*, 30(1): 57–63.

De Witte, H. (1999). Job Insecurity and Psychological Well-Being: Review of the Literature and Exploration of Some Unresolved Issues. *European Journal of Work and Organizational Psychology*, 8(2): 155–77.

—— (2005). Job Insecurity: Review of the International Literature on Definitions, Prevalence, Antecedents and Consequences. *SA Journal of Industrial Psychology*, 31(4): 1–6.

Dieckhoff, M. (2007). Does it Work? The Effect of Continuing Training on Labour Market Outcomes: A Comparative Study of Germany, Denmark, and the United Kingdom. *European Sociological Review*, 23(3): 295–308.

—— and Gash, V. (2012). *The Social Consequences of Unemployment in Europe: A Two-Stage Multilevel Analysis.* CCSR Paper 2012-04. Manchester: The Cathie Marsh Centre for Census and Survey Research.

—— and Steiber, N. (2011). A Re-Assessment of Common Theoretical Approaches to Explain Gender Differences in Continuing Training Participation. *British Journal of Industrial Relations*, 49(S1): s135–s157.

Diener, E. and Suh, E. (1997). Measuring Quality of Life: Economic, Social, and Subjective Indicators. *Social Indicators Research*, 40(1–2): 189–216.

Dietz, M., Stops, M., and Walwei, U. (2010). Safeguarding Jobs through Labor Hoarding in Germany. In *The Economy, Crises, and the Labor Market: Can Institutions Serve as a Protective Shield for Employment?* ed. K. F. Zimmermann and C. Wey, pp. 125–50. Berlin: Duncker & Humblot.

Dolls, M., Fuest, C., and Peichl, A. (2011). Automatic Stabilizers, Economic Crisis and Income Distribution in Europe. *Research in Labor Economics*, 32: 227–55.

Dordevic, B. (2004). Employee Commitment in Times of Radical Organizational Changes. *Facta Universitatis. Series Economics and Organization*, 2(2): 111–17.

Drobnic, S. (2011). Introduction: Job Quality and Work–Life Balance. In *Work–Life Balance in Europe: The Role of Job Quality*, ed. S. Drobnic and A. Guillen, pp. 1–16. Basingstoke: Palgrave Macmillan.

—— and Guillen Rodriguez, A. (2011). Tensions between Work and Home: Job Quality and Working Conditions in the Institutional Contexts of Germany and Spain. *Social Politics*, 18(2): 232–68.

Dunne, T., Roberts, M. J., and Samuelson, L. (1989). The Growth and Failure of U.S. Manufacturing Plants. *Quarterly Journal of Economics*, 104(4): 671–98.

Durand, J. P. and Hatzfeld, N. (2003). *Living with Labour: Life on the Line at Peugeot France.* Basingstoke: Palgrave Macmillan.

Dysvik, A. and Kuvaas, B. (2011). Intrinsic Motivation as a Moderator on the Relationship between Perceived Job Autonomy and Work Performance. *European Journal of Work and Organizational Psychology*, 20(3): 367–87.

Easterlin, R. A. (1974). Does Economic Growth Improve the Human Lot? In *Nations and Households in Economic Growth: Essays in Honor of Moses Abramovitz*, ed. P. A. David and M. W. Reder, pp. 98–125. New York: Academic Press.

—— (1995). Will Raising the Incomes of All Increase the Happiness of All? *Journal of Economic Behaviour and Organisation*, 27(1): 35–48.

—— (ed.) (2002). *Happiness in Economics.* Cheltenham: Edward Elgar Publishers.

Easton, D. (1975). A Re-assessment of the Concept of Political Support. *British Journal of Political Science*, 5(4): 435–57.

The Economist (2007). The Economist Intelligence Unit's Index of Democracy. Available at: <http://files.meetup.com/206829/DEMOCRACY_INDEX_2007_v3.pdf> (accessed 9 May 2012).

Edlund, J. (1999). Trust in Government and Welfare Regimes: Attitudes to Redistribution and Financial Cheating in the USA and Norway. *European Journal of Political Research*, 35(3–4): 341–70.

—— and Grönlund, A. (2008). Protection of Mutual Interests? Employment Protection and Skill Formation in Different Labour Market Regimes. *European Journal of Industrial Relations*, 14(3): 245–64.

Edwards, R. C. (1979). *Contested Terrain: The Transformation of the Workforce in the Twentieth Century*. New York: Basic Books.

El País (2011). Hasta 8,5 millones de españoles apoyan el Movimiento 15-M. *El País*. Available at: <http://politica.elpais.com/politica/2011/08/03/actualidad/1312388649_737959.html> (accessed 6 June 2012).

Elsby, M. W., Hobijn, B., and Sahin, A. (2010). The Labor Market in the Great Recession. *Brookings Papers on Economic Activity*, Spring: 1–48.

Employment Committee (EMCO) (2010). *Ad Hoc Group report on the 2010 Thematic Review. Part 2: 'Quality in Work'. Report endorsed by EMCO on 24 November 2010.* EMCO Reports Issue 6, November. Available at: <http://ec.europa.eu/emco>.

Esping-Andersen, G. (1990). *The Three Worlds of Welfare Capitalism*. Princeton: Princeton University Press.

—— and Regini, M. (2000). *Why Deregulate Labour Markets?* Oxford: Oxford University Press.

Esser, I. (2009). Has Welfare Made Us Lazy? Employment Commitment in Different Welfare States. In *British Social Attitudes: The 25th Report*, ed. A. Park, J. Curtice, K. Thomson, M. Phillips, and E. Clery, pp. 79–106. London: Sage Publications.

—— and Olsen, K. M. (2012). Perceived Job Quality: Autonomy and Job Security within a Multi-Level Framework. *European Sociological Review*, 28(4): 443–54.

Estevez-Abe, M. (2005). Gender Bias in Skills and Social Policies: The Varieties of Capitalism Perspective on Sex Segregation. *Social Politics*, 12(2): 180–215.

—— Iversen, T., and Soskice, D. (2001). Social Protection and the Formation of Skills: A Reinterpretation of the Welfare State. In *Varieties of Capitalism: The Institutional Foundations of Comparative Advantage*, ed. P. A. Hall and D. Soskice, pp. 145–83. Oxford: Oxford University Press.

European Commission (2007). Working Time, Work Organisation and Internal Flexibility- Flexicurity Models in the EU. *Employment in Europe 2007*. Luxembourg: Office for Official Publications of the European Communities.

—— (2009). *Industrial Relations in Europe 2008*. Luxembourg: Office for Official Publications of the European Communities.

—— (2010a). *Combating Poverty and Social Exclusion 2010 Edition: A Statistical Portrait of the European Union 2010*. Luxembourg: Publications Office of the European Union.

—— (2010b). *Employment in Europe 2010*. Directorate-General for Employment, Social Affairs and Equal Opportunities. Unit D.1. Luxembourg: Publications Office of the European Union.

—— (2011a). *Industrial Relations in Europe 2010*. Luxembourg: Publications Office of the European Union.

—— (2011b). *Quality of Work: Streamlining the Policy Concept and Review of Indicators*. Discussion note (rev.) INDIC/18/271011/EN.

—— (2012). *EU Employment and Social Situation*. Quarterly Review: September.

Eurostat (2010). *Combating Poverty and Social Exclusion: A Statistical Portrait of the European Union*. Luxembourg: Publications Office of the European Union.

—— (2012a). *Wachstumsrate des realen BIP-Volumen*. Available at: <http://epp.eurostat.ec.europa.eu/tgm/table.do?tab=table&init=1&plugin=0&language=de&pcode=tec00115> (accessed 16 September 2012).

—— (2012b). *Arbeitslosenquoten—jährliche Daten*. Available at: <http://epp.eurostat. ec.europa.eu/tgm/table.do?tab=table&init=1&plugin=0&language=de&pcode=tip sun20> (accessed 16 September 2012).

—— (2012c). *Employment and Unemployment Dataset*. Available at: <http://epp.eurostat. ec.europa.eu/portal/page/portal/employment_unemployment_lfs/data/database> (accessed 11 September 2012).

—— (2012d). *Real GDP Growth Rate*. Available at: <http://epp.eurostat.ec.europa. eu/tgm/table.do?tab=table&init=1&plugin=1&language=en&pcode=tsieb020> (accessed 9 May 2012).

Fagan, C. (2003). *Working-Time Preferences and Work–Life Balance in the EU: Some Policy Considerations for Enhancing the Quality of Life*. Dublin: European Foundation for the Improvement of Living and Working Conditions.

—— and Walthery, P. (2011). Job Quality and the Perceived Work–Life Balance Fit between Work Hours and Personal Commitments. In *Work–Life Balance in Europe: The Role of Job Quality*, ed. S. Drobnic and A. Guillen, pp. 69–94. Basingstoke: Palgrave Macmillan.

Fahey, T. (2007). How Do We Feel? Economic Boom and Happiness. In *Best of Times? The Social Consequences of the Celtic Tiger*, ed. T. Fahey, H. Russell, and C. T. Whelan, pp. 11–26. Dublin: Institute of Public Administration.

—— and Smyth, E. (2004). Do Subjective Indicators Measure Welfare? Evidence from 33 European Societies. *European Societies*, 6(1): 5–27.

Feldman, S. and Zaller, J. (1992). The Political Culture of Ambivalence: Ideological Responses to the Welfare State. *American Journal of Political Science*, 36(1): 268–307.

Felstead, A. and Green, F. (1994). Training during the Recession. *Work, Employment & Society*, 8(2): 199–219.

—— and Jewson, N. (2011). *The Impact of the 2008–9 Recession on the Extent, Form and Patterns of Training at Work*. LLAKES Research Paper 22. London: LLAKES Centre, Institute of Education.

Fernandez-Macias, E., Hurley, J., and Storrie, D. (eds.) (2012). *Transformation of the Employment Structure in the EU and USA, 1995–2007*. Basingstoke: Palgrave Macmillan.

Ferragina, E., Seeleib-Kaiser, M., and Tomlinson, M. (2012). Unemployment Protection and Family Policy at the Turn of the 21st Century: A Dynamic Approach to Welfare Regime Theory. *Social Policy & Administration*, advance access.

Ferrera, M. (1996). The 'Southern Model' of Welfare in Social Europe. *Journal of European Social Policy*, 6(1): 17–37.

Ferrie, J. E., Shipley, M. J., Marmot, M. G., Stansfeld, S., and Smith, G. D. (1998). The Health Effects of Major Organisational Change and Job Insecurity. *Social Science & Medicine*, 46(2): 243–54.

—— —— and Stansfeld, S. A. M. M. G. (2002). Effects of Chronic Job Insecurity and Change in Job Security on Self-Reported Health, Minor Psychiatric Morbidity, Physiological Measures, and Health Related Behaviours in British Civil Servants: The Whitehall II Study. *Journal of Epidemiological & Community Health*, 56: 450–4.

Fiorio, C. V. and Saget, C. (2010). *Reducing or Aggravating Inequality? Preliminary Findings from the 2008 Financial Crisis*. Working Paper No. 95. Geneva: International Labour Office, Policy Integration Department.

Follesdal, A. and Hix, S. (2006). Why There is a Democratic Deficit in the EU: A Response to Majone and Moravcsik. *Journal of Common Market Studies*, 44(3): 533–62.

Franzese, R. J. (2005). Empirical Strategies for Various Manifestations of Multilevel Data. *Political Analysis*, 13(4): 430–46.

Frey, B. and Stutzer, A. (2001). *Happiness and Economics: How the Economy and Institutions Affect Human Well-Being*. Princeton: Princeton University Press.

—— (2002). What Can Economists Learn from Happiness Research? *Journal of Economic Literature*, 40(2): 402–35.

Frone, M., Russell, M., and Cooper, M. (1992). Prevalence of Work–Family Conflict: Are Work and Family Boundaries Asymmetrically Permeable? *Journal of Organizational Behavior*, 13(7): 723–9.

Fryer, D. (1992). Psychological or Material Deprivation: Why Does Unemployment Have Mental Health Consequences? In *Understanding Unemployment: New Perspectives on Active Labour Market Policies*, ed. E. McLaughlin, pp. 103–25. London: Routledge.

Gallie, D. (1993). *Are the Unemployed an Underclass? Some Evidence from the Social Change and Economic Life Initiative*. Estudio Working Paper 1998/124. Madrid: Juaqn March Institute of Study and Research.

—— (2003). The Quality of Working Life: Is Scandinavia Different? *European Sociological Review*, 19(1): 61–79.

—— (2005). Work Pressure in Europe 1996–2001: Trends and Determinants. *British Journal of Industrial Relations*, 43(3): 351–75.

—— (2007a). Welfare Regimes, Employment Systems and Job Preference Orientations. *European Sociological Review*, 23(3): 279–93.

—— (2007b). *Employment Regimes and the Quality of Work*. Oxford: Oxford University Press.

—— (2009). Institutional Regimes and Employee Influence at Work: A European Comparison. *Cambridge Journal of Regions, Economy and Society*, 2(3): 379–93.

—— (2011). *Production Regimes, Employee Job Control and Skill Development*. LLAKES Research Paper 31. London: LLAKES Centre, Institute of Education.

—— and Alm, S. (2000). Unemployment, Gender and Attitudes to Work. In *Welfare Regimes and the Experience of Unemployment in Europe*, ed. D. Gallie and S. Paugam, pp. 109–33. Oxford: Oxford University Press.

—— and Paugam, S. (eds.) (2000). *Welfare Regimes and the Experience of Unemployment in Europe*. Oxford: Oxford University Press.

—— and Russell, H. (1998). Unemployment and Life Satisfaction: A Cross-Cultural Comparison. *European Journal of Sociology*, 39(2): 248–80.

—— —— (2009). Work–Family Conflict and Working Conditions in Western Europe. *Social Indicators Research*, 93(3): 445–67.

—— and Vogler, C. (1993). Unemployment and Attitudes to Work. In *Social Change and the Experience of Unemployment*, ed. D. Gallie, C. Marsh, and C. Vogler, pp. 115–53. Oxford: Oxford University Press.

—— Jacobs, S., and Paugam, S. (2000). Poverty and Financial Hardship Among the Unemployed. In *Welfare Regimes and the Experience of Unemployment in Europe*, ed. D. Gallie and S. Paugam, pp. 47–68. Oxford: Oxford University Press.

—— Marsh, C., and Vogler, C. (eds.) (1994). *Social Change and the Experience of Unemployment*. Oxford: Oxford University Press.

—— White, M., Cheng, Y., and Tomlinson, M. (1998). *Restructuring the Employment Relationship*. Oxford: Clarendon Press.

—— Paugam, S., and Jacobs, S. (2003). Unemployment, Poverty and Social Isolation: Is There a Vicious Circle of Social Exclusion? *European Societies*, 5(1): 1–32.

Gash, V. (2008a). Bridge or Trap? To What Extent do Temporary Workers Make More Transitions to Unemployment than to the Standard Employment Contract? *European Sociological Review*, 24(5): 651–68.

—— (2008b). Preference or Constraint? Part-time Workers' Transitions in Denmark, France and the United-Kingdom. *Work, Employment & Society*, 22(4): 655–74.

—— Mertens, A., and Romeu-Gordo, L. (2007). Are Fixed-Term Jobs Bad for your Health? A Comparison of Spain and Germany. *European Journals*, 9(3): 429–58.

—— (2012). The Influence of Changing Hours of Work on Women's Life Satisfaction. *The Manchester School*, 80(1): 51–74.

Gasper, D. (2007). Uncounted or Illusory Blessings? Competing Responses to the Easterlin, Easterbrook and Schwartz Paradoxes of Well-Being. *Journal of International Development*, 19(4): 473–92.

Gelderblom, A. and De Koning, J. (2002). Exclusion of Older Workers, Productivity and Training. In *Education, Training and Employment Dynamics: Transitional Labour Markets in the European Union*, ed. K. Schömann and P. J. O'Connell, pp. 243–59. Cheltenham: Edward Elgar Publishers.

Gershuny, J. and Marsh, C. (1993). Unemployment in Work Histories. In *Social Change and the Experience of Unemployment*, ed. D. Gallie, C. Marsh, and C. Vogler, pp. 66–114. Oxford: Oxford University Press.

Giuliano, P. and Spilimbergo, A. (2009). *Growing Up in a Recession: Beliefs and the Macroeconomy*. Working Paper 15321. Cambridge, MA: National Bureau of Economic Research.

Goldin, C. and Katz, L. F. (2007). *The Race between Education and Technology*. Cambridge, MA: Harvard University Press.

Goldthorpe, J. H. (1996). Class and Politics in Advanced Industrial Societies. In *Conflicts about Class: Debating Inequality in Late Industrialism*, ed. D. J. Lee and B. S. Turner, pp. 196–208. New York: Longman.

—— Lockwood, D., Bechhofer, F., and Platt, J. (1969). *The Affluent Worker in the Class Structure*. Cambridge: Cambridge University Press.

Gollac, M. (2011). *Mesurer les facteurs psychosociaux de risque au travial pour les maitriser. Rapport du College d'expertise sur le suivi des risques psychosociaux au travail*. Paris: Ministère du travail, des relations sociales et de la solidarité.

Goode, W. J. (1960). A Theory of Role Strain. *American Sociological Review*, 25(4): 483–96.

Goos, M. and Manning, A. (2007). Lousy and Lovely Jobs: The Rising Polarization of Work in Britain. *Review of Economics and Statistics*, 89(1): 118–33.

—— and Salomons, A. (2009). Job Polarization in Europe. *American Economic Review*, 99(2): 58–63.

Gordo, L. R. (2006). Effects of Short- and Long-Term Unemployment on Health Satisfaction: Evidence from German Data. *Applied Economics*, 38(20): 2335–50.

Gornick, J. C. and Meyers, M. K. (2003). *Families That Work: Policies for Reconciling Parenthood and Employment*. New York: Russell Sage Foundation.

Green D., Palmquist, B., and Schickler, E. (2002). *Partisan Hearts and Minds*. New Haven: Yale University Press.

Green, F. (2001). It's Been a Hard Day's Night: The Concentration and Intensification of Work in Late Twentieth-Century Britain. *British Journal of Industrial Relations*, 39(1): 53–80.

—— (2003). *The Rise and Decline of Job Insecurity*. Department of Economics Discussion Paper 05/03. Canterbury: University of Kent.

—— (2009). Subjective Employment Insecurity around the World. *Cambridge Journal of Regions, Economy and Society*, 2(3): 343–63.

—— Felstead, A., and Gallie, D. (2003). Computers and the Changing Skill-Intensity of Jobs. *Applied Economics*, 35: 1561–76.

Greenhaus, J. H. and Beutell, N. J. (1985). Sources of Conflict between Work and Family Roles. *Academy of Management Review*, 10(1): 76–88.

Gregg, P., Scutella, R., and Wadsworth, J. (2010). Reconciling Workless Measures at the Individual and Household Level: Theory and Evidence from the United States, Britain, Germany, Spain and Australia. *Journal of Population Economics*, 23(1): 139–67.

Gregory, M. and Connolly, S. (2008). The Price of Reconciliation: Part-Time Work, Families and Women's Satisfaction. *Economic Journal*, 118(526): F1–F7.

Habermas, J. (1973). *Legitimation Crisis*. Boston: Beacon.

Hall, P. A. and Soskice, D. (eds.) (2001). *Varieties of Capitalism: The Institutional Foundations of Comparative Advantage*. Oxford: Oxford University Press.

Handel, M. J. (2003). *Implications of Information Technology for Employment, Skills and Wages: A Review of Recent Research*. Final Report. SRI Project Number P10168. Menlo Park, CA: SRI International.

Hanushek, E. A. and Woessmann, L. (2008). The Role of Cognitive Skills in Economic Development. *Journal of Economic Literature*, 46(3): 607–68.

Hasenfeld, Y. and Rafferty, J. A. (1989). The Determinants of Public Attitudes Toward the Welfare State. *Social Forces*, 67(4): 1027–48.

Hauser, R., Nolan, B., Mörsdorf, K., and Strengmann-Kuhn, W. (2000). Unemployment and Poverty: Change over Time. In *Welfare Regimes and the Experience of Unemployment in Europe*, ed. D. Gallie and S. Paugam, pp. 25–46. Oxford: Oxford University Press.

Heady, P. and Smyth, M. (1989). *Living Standards during Unemployment: A Report of a Survey of Families Headed by Unemployed People*. London: HMSO.

Heller, F., Pusic, E., Strauss, G., and Wilpert, B. (1998). *Organizational Participation: Myth and Reality*. Oxford: Oxford University Press.

Herrigel, G. and Sabel, C. F. (1999). Craft Production in Crisis: Industrial Restructuring in Germany during the 1990s. In *The German Skills Machine: Sustaining Comparative Advantage in a Global Economy*, ed. P. P. Culpepper and D. Finegold, pp. 77–114. Oxford and New York: Berghahn Books.

Hout, M., Brooks, C., and Manza, J. (1995). The Democratic Class Struggle in the United States, 1948–1992. *American Sociological Review*, 60(6): 805–28.

Hult, C. and Stattin, M. (2010). Age, Policy Changes and Work Orientation: Comparing Changes in Commitment to Paid Work in Four European Countries. *Journal of Population Ageing*, 2(3–4): 101–20.

—— and Svallfors, S. (2002). Production Regimes and Work Orientations: A Comparison of Six Western Countries. *European Sociological Review*, 18(3): 315–31.

Hyggen, C. (2008). Change and Stability in Work Commitment in Norway: From Adolescence to Adulthood. *Journal of Social Policy*, 37(1): 103–23.

Hyman, H. H. and Wright, C. R. (1979). *Education's Lasting Influence on Values*. Chicago: University of Chicago Press.

ILO (International Labour Office) (2010). *Global Wage Report 2010/11: Wage Policies in Times of Crisis*. Geneva: International Labour Office.

Immervoll, H. and O'Donoghue, C. (2004). What Difference Does a Job Make? The Income Consequences of Joblessness in Europe. In *Resisting Marginalization: Unemployment Experience and Social Policy in the European Union*, ed. D. Gallie, pp. 105–39. Oxford: Oxford University Press.

Inanc, H. (2010). *Labour Market Insecurity and Family Relationships*. EMPLOY State-of-the-art-Report. Equalsoc.

—— (2012). *Labour Market Insecurity and Family Relations in the United Kingdom*. Working Paper. Department of Sociology, University of Oxford.

Inglehart, R. (1977). *The Silent Revolution: Changing Values and Political Styles among Western Publics*. Princeton: Princeton University Press.

—— (1990). *Culture Shift in Advanced Industrialized Societies*. Princeton: Princeton University Press.

Jackman, M. R. and Muha, M. J. (1984). Education and Intergroup Attitudes. *American Sociological Review*, 49(6): 751–69.

Jackson, P. R. and Warr, P. B. (1984). Unemployment and Psychological Ill-Health: The Moderating Role of Duration and Age. *Psychological Medicine*, 14(3): 605–14.

Jacobs, J. A. and Gerson, K. (2004). *The Time Divide: Work, Family and Gender Inequality*. Cambridge, MA: Harvard University Press.

Jacoby, W. G. (1994). Public Attitudes toward Government Spending. *American Journal of Political Science*, 38(2): 336–61.

Jahoda, M. (1982). *Employment and Unemployment: A Social-Psychological Analysis*. Cambridge: Cambridge University Press.

—— Lazersfeld, P., and Zeisal, H. (1972). *Marienthal: The Sociography of an Unemployed Community*. London: Tavistock Publications.

Johnson, J. V. and Johansson, G. (eds.) (1991). *The Psychosocial Work Environment: Work Organization, Democratisation and Health—Essays in Memory of Bertil Gardell*. Amityville, NY: Baywood Publishing Company.

Jones, M. K., Jones, R. J., Latreille, P. L., and Sloane, P. J. (2009). Training, Job Satisfaction, and Workplace Performance in Britain: Evidence from WERS 2004. *Labour*, 23(S1): S139–S175.

Kaase, M. and Newton, K. (1995). *Beliefs in Government*. New York: Oxford University Press.

Kahn, L. B. (2010). The Long-Term Labour Market Consequences of Graduating from College in a Bad Economy. *Labour Economics*, 17(2): 303–16.

Kahneman, D. and Tversky. A. (1984). Choices, Values, Frames. *American Psychologist,* 39(4): 341–50.

Kalleberg, A. L. (2011). *Good Jobs, Bad Jobs: The Rise of Polarized and Precarious Employment Systems in the United States, 1970s to 2000s.* New York: Russell Sage Foundation.

—— and Vaisey, S. (2005). Pathways to a Good Job: Perceived Work Quality among the Machinists in North America. *British Journal of Industrial Relations,* 43(3): 431–54.

—— Reskin, B., and Hudson, K. (2000). Bad Jobs in America: Standard and Nonstandard Employment Relations and Job Quality in the United States. *American Sociological Review,* 65: 256–78.

Kam, C. and Nam, Y. (2008). Reaching Out or Pulling Back: Macroeconomic Conditions and Public Support for Social Welfare Spending. *Political Behavior,* 30(2): 223–58.

Karamessini, M. (2008). Continuity and Change in the Southern European Social Model. *International Labour Review,* 147(1): 43–70.

Karasek, R. A. (1979). Job Demands, Job Decision Latitude, and Mental Strain: Implications for Job Redesign. *Administrative Science Quarterly,* 24(2): 285–308.

—— and Theorell, T. (1990). *Healthy Work, Stress, Productivity and the Reconstruction of Work Life.* New York: Basic Books.

Kenworthy, L. (2001). Wage-Setting Measures: A Survey and Assessment. *World Politics,* 54(1): 57–98.

—— (2010). Institutions, Wealth, and Inequality. In *The Oxford Handbook of Comparative Institutional Analysis,* ed. G. Morgan, J. Campbell, C. Crouch, O. K. Pedersen, and R. Whitley, pp. 399–420. Oxford: Oxford University Press.

Kern, H. and Schumann, M. (1987). Limits of the Division of Labour: New Production and Employment Concepts in West German Industry. *Economic and Industrial Democracy,* 8(1): 151–70.

Kessler, R., Blake, S., Turner, J., and House, J. S. (1988). Effect of Unemployment in a Community Sample: Main Modifying and Mediating Effects. *Journal of Social Issues,* 44(4): 69–85.

Kinder, D. R. and Kiewiet, R. (1981). Sociotropic Politics: The American Case. *British Journal of Political Science,* 11(2): 129–61.

Korpi, W. (1983). *The Democratic Class Struggle.* London: Routledge & Kegan Paul.

—— (2006). Power Resources and Employer-Centered Approaches in Explanations of Welfare States and Varieties of Capitalism. Protagonists, Consenters and Antagonists. *World Politics,* 58(2): 167–206.

—— and Levin, H. (2001). Precarious Footing: Temporary Employment as a Stepping Stone out of Unemployment in Sweden. *Work, Employment & Society,* 15(1): 127–48.

Kotowska, I., Matysiak, A. S. M., Pailhe, A., Solaz, A., and Vignoli, D. (2010). *Second European Quality of Life Survey: Family Life and Work.* Luxembourg: Office for Official Publications of the European Communities.

Krugman, P. (1994). Past and Prospective Causes of High Unemployment. *Economic Review: Federal Reserve Bank of Kansas City,* January: 49–98.

Lampard, R. (1993). An Examination of the Relationship between Marital Dissolution and Unemployment. In *Social Change and the Experience of Unemployment,* ed. D. Gallie, C. Marsh, and C. Vogler, pp. 264–98. Oxford: Oxford University Press.

Layard, R. (2005). *Happiness: Lessons from a New Science.* New York: Penguin.

Leggett, J. C. (1964). Economic Insecurity and Working Class Consciousness. *American Sociological Review*, 29(2): 226–34.

Leibfried, S. (1992). Towards a European Welfare State? In *Social Policy in Changing Europe*, ed. F. Zsuza and J. E. Kolberg, pp. 245–79. Frankfurt: Campus.

Lewis, J. B. (2000). *Edvreg (Version 1.1)* [Computer program]. Available at: <http://svn.cluelessresearch.com/twostep/trunk/edvreg.ado> (accessed 1 October 2010).

—— and Linzer, D. A. (2005). Estimating Regression Models in which the Dependent Variable is Based on Estimates. *Political Analysis*, 13(4): 345–64.

Lewis-Beck, M. S. and Stegmaier, M. (2000). Economic Determinants of Electoral Outcomes. *Annual Review of Political Science*, 3(1): 183–219.

Liem, R. and Liem, J. (1988). Psychological Effects of Unemployment on Workers and their Families. *Journal of Social Issues*, 44(4): 87–105.

Lindbeck, A. and Snower. D. (1988). *The Insider–Outsider Theory of Employment and Unemployment*. Cambridge, MA: MIT Press.

Linde, J. and Ekman, J. (2003). Satisfaction with Democracy: A Note on a Frequently Used Indicator in Comparative Politics. *European Journal of Political Research*, 42(3): 391–408.

Linn, M. W., Sandlifer, R., and Stein, S. (1985). Effects of Unemployment in Mental and Physical Health. *American Journal of Psychological Health*, 75(5): 502–6.

Lipset, S. M. (1960). *Political Man*. New York: Vintage Books

—— (1994). The Social Requisites of Democracy Revisited. *American Sociological Review*, 59(1): 1–22.

—— and Rokkan, S. (1967). Cleavage Structures, Party Systems, and Voter Alignments: An Introduction. In *Party Systems and Voter Alignments*, ed. S. M. Lipset and S. Rokkan, pp. 1–64. New York: Free Press.

Lockwood, D. (1966). Sources of Variation in Working-Class Images of Society. *The Sociological Review*, 14(3): 249–67.

Lohmann, H. (2009). Welfare States, Labour Market Institutions and the Working Poor: A Comparative Analysis of 20 European Countries. *European Sociological Review*, 25(4): 489–504.

Luechinger, S., Meier, S., and Stutzer, A. (2010). Why Does Unemployment Hurt the Employed? Evidence from the Life Satisfaction Gap between the Public and the Private Sector. *Journal of Human Resources*, 45(4): 998–1045.

McGinnity, F. (Forthcoming). Work–Life Conflict in Europe. In *Encyclopedia of Quality of Life and Well-Being Research*, ed. A. C. Michalos. Dordrecht: Springer.

—— and Calvert, E. (2009). Work–Life Conflict and Social Inequality in Western Europe. *Social Indicators Research*, 93(3): 489–508.

—— and Whelan, C. T. (2009). Reconciling Work and Family Life: Evidence from the European Social Survey. *Social Indicators Research*, 93(3): 433–45.

McGovern, P., Hill, S., Mills, C., and White, M. (2007). *Market, Class and Employment*. Oxford: Oxford University Press.

McKee-Ryan, F., Song, Z., Wanberg, C. R., and Kinicki, A. J. (2005). Psychological and Physical Well-Being during Unemployment: A Meta-Analytic Study. *The Journal of Applied Psychology*, 90(1): 53–76.

Macpherson, C. B. (1977). *The Life and Times of Liberal Democracy*. Oxford: Oxford University Press.

Majumdar, S. (2007). Market Conditions and Worker Training: How Does it Affect and whom? *Labour Economics*, 14(1): 1–23.

Manning, A. and Petrongolo, B. (2008). The Part-Time Pay Penalty for Women in Britain. *Economic Journal*, 118(526): F28–F51.

Manza, J. and Brooks, C. (1996). Does Class Analysis Still Have Anything to Contribute to the Study of Politics? Comments. *Theory and Society*, 25(5): 717–24.

Marmot, M. (2004). *Status Syndrome: How Your Social Standing Directly Affects Your Health and Life Expectancy*. London: Bloomsbury.

—— and Smith, G. D. (1991). Health Inequalities among British Civil Servants: The Whitehall II Study. *Lancet*, 337(8754): 1387.

Marsh, C. and Alvaro, J. L. (1990). A Cross-Cultural Perspective on the Social and Psychological Distress Caused by Unemployment: A Comparison of Spain and the United Kingdom. *European Sociological Review*, 6(3): 237–56.

Marshall, G., Rose, D., Newby, H., and Vogler, C. (1988). Political Quiescence among the Unemployed in Modern Britain. In *Social Stratification and Economic Change*, ed. D. Rose, pp. 193–225. London: Hutchinson.

Marshall, T. H. (1964). *Class, Citizenship and Social Development*. Garden City, NY: Doubleday.

Maslow, A. H. (1954). *Motivation and Personality*. New York: Harper.

Mason, G. and Bishop, K. (2010). *Adult Training, Skills Updating and Recession in the UK: The Implications for Competitiveness and Social Inclusion*. LLAKES Research Paper 10. London: LLAKES Centre, Institute of Education.

Mau, S., Mewes, J., and Schöneck, N. M. (2012). What Determines Subjective Socio-Economic Insecurity? Context and Class in Comparative Perspective. *Socio-Economic Review*, 10(4): 655–82.

Melero, E. (2010). Training and Promotion: Allocation of Skills or Incentives? *Industrial Relations*, 49(4): 640–67.

Meltzer, A. H. and Richard, S. F. (1981). A Rational Theory of the Size of Government. *Journal of Political Economy*, 89(5): 914–27.

Möller, J. (2010). The German Labour Market Response in the World Recession: De-mystifying a Miracle. *Zeitschrift für ArbeitsmarktForschung*, 42(4): 325–36.

Mood, C. (2010). Logistic Regression: Why we Cannot Do What We Think We Can Do, and What We Can Do About It. *European Sociological Review*, 26(1): 67–82.

Morris, L. (1990). *The Workings of the Household: A US–UK comparison*. Cambridge: Polity Press.

Morrison, E. W. and Robinson, S. L. (1997). When Employees Feel Betrayed: A Model of How Psychological Contract Violation Develops. *The Academy of Management Review*, 22(1): 226–56.

Mughan, A. and Lacy, D. (2002). Economic Performance, Job Insecurity and Electoral Choice. *British Journal of Political Science*, 32(3): 513–33.

Narendranathan, W. and Stewart, M. B. (1993). How Does Benefit Effect Vary as Unemployment Spells Lengthen? *Journal of Applied Econometrics*, 8: 361–81.

NasséNew, P. and Legeron, P. (2008). *Rapport sur la* détermination, *la mesure et le suivi des risques psychosociaux au travail*. Paris: Ministère du travail, des relations sociales et de la solidaritéNew.

Neesham, C. and Tache, I. (2010). Is there an East-European Social Model? *International Journal of Social Economics*, 37(5): 344–60.

Nickell, S. (1997). Unemployment and Labor Market Rigidities: Europe versus North America. *Journal of Economic Perspectives*, 11(3): 55–74.

—— Narendranathan, W., Stern, W., and Garcia, J. (1989). *The Nature of Unemployment in Britain: Studies of the DHSS Cohort*. Oxford: Oxford University Press.

Nordenmark, M. and Strandh, M. (1999). Towards a Sociological Understanding of Mental Well-Being among the Unemployed: The Role of Economic and Psychosocial Factors. *Sociology*, 33(3): 577–97.

—— and Layte, R. (2006). The Impact of Unemployment Benefit System on the Mental Well-Being of the Unemployed in Sweden, Ireland and Great Britain. *European Societies*, 8(1): 83–110.

North, D. (1990). *Institutions, Institutional Change and Economic Performance*. Cambridge: Cambridge University Press.

O'Connell, P. (1999). *Adults in Training: An International Comparison of Continuing Education and Training*. OECD Working Paper. Paris: OECD.

—— and Byrne, D. (2012). The Determinants and Effects of Training at Work: Bringing the Workplace Back In. *European Sociological Review*, 28(3): 283–300.

OECD (Organisation for Economic Co-operation and Development) (1999). *OECD Employment Outlook*. Paris: Organisation for Economic Co-operation and Development.

—— (2004). *OECD Employment Outlook*. Paris: Organisation for Economic Co-operation and Development.

—— (2006). *OECD Employment Outlook*. Paris: Organisation for Economic Co-operation and Development.

—— (2008). OECD Stat (Database: Employment protection in OECD and selected non-OECD countries, 2008) Available at: <http://www.oecd.org/employment/emp/oecdindicatorsofemploymentprotection.htm> (accessed 2 October 2012).

—— (2010). *OECD Employment Outlook*. Paris: Organisation for Economic Co-operation and Development.

—— (2011). *OECD Employment Outlook*. Paris: Organisation for Economic Co-operation and Development.

—— (2012). *OECD Stat (Database: Strictness of employment protection—overall)*. Available at: <http://stats.oecd.org/Index.aspx?QueryId=19465#> (accessed 19 October 2012).

Oesch, D. and Lipps, O. (2012). Does Unemployment Hurt Less if There is More of it Around? A Panel Analysis of Life Satisfaction in Germany and Switzerland. *European Sociological Review*. Available at: <http://www.iza.org/conference_files/ReDisWeBe2010/oesch_d6590.pdf>.

—— and Rodriguez Menes, J. (2011). Upgrading or Polarization? Occupational Change in Britain, Germany, Spain and Switzerland, 1990–2008. *Socio-Economic Review*, 9(3): 503–32.

Offe, C. (1984). *Contradictions of the Welfare State*. London: Hutchinson.

—— (2000). The Democratic Welfare State in an Integrating Europe. In *Democracy Beyond the State? The European Dilemma and the Emerging Global Order*, ed. M. T. Greven and L. W. Pauly, pp. 63–90. Oxford: Rowman & Littlefield.

—— (2003). The European Model of 'Social' Capitalism: Can It Survive European Integration? *Journal of Political Philosophy*, 11(4): 437–69.

Ok, W. and Tergeist, P. (2003). *Improving Workers' Skills: Analytical Evidence and the Role of Social Partners*. OECD Social, Employment and Migration Working Papers. Paris: Organisation for Economic Co-operation and Development.

Paugam, S. and Russell, H. (2000). The Effects of Employment Precarity and Unemployment on Social Isolation. In *Welfare Regimes and the Experience of Unemployment in Europe*, ed. D. Gallie and S. Paugam, pp. 243–64. Oxford: Oxford University Press.

—— and Zhou, Y. (2007). Job Insecurity. In *Employment Regimes and the Quality of Work*, ed. D. Gallie, pp. 179–204. Oxford: Oxford University Press.

Paul, K. I. and Moser, K. (2009). Unemployment Impairs Mental Health: Meta-Analyses. *Journal of Vocational Behavior*, 74(3): 264–82.

Pfeifer, M. (2012). Comparing Unemployment Protection and Social Assistance in 14 European Countries: Four Worlds of Protection for People of Working Age. *International Journal of Social Welfare*, 21(1): 13–25.

Piore, M. J. and Sabel, C. F. (1984). *The Second Industrial Divide: Possibilities for Prosperity*. New York: Basic Books.

Polavieja, J. G. (2001). *Insiders and Outsiders: Structure and Consciousness Effects of Labour Market Deregulation in Spain (1984–1997)*. Madrid: Ediciones Peninsular.

—— (2003). *Estables y Precarios: Desregulación Laboral y Estratificación Social en España*. Madrid: Centro de Investigaciones Sociológicas.

Primo, D. M., Jacobsmeier, M. L. and Milyo, J. (2007). Estimating the Impact of State Policies and Institutions with Mixed-Level Data. *State Politics and Policy Quarterly*, 7(4): 446–59.

Putnam, R. D. (1993). *Making Democracy Work: Civic Traditions in Modern Italy*. Princeton: Princeton University Press.

Rhodes, M. (ed.) (1997). *Southern European Welfare States: Between Crisis and Reform*. London: Frank Cass.

Robinson, P. (2000). Insecurity and Flexible Workforce: Measuring the Ill-defined. In *The Insecure Workforce*, ed. E. Heery and J. Salmon, pp. 25–38. London: Routledge.

Robinson, R. V. and Bell, W. (1978). Equality, Success and Social Justice in England and the United States. *American Sociological Review*, 43(1): 125–43.

Rosenfeld, R. (1992). Job Mobility and Career Processes. *Annual Review of Sociology*, 18: 39–61.

Rousseau, D. M. (1995). *Psychological Contracts in Organizations: Understanding Written and Unwritten Agreements*. Thousand Oaks, CA: Sage Publications.

Ruiz-Rufino, R. (2013). Satisfaction with Democracy in Multi-ethnic Countries: The Effect of Representative Political Institutions on Ethnic Minorities. *Political Studies*, 61(1): 101–18.

Russell, H. (1999). Friends in Low Places: Gender, Unemployment and Sociability. *Work, Employment & Society*, 13(2): 205–24.

—— and McGinnity, F. (2011). *Workplace Equality in the Recession? The impact and incidence of equality policies and flexible working*. Dublin: ESRI/Equality Authority.

—— (2013). Under Pressure: The Impact of Recession on Employees in Ireland. *British Journal of Industrial Relations*. doi: 10.1111/bjir.12018

Ryan, R. M. and Deci, E. L. (2001). On Happiness and Human Potentials: A Review of Research on Hedonic and Eudaimonic Well-Being. *Annual Review of Psychology*, 52(1): 141–66.

Saraceno, C. (1994). The Ambivalent Familism of the Italian Welfare State. *Social Politics*, 1: 60–82.

Scharpf, F. W. (1997). Economic Integration, Democracy and the Welfare State. *Journal of European Public Policy*, 4(1): 118–36.

Scherer, S. (2009). The Social Consequences of Insecure Jobs. *Social Indicators Research*, 93(3): 469–88.

—— and Steiber, N. (2007). Work and Family in Conflict? The Impact of Work Demands on Family Life. In *Employment Regimes and the Quality of Working Life*, ed. D. Gallie, pp. 137–78. Oxford: Oxford University Press.

Schieman, S., Milkie, M., and Glavin, P. (2009). When Work Interferes with Life: Work-Nonwork Interference and the Influence of Work-Related Demands and Resources. *American Sociological Review*, 74(6): 966–88.

Schils, T. (2005). *Early Retirement Patterns in Europe: A Comparative Panel Study*. Amsterdam: Dutch University Press.

Schimmack, U. and Oishi, S. (2005). The Influence of Chronically and Temporarily Accessible Information on Life Satisfaction Judgments. *Journal of Personality and Social Psychology*, 89(3): 395–406.

Schlozman, K. L. and Verba, S. (1979). *Injury to Insult: Unemployment, Class and Political Response*. Cambridge, MA: Harvard University Press.

Schumpeter, J. A. (1970). *Capitalism, Socialism and Democracy*. London: Routledge.

Sen, A. (1985). *Commodities and Capabilities*. Amsterdam: North-Holland.

Shields, M. A., Wheatley Price, S., and Wooden, M. (2009). Life Satisfaction and the Economic and Social Characteristics of Neighbourhoods. *Journal of Population Economics*, 22: 421–43.

Shimer, R. (2012). Reassessing the Ins and Outs of Unemployment. *Review of Economic Dynamics*, 15(2): 127–48.

Smith, V. (1994). Braverman's Legacy: The Labor Process Tradition at 20. *Work and Occupations*, 21(4): 403–21.

Solon, G., Barsky, R., and Parker, J. A. (1994). Measuring the Cyclicality of Real Wages: How Important is Composition Bias? *Quarterly Journal of Economics*, 109(1): 1–25.

Soskice, D. (1999). Divergent Production Regimes: Coordinated and Uncoordinated Market Economies in the 1980s and 1990s. In *Continuity and Change in Contemporary Capitalism*, ed. H. Kitschelt, P. Lange, G. Marks, and J. Stephens, pp. 101–34. Cambridge: Cambridge University Press.

Spiegel, P. and Mallet, V. (2012). Spain Seeks Eurozone Bailout. *Financial Times*. Available at: <http://www.ft.com/intl/cms/s/0/b4deeb3a-b256-11e1-99ff 00144feabdc0.html#axzz1y8DI7HwF> (accessed 15 May 2012).

Spiezia, V. (2000). The Effects of Benefits on Unemployment and Wages: A Comparison of Unemployment Compensation Schemes. *International Labour Review*, 139(1): 73–87.

Spitz-Oener, A. (2006). Technical Change, Job Tasks, and Rising Educational Demands: Looking Outside the Wage Structure. *Journal of Labor Economics*, 24(2): 235–70.

Steger, M. F. and Kashdan, T. B. (2007). Stability and Specificity of Meaning and Life Satisfaction over One Year. *Journal of Happiness Studies*, 8: 161–79.

Steiber, N. (2008). *How Many Hours Would You Want to Work a Week? Job Quality and the Omitted Variables Bias in Labour Supply Models*. SOEP papers on Multidisciplinary Panel Data Research No. 121. DIW, Berlin.

—— (2009). Reported Levels of Time-Based and Strain-Based Conflict between Work and Family Roles in Europe: A Multi-Level Approach. *Social Indicators Research*, 93(3): 469–88.

Stigler, S. M. (1997). Regression towards the Mean, Historically Considered. *Statistical Methods in Medical Research*, 6(2): 103–14.

Stjórnlagaráðs (2011). The Constitutional Council—General Information. Available at: <http://stjornlagarad.is/english/> (accessed 7 June 2012).

Stovicek, K. and Turrini, A. (2012). *Benchmarking Unemployment Benefits in the EU*. IZA Policy Paper No. 43. Bonn: Forschungsinstitut zur Zukunft der Arbeit GmbH (IZA).

Strandh, M. and Nordenmark, N. (2006). The Interference of Paid Work with Household Demands in Different Social Policy Contexts: Perceived Work-Household Conflict in Sweden, the UK, the Netherlands, Hungary, and the Czech Republic. *The British Journal of Sociology*, 57(4): 597–617.

Streeck, W. (1992). Training and the New Industrial Relations: A Strategic Role for Unions? In *The Future of Labour Movements*, ed. M. Regini, pp. 250–69. London, Newbury Park, CA and New Delhi: Sage Publications.

Svallfors, S. (1997). Worlds of Welfare and Attitudes to Redistribution: A Comparison of Eight Western Nations. *European Sociological Review*, 13(3): 283–304.

Sverke, M., Hellgren, J., and Näswall, K. (2002). No Security: A Meta-Analysis and Review of Job Insecurity and its Consequences. *Journal of Occupational Health Psychology*, 7(3): 242–64.

—— (2006). Job Insecurity: A Literature Review. Stockholm: National Institute for Working Life.

Tåhlin, M. (2004). Do Opposites Attract? How Inequality Affects Mobility in the Labor Market. *Research in Social Stratification and Mobility*, 20: 255–82.

—— (2007). Skills and Wages in European Labour Markets: Structure and Change. In *Employment Regimes and the Quality of Work*, ed. D. Gallie, pp. 35–76. Oxford: Oxford University Press.

Tavora, I. (2012). The Southern European Social Model: Familialism and the High Rates of Female Employment in Portugal. *Journal of European Social Policy*, 22(1): 63–76.

Taylor, P. and Walker, A. (1998). Employers and Older Workers: Attitudes and Employment Practices. *Ageing and Society*, 18(6): 641–58.

Theorell, T. (2007). Psychosocial Factors in Research on Work Conditions and Health in Sweden. *Scandinavian Journal of Work and Environment Health*, 33(1): 20–6.

—— and Karasek, R. (1996). Current Issues Relating to Psychosocial Job Strain and Cardiovascular Disease Research. *Journal of Occupational Health and Psychology*, 1(1): 9–26.

Turunen, T. (2011). Commitment to Employment and Organisation: Finland in a European Comparison. *Research on Finnish Society*, 4(1): 55–66.

Tversky, A. and Kahneman, D. (1974). Judgment under Uncertainty. *Science*, 185(4157): 1124–31.

Van den Berg, A. and Masi, A. (2005). Responses to Downsizing under Different Adjustment Regimes: A Two-Country Comparison. In *Job Insecurity, Union Involvement and Union Activism*, ed. H. D. Witte, pp. 155–86. Aldershot: Ashgate.

Van der Lippe, T., Jager, A., and Kops, Y. (2006). Combination Pressure: The Paid Work–Family Balance of Men and Women in European Countries. *Acta Sociologica*, 49(3): 303–19.

Van Vliet, O. and Caminada, K. (2012). *Unemployment Replacement Rates Dataset among 34 Welfare States 1971–2009: An Update, Extension and Modification of the Scruggs, Welfare State Entitlements Data Set*. NEUJOBS Special Report No. 2. Leiden: Leiden University.

Veenhoven, R. (1993). *Happiness in Nations*. RISBO 127. Rotterdam: Erasmus University.

—— (2002a). Why Social Policy Needs Subjective Indicators. *Social Indicators Research*, 58(1): 33–45.

—— (2002b). Why Social Policy Needs Subjective Indicators. In *Assessing Quality of Life and Living Conditions to Guide National Policy*, ed. M. R. Hagerty, J. Vogel, and V. Møller, pp. 33–46. Dordrecht: Kluwer.

—— (2009). How Do We Assess How Happy We Are? Tenets, Implications and Tenability of Three Theories. In *Happiness, Economics and Politics: Towards a Multi-Disciplinary Approach*, ed. A. Dutt and B. Radcliff, pp. 45–69. Cheltenham: Edward Elgar Publishers.

Venn, D. (2009). *Legislation, Collective Bargaining and Enforcement: Updating the OECD Employment Protection Indicators*. OECD Social, Employment and Migration Working Papers. Paris: Organisation for Economic Co-operation and Development.

—— (2012). *Eligibility Criteria for Unemployment Benefits: Quantitative Indicators for OECD and EU Countries*. OECD Social, Employment and Migration Working Papers. Paris: Organisation for Economic Co-operation and Development.

Visser, J. (2011). *Database on Institutional Characteristics of Trade Unions, Wage Setting, State Intervention and Social Pacts in 34 Countries between 1960 and 2007*. Amsterdam: Institute for Advanced Labour Studies, University of Amsterdam. Available at: <http://www.uva-aias.net/207> (accessed 1 May 2011).

Voydanoff, P. (2005). Toward a Conceptualization of Perceived Work–Family Fit and Balance: A Demands and Resources Approach. *Journal of Marriage and Family*, 67(4): 822–36.

Wall, T. D., Cordery, J. L., and Clegg, C. W. (2002). Empowerment, Performance, and Operational Uncertainty: A Theoretical Integration. *Applied Psychology*, 51(1): 146–69.

Walsh, B. (2011). *The Influence of Macroeconomic Conditions and Institutional Quality on National Levels of Life Satisfaction*. UCD Centre for Economic Research, Working Paper Series, WP12/08.

Walton, R. E. (1985). From Control to Commitment in the Workplace. *Harvard Business Review*, 85(2): 77–84.

Warr, P. (1982). A National Study of Non-Financial Employment Commitment. *Journal of Occupational Psychology*, 55(4): 297–312.

—— (1987). *Work, Unemployment and Mental Health*. Oxford: Oxford University Press.

—— and Jackson, P. (1984). Men without Jobs: Some Correlates of Age and Length of Unemployment. *Journal of Occupational Psychology*, 57(1): 77–85.

—— (1987). Adapting to the Unemployed Role: A Longitudinal Investigation. *Social Science & Medicine*, 25(11): 1219–24.

—— and Lovatt, J. (1977). Retraining and Other Factors Associated with Job Finding after Redundancy. *Journal of Occupational Psychology*, 50(2): 67–84.

Whelan, C. T. (1992). The Role of Income, Life-Style Deprivation and Financial Strain in Mediating the Impact of Unemployment on Psychological Distress: Evidence from the Republic of Ireland. *Journal of Occupational Psychology*, 65(4): 331–44.

—— and McGinnity, F. (2000). Unemployment and Satisfaction: A European Analysis. In *Welfare Regimes and the Experience of Unemployment in Europe*, ed. D. Gallie and S. Paugam, pp. 286–306. Oxford: Oxford University Press.

White, M., Hill, S., McGovern, P., Mills, C., and Smeaton, D. (2003). High-Performance Management Practices, Working Hours and Work–Life Balance. *British Journal of Industrial Relations*, 41(2): 175–95.

Wilthagen, T. and Tros, F. (2004). The Concept of Flexicurity: A New Approach to Regulating Employment and Labour Markets. *Transfer: European Review of Labour and Research*, 10(2): 166–86.

Winkelmann, L. and Winkelmann, R. (1998). Why Are the Unemployed so Unhappy? Evidence from Panel Data. *Economica*, 65: 1–15.

Womack, J. P., Jones, D. T., and Roos, D. (1990). *The Machine That Changed the World*. New York: Macmillan.

Wood, S. (2001). Business, Government, and Patterns of Labor Market Policy in Britain and the Federal Republic of Germany. In *Varieties of Capitalism: The Institutional Foundations of Comparative Advantage*, ed. P. Hall and D. Soskice, pp. 247–74. Oxford: Oxford University Press.

Woodward, J. (ed.) (1970). *Industrial Organization: Behaviour and Control*. Oxford: Oxford University Press.

Wright, E. O. and Dwyer, R. E. (2003). The Patterns of Job Expansions in the USA: A Comparison of the 1960s and 1990s. *Socio-Economic Review*, 1(3): 289–325.

Zhou, Y. (2009). *British Employees' Organizational Participation: Trends, Determinants and Impact*. Berlin: VDM Verlag Dr Muller.

Author Index

Aaberge, R. 84
Acemoglu, D. 32, 90, 94
Aidukaite, J. 202
Alderfer, C. P. 199
Allard, G. J. 204
Allen, T. 169
Allison, P. D. 96
Alm, S. 15 197
Almond, G. 257
Alt, J. E. 260
Altindag, D. 17
Alvaro, J. L. 250
Amable, B. 13
Anderson, C. J. 198
Andress, H.-J. 260
Anxo, D. 25, 204, 233
Armstrong-Stassen, M. 198
Arulampalam, W. 15, 95–96, 234
Aspalter, C. 202
Atkinson, A. B. 23
Atkinson, J. 11
Auer, P. 12
Autor, D. 11, 73, 80, 280
Avram, S. 232
Axinn, J. 260

Barbieri, P. 144–145, 303
Bardasi, E. 143
Barker, K. 11
Barlevy, G. 84
Barnes, S. 257
Barsky, R. 84
Bassi, L. 11, 132
Basuil, D. 198
Bechhofer, F. 258
Becker, G. S. 89, 91
Bell, D. 115, 230
Bell, W. 259
Bermeo, N. 257, 295
Beutell, N. J. 170
Bewley, T. F. 94
Bianchi, S. 172
Bishop, J. H. 90
Bishop, K. 89
Björklund, A. 84

Blake, S. 229
Blanchflower, D. 230
Blauner, R. 10, 115
Blekesaune, M. 260
Blumberg, P. 9
Bohle, P. 160–161
Bonoli, G. 202
Booth, A. L. 95–96
Brand, J. E. 197
Brannen, P. 9
Braverman, H. 8, 115
Brockner, J. 198
Brooks, C. 258
Bruck, C. 169
Brüderl, J. 34
Brunello, G. 89–90
Bryan, M. 95
Burchell, B. 16, 160–161, 196–197,
    217, 223
Burgard, C. 91
Burgard, S. A. 197
Burns, T. 9, 123
Byron, K. 172

Calvert, E. 172–173, 182
Cameron, D. R. 295
Caminada, K. 204–205, 226
Canache, D. 262
Capelli, P. 11, 132
Caponi, V. 88–90
Card, D. 94
Castles, F. G. 18
Cazes, S. 12
Cedefop, 73, 80, 280
Chamberlain, K. 233
Chandola, T. 136
Cheng, Y. 181
Christensen, K. 11
Chung, H. 173–174, 200
Clark, A. E. 16, 197, 230–231, 235
Clark, S. C. 170
Clarke, H. D. 257–258
Clegg, C. W. 9, 123
Connolly, S. 143
Cooper, C. L. 198

Cooper, M. 171
Cordery, J. L. 9, 123
Cressy, R. 34
Crompton, R. 171, 173

Datta, D. K. 198
Deaton, A. 243
Deci, E. L. 231, 234
DeJong, D. N. 88
Dekker, S. W. A. 160
De Koning, J. 91
De Witte, H. 16, 197–198
Dieckhoff, M. 27–28, 88, 93, 95, 197, 203, 282–283, 297
Diener, E. 234
Dietz, M. 92
Dolls, M. 43
Dordevic, B. 15
Drobnic, S. 171, 173, 182, 190
Dunne, T. 34
Durand, J. P. 115
Dutt, N. 257–258
Dwyer, R. E. 11, 280
Dysvik, A. 196

Easterlin, R. A. 231, 243
Edlund, J. 93, 110, 260
Edwards, R. C. 8
Ekman, J. 262
El País 277
Elsby, M. W. 52, 59
Employment Committee (EMCO) 3
Ericson, T. 25, 204, 233
Esping-Andersen, G. 13, 18, 44, 144, 201
Esser, I. 201, 203
Estevez-Abe, M. 13, 92
European Commission 3, 21–22, 59, 200

Fagan, C. 172
Fahey, T. 231, 243
Feldman, S. 259
Felstead, A. 88–90, 101, 280
Fernandez-Macias, E. 11
Ferragina, E. 203
Ferrera, M. 18, 202
Ferrie, J. E. 16, 160
Fiorio, C. V. 84
Follesdal, A. 275
Franzese, R. J. 96
Frey, B. 230–231, 234, 243
Frone, M. 171
Fryer, D. 229
Fuest, C. 43

Gallie, D. 1, 10, 13, 15–16, 18, 21, 23, 25, 27–28, 42, 88, 92–94, 101, 115, 130, 132–133, 135, 148, 167, 171–172, 174, 195,

197, 199–201, 203, 210, 217, 229–233, 250, 258, 279
Garcia, J. 15
Gash, V. 27, 142, 159–161, 197, 285–286
Gasper, D. 233
Georgellis, Y. 230, 235
Gershuny, J. 10
Gerson, K. 172
Giuliano, P. 15, 17
Glavin, P. 172–173, 181
Goldin, C. 73
Goldthorpe, J. H. 258
Gollac, M. 302
Goode, W. J. 170
Goos, M. 11, 73, 80, 280
Gordo, L. R. 160, 197
Görlitz, K. 91
Gornick, J. C. 143, 169
Green, D. 132–133, 160, 162, 258, 280
Green, F. 88–89
Greenhaus, J. H. 170
Gregg, P. 179
Gregory, M. 143
Grönlund, A. 93, 110
Grover, S. 198
Guillen Rodriguez, A. 173, 182, 190
Guthrie, J. P. 198
Gelderblom, A. 91

Habermas, J. 258
Hall, P. A. 12–13, 89, 92–93, 130, 148, 203
Handel, M. J. 280
Hanushek, E. A. 76
Hasenfeld, Y. 259–260
Hatzfeld, N. 115
Hauser, R. 232
Heady, P. 161
Heien, T. 260
Heller, F. 9
Hellgren, J. 16, 198
Herrigel, G. 280
Herst, D. 169
Hill, S. 12, 181
Hix, S. 275
Hobijn, B. 52, 59
House, J. S. 197, 229
Hout, M. 258
Hudson, K. 142
Hult, C. 201
Hurley, J. 11
Hyggen, C. 197
Hyman, H. H. 257, 259

ILO (International Labour Office) 73, 84
Immervoll, H. 233
Inanc , H. 16, 27, 50, 124, 142, 161, 230, 285–286
Inglehart, R. 257

Ingram, B. F. 88
Iversen, T. 92

Jackman, M. R. 264
Jackson, P. 161, 197
Jacobs, J. A. 172
Jacobs, S. 16, 233
Jacobsmeier, M. L. 96
Jacoby, W. G. 259
Jager, A. 171, 173
Jahoda, M. 15–16, 195–196, 229, 258
Jäntti, M. 84
Jewson, N. 89–90, 101
Jinsoo, K. 202
Johansson, G. 115
Johnson, J. V. 115
Jones, D. T. 9
Jones, M. K. 88
Jones, R. J. 88

Kaase, M. 257
Kahn, L. B. 74
Kahneman, D. 33
Kalleberg, A. L. 10–11, 115, 142, 280
Kam, C. 259–260
Karamessini, M. 202–203
Karasek, R. 115, 133, 135, 172
Kashdan, T. B. 233
Katz, H. 11, 132
Katz, L. F. 73
Kayahan, B. 88–90
Kenworthy, L. 19–20, 45
Kern, H. 9
Kessler, R. 229
Kiewiet, R. 259
Kinder, D. R. 259
Kinicki, A. J. 197, 229, 231, 240
Knoke, D. 11, 132
Kops, Y. 171, 173
Kornberg, A. 257–258
Korpi, W. 13, 57, 234
Kotowska, I. 169
Krugman, P. 35
Kuvaas, B. 196

Lacy, D. 258
Lampard, R. 16
Lapido, D. 16
Latreille, P. L. 88
Layard, R. 32
Layte, R. 232
Lazersfeld, P. 16, 229, 258
Lee Dewitt, R. 198
Legeron, P. 302
Leggett, J. C. 258
Leibfried, S. 18, 202
Lemieux, T. 94

Levin, H. 234
Levy, F. 11, 73, 80, 280
Lewis, J. B. 96, 208, 262
Lewis-Beck, M. S. 259
Liem, J. 230
Liem, R. 230
Lindbeck, A. 32
Linde, J. 262
Linn, M. W. 16
Linzer, D. A. 96, 208, 262
Lipps, O. 197, 231
Lipset, S. M. 257–258
Lockwood, D. 258
Lohmann, H. 202
Lovatt, J. 196
Luechinger, S. 200
Lyonette, C. 171, 173

Macpherson, C. B. 258
Majumdar, S. 89–90
Manning, A. 11, 73, 80, 143, 280
Manza, J. 258
Marmot, M. 16, 115
Marsh, C. 10, 197, 229, 250
Marshall, G. 258
Marshall, T. H. 256
Masi, A. 198–199
Maslow, A. H. 199
Mason, G. 89
Matysiak, A. S. M. 169
Mau, S. 200–201, 203
Mayhew, C. 160–161
McGinnity, F. 27, 135, 169, 171–173, 175,
    182, 189, 229, 236, 287, 291
McGovern, P. 12, 181
McKee-Ryan, F. 197, 229, 231, 240
Meier, S. 200
Melero, E. 88
Meltzer, A. H. 260
Mertens, A. 160
Mewes, J. 200–201, 203
Meyers, M. K. 169
Mickelwright, J. 23
Milkie, M. 172–173
Mills, C. 12, 181
Milyo, J. 96
Mocan, N. 17
Möller, J. 89–90
Mondak, J. J. 262
Mood, C. 96
Morris, L. 230
Morrison, E. W. 198
Mörsdorf, K. 232
Moser, K. 229
Mughan, A. 258
Muha, M. J. 264
Murnane, R. J. 11, 73, 80, 280

Nam, Y. 259–260
Narendranathan, W. 15
Nassé New, P. 302
Näswall, K. 16, 198
Neesham, C. 202
Newby, H. 258
Newton, K. 257
Nickell, S. 15, 32
Nolan, B. 232
Nordenmark, M. 173, 229, 232
North, D. 31

O'Connell, P. 91, 95–96
O'Donoghue, C. 233
OECD 5–6, 24, 26, 43, 84–85, 88, 91, 103,
   112, 142–144, 148–149, 204–205, 219,
   225–226, 232, 271
Oesch, D. 11, 197, 231, 280
Offe, C. 256, 258, 275
Oishi, S. 233
Ok, W. 93
Olsen, K. M. 203
Osterman, P. 11, 132
Oswald, A. J. 16, 231

Pailhe, A. 169
Palmquist, B. 258
Pandey, A. 198
Parker, J. A. 84
Paugam, S. 16, 18, 23, 25, 160, 203, 229,
   232–233, 250
Paul, K. I. 229
Pedersen, P. J. 84
Peichl, A. 43
Petrongolo, B. 143
Pfeifer, M. 203
Piore, M. J. 10
Pischke, J.-S. 32, 90, 94
Platt, J. 258
Plesca, M. 88–90
Polavieja, J. G. 27, 142, 256, 258,
   292–293, 300
Pontusson , J. 198, 295
Preisendörfer, P. 34
Primo, D. M. 96
Pusic, E. 9
Putnam, R. D. 257

Quadagno, J. 260
Quick, J. C. 198
Quinlan, M. 160–161

Rafferty, J. A. 259–260
Reed, T. F. 198
Regini, M. 144
Reskin, B. 142
Rhodes, M. 18

Richard, S. F. 260
Riddell, W. 94
Roberts, M. J. 34
Robinson, P. 145
Robinson, R. V. 259
Robinson, S. L. 198
Rodriguez Menes, J. 11, 280
Rokkan, S. 258
Romeu-Gordo, L. 160
Roos, D. 9
Rose, D. 258
Rosenfeld, R. 34
Rousseau, D. M. 198
Ruiz-Rufino, R. 262
Russell, H. 16, 27–28, 135, 169, 171–172,
   174–175, 189, 229–231, 287, 291
Russell, M. 171
Ryan, R. M. 231, 234

Sabel, C. F. 10, 280
Saget, C. 84
Sahin, A. 52, 59
Salomons, A. 11, 80
Samuelson, L. 34
Sandlifer, R. 16
Sanfey, P. 230, 235
Saraceno, C. 18
Scharpf, F. W. 275
Schaufeli, W. B. 160
Scherer, S. 172–173, 175, 230, 287
Schickler, E. 258
Schieman, S. 172–173, 181
Schils, T. 91, 107
Schimmack, U. 233
Schlozman, K. L. 258
Schöneck, N. M. 200–201, 203
Schumann, M. 9
Schumpeter, J. A. 9
Scutella, R. 179
Seeleib-Kaiser, M. 203
Seligson, M. A. 262
Sen, A. 234
Shields, M. A. 231
Shimer, R. 52
Shipley, M. J. 16, 160
Sloane, P. J. 88
Smeaton, D. 181
Smith, G. D. 16
Smith, N. 84
Smith, V. 8
Smyth, E. 231
Smyth, M. 161
Snower, D. 32
Sojeung, P. 202
Solaz, A. 169
Solon, G. 84
Song, Z. 197, 229, 231, 240

Soskice, D. 12–13, 19, 92–93, 130, 148, 202–203
Spiegel, P. 256
Spiezia, V. 15
Spilimbergo, A. 15, 17
Spitz-Oener, A. 73
Stalker, G. M. 9, 123
Stansfeld, S. 16, 160
Stattin, M. 201
Steger, M. F. 233
Stegmaier, M. 259
Steiber, N. 27–28, 95, 170, 172–173, 195, 199, 203, 249, 287, 289, 299
Stein, S. 16
Stern, M. J. 260
Stern, W. 15
Stewart, M. B. 15
Stigler, S. M. 33
Stjórnlagaráðs 277
Stops, M. 92
Storrie, D. 11
Stovicek, K. 24, 232
Strandh, M. 173, 229
Strauss, G. 9
Streeck, W. 94
Strengmann-Kuhn, W. 232
Stutzer, A. 200, 230–231, 234, 243
Suh, E. 234
Sutherland, H. 232
Sutton, M. 169
Svallfors, S. 201, 260
Sverke, M. 16, 198

Tache, I. 202
Tåhlin, M. 27–28, 30, 32, 58, 96, 101, 280–282, 295–297
Tasseva, I. 232
Tavora, I. 202
Taylor, M. P. 234
Taylor, P. 91
Tergeist, P. 93
Theorell, T. 115, 133, 135
Tomlinson, M. 10, 115, 203
Tros, F. 199
Tsiddon, D. 84
Tumino, A. 232
Turner, J. 229
Turrini, A. 24, 232
Turunen, T. 209
Tversky, A. 33

Useem, M. 11, 132

Vaisey, S . 115
Van den Berg, A. 198
Van der Lippe, T. 171, 173
Van Oorschot, W. 200
Van Vliet, O. 204–205, 226
Veenhoven, R. 159, 233–234
Venn, D. 112
Verba, S. 257–258
Vignoli, D. 169
Visser, J. 19–20, 22, 43, 103, 112, 126–127, 131
Vogler, C. 15, 197, 229, 258
Voydanoff, P. 170

Wadsworth, J. 179
Walker, A. 91
Wall, T. D. 9, 123
Walsh, B. 243
Walthery, P. 172
Walton, R. E. 115
Walwei, U. 92
Wanberg, C. R. 197, 229, 231, 240
Warr, P. 16, 161, 196–197, 229
Watson, D. 27–28, 229, 291
Wennemo, T. 84
Wheatley Price, S. 231
Whelan, C. T. 169, 171, 229, 236
White, M. 10, 12, 115, 181
Wilkinson, F. 16
Wilpert, B. 9
Wilthagen, T. 199
Winkelmann, L. 290
Winkelmann, R. 290
Woessmann, L. 76
Womack, J. P. 9
Wood, S. 148
Wooden, M. 231
Woodward, J. 10
Wright, C. R. 257, 259
Wright , E. O. 11, 280

Zaller, J. 259
Zeisal, H. 16, 229, 258
Ziegler, R. 34
Zika, S. 233
Zhou, Y. 27, 115, 160

Subject Index

active labour market policies (ALMP), 25, 43,
   45, 95, 198–199, 204, 232, 296, 299
age, 14, 29, 51, 54, 58–60, 62–64, 66, 68–72,
   77, 83, 86, 95–100, 102, 105, 107–108,
   111, 113–114, 118–122, 124, 129–130,
   134–135, 139–140, 144, 151–152, 155,
   164–165, 167, 169–170, 172, 175–176,
   181–184, 192, 194, 200, 205–213,
   216, 218, 221, 223–225, 227–228, 235,
   238–239, 241, 244, 252, 254, 261, 263,
   265, 271, 278, 288–289, 303
   age group, 29, 100, 105, 114, 144, 146,
      150–151, 153–154, 212, 225, 227–228,
      238, 252, 254
   age inequality, 87, 107–108, 110, 283
   mid/prime-age, 62–64, 66, 68, 70–72, 72,
      87, 108
   older age, 63, 108
   youth, 59, 62–63, 65–66, 70, 72, 87, 200
automatic stabilizers, 32, 295
automation, theories of, 10–11

bailout, 256, 275–276
Belgium, 3–7, 20–21, 23–25, 27–28, 37–38,
   44–46, 49, 55, 61–63, 68, 75, 85, 93–95,
   99–100, 105, 107–108, 110–112, 114,
   117–118, 128, 145, 152, 159, 185, 193,
   196, 204, 208–209, 225–226, 232, 252,
   261, 267–269, 280, 285–286, 294, 302
benefits
   benefits coverage, 18, 23–25, 232, 252
   housing benefits, 24
   replacement rates, 23–25, 32, 204–205, 218,
      226, 232, 252
border theory, 41, 54, 57, 170, 181
bumping-down, 73, 281

Caetano, Marcello, 303
career
   career advancement/development/
      progression/trajectories, 142, 160–161,
      171, 286
   career opportunities, 15, 286
   career outcome, 142
Carnation revolution, 303

Catholic Church, 303
childcare, 36, 50, 145
   childcare policy, 173
   childcare provision, 287
civic culture, 257
class, 13, 44, 96–98, 100, 105, 108, 119,
   119–124, 129–130, 134–135, 139,
   153–154, 164–165, 172, 180–184, 192,
   194, 206–207, 224, 227–228, 238–239,
   241, 258, 263–266, 284–285, 304
   class inequalities, 87, 119–120, 133,
      297, 301
   class polarization, 122, 133–134, 138,
      140, 285
collective bargaining, 21, 43, 93–96, 103–104,
   110, 112, 296
   bargaining centralization, 43
   bargaining coordination, 19–21, 43, 93,
      130–132, 141, 302–303
   bargaining coverage, 21–22, 43, 93–96,
      103–104, 110, 112, 296, 302–303
   bargaining power, 43, 147, 174, 178
   bargaining practices/procedure, 12, 19
   bargaining rights, 22
   bargaining synchronization, 19
   firm-level/industry bargaining, 20, 112
   fragmented bargaining, 20, 103, 112
   government involvement in
      bargaining, 43
   regularized pattern bargaining, 19–20
computerization, 10–11, 280
contract type, 96, 151, 155, 157–158, 160,
   163, 166
   atypical/non standard contract/work, 2, 11,
      13, 122, 142–145, 147–148, 151–155, 157,
      159–163, 165–168, 285–286, 293–294
   fixed-term/short-term/temporary/time
      limited contract/employee/employment/
      job/work, 11–12, 35, 47, 55, 59, 96, 112,
      122, 140, 142, 145–161, 163, 166–168,
      172, 203, 284–287, 294
   full-time/permanent contract/regular/
      employee/employment/job, 59, 143,
      145, 147, 153, 158, 160, 166, 168, 285,
      293–294

contract type (*Cont.*)
part-time employee/employment/job/work,
121–122, 139–140, 142–147, 150–155,
158–161, 163, 166–168, 285–286, 294
permanent employee/employment, 149,
156, 158, 286
standard contract, 147–148, 163, 166, 168,
285–286
coordinated market economy, 12–13, 19, 21,
92, 149, 202, 302
corruption, 77, 243, 271
country groups
Anglo-Saxon/Anglo countries, 18, 24–25,
37, 45, 61, 145, 285–286, 291, 294–295,
297–299, 301, 304–305
Benelux countries, 19
Continental countries/regime, 3, 5–6, 13,
18, 20–21, 23–25, 27, 37–39, 44–46,
49, 61, 68, 93, 98–100, 105–106, 108,
111–112, 118, 120–124, 126–128, 130,
132–133, 137–141, 144, 146–147, 149,
151–152, 155–156, 158–159, 163–168,
185–186, 202–203, 208–209, 212, 216–
228, 232–233, 238, 241, 243, 245–248,
251–252, 281, 283–286, 289, 294–299,
301–305
Eastern/East European/ East-Central
European countries, 3, 5–7, 13, 18–19,
21, 23, 25, 27, 37–40, 45–46, 49, 61,
63–64, 67–69, 76, 117, 202, 219, 221–222,
283–284, 291, 294–295, 297–298, 300,
303–305
European/EU/Eurozone countries, 3–4, 6,
19, 27, 37, 44, 59, 80, 88, 137, 142, 144–
145, 150, 153–155, 167, 169, 171, 173,
201, 256, 259, 261, 270–271, 273–275,
277, 280, 299–302
Liberal countries, 13, 18, 23–25, 27, 93–94,
98–102, 106, 108, 110–112, 118, 120–127,
130, 132–133, 137–141, 145–148, 150,
152, 154–156, 158–159, 162–168,
185–186, 201–203, 208–209, 212, 216,
218, 220–221, 223–228, 232–233, 235,
237–238, 240–241, 245–248, 250–253,
255, 283–286, 294–295, 297–299, 301,
303–305
Mediterranean countries, 93–94, 203, 303
Nordic countries, 2–3, 5–6, 18–19, 21,
23–25, 27, 37, 39, 44–45, 49, 51–52, 55,
61–62, 67–69, 84, 98, 100–101, 105, 108,
111–112, 117–130, 132–133, 137–141,
145–146, 149, 152, 154–156, 158–159,
162–168, 185–186, 201, 203, 208–209,
216, 225–226, 232–233, 235, 237–238,
240–243, 246–249, 251–253, 255, 283,
286, 294, 296–299, 301–302, 304–306
North Western countries, 3, 5, 39, 45, 76

OECD countries, 58, 72, 149
Scandinavian countries, 13, 43–44, 93–94,
106, 110, 200–203, 209, 212, 216–221,
223–224, 227–228, 289, 299
Southern countries, 2–3, 5–7, 13, 18–19,
21–25, 27, 43, 45–46, 49, 61, 76, 93,
98, 100–101, 105, 107–108, 110–112,
117–128, 130, 132–133, 137–141, 144–
147, 149, 152, 154–156, 158–159, 162,
164–168, 185–186, 191, 202–204, 209,
211–212, 216–217, 219–222, 232–233,
235, 237–238, 240–243, 246–253, 255,
284–287, 289–290, 294–295, 297–300,
302–305
Transition countries, 21, 24–25, 27, 77, 94,
98–102, 105, 107–108, 110–112, 118–128,
130, 132–133, 137–141, 145–147,
150–152, 154–156, 158–159, 162–168,
185–186, 191, 204, 208–209, 211–212,
216–228, 232–233, 235, 237–238,
240–241, 243, 245–248, 251–253, 255,
285–287, 289–291, 294, 298–299, 304
creative destruction, theory of, 9–10, 14, 116,
280–281

decommodification, 201–202
demand-control model/theory, 137
democracy, 14, 17–18, 27, 256–258, 260–262,
264–277, 292–294, 300
democratic culture/values, 257, 262, 264
democratic legitimacy/diffuse support, 257,
262, 274–275
democratic performance, 262
democratic representation, 271
dissatisfaction/satisfaction with democracy,
262, 266, 268, 271–273, 275
Denmark, 3–7, 20, 24–25, 27–28, 36–38,
44, 46, 48, 51, 60–63, 93, 95, 99–100,
105, 107–114, 117, 128, 145, 147, 150,
152, 159, 185, 190, 193, 196, 200, 204,
208–209, 221, 225–226, 229, 232, 252,
261, 267–269, 283, 286–287, 294
downsizing, 198–199, 207, 220–221, 228
dualism
variants of dualism, 303

earnings (*see also* wage)
distribution of earnings, 24, 43, 84–87
earnings growth, 74
earnings inequality, 84–85
low earnings, 85–87
median earnings, 86–87
economic crisis
accentuating effect of flexibility, 55–56
country variations in severity, 4–8, 36–37
definition of economic crisis, 4
differential severity for social groups, 66–72

effect of prior growth rates, 38–39
implications for quality of work policy, 2–3
mitigating effect of equality-promoting institutions, 42–49
role of construction industry in economic crisis, 39–40
economy, changes in, 4, 17, 89–90, 92, 161, 231, 256, 263, 266–267, 274, 295
economic contraction, 32, 35, 39, 47, 55–56, 59, 66, 71, 73–74, 77–78, 81, 84–94, 96, 98, 104, 107, 176, 185, 195, 223, 242, 248, 261
economic cycle, 116, 132, 280, 295
economic development, 44, 295–296
economic growth, 1, 3, 31, 35, 38–39, 41, 49, 55, 57, 142, 169, 243, 259, 284, 287, 293
economic volatility, 296
economic wealth, 44, 46, 61–62, 75–76
education, 36, 50, 58–59, 64–66, 68–78, 83, 86, 91, 95–98, 100, 105–106, 108, 110, 113–114, 145, 147, 151–152, 155, 164–165, 167, 206–207, 214, 224, 227–228, 238, 259, 264, 281–283, 292
education differences / inequality, 68, 105–107, 110, 281, 283
education gradient, 66
education shortage, 75
educational enrolment, 73
over education, 75, 77
education level/type, 65, 74–75, 91, 98, 105–106, 151–152, 155, 164–165, 167, 214, 281–282
educational attainment/experience, 73, 292
highly/well educated, 58, 64, 73, 104, 106–107, 111, 235, 281, 283
low/less educated, 58, 64–66, 72, 74–75, 107, 283
secondary education, 66, 68–69, 72, 100, 105–106, 108, 113–114, 281, 283
tertiary education, 64–66, 74, 100, 105–106, 108, 113, 281, 283
vocational education/learning/training, 12, 73, 92, 95, 280
egocentric effects, 259–260, 263, 266, 292
employee, occupational type of
agricultural worker, 74
clerical employee, 74, 81, 83
craft worker, 74, 81–83, 86, 297
elementary worker, 74, 81, 83, 282, 297
factory worker, 74, 81, 83, 282, 297
managers, 74, 81, 83, 100, 105, 108, 120–121, 134, 138, 153, 173, 181–183, 194, 264–265, 284, 304
manual worker, 80–82, 86–87, 119–121, 123–124, 134, 139, 263, 282, 284, 297

professionals, 74, 81, 83, 97, 100, 105, 108, 120–121, 134, 138, 153, 172–173, 181–183, 192, 194, 264–265, 282, 284, 297
working class, 124, 258
employee representation/representatives, 127–130
employer coordination, 12, 19–20, 130, 294, 301
employer training, 90, 95, 293
employment commitment, 14–15, 195–197, 199–203, 205–213, 216, 218, 220–222, 224, 250, 279, 288–290, 299, 305
country differences in employment commitment, 208–211, 223
debates about employment commitment, 196–200
employment commitment and job insecurity, 27, 196–201, 205, 207–208, 217–223, 227–228, 289–290
employment commitment and unemployment, 196–201, 203–208, 211–220, 222–228
implications of welfare regimes for employment commitment, 201–205
employment policy, 18
employment protection, 32, 43, 45, 94–96, 103–104, 110, 112, 145, 148–149, 155, 167, 204, 298
employment regulation, 13, 122, 203, 294, 301, 305–306
employment rates/levels, 1–3, 8, 33, 36–37, 40, 51, 56, 58, 60–66, 83, 148–149, 157–158, 285, 288
employment fall/rise, 30, 33–41, 43, 46–49, 50, 52–53, 55–59, 65–72, 77–79, 81–83, 85–87, 158–159, 178, 281–282, 295–297
employment volatility, 32–33, 36, 47–49, 56–57, 59
employment regime, 12–13, 21, 23, 92–94, 106, 110–111, 118, 120, 130, 141, 148–149, 167, 173, 201, 203, 210, 301–302
employment status, 18, 123, 201–202, 230–231, 233–240, 242, 245, 251, 263
EMU membership, 270–272
equality promotion, 32–33, 35, 38, 42–49, 54–55, 58, 62, 70–72, 83, 86, 296–297
European model of social capitalism, 256, 274
European Monetary Union (EMU), 259, 261–262, 269–273, 300
European Social Survey (ESS), 7, 26, 28–30, 95, 98, 117, 143, 162–165, 167, 175, 177, 179, 186–188, 196, 200, 205, 207, 237, 240, 257, 261, 273, 276–277, 279

European Union Labour Force Survey (EULFS), 26, 28–29, 37, 60, 73, 124, 143, 146, 149–156, 165
Eurozone, 256, 259, 261, 270–271, 273–275, 300

family life, 44, 169–172, 174–175, 181, 184–185, 188, 190, 287–288, 305
financial deprivation
   financial cutbacks, 188–191, 194, 236–237, 239–240, 249, 251, 253
   financial difficulty/insecurity, 135, 161
   financial pressure/strain/stress, 179, 188, 235, 238–239, 241, 249
firm financial difficulties, 189, 194
France, 3–7, 13, 20–21, 23–25, 27–28, 37, 39, 44, 46, 50, 55, 61, 63, 68, 75, 93–95, 98–100, 105, 108, 111–112, 117–128, 130, 132–133, 137–141, 144, 149, 177, 179, 196, 204, 208–212, 223–226, 252, 261, 267–269, 271, 275, 280, 284–285, 291, 293–294, 298, 302
Franco, 303

gender/sex, 29, 58–59, 62, 66–67, 70–72, 83, 86, 100, 105, 108, 118–122, 124, 129–130, 134–135, 139, 147, 151–152, 154–155, 160, 163–164, 169, 173, 183, 206–207, 209, 212, 224, 227–228, 238–239, 241, 286
   gender differences/gap/inequality, 44, 69, 87, 154, 173, 208–211, 224, 227–228, 286
   gender employment gap, 69–72
   gender interactions/relations, 44, 180
   gender role, 173, 175, 182–183, 192, 194
Germany, 3–7, 13, 19–25, 27–28, 36–38, 44, 46–47, 49, 55, 61, 63, 68, 73, 93–95, 99–101, 105, 108, 110–112, 117–118, 128–129, 144–145, 147, 149–152, 157–158, 160, 185, 193, 196, 201–202, 205, 208–209, 211, 214, 219, 221, 225–226, 231–232, 252, 261, 267–269, 280, 285–286, 294, 302
governance
   governance quality, 77
   political governance, 288
Great Depression, 14
Greece, 3–7, 20–21, 24–25, 27–28, 36–37, 45, 49, 51–52, 55, 61–62, 65, 75, 93, 95, 99–100, 105, 108, 110–112, 117, 128–130, 152, 158, 185–187, 191, 193, 196, 200–201, 204, 208–209, 211, 213, 225–226, 232, 249, 252, 256, 261, 267–269, 273, 275–276, 286–287, 293–294, 297, 300, 303
Gross Domestic Product (GDP), 4–5, 7, 23–24, 26–27, 30, 38–41, 43–44, 46–47, 61–62, 76–77, 96, 101–104, 109–110, 112, 173, 186, 226, 231, 242–243, 248, 250, 253, 255–256, 261, 268–274, 280, 283, 293, 295–296

health
   blood pressure, 136
   cardiovascular/heart disease, 115, 136
   physical health, 115, 133, 135–136, 138, 141, 197, 284, 298, 301, 303
household
   composition, 24, 172, 236
   household/family spending cutbacks (see financial deprivation, financial cutbacks)
   household income, 162, 166–167, 170, 189, 237, 263
housework, 170, 206
housing assistance/benefit, 24
human capital, 89, 91, 98, 142

immigrant, 59, 276
income, 14, 16, 23–25, 143, 162, 173, 178–179, 183, 191–192, 194–195, 198–199, 202, 204–205, 214, 217–219, 223, 226, 229–230, 232–234, 236–238, 251–252, 262–263, 299
   household income (see household)
   income (re)distribution, 84, 257, 262–264, 266, 274
   income inequality, 84, 243, 297
industrial structure, 57
industry
   construction industry, 34, 39–41, 47, 57, 80–81, 87, 178, 282, 295
   manufacturing industry, 59, 80–81, 87, 281–282
insiders/insider-outsider, 32–33, 35, 47, 93, 199
Institutional Characteristics of Trade Unions, Wage Setting, State Intervention and Social Pacts (ICTWSS), 19–20, 22, 43, 112, 126, 130–132
institutions
   democratic institutions, 17, 256–258, 260, 262, 271, 273–274
   equality-promoting/equalizing/equality-related institutions, 32–33, 35–36, 38, 42–49, 54–55, 57, 71, 83, 86, 296–297
   labour market institutions, 31, 42–43, 54, 57, 59, 70–72, 83, 85–87, 92, 110, 296–297
   political institutions, 17, 258–260, 263–264, 271, 274, 292, 300
   welfare institutions, 27, 300, 305
International Labour Organization (ILO), 73
International Standard Classification of Occupations (ISCO), 29, 73–74, 81, 282
interwar period, 17

job change, 189, 194
job control, 27, 115–121, 123–126, 129–130,
    132–133, 135–136, 139–141, 172, 177,
    182, 192, 194, 279, 284, 293, 298,
    301–302, 304
  effects of economic crisis on job control,
    123–125, 140–141
  employee/job involvement, 2, 115,
    122–123, 125, 140, 182, 198, 284, 288,
    301, 303
  implications for effects of work intensity,
    133, 135–138
  implications for work motivation, 115,
    195, 198
  indicators of job control, 117
  influence of employee representatives on
    job control, 127–130
  job autonomy, 10, 115, 170, 172, 175, 182
  organizational commitment, 115, 195, 198
  polarization in job control, 119–122
  task discretion, 11, 117, 203, 210, 216
  trends in job control, 117–118, 139
job finding rate, 51–52
job insecurity, 2–4, 11, 14, 16–17, 27,
    142–143, 159–164, 167, 170–173, 175,
    179, 182, 184, 190–191, 196–200, 205,
    207–208, 217–220, 222–223, 227–228,
    234, 242, 249, 279, 285–287, 289–290,
    294, 298–299, 301–302, 304–305
  change over time in job insecurity, 4, 14,
    143–147, 160, 162–168, 175, 285, 294,
    298–299
  and contract type, 142–168, 285–286
  effects of economic crisis on job insecurity,
    155–159
  and employment commitment, 27,
    196–201, 205, 207–208, 217–223,
    227–228, 289–290
  entrapment in job insecurity, 163
  polarization in job insecurity, 149–152
  and psychological/subjective well-being,
    3, 16, 197–200, 230–231, 234, 242,
    248–249, 290
  subjective job insecurity, 160–162
  and work-family conflict, 171–173, 175,
    179, 182, 184–185, 187, 190–191, 287
job loss, 8, 14, 16–17, 84, 87, 91, 142–143,
    155–156, 160–163, 168, 175, 196–201,
    205, 207, 213–214, 217, 219, 222–223,
    229, 242, 285, 289
job mobility, 84
job pressure (see also work intensity), 177, 183,
    192, 194
job quality, 8, 10, 116, 145, 161, 206–207, 210,
    218, 220, 222, 224, 227–228, 284
job resources, 172, 175
job satisfaction, 88, 115, 169

job strain types, 136–137, 139
  active job, 136–137, 139, 206
  class variations in job strain types, 139
  country variation in job strain types,
    137–138
  high strain job, 136–141, 301, 303
  low strain job, 136–137
  passive job, 136–137, 304
  polarization in job strain types, 138–140
  theory of job strain types, 133
job tasks, 10–11, 73, 80, 126

labour costs, 10, 12, 147
labour demand, 34–35, 54, 62–63, 80, 148
labour hoarding, 89–91, 109
labour market
  labour market dualism/segmentation, 2, 10,
    143, 203, 285
  labour market flexibility, 54, 56, 72, 83
  labour market flows, 50
  labour market/force entry, 92, 95, 199, 280
  labour market institutions, 31, 42–43,
    54, 57, 59, 70–72, 83, 85–87, 92, 110,
    296–297
  labour market participation, 63, 179
  labour market regulation, 173
latent deprivation, 196–197, 199–200, 211,
    216, 222
left party, 43
Liberal Market Economy (LME), 12–13, 19, 21,
    148, 203, 209
life satisfaction, 16, 136–137, 161, 169,
    230–231, 234–250, 252, 278, 290–291,
    299–300, 305
Lisbon Strategy, 2
loss aversion, 33

MEDEF, 302

neo-institutional approach/theories, 118, 294
neo-Marxian theory, 8, 115

occupation skill level, 12, 74–79, 82–83, 86,
    281–282
  high-skill occupation/job/work, 11–12, 59,
    73, 76–77, 80, 82–84, 87, 90–92, 109, 142,
    195, 202–203, 214, 225, 281, 283, 304
  low-skill occupation/job/work, 2, 11–12,
    59, 73–74, 77, 79–80, 82–83, 87, 105–106,
    123, 143, 214, 225, 281, 293, 304
  skilled manual occupation, 80
occupation structure, 59, 71, 74–77, 79–80,
    82–83, 85–87, 195, 297
Oliveira Salazar, Antonio de, 303

parental leave, 173
parliament, 17, 262, 276

Subject Index

part-time work, 122, 139, 142–143, 146–147, 151–152, 154–155, 158–161, 163, 166, 168, 285–286
path dependency, 116, 298
peripheral workforce, 2, 142–143, 149, 280, 285, 293
political attitudes, 17, 258, 262–267, 269, 271, 273, 293
  change over time in political attitudes, 266–267
  changes in Greece in political attitudes, 268, 275–277
  effect of class position on political attitudes, 264–265
  effect of economic crisis on political attitudes, 269–271, 274
  effect of education on political attitudes, 264
  effect of financial stress on political attitudes, 265–266
  effect of membership of the Eurozone on political attitudes, 259, 277–278
  effect of political socialization on political attitudes, 257, 259, 264–265
  effect of unemployment on political attitudes, 264–265
  indicators of political attitudes, 261–263
  political culture, 257–258, 263–264, 274, 292
  political dissatisfaction, 260, 275
  political distrust/trust, 17, 257, 259–262, 264–276, 292–294, 300
  political legitimacy, 14, 256, 259, 266, 268, 270–271, 275, 277, 279, 292–293, 300
  sociotropic effects, 259–260, 263, 266, 270, 274, 292
  theories of political attitudes, 257–261
political economy, 257–260, 263–265, 274
political system, 4, 256–260, 263
poverty rate, 233–234, 252
power resource theory, 8, 13, 116, 130, 141, 294, 301
production regime, 12–13, 19, 21, 92–93, 130, 141, 148, 202, 209, 294, 296, 301–302
psychological contract theory, 198–199, 217, 221

recruitment, 73, 132, 148, 296
redistribution
  attitudes towards redistribution, 260–270, 274, 292–293
  income redistribution, 257, 262, 264, 266, 274
  redistributive policies, 260–261
  welfare state redistribution, 43, 256–257, 264, 269, 273–274

replacement rate, 23–25, 32, 204–205, 218, 226, 232, 252
representative influence, 129–131
role theory, 170

scarring effect, 230, 234, 242
self-employed, 206, 224, 227–228
self-development, 115, 136, 199, 301, 304
self-realization, 91, 115
skill-biased change
  skill-biased employment change, 87
  skill-biased labour demand change, 80
  skill-biased technological development, 11
skill demand/requirement, 2, 58, 73–75, 79, 281, 304
skill formation, 12, 92, 280, 294, 301
skill level, 12, 74–79, 82–83, 86, 281–282
  high-skill occupation/job/work, 11–12, 59, 73, 76–77, 80, 82–84, 87, 90–92, 109, 142, 195, 202–203, 214, 225, 281, 283, 304
  low-skill occupation/job/work, 2, 11–12, 59, 73–74, 77, 79–80, 82–83, 87, 105–106, 123, 143, 214, 225, 281, 293, 304
  skilled manual occupation, 80
skill matching/mismatch, 73–77, 204
skill/occupational polarization, 58–59, 72, 80, 82–84, 86–87, 280–282, 297
skill structure, 3, 73, 77–78, 80–81, 86, 120, 153, 281–282, 297
skill supply, 73–75, 77–78, 84
skill upgrading, 58–59, 72, 74, 78–79, 82–84, 86, 280–282, 293, 297
  transferable skill, 90
social assistance, 24–25
social cohesion, 256, 259, 262
social integration, 1, 3–4, 14, 16–18, 26–27, 197, 235, 237, 239–240, 249, 279, 288, 290–295, 299–300, 305–306
social norm, 197
social pact, 112
social protection, 145, 201–202, 210, 231–232
social support, 16, 229, 237, 239–241, 249, 291
  familial support, 233
  social contact, 196–197, 238, 240, 249
  social exclusion/isolation, 16, 197, 229, 262, 300
  social networks, 16, 231, 277, 290–291
  social relations/relationships, 14, 171, 198, 290
  supportive partner, 170
socialization, 259, 292
  political socialization, 257, 259, 264–265
sociotropic effects/impact/reactions/views, 259–260, 263, 266, 270, 274, 292
Southern distinctiveness, 249–250

Spain, 3–8, 20–22, 24, 27–28, 35–37, 39–40, 45–46, 48, 52–53, 55, 57, 61–63, 65, 67, 69, 75, 87, 93, 95, 99–100, 105–108, 110–113, 117–118, 128, 130, 144–145, 147, 150, 152, 157–160, 168, 185, 191, 196, 200–201, 204, 208–209, 213, 217, 225–227, 232, 242, 248–250, 252–253, 255–256, 261, 267–269, 275, 277, 280, 283, 285–286, 293–294, 303
state intervention, 20–21, 112
stigma, 15, 229, 231, 235, 248, 290
stress
    financial stress, 179, 238–239, 241
    housework stress, 170
    work stress, 27, 115–116, 132–133, 135, 141, 171, 284, 302
subjective well-being, 3, 16, 27, 229–233, 235–236, 240, 242–243, 248–250, 278–279, 290–291, 305
    affective/emotional-cognitive dimensions, 234
    change in subjective well-being, 243–248
    country group variation in subjective well-being, 240–241
    financial pressure/strain/stress, 179, 188, 235, 238–239, 241, 249
    implications of welfare state for subjective well-being, 231–233
    indicators of subjective well-being, 233–234, 237
    psychological distress, 16, 136, 239
    subjective distress, 135
    subjective well-being and job insecurity, 3, 16, 197–200, 230–231, 234, 242, 248–249, 290
    subjective well-being and social support, 240, 249
    subjective well-being and unemployment, 229–255
survivor syndrome, 10, 15, 198–199, 220–221

task-biased labour market change, 80
task discretion, 11, 117, 203, 210, 216
technical change, 2, 11
technology, 10
    computer technology, 80
    skill-biased technological development, 11
    technological change, 10, 80, 195, 281
    technological replacement, 80
    technologically advanced sectors, 10, 116
temporary work, 12, 47, 122, 139, 142, 145–147, 150–153, 155, 157–158, 160, 285–286
trade union/organized labour, 22, 35, 93–94, 112, 130–131, 141, 148, 298, 301, 303
    trade union and job control, 127, 130–132, 141

trade union density, 130–131, 298
trade union strength, 32, 130, 132, 298
training, 10, 88–111, 113–114, 142–143, 145, 149, 203, 282–283, 293, 297–298, 301, 304–305
    continuing training, 88–91, 93, 95–100, 102, 104–111, 203, 297, 301
    country patterns, 98–102
    distribution by age, 107–108
    distribution by education, 104–107
    effect of change in GDP growth rates on training, 101–102
    effect of employment protection on training, 93–96, 103–104, 110, 112
    theories of training, 89–94
    training costs, 91–92, 94, 104, 106, 111
    training cuts, 89–90, 94, 101, 110–111
    training inequality/stratification, 91, 107, 109
    training opportunities, 27, 90–91, 93, 96, 109–111, 145, 293, 298
    training participation, 88–91, 94, 98, 103–111
    training provision, 1, 89, 92–94, 96, 104, 109–110, 283, 297–298, 301
    vocational education/learning/training, 12, 73, 92, 95, 280

unemployment, 196, 204, 211–216, 219, 222, 224, 226, 232, 249
    level/rate of unemployment, 4–7, 15–16, 27, 36–37, 43, 59–61, 63, 65, 123, 157, 160, 176, 179, 187–188, 199–200, 204, 213–215, 219, 225, 229–231, 248, 250, 280, 288, 290–292
    long-term unemployment, 213–214, 222, 225
    Marienthal unemployment, 16
    regional unemployment, 231
    unemployment and employment commitment, 196–201, 203–208, 211–220, 222–228
    unemployment and psychological/subjective well-being, 229–255
    unemployment and work-family conflict, 169, 174, 176, 178–180, 185, 187–188, 191
    unemployment duration, 216, 227, 236
    unemployment experience, 228, 234, 238, 242, 249, 263, 292
    unemployment risk, 32, 88, 234
    unemployment welfare systems, 203, 205, 232

vocational education/learning/training, 12, 73, 92, 95, 280

wage (*see also* earnings)
  wage compression/growth, 84, 94
  wage dispersion, 43, 296
  wage inequality, 32, 35, 58–59, 84–87, 297
  wage setting, 96, 103, 110, 112
  wage structure, 58, 84
wealth, 34, 44–46, 61–62, 75–76, 229, 243, 250
weighting, 26, 28–29, 208
welfare institutions, 27, 300, 305
welfare regime/system, 13–14, 18, 23, 25, 173,
    176, 201–203, 205, 208, 231–233, 235,
    240, 249, 279, 294, 299, 305
  unemployment welfare systems, 203,
    205, 232
welfare state, 18, 42–43, 202, 231, 256–257,
    259, 261–262, 274, 296
work ethic/values, 197, 199, 201, 203, 222,
    250, 289
work-family/work-life conflict, 3, 27, 135,
    169–178, 180–192, 194, 279, 287–288, 293
  change over time in work-family conflict,
    180–187
  effect of economic crisis on work-family
    conflict, 174–176, 188–191
  effect of work intensity on work-family
    conflict, 183–184, 187
  indicators of work-familiy conflict, 176
  theories of work-family conflict, 170–174
  work-family conflict and child
    development, 169–170, 172–173, 175,
    182–184, 191–192, 194
  work-family conflict and financial difficulty/
    stress, 179, 189
  work-family conflict and job insecurity,
    171–173, 175, 179, 182, 184–185, 187,
    190–191, 287
  work-family conflict and scheduling,
    171–174, 180–181, 183–184, 187, 192
  work-family conflict and unemployment,
    169, 174, 176, 178–180, 185, 187–188, 191
work intensity, 15, 27, 115–116, 132–137, 141,
    177, 279, 284–285, 287–288, 290, 293,
    298, 302
work organization/reorganization, 1–2, 8–10,
    116, 132, 140, 177, 183, 192, 194–195,
    206–207, 224, 227–228, 280, 303–305

work motivation, 15, 115, 195–196, 199,
    202–203, 206, 213, 222–223, 289
work-related suicide, 141, 302
work type
  paid work, 169–173, 182, 190, 197, 200,
    205–206, 211–213, 217, 222, 224
  unpaid work, 173, 182
worker productivity, 32
workforce polarization, 10, 140, 149,
    283–284
workforce reductions, 7–8, 10, 123, 135, 148,
    196, 214
working age, 14, 205, 235, 271, 288–289
working conditions, 2, 8–13, 119, 123,
    127, 136, 141–144, 160–163, 165–166,
    168, 172, 174–175, 178, 180, 182, 185,
    187–188, 210, 280, 287–288, 290, 293,
    299, 301, 303
  health and safety, 178–179, 183, 192, 194
  work colleagues, 170, 172, 175, 178–179,
    184, 190
  work demands/pressure, 132–135, 170–172,
    174–175, 177, 182–184, 186–187, 190,
    192, 218, 284, 287–288
  work stress, 27, 115–116, 132–133, 135, 141,
    171, 284, 302
working hours, 35, 47, 59, 71, 97, 113–114,
    140, 146, 148, 151, 154, 157, 159,
    170–175, 177, 179–181, 183–184, 187,
    190, 192, 194, 287, 296
  35-hour work week, 302
  overtime, 170–171, 174, 178–181, 183–184,
    190, 192, 194, 287
  scheduling, 171–174, 180–181, 183–184,
    187, 192
  unsocial hours, 170–171, 174, 180–181,
    183–184, 190, 192, 194, 200, 287
  work evenings/nights/weekends, 171,
    178–179, 181, 183, 192, 194, 287
  working time, 96, 100, 105, 108, 163–164,
    171, 173–174, 178, 180–181, 183,
    197, 287
workplace participatory mechanisms, 126
workplace representation/representatives,
    126–127, 129–131, 141, 298
works councils, 126–129